THE ART OF ELOQUENCE

The Art of Eloquence

Byron, Dickens, Tennyson, Joyce

MATTHEW BEVIS

OXFORD
UNIVERSITY PRESS

OXFORD

UNIVERSITY PRESS

Great Clarendon Street, Oxford OX2 6DP

Oxford University Press is a department of the University of Oxford.
It furthers the University's objective of excellence in research, scholarship,
and education by publishing worldwide in

Oxford New York

Auckland Cape Town Dar es Salaam Hong Kong Karachi
Kuala Lumpur Madrid Melbourne Mexico City Nairobi
New Delhi Shanghai Taipei Toronto

With offices in

Argentina Austria Brazil Chile Czech Republic France Greece
Guatemala Hungary Italy Japan Poland Portugal Singapore
South Korea Switzerland Thailand Turkey Ukraine Vietnam

Oxford is a registered trade mark of Oxford University Press
in the UK and in certain other countries

Published in the United States
by Oxford University Press Inc., New York

British Library Cataloguing in Publication Data

Data available

Library of Congress Cataloging in Publication Data

Data available

Typeset by Laserwords Private Limited, Chennai, India
Printed in Great Britain
on acid-free paper by
Biddles Ltd., King's Lynn, Norfolk

ISBN 978–0–19–925399–9

1 3 5 7 9 10 8 6 4 2

For my mother

Acknowledgements

The introduction to this book includes some observations first published in 'Volumes of Noise', *Victorian Literature and Culture*, 31 (2003), 577–91. The chapter on Tennyson contains passages that first appeared as 'Tennyson's Civil Tongue', *Tennyson Research Bulletin*, 7 (1999), 113–25; a couple of paragraphs from 'Fighting Talk: Victorian War Poetry', in Tim Kendall (ed.), *A Handbook of Twentieth-Century British and Irish War Poetry* (Oxford: Oxford University Press, 2007); and a couple from 'Tennyson, Ireland, and "The Powers of Speech"', *Victorian Poetry*, 39 (2001), 345–64. The chapter on Dickens includes sections from two earlier pieces: 'Temporizing Dickens', *Review of English Studies*, 52 (2001), 171–91, and 'Dickens in Public', *Essays in Criticism*, 51 (2001), 330–52. None of these articles is reproduced exactly, but I thank the publishers for permission to reprint.

I am grateful to the British Academy and to St John's College, Cambridge, for funding me during the early stages of writing this book, and to the Arts and Humanities Research Council for awarding me matching leave to complete it. I am also especially thankful to the universities of Cambridge, Sheffield, and York for providing friendly and supportive environments in which to work. At Oxford University Press, I appreciate the guidance and expertise of Jacqueline Baker, Sophie Goldsworthy, Andrew McNeillie, Tom Perridge, and Val Shelley.

The errors in this book are mine, and there would have been more if it were not for the help of many people. I would like to thank everyone who gave me ideas, criticism, and encouragement, especially those who read draft chapters: the two anonymous readers at the Press, Jean van Altena, Derek Attridge, Kathryn Bevis, Stefan Collini, Matthew Creasy, Cathal Dowling, Robert Douglas-Fairhurst, Paul Faulkner, John Haffenden, Hugh Haughton, Judith Hepper, Jean Holloway, Ray Holloway, Alex Houen, Daniel Karlin, Claire Lockwood, Catrin Lowe, Seamus Perry, Adam Piette, Adrian Poole, Matthew Reynolds, Erica Sheen, Marcus Waithe, Stephen Wall, and Timothy Webb.

I owe a huge debt to the eloquence, patience, and generosity of a few people in particular: Matthew Campbell, for his good cheer and his good advice; Freya Johnston, for her insight into the little details that make a big difference; and Brigid Lowe, for her sympathetically searching questions. My greatest debt is to Eric Griffiths, who taught me to listen more carefully to what I was reading.

M. B.

Contents

Abbreviations

Aristotle, *On Rhetoric*	Aristotle, *Aristotle, On Rhetoric: A Theory of Civic Discourse*, ed. and trans. George Kennedy (Oxford: Oxford University Press, 1991)
BCP	*Lord Byron: The Complete Miscellaneous Prose*, ed. Andrew Nicholson (Oxford: Clarendon Press, 1991)
BLJ	*Byron's Letters and Journals*, ed. Leslie A. Marchand, 11 vols. (London: John Murray, 1973–81)
BPW	*Lord Byron: The Complete Poetical Works*, ed. Jerome McGann, 7 vols. (Oxford: Clarendon Press, 1980–93)
Cicero, *De Oratore*	Cicero, *De Oratore*, trans. E. W. Sutton and H. Rackham, 2 vols. (London: Heinemann, 1976)
DJ	*The Dent Uniform Edition of Dickens' Journalism*, ed. Michael Slater, 4 vols. (London: Dent, 1994–2001)
DL	*The Pilgrim Edition of the Letters of Charles Dickens*, ed. Graham Storey, Kathleen Tillotson, and Madeline House, 12 vols. (Oxford: Clarendon Press, 1982–2002)
DS	*The Speeches of Charles Dickens: A Complete Edition*, ed. K. J. Fielding (Brighton: Harvester Press, 1988)
Hansard	*Hansard's Parliamentary Debates*
JCW	*The Critical Writings of James Joyce*, ed. Ellsworth Mason and Richard Ellmann (New York: Viking, 1959)
JL	*Letters of James Joyce*, ed. Stuart Gilbert and Richard Ellmann, 3 vols. (London: Faber & Faber, 1957–66)
PD	*Cobbett's Parliamentary Debates 1803–1812*
PH	*Cobbett's Parliamentary History of England to 1803*
Quintilian, *Institutio*	Quintilian, *Institutio Oratoria*, trans. H. E. Butler, 4 vols. (London: Heinemann, 1968)
TL	*The Letters of Alfred Lord Tennyson*, ed. Cecil Y. Lang and Edgar F. Shannon jun., 3 vols. (Oxford: Clarendon Press, 1982–90)
TP	*The Poems of Tennyson*, ed. Christopher Ricks, 2nd edn., 3 vols. (London: Longman, 1987)

We compensate, we reconcile, we balance. We are enabled to unite into a constituent whole the various anomalies and contending principles that are found in the minds and affairs of men. From hence arises, not an excellence in simplicity, but one far superior, an excellence in composition.

Edmund Burke

Introduction: Literary Persuasions

In *Great Expectations* (1860–1), Pip and Herbert watch Mr Wopsle perform the lead role in *Hamlet*. Nearly everything that could go wrong does go wrong, and soon even the Prince of Denmark himself is the subject of the audience's laughter:

Upon my unfortunate townsman all these incidents accumulated with playful effect. Whenever that undecided Prince had to ask a question or state a doubt, the public helped him out with it. As for example; on the question whether 'twas nobler in the mind to suffer, some roared yes, and some no, and some inclining to both opinions said 'toss up for it;' and quite a Debating Society arose. When he asked what should such fellows as he do crawling between earth and heaven, he was encouraged with loud cries of 'Hear, hear!'[1]

The drama begins to resemble a scene from the floor of the House of Commons, with some members chiming in 'Hear, hear', others murmuring their disapproval from the back benches. Wopsle is translated from player to orator, and Pip finds himself 'feeling keenly for him, but laughing, nevertheless, from ear to ear' (p. 255); even Pip's recollection is inflected with the audience's cries, for 'ear to ear' echoes 'Hear, hear'. After the farcical performance, Herbert and Pip dine with Wopsle, sitting up with him until two in the morning to indulge him in his pipe dreams for 'reviving the Drama'. When Pip retires to bed, mulling over his chances with Estella, we begin to sense one reason why he felt so keenly for the actor. The chapter ends as he falls asleep: '[I] miserably dreamed that my expectations were all cancelled, and that I had to give my hand in marriage to Herbert's Clara, or to play Hamlet to Miss Havisham's Ghost, before twenty thousand people, without knowing twenty words of it' (p. 258). It's as though Pip sees his own predicament in

---

[1] Charles Dickens, *Great Expectations*, ed. Charlotte Mitchell (London: Penguin, 1996), 254. Subsequent page references are given parenthetically in the text.

Wopsle's—full of great expectations, haunted as well as taunted by voices off-stage, a public figure faced by the nightmare of a demanding audience.

This scene, like many others in *Great Expectations*, is itself haunted by a book that appeared a year before it began its serial run: Samuel Smiles's *Self-Help* (the phrase 'great expectations' is employed by an orator in the first chapter of Smiles's book).[2] *Self-Help* (1859) tells of another who was trying to make his way in the world, Benjamin Disraeli:

As an orator too, his first appearance in the House of Commons was a failure. It was spoken of as 'more screaming than an Adelphi farce'. Though composed in a grand and ambitious strain, every sentence was hailed with 'loud laughter'. 'Hamlet' played as a comedy were nothing to it. But he concluded with a sentence which embodied a prophecy. Writhing under the laughter with which his studied eloquence had been received, he exclaimed, 'I have begun several things many times, and have succeeded in them at last. I shall sit down now, but the time will come when you will hear me.'[3]

The Times report of the speech makes for entertaining reading—' "Nothing was so easy as to laugh" (Increased laughter)'[4]—and when Disraeli finishes up with the prophecy 'you will hear me', his audience eagerly chimes in: 'Hear, hear.'[5] Like Wopsle's, Disraeli's 'grand and ambitious strain' is the occasion for 'playful effects', something akin to *Hamlet* performed as a comedy of errors. But Disraeli was proved right (this is why Smiles is telling the story), rising to the top of the greasy pole of politics despite his inauspicious start. Significantly, when we come across Wopsle again later in Dickens's novel, we find that he is no longer playing the Prince who loiters at the edge of court, but 'a plenipotentiary of great power' who has 'a gracious dignity' and is addressed as 'Your Honour' (pp. 383–4).

Much of Dickens's fiction—and much other nineteenth-century writing—is shadowed in this way by oratorical trials and tribulations. When Wopsle finds his soliloquies reshaped into dialogues by a 'Debating Society', his predicament is a miniature version of a larger development that sees literary rumination involved in scenes of debate and persuasion. On the jubilee of the Oxford Union in 1873, a reporter for *The Times* enthused:

In the course of these fifty years we have become a nation of public speakers. Everyone speaks now...Eloquence is but a facility, or instrument, or weapon, or accomplishment, or, in academic terms, an art...We are now more than ever a debating, that is, a Parliamentary people.[6]

---

[2] Samuel Smiles, *Self-Help: With Illustrations of Character, Conduct, and Perseverance*, ed. Peter W. Sinnema (Oxford: Oxford World's Classics, 2002), 19.

[3] Ibid. 34.   [4] *The Times*, 8 Dec. 1837, 3e–f.   [5] Ibid. 3f.

[6] *The Times*, 23 Oct. 1873, 7b.

These multiple definitions of 'eloquence' invite a question. If eloquence might be an art in a nation of public speakers, then what could art become? During the nineteenth century, a commitment to literary eloquence involved consideration of how far it might, or should, be both a 'weapon' and an 'art'. This book explores how four writers responded to a debating, parliamentary people, and examines the ways in which they and their publics conceived the relations between political speech and literary endeavour. It envisages literary 'persuasion' not just as an attempt to get someone to adopt a position (although it is sometimes that), but also as a certain kind of disposition—one drawn to the study of conflicting allegiances and principles. Such a persuasion—asking questions, stating doubts—partakes of the nature of 'that undecided Prince' that Wopsle was playing, and it echoes throughout the period.

As *The Times* suggests, the century witnessed an expansion in audiences for political debate. A demand for public speaking stimulated discussion about whether the rhetorical impulse of oratory to move listeners to action should be combined with or kept at a remove from the aesthetic impulse of literature. Alongside the growth of the talking world ran an emerging conception of art as a sphere detached from the encroachments of contemporary socio-political debate. The influence of Kant's *Critique of Judgement* (1790) helped to foster these visions of detachment, as Coleridge and others imported the philosopher's notions of aesthetic disinterestedness into discussions of literature.[7] Kant's *Critique* includes a distinction between poetry and rhetoric: poetry 'expands the mind by setting the imagination free', whereas rhetoric—a duplicitous ally in the war for freedom and enlightenment—'borrows from the art of poetry only as much as it is necessary to win minds over to the advantage of the speaker before they can judge and to rob them of their freedom'.[8] However, a subsequent footnote gestures towards a less stable sense of opposition that would be echoed throughout the forthcoming century:

I must confess that a beautiful poem has always given me a pure enjoyment, whereas reading the best speech of a Roman popular speaker or a contemporary speaker in parliament . . . has always been mixed with the disagreeable feeling of disapproval of a deceitful art, which understands how to move people, like machines, to a judgment in important matters which must lose all weight for them in calm reflection.[9]

This confession of 'mixed' feelings comes from an appreciation that trying to move people to consideration of 'important matters' is not merely to be

---

[7] See Paul Kristeller, 'The Modern System of the Arts: A Study in the History of Aesthetics', repr. in Peter Kivy (ed.), *Essays on the History of Aesthetics* (New York: University of Rochester Press, 1992), 3–64.

[8] Immanuel Kant, *Critique of the Power of Judgment*, ed. Paul Guyer, trans. Paul Guyer and Eric Matthews (Cambridge: Cambridge University Press, 2000), 203–4.

[9] Ibid. 205.

scorned. Arguments for a rigid separation of political from 'calm' aesthetic judgements may lead to an inert quietism—what, one might ask, are people meant to be *reflecting on* when they partake of their 'pure enjoyments'? Kant was alert to this danger, and conceived aesthetic experience as distinct, yet not wholly dissociated from, the interests of practical reason and morality.[10] His sense that the art of the orator 'borrows' and breaks from that of the poet also suggests an enduring link between poetics and rhetoric. Here, though, it is worth noting that his reference to the 'contemporary speaker' alongside the classical orator is a microcosm of a more general nineteenth-century development in which literary writing is seen to be steadily more specialized as the political public expands.

The *OED* helps to chart this shift. As the earlier, broader sense of 'literature' as 'polite or humane learning' starts to become '*rare* and *obsolescent*' (the last citation of this meaning dates from 1880), so the dictionary observes the rise of literature as a particular 'body of writings' (1812): 'applied to writing which has claim to consideration on the ground of beauty of form or emotional effect' (a new set of cognates also highlights increased specialization: 'literarily' (1825), 'literatize' (1836), 'literarian' (1866), 'literariness' (1877), 'literaryism' (1879), 'literose' (1888)). The temporal overlap in the primary definition between old and new meanings of 'literature' suggests an ambiguity concerning exactly what 'claims to consideration' this form of expression had in the period. From one perspective, the writer is required to make himself heard from amid a cacophony of political voices, and to address the concerns raised by a 'parliamentary people'. (Another set of neologisms alerts us to the company that writers kept: the first citation of 'oratorical' to describe a person is in 1801; one can 'oration' oneself from 1802; 'oratorize' is cited as a transitive verb from 1853; 'oratiuncle' (1832), 'orational' (1840), 'oration-like' (1845), and 'oratist' (1860) also appear on the scene.) From another perspective, 'literature' is itself increasingly defined as a world away from such voices, a space where one might escape the din of the oratists and their oratiuncles.

In a speech on 'Politics and Literature', William Gladstone hinted at these seemingly opposed trends. The politician hoped that

the *absolute integrity of mental labour and enquiry* might never be compromised in whole or in part by the seductions of immediate popular applause. (Hear, Hear). With this reservation he rejoiced that men like Sir Walter Scott, Charles Dickens and Alfred Tennyson had received from the public such an acknowledgement of their works as was a substantial evidence of gratitude, if not an adequate reward, and in the nature

---

[10] See Paul Guyer, *Kant and the Experience of Freedom: Essays on Aesthetics and Morality* (Cambridge: Cambridge University Press, 1993).

of an *absolute guarantee of the freedom and independence* of the modern literary work. (Cheers).[11]

The studied sentences and polished periods have their charm, but 'Hear, Hear' follows so quickly on the heels of Gladstone's worries about 'applause' that we are perhaps inclined to smile rather than to cheer. Having more time than the audience, a reader can note that the orator's 'absolute's point to a mixed state of affairs: the first suggests that literature's relations with the 'immediate' are to be avoided; the second asserts that, for these writers, the contemporary public has been the guarantee of 'freedom'.

The writers who appear in the following chapters would not have been entirely at ease with Gladstone's eulogy. Their negotiations with an increasingly political public show that the integrity of 'the modern literary work' often involved a mediation between the 'immediate' and the 'independent'. The politician may vaunt the 'freedom' of literature from immediate public debate, but the cost of such freedom might entail a view of literary achievement that precludes formative socio-political influence. Even as they felt the need for a form of eloquence in which immediate commitment could be tempered by other considerations, Byron, Dickens, Tennyson, and Joyce were aware that a disinterested independence might shade into an irresponsible indifference. One reason for focusing on these writers is that their struggles are representative of a dilemma faced by others in the period. As Philip Davis has observed:

Two opposite but mutually linked tendencies were going on at the same time, as though struggling to belong together: on the one hand, the establishment of literature as a distinct and defended area, also a separate profession and even an industry; on the other, within those forms, a counter-tendency which internally recommitted art — in its content, in its urgency — to the service of the world outside.[12]

My interest lies in how writers sought to bring these opposing tendencies into fruitful dialogue, and in how they aimed to cultivate a 'literary' detachment that could gain critical purchase on political arguments without being conceived as a culpable isolation from them. Such a study needs to reflect on the kinds of responsibility that writers have when they seek to address political issues in their work, and to examine the ways in which a style of writing might act as a spur to, or disclaimer of, political sympathies.

Matthew Arnold's deliberations over the value of 'Culture' and 'disinterest-edness' bring these questions into sharper focus. Arnold's presence at many of the 1866–7 reform debates in Parliament prompted him to write those articles that would make up *Culture and Anarchy* (1869), a book that continually

---

[11] *The Times*, 16 June 1879, 6a; my emphasis.
[12] Philip Davis, *The Victorians* (Oxford: Oxford University Press, 2002), 238.

objected to the uncultured polemics of contemporary political argument. 'Culture is of like spirit with poetry,' he claimed, and this spirit was being neglected by the party spirit at Westminster. Arnold's book takes its bearings from the speech it hears, opening with the words 'In one of his speeches a short time ago . . .', going on to criticize those orators who were for and those who were against reform, and dreaming at its close of an eloquence that would contain a 'power of disinterested play of consciousness' to answer 'any House of Commons' orator, or practical operator in politics'.[13] This emphasis on the 'power' of disinterestedness and the alignment of 'culture' with 'poetry' suggest that the aesthetic realm might help to address and redress political problems.

This suggestion is full of promise and fraught with danger. Arnold asserts that the disinterested business of the believer in culture is 'to get the present believers in action, and lovers of political talking and doing, to make a return on their own minds'.[14] This mention of 'a return' is a return to a passage in Arnold's earlier lecture 'The Function of Criticism at the Present Time' (1864). There he asked writers to cultivate an impulse that pulls against the polemical. His gloss on Burke's ending to *Thoughts on French Affairs* (1791) explains the quality of this impulse:

That return of Burke upon himself has always seemed to me one of the finest things in English literature, or indeed in any literature. That is what I call living by ideas: when one side of the question has long had your earnest support, when all your feelings are engaged, when you hear all round you no language but one, when your party talks this language like a steam-engine and can imagine no other,—still to be able to think, still to be irresistibly carried, if so it be, by the current of thought to the opposite side of the question.[15]

Just as Kant felt that rhetoric could 'move people, like machines', so Arnold fears the growth of party-political language that can encourage you to talk like 'a steam-engine'. This 'return upon' the self is praised as a model of '*disinterestedness*',[16] but admirers of such a return should also note its proximity to what Arnold in his 'Preface to *Poems*' (1853) denounces as 'the dialogue of the mind *with* itself, a dialogue in which 'disinterested objectivity' is not intensified but dissipated by a situation where 'there is everything to be endured, nothing to be done'.[17] For Arnold, literature must lend its peculiar

---

[13] Matthew Arnold, *Culture and Anarchy and Other Writings*, ed. Stefan Collini (Cambridge: Cambridge University Press, 1993), 67, 55, 186.

[14] Ibid. 184.   [15] Ibid. 35.

[16] Ibid. 37; Arnold's emphasis. This quality is again conceived by Arnold as 'keeping aloof from what is called "the practical view of things" . . . leav[ing] alone all questions of practical consequences and application'.

[17] Matthew Arnold, 'Preface to *Poems*', in *The Poems of Matthew Arnold*, ed. Miriam Allott, 2nd edn. (London: Longman, 1979), 656; my emphasis.

eloquence to 'the opposite side of the question', but this eloquence must not tend towards a reflexivity that turns political amplitude into a passive or unprincipled loss of bearings. In the passage above, Arnold's own oscillation between active and passive voices ('still to be able to think, still to be irresistibly carried') gives distilled expression to this dilemma.

Arnold's enquiries into the varying implications of disinterestedness point to how difficult it is to achieve—and to define—a balance between affirmation and concession that is at once politically responsive and responsible. As Henry Sidgwick astutely observed in a review of Arnold's work: 'All this criticism of action is very valuable; but it is usually given in excess, just because, I think, culture is a little sore in conscience, is uncomfortably eager to excuse its own evident incapacity for action.'[18] Such excuses can also lead to claptrap, as George Eliot (an admirer of Arnold and of disinterestedness) suggests when her narrator swoops on Mr Brooke in *Middlemarch* (1871–2):

And here I must vindicate a claim to philosophical reflectiveness, by remarking that Mr Brooke on this occasion little thought of the Radical speech which, at a later period, he was led to make on the incomes of the bishops . . . if he had foreknown this speech, it might not have made any great difference. To think with pleasure of his niece's husband having a large ecclesiastical income was one thing—to make a Liberal speech was another thing; and it is a narrow mind which cannot look at a subject from various points of view.[19]

From this angle, a return upon the self that goes beyond the language of 'your party' is a disingenuous rhetorical manœuvre: self-interest masquerades as large-mindedness. Still, Eliot's wry take on Brooke's pale imitation of disinterestedness is itself disinterested, for the free indirect style through which we learn that 'it is a narrow mind which cannot look at a subject from various points of view' is a model of what it describes. The compound narrative voice belongs to the author and to Mr Brooke, acknowledging the value of Arnold's ideal even as it draws attention to how it might be misused.

The ideal has fared less well since Sidgwick and Eliot offered their even-handed contributions to the debate. A hundred years later, Paul Goodman conceded that 'Some of us . . . have been fighting a losing fight to save "disinterested"', before stressing that the term should not be seen as a synonym for either 'uninterested' or 'impartial', but might be better defined as a 'non-attached attitude'.[20] William Empson also spotted a sea-change when reviewing Raymond Williams's *Keywords* (1976) a few years later. Williams had expressed

---

[18] Henry Sidgwick, 'The Prophet of Culture', *MacMillan's Magazine*, 16 (Aug. 1867), 271–80, pp. 279–80.
[19] George Eliot, *Middlemarch*, ed. David Carroll (Oxford: Oxford World's Classics, 1998), 61.
[20] Paul Goodman, *Speaking and Language: Defence of Poetry* (New York: Random House, 1971), 132–3.

consternation that 'Disinterested is still used, with what are intended to be positive implications' by 'those' who wish to associate the word with ' "undogmatic" concern'. Empson intimates that ' "Those" are the bosses . . . deceiving the workers with their tainted words', and he is bracingly direct about the tainted aspect of Williams's own words: 'why *still*, and where does *dogma* come from? Surely, at any date, in a football match, you want a ref who hasn't been nobbled by either side? . . . I grant that the ref should not be too bored to pay attention, but an appearance of decent coolness is expected of him.'[21]

Empson's metaphor usefully conceives disinterestedness as a form of engaged yet fair-minded arbitration, but subsequent contributions to the debate by both deconstructive and Marxist critics tend towards suspicion. Jacques Derrida sees those who appeal to the concept as making a disingenuous claim to 'interestlessness', while Pierre Bourdieu claims that the term 'really' means 'indifference . . . the refusal to invest oneself and take things seriously'.[22] The term is, I think, redeemable, and it can be made to allow for a more capacious sense of how literary writers conduct their political investigations. But it needs to be considered less as a specific ideology or as a set of prescriptions, more as a method—a *form* of enquiry, rather than a repository for a settled political *content*. Hazlitt, for example, would have baulked at some aspects of Arnold's politics, but his passionate defence of disinterestedness as a fulcrum, not a terminus, is based on his faculty, as David Bromwich puts it, 'of holding two opposed ideas in his mind at the same time': 'he believed "disinterestedness" meant not excluding all interests but being open to an unpredictable plurality of them . . . if [the action] is responsive to many interests, and settled in its service to none, we are making sense when we praise it as disinterested.'[23]

Instead of approaching or reproaching literary texts primarily for their political commitments, we might focus on how writers negotiate contending political demands in and through their work, and on how the literary arena can be considered one in which political questions are raised, entertained, and tested—not only decided or 'settled'. The conflicts and divided loyalties embodied in this arena need not be construed as a merely impracticable or disingenuous hedging of bets. They might also be seen as models of responsible political conduct, for their willingness to engage with multiple and sometimes

[21] William Empson, 'Compacted Doctrines' (1977), in *Argufying: Essays on Literature and Culture*, ed. John Haffenden (London: Chatto & Windus, 1987), 185–6.

[22] Jacques Derrida, 'Economimesis', *Diacritics*, 11 (June 1981), 3–25, p. 15; Pierre Bourdieu, *Distinction: A Social Critique of the Judgement of Taste*, trans. Richard Nice (London: Routledge & Kegan Paul, 1984), 34.

[23] David Bromwich, *Hazlitt: The Mind of a Critic*, 2nd edn. (New Haven and London: Yale University Press, 1999), 22, 80, 86.

contradictory values can prepare the ground for a richer political response in future. Like Arnold, Hazlitt appreciated the literary aspect of Burke's oratory for precisely this reason; he once asserted that 'Burke's eloquence was that of the poet,' and compared it with Chatham's:

I cannot help looking upon him [Burke] as the chief boast and ornament of the English House of Commons . . . Chatham's eloquence was calculated to make men *act*; Burke's was calculated to make them *think* . . . Chatham supplied his hearers with motives to immediate action: Burke furnished them with *reasons* for action which might have little effect upon them at the time, but for which they would be wiser and better all their lives after. [24]

Investigating the grounds of action might sometimes be preferable to inciting it; Burke's disinterested exploration of 'reasons' would often involve the weighing up of opposing claims and incompatible goods. This book is a defence of such a process, and of the potential strength of a politically divided as well as a decisive mind. It envisages disinterestedness as a form of internal struggle, and as a detached yet enabling form of curiosity—an impulse, to adopt Arnold's praise of Burke, that is sympathetically drawn towards 'the opposite side of the question' even as it seeks to engage critically with that opposition.[25]

Debates about disinterestedness are now seen as primarily aesthetic in nature and context, but it is striking how often nineteenth-century defences of the ideal return to oratorical figures or to scenes of rhetorical persuasion: Arnold's sense of the 'opposite side of the question' is shaped by his engagement with the voices in Parliament; Hazlitt's praise of 'poetic' eloquence leads him to the 'chief boast' of the House of Commons. Others who echoed Arnold's terms, if not his politics, also found themselves gravitating towards oratorical debate. When John Stuart Mill in *On Liberty* (1859) supports the need to 'attend equally . . . to both sides', he begins by praising Cicero's willingness to study his adversary's case with greater intensity than his own: 'What Cicero practised as the means of forensic success, requires to be imitated by all who study any subject in order to arrive at the truth.'[26] Mill's subsequent emphasis on disinterestedness is based on this oratorical model, although he revises Cicero's position as enlightened

[24] William Hazlitt, 'Character of Mr Burke' (1807), in *The Complete Works of William Hazlitt*, ed. P. P. Howe, 21 vols. (London: Dent, 1930–4), vii. 302–3.

[25] For other discussions that pursue this line of enquiry, see David Bromwich, 'The Genealogy of Disinterestedness', in *A Choice of Inheritance: Self and Community from Edmund Burke to Robert Frost* (Cambridge, Mass.: Harvard University Press, 1989), 106–32; Eugene Goodheart, *The Reign of Ideology* (New York: Columbia University Press, 1997), 62–81; and Amanda Anderson, *The Powers of Distance: Cosmopolitanism and the Cultivation of Detachment* (Princeton: Princeton University Press, 2001).

[26] John Stuart Mill, *On Liberty and Other Essays*, ed. John Gray (Oxford: Oxford World's Classics, 1991), 42–3.

'advocate' to a focus on that 'judicial faculty which can sit in intelligent judgement between two sides of a question': 'it is not on the impassioned partisan, it is on the calmer and more disinterested bystander, that this collision of opinions works its salutary effect.'[27] Note '*more* disinterested': Mill is not claiming that the bystander is not emotionally involved; disinterestedness is not absence of interest, but an attempt to mediate between interests.[28]

To view disinterestedness, then, exclusively as a retreat into an autotelic aesthetic realm is to overlook other sources of its hold on nineteenth-century imaginations. The versions of disinterestedness formulated by Hazlitt, Mill, and Arnold are also indebted to a long-standing ideal of *public* debate; as Quentin Skinner notes, a central feature of classical rhetorical theory is 'the contention that there are two sides to every question, and thus that one can always argue *in utramque partem*'.[29] This was an informing principle of the Sophists. Aristotle would subsequently note that 'one should be able to argue persuasively on either side of a question', and Cicero observes that 'we must argue every question on both sides'.[30] The modern vocabulary of disinterestedness has much in common with the earlier classical tradition, just as some modern concerns about this vocabulary mirror older criticisms of the role of rhetoric in society. The central ideal, *in utramque partem*, was seen by its defenders as evidence of sophisticated probity in matters of civic concern, but denounced by others—Plato, most prominently—as an indication of sophistical relativism or irresponsible demagoguery.[31]

This debate is echoed in Arnold's sense that disinterestedness can help to create an enlightened 'return upon' the self through an engagement with 'the opposite side of the question', and in his corresponding fear that 'the dialogue of the mind with itself' may lead to cultural and socio-political paralysis. It is significant in this respect that Arnold's concern in his 1853 Preface about the state of modern poetics is accompanied by his decision to cut his poem 'Empedocles upon Etna' from his collection, for Empedocles was seen as the supreme *rhetor* (sometimes even as the inventor of the study of rhetoric) and was teacher of Gorgias (father of the Sophists). Arnold observes that Empedocles has lived on to a time when 'the influence of the Sophists [had begun] to prevail' over a spirit of 'disinterested objectivity'.[32] Behind

---

[27] John Stuart Mill, *On Liberty and Other Essays*, 58–9.

[28] In *Utilitarianism* (1861), Mill associates disinterestedness with 'devotion', 'duty', and 'love', and in *Considerations on Representative Government* (1861) with a 'zeal to benefit others', 'conscience', and 'public spirit'; see *On Liberty and Other Essays*, 160–1, 171, 251, 298.

[29] Quentin Skinner, *Reason and Rhetoric in the Philosophy of Hobbes* (Cambridge: Cambridge University Press, 1996), 10.

[30] Aristotle, *On Rhetoric*, I. i. 1; Cicero, *de Oratore*, I. xxxv. 158.

[31] See Brian Vickers, *In Defence of Rhetoric* (Oxford: Oxford University Press, 1988), 128.

[32] Arnold, 'Preface to *Poems*', 656.

his distrust and suppression of this poetic voice, then, lies a larger concern about where a rhetorical commitment to dialogue might lead in both literary and political realms. Arnold's shifting attitude towards his own work stages a broader crisis: if modern literary expression harbours a rhetorical desire to engage and persuade audiences, then its own inclination towards 'the opposite side of the question' will need to be watched, lest this movement inspires a slide from 'disinterested objectivity' to dispiriting apathy or sophistry.

Consideration of the opportunities and the risks presented by the search for disinterestedness involves an engagement with recent debates about the political inflections of the aesthetic realm. Since the last decades of the twentieth century, a 'hermeneutics of suspicion' has denigrated the category of the aesthetic and its associated value of disinterestedness, seeing it as a form of indifference towards politics, or as a disguised mode of ideological assimilation—a continuation of circumspect (usually translated as 'right-wing') politics by indirect means.[33] Terry Eagleton has recently complained that disinterestedness is a notion 'almost universally scorned by the cultural left nowadays',[34] but he declines to mention that his work has helped to foster and maintain such scorn. His final reference to the term in his *The Ideology of the Aesthetic*, for instance, claims that the relation between 'truth' and 'disinterestedness' is merely 'one of the most powerful ideological ploys of liberal humanist thought . . . which it is important that radicals should sever'.[35]

Eagleton's book is, in fact, a microcosm of the larger historical shift in attitudes. It begins by warning against a facile equation of the aesthetic with any particular ideological position, announcing that aesthetic achievement need not only be a form of indifferent quietism or a cipher for the prevailing ideology, but can also provide the foundation for an enabling critical insight into political praxis. Attentiveness to dual potential, however, soon turns into a narrative of steady decline, as the focus moves from the aesthetic as formative self-analysis to the aesthetic as failed social activism. By the time we get to Eagleton's digest of Adorno, the category has become 'a rationale for political inertia':

praxis is a crude, blundering affair, which could never live up to the exquisite many-sidedness of our theoretical insights. It is remarkable how this Arnoldian doctrine is still alive and well today, occasionally in the most 'radical' of circles . . . From Romanticism to modernism, art strives to turn to advantage the autonomy which its commodity status has forced upon it, making a virtue out of grim necessity. Autonomy in the worrying sense—social functionlessness—is wrenched into autonomy in a more

---

[33] See, e.g. Paul de Man, *Aesthetic Ideology*, ed. Andrzej Warminski (Minneapolis: University of Minnesota Press, 1996).

[34] Terry Eagleton, *After Theory* (London: Allen Lane, 2003), 133.

[35] Eagleton, *The Ideology of the Aesthetic* (Oxford: Blackwell, 1990), 378.

productive sense: art as a deliberate turning in upon itself, as a mute gesture of resistance to a social order which, in Adorno's phrase, holds a gun to its head . . . this negative aesthetics thus proves too feeble a basis on which to found a politics.[36]

This is a characteristic move of Eagleton's book—impersonating an argument by caricaturing it—for Adorno does not see either '*praxis*' or 'art' in these terms. What speaks volumes here, though, is Eagleton's own language. While art's deliberate 'turning in upon itself' reminds one of Arnold's admiration for Burke's disinterested 'return upon the self', Eagleton's crucial addition 'turning *in*' reduces the Arnoldian goal of ameliorative self-reflexivity to an impotent, self-involved posturing. Earlier, Eagleton is more accommodating, referring not to a 'doctrine', but to 'an Arnoldian large-mindedness, impartially weighing competing interests with an eye to the affirmative whole'.[37] During the course of the book, this conception of Arnold's ideal has been pessimistically pared down to a one-sided view of his work. Moreover, by claiming that autonomy was originally something 'forced upon' art, Eagleton indulges in a determinism through which art becomes the mere repository of socio-political change rather than, as he previously suggested, an impetus to it. The verbs continue to conspire against art even when the critic admits that autonomy may be 'productive' (this form of autonomy seems untenable when it is described as being 'wrenched' from the 'grim necessity' of the preceding form). There are no human agents here ('art strives to turn'), just 'isms' and passive structures ('Autonomy . . . is wrenched into'). From an initial recognition of the artist's ability to effect change, we have reached a dead end in which aesthetic expression proves itself feeble in the face of political exigency.

Eagleton's language enshrines an approach that has exerted lasting influence on literary studies. Discussion of the aesthetic as a way to expand conceptual horizons gives way to a view of the aesthetic as an indifferent or impotent stance on any practical political effort whatsoever. Adorno offers a way out of this dismal end-game, for he has a more mobile sense of how the aesthetic might help to 'found a politics'. He points out that artists need not advocate 'a particular partisan position' to be considered 'committed'; they may rather 'work toward an attitude': 'Art is not a matter of pointing up alternatives but rather of resisting, solely through artistic form, the course of the world, which continues to hold a pistol to the head of human beings.'[38] Adorno, then, considers artistic form not as 'mute' (as Eagleton suggests), but as the most powerful means available to artists to appeal to their audiences, for

---

[36] Terry Eagleton, *The Ideology of the Aesthetic*, 363, 370.   [37] Ibid. 163.

[38] Theodor Adorno, 'Commitment', in *Notes to Literature*, ed. Rolf Tiedemann, trans. Shierry Weber Nicholsen, 2 vols. (New York: Columbia University Press, 1991–2), ii. 79–80.

his emphasis on form rather than content accords art a non-propositional character that can lead to a different way of life.[39]

In *Aesthetic Theory* (1970), Adorno's dialectical conception of art as 'autonomous' and as '*fait social*' leads to the assertion that 'art does not come to rest in disinterestedness. For disinterestedness immanently reproduces—and transforms—interest.'[40] That is, disinterestedness is achieved not in spite, but because, of an attentiveness to other points of view. Disinterestedness stays interested even as it seeks to resist certain forms of interest, and this resistance is a form of *response*. The emphasis on 'transformation' again leads Adorno to artistic form: 'Real denunciation is probably only a capacity of form . . . Artworks exercise a practical effect, if they do so at all, not by haranguing but by the scarcely apprehensible transformation of consciousness.'[41] Praxis, then, is not seen as 'a crude, blundering affair' by Adorno; on the contrary, it is part of what art *is*. His proposal that art 'is less than praxis and more . . . as the negation of practical life, it is itself praxis'[42] is similar to Arnold's view that 'it is only by remaining collected, and refusing to lend himself to the point of view of the practical man, that the critic can do the practical man any service'.[43] In contrast to demands for propositions and a directly political content in art, a step back from the terms of the debate—and from the terminology of the debaters—is here envisaged as the way to ameliorative action through art.[44]

Adorno's stridency about form ('*solely* through artistic form') has its own hesitancies ('*probably* only a capacity of form'), and while the writers I discuss were often averse to 'haranguing' their audiences, they were also aware that dedication to a 'scarcely apprehensible transformation of consciousness' might be a luxury that urgent political circumstances do not always grant. Each sought to develop a form of public eloquence that could mediate between a commitment to circumstance and a need for circumspection, and a study of this dual concern needs to be attuned to the outspoken as well as to the oblique political inflections of literary writing—to content as well as to form.

Instead of abstract discussions of the politics of the aesthetic, George Levine calls for another kind of emphasis:

There must be a distinction between aspiration to some impossible ideal disinterested stance, and the effort to resist, in certain situations, the political thrust of one's own

---

[39] See Simon Jarvis, *Adorno: A Critical Introduction* (Cambridge: Polity, 1998), 90–147.

[40] Theodor Adorno, *Aesthetic Theory*, ed. Gretel Adorno and Rolf Tiedemann, trans. Robert Hullot-Kentor (London: Athlone, 1997), 13.

[41] Ibid. 230, 243.   [42] Ibid. 241.   [43] Arnold, *Culture and Anarchy*, 41.

[44] Adorno and Arnold thus echo what Paul Guyer refers to as the 'deepest lesson' of Kant's aesthetics, a lesson also explored in Schiller's *On The Aesthetic Education of Man* (1795); see Guyer, *Kant and the Experience of Freedom*, 94–130.

interest in order—in those situations—to keep open to new knowledge of alternative possibilities and to avoid the consequences of simple partisanship. There is something utterly nihilistic, not to say counterproductive, about the extension of the truism that everything is political into a practical obliteration of all grades of interest in all circumstances . . . If *everything* is political, discriminations between, say, a classroom debate and a political debate, between a novel and a campaign speech, are mere mystifications.[45]

Levine's language is cagey, but responsibly so, for locating and defining distinctions between 'grades of interest' is a difficult business. Discriminating between the political tenor of a literary text and a campaign speech is one way of doing this, however, and an instructive way forward if we are to test and revise the thesis that a 'disinterested stance' is either impossible or inconsequential. By focusing on oratorical as well as on literary styles between the early nineteenth and twentieth centuries, this book suggests correction along the lines hinted at by Levine when he notes that 'literature cannot be imagined as somehow divorced, by way of the aesthetic, from moral and political issues; yet no criticism that refuses distinctions between aesthetic and instrumental functions of language can do justice to either the aesthetic or the ideological'.[46] I aim to calibrate the ways in which writers resisted a 'divorce' between literature and politics even as they attempted to formulate distinctions between aesthetic and instrumental languages in their work.

Calls for an understanding of literature as rhetorically motivated yet also rhetorically hesitant continue to be made by writers as well as by critics. One of the perplexed voices in Geoffrey Hill's recent collection *Speech! Speech!* asks: 'Why and how|in these orations do I twist my text?'[47] The following chapters return frequently to these questions. In search of a way in which a politically engaged imagination might effect a *rapprochement* between positive 'action' and contemplative 'return', Hill has voiced the need for writing that includes 'cross-rhythms and counterpointings' and 'the antiphonal voice of the heckler' within its own structure; he praises a style that is 'a recognition and a resistance; it is parenthetical, antiphonal, it turns upon itself'.[48] Again, this definition of literary achievement involves an oratorical imagining ('the antiphonal voice of the heckler'). It also echoes the language of Arnold himself. Hill's words recall Arnold's 'return upon the self', and while he expresses concern about Arnold's 'trim formulas', he goes on to observe:

---

[45] George Levine, 'Reclaiming the Aesthetic', in Levine (ed.), *Aesthetics and Ideology*, (New Brunswick, NJ: Rutgers University Press, 1994), 3, 14–15.

[46] Ibid. 9.   [47] Geoffrey Hill, *Selected Poems* (London: Penguin, 2006), 205.

[48] Hill, *The Lords of Limit* (London: André Deutsch, 1984), 90, 94.

When Arnold praised a paragraph in Burke's 'Thoughts on French Affairs' as 'one of the finest things in English Literature' he reversed significantly an order of precedence. Burke's concern was not with 'literature' in the hypostatically pure form. In Arnold's statement the 'literature' is central, the politics a catalyst in the creation of the integral substance. This is not to suggest that Arnold was unconcerned with the politics but rather that he saw literature as containing politics within a sphere of more precisely adjusted anxieties.[49]

What Hill means by 'literature' in 'the hypostatically pure form' is, I take it, something akin to the *OED*'s modern definition of literature as a specialized, imaginative 'body of writings'. Arnold's reversal of 'an order of precedence' would seem to point towards that shift whereby literature becomes steadily more isolated from 'polite and humane learning'. However, such a reversal of precedence cannot be complete while literature is still seen as 'containing politics'. Hill's language raises the question of how literature 'contains' politics (to contain is 'to hold, comprise, include' but also 'to restrain, hold in, keep in check'), and to what, exactly, literary anxieties are being 'adjusted' when they attempt such containment. These questions preoccupied many writers between the early nineteenth and twentieth centuries. For them, politics was not only a 'catalyst' for literary expression (catalysts do not themselves change during the chemical process); it was a realm that could be influenced and shaped by that form's creative interventions. That is to say, literature itself was conceived as a mode of rhetorical persuasion and as a 'hypostatically pure form'.

DEBATING SOCIETIES

A 'Debating Society arose' when Wopsle took to the stage, and any argument for rereading literature from within the context of nineteenth-century oratorical developments needs to defend its interest in speaking places as well as in written pages. It did not always prove easy to disentangle the two realms; Carlyle, as ever, was tetchily alert to the signs of the times:

But does not, though the name Parliament subsists, the parliamentary debate go on now, everywhere and at all times, in a far more comprehensive way, *out* of Parliament altogether? Burke said there were Three Estates in Parliament; but, in the Reporters' Gallery yonder, there sat a *Fourth Estate* more important far than they all. It is not a figure of speech, or a witty saying; it is a literal fact,—very momentous to us in these times. Literature is our Parliament too![50]

---

49 Ibid. 107.
50 Thomas Carlyle, *On Heroes, Hero-Worship and the Heroic in History* (1841), in *The Works of Thomas Carlyle*, ed. H. D. Traill, 30 vols. (London: Chapman & Hall, 1896–9), v. 164.

Carlyle's sense of 'literature' hovers between older and newer senses of the word, referring to press and print culture generally but also gesturing towards the implications of these developments for writers of fiction, drama, and poetry. The shift from the figurative to the literal is tempting—we might see the literary realm itself as a parliament in which different voices are represented—but it should also be noted that writers often tried to resist the evolving party-political terms of debate, and to circumvent and extend parliamentary procedures in their work.

Carlyle's strictures echo the observation in *The Times* that 'We are now more than ever a debating, that is, a Parliamentary people'. The nineteenth century was the most insistently parliamentary age in Britain's history. As Henry Reeve observed when discussing the effects of the 1832 Reform Bill: 'Parliamentary Government has been established in this country with greater purity and efficiency than it ever possessed before'.[51] For many, parliamentary rule meant government by talk. During the early decades of the century, as Boyd Hilton observes, 'the focal point of politics was no longer the closet nor yet the ballot box but the division lobby . . . what was said in the Commons actually swayed the outcome of legislation'.[52] At certain times, the Commons could make and unmake governments: between 1841 and 1865, of the six parliaments elected, each brought down at least one ministry without recourse to a general election.[53] That is not to say that oratorical prowess was the consistently predominant factor in shaping either policy or votes.[54] Still, although a speech might fail to change immediate opinion or personnel in Westminster, eloquence had a considerable effect on the longer-term balance of power in the Commons—as Burke observed: 'If a man speaks well, he gradually establishes a certain reputation and consequence . . . though not one vote is gained a good speech has its effect.'[55]

Many subsequent politicians shared this outlook. Looking back to a time when 'the pen was . . . a more formidable political engine than the tongue', Macaulay remarked how times had changed and how 'the orator . . . has to a

---

[51] Henry Reeve, 'Earl Grey on Parliamentary Government', *Edinburgh Review*, 108 (July 1858), 271–97, p. 272.

[52] Boyd Hilton, *A Mad, Bad, and Dangerous People? England, 1783–1846* (Oxford: Clarendon Press, 2006), 209.

[53] T. A. Jenkins, *Parliament, Party and Politics in Victorian Britain* (Manchester: Manchester University Press, 1996), 36.

[54] See Michael Rush, *The Role of the Member of Parliament since 1868: From Gentlemen to Players* (Oxford: Oxford University Press, 2001), 183–7.

[55] Edmund Burke, cited in James Boswell, *Boswell's Life of Johnson*, ed. George Birkbeck Hill and L. F. Powell, 6 vols. (Oxford: Oxford University Press, 1934–50), iii. 233–4.

great extent superseded the pamphleteer'.[56] The *OED* documents the shift: in 1839 *Blackwood's* coined a phrase when it referred to 'the parliamentaryism of the nineteenth century'; 'parliamentarian' began to refer to 'a skilled and experienced parliamentary debater'(1834), while the adjective 'parliamentary' to describe the language of Parliament is recorded as dating from 1818. Alongside these developments came new words for those engaged in debate: 'speech' was used as a verb (meaning 'to direct a speech *at* a person' (1826)), and its cognates took on increasingly varied shapes as public speakers came to the foreground of national attention: 'speechification' (1809), 'speechment' (1826), 'speechful' (1842).

As Carlyle observed, a crucial factor in the development of the age of 'speechification' was the expansion of the press. During the eighteenth century, the standing order prohibiting the recording or publication of parliamentary debates meant that access to such voices was sporadic. Digests and recollections in public journals were renowned for the artistic licence of their 'recreations'—as Dr Johnson handsomely remarked of his methods: 'I took care that the WHIG DOGS should not have the best of it.'[57] This state of affairs began to change; by 1780, the *Morning Chronicle* noted 'the present rage for Debate, which seems to inflame all ranks of people',[58] and the flames were fanned by changing rules and attitudes in the House. Discussions lengthened when the rule stipulating that an MP could speak only once in a debate was relaxed,[59] and although at the end of the 1700s one could still be jailed for reporting debates, Westminster had abandoned its efforts to enforce the standing order.

MPs duly began to refashion themselves rhetorically by developing styles that could mediate between those listening at Westminster and those reading the newspapers. Print 'historicized the speech (or a version of it), took possession of it and gave it an extra-parliamentary dimension. It brought wider opportunities for the critical discussion and interpretation of debates and for the assessment of an orator's performance and reputation.'[60] What was

[56] Thomas Babington Macaulay, 'The Life and Writings of Addison', *Edinburgh Review*, 78 (July 1843), 193–260, p. 221.

[57] Samuel Johnson, cited in Benjamin Beard Hoover, *Samuel Johnson's Parliamentary Reporting: Debates in the Senate of Lilliput* (Berkeley and Los Angeles: University of California Press, 1953), 55.

[58] *Morning Chronicle*, 5 Apr. 1780.

[59] P. D. G. Thomas, *The House of Commons in the Eighteenth Century* (Oxford: Clarendon Press, 1971), 193.

[60] Christopher Reid, 'Whose Parliament? Political Oratory and Print Culture in the Later Eighteenth Century', *Language and Literature*, 9 (May 2000), 122–34, p. 127.

once perceived by MPs as a threat (the 'critical' discussion of their speeches) would slowly come to be seen as an opportunity, for if print took possession of their words, it also allowed their words to take possession of the public. In 1850 the opening of the new Houses of Parliament was delayed for two years while a glass roof was installed so that speeches could be heard in the reporters' gallery. Bagehot remarked how times had changed: 'only those members have been discontented whose speeches have *not* been adequately reported.'[61]

William Cobbett's *Parliamentary Debates* (1802–) were the first elaborate and connected record of parliamentary discussion published in England, and *Hansard's Parliamentary Debates* came into official being in 1812 when Cobbett's *Debates* was sold to the Hansard family. Never before or since had so many pages of print been devoted to political oratory, and the rise of *The Times* was an important influence on these developments. While Parliament was in session, between a half and three-quarters of its news columns were dedicated to parliamentary reports.[62] *The Satirist* referred to an 'age of oratory and politics . . . we have so many volumes of parliamentary debates',[63] and Hazlitt proclaimed that 'the manufacture of newspapers and parliamentary speeches, have exceeded all former example'.[64] Examples continued to be exceeded; fifty years later, Henry Traill calculated that *The Times* devoted approximately 1,500 lines of print per day to a 'deluge of political talk'.[65] Looking back on the nineteenth century, William Murphy recalled: 'Then was the era of the political orator's power. A speech delivered in the House of Commons in the evening was read next morning at a million breakfast tables, and discussed in the afternoon in thousands of workshops and mills.'[66]

G. H. Francis spoke for many when he emphasized the importance of contributing to the deluge: 'publicly and ostensibly powerful you will never be, unless you have mastered the art of oratory'.[67] Francis's 'you' is referring not only to those inside the House; it points to the links between public speaking and the development of democracy—much to the chagrin of Carlyle, who complained in his journal that '*Democracy*' involved 'the Talking

[61] Walter Bagehot, 'Parliament and the Press' (1875), in *The Collected Works of Walter Bagehot*, ed. Norman St John-Stevas, 15 vols. (London: *The Economist*, 1965–86), vii. 300.

[62] See W. F. Monypenny and G. E. Buckle, *The Life of Benjamin Disraeli, Earl of Beaconsfield*, 6 vols. (London: John Murray, 1910–20), ii. 840.

[63] *The Satirist*, 1 Mar. 1811, 234.

[64] Hazlitt, 'Standard Novels and Romances' (1815), in *Complete Works*, xvi. 20.

[65] Henry Traill, 'The Plague of Tongues', *National Review*, 6 (Jan. 1886), 616–30, pp. 618, 630.

[66] William S. Murphy, *The Genesis of British War Poetry* (London: Simpkin, Marshall & Co., 1918), 39.

[67] G. H. Francis, *Orators of the Age* (London: Nickisson, 1847), 2.

Necessity'.[68] In 1850 he growled: 'Talk, talk... To wag the tongue with dextrous acceptability, there is for human worth and faculty, in our England of the Nineteenth Century, that one method of emergence and no other... Vox is the God of this Universe.'[69] *Vox* was not yet *vox populi*, but it was loud enough to be heard by many as a portent of things to come. Marx also emphasized how parliamentary systems created the tastes by which they were to be relished:

The war of the orators at the rostrum evokes the war of the printing presses; parliamentary debaters are necessarily supplemented by debaters in the salons and saloon bars... The parliamentary regime leaves everything to majority decision, why then should the great majorities outside parliament not want to make decisions? When you call the tune at the pinnacles of power, is it a surprise when the underlings dance to it?[70]

The movement from spoken oratory to the printed page, and then from the need to discuss it over a drink to the formation of a written petition, forms an analogy that accords with Marx's sense of the public as an imitation parliament. The increased focus on the speaking place at Westminster ('*parler-ment*': 'speaking-place') was to lead to another development that raised the volume still further: the platform.

Political movements made increased use of the platform in the early decades of the century.[71] Moreover, politicians began to use new spaces to influence the public, from the growth of the 'political dinner' as a mode of public address to the increased focus on speech making at elections.[72] Extra-parliamentary oratory and rituals went some way towards drawing new members of the community into the political process; non-voters also played an active part in the election drama, through heckling and joining (illicitly) in the show of hands during voting. The platform was effecting a shift in conceptions of the political nation. By 1845, Francis could observe that 'The "pressure from

---

[68] Thomas Carlyle, quoted in James Froude, *Thomas Carlyle: A History of his Life in London*, 2 vols. (London: Longman, 1884), i. 429.

[69] Carlyle, *Latter-Day Pamphlets* (1850), ed. M. K. Goldberg and J. P. Seigel (Ottawa: Canadian Federation for the Humanities, 1983), 15, 241.

[70] Karl Marx, 'The Eighteenth Brumaire of Louis Bonaparte' (1852), in *Marx: Later Political Writings*, ed. and trans. Terrell Carver (Cambridge: Cambridge University Press, 1996), 71.

[71] See John Belchem, 'Radical Language and Ideology in Early Nineteenth-Century England: The Challenge of the Platform', *Albion*, 20 (1988), 246–60; James Epstein, *Radical Expression: Political Language, Ritual and Symbol in England, 1790–1850* (Oxford: Oxford University Press, 1994).

[72] See Peter Brett, 'Political Dinners in Early Nineteenth-Century Britain: Platform, Meeting Place and Battleground', *History*, 81 (Oct. 1996), 527–52; Frank O'Gorman, 'Campaign Rituals and Ceremonies: The Social Meaning of Elections in England, 1780–1860', *Past and Present*, 135 (May 1992), 79–115.

without" is now looked to as the ready solution of all political difficulties and dilemmas . . . The whole empire is from time to time under the influence of public speakers.'[73] Many groups employed public speeches and lectures to further their causes, and the platform steadily gained respectability as the century progressed.

Gladstone's career highlights the shift in attitude. In 1856 he expressed concern that 'The inter-sessional speeches of members to their constituents present us with the picture of something like a confessional for politics, brought under the public eye.'[74] However, the reform crisis of 1866–7 encouraged more MPs than ever to take to platforms outside the House. In the first extended study of the phenomenon to appear in England, Henry Jephson observed:

That every minister who had to undergo re-election had felt himself compelled to appear on the Platform before his constituents, and to take them, and through them, the country, into his confidence, was such a recognition of the Platform as had in earlier times never been dreamed of.[75]

Jephson's shift from 'constituents' to 'country' underlines the growth of the political nation that the 1867 Act helped to secure, and the platform was increasingly 'recognized' after the act. The growing challenge to the authority of the Commons through appeals to 'the people' was exploited by Gladstone himself in his widely publicized Midlothian tours, and the sense of an audience outside Westminster became a key part of political oratory. From the 1870s, many important policy statements were made *outside* parliament,[76] and the rise of the figure of the 'charismatic leader' centred on the image of the orator moving mass crowds.[77]

By 1883, John Wodehouse could complain that public speeches were more of a necessity than an opportunity:

They are one of the duties in public life with which unfortunately one cannot dispense, and I am sorry to say that in this country 'going to the stump' has become a recognised

[73] [G. H. Francis], 'Contemporary Orators: Sir Robert Peel', *Fraser's Magazine*, 31 (Apr. 1845), 379–91, pp. 380–1.

[74] William Gladstone, 'The Declining Efficiency of Parliament', *Quarterly Review*, 99 (Sept. 1856), 521–60, p. 554.

[75] Henry Jephson, *The Platform: Its Rise and Progress*, 2 vols. (1892; repr. London: Cass, 1968), ii. 442.

[76] See H. C. G. Matthew, 'Gladstone, Rhetoric, and Politics', in Peter Jagger *Gladstone*, (ed.), (London: Hambledon, 1998), 213–34.

[77] See Eugenio Biagini, *Liberty, Retrenchment and Reform: Popular Liberalism in the Age of Gladstone, 1860–1880* (Cambridge: Cambridge University Press, 1992), 369–425.

part of the business of politics and will become more and more indispensable, every year, as democracy gains in strength.[78]

Although the business is recognized, Wodehouse's quotation-marks try to hedge off the new language it creates. The verb 'to platform' is recorded as being first used in 1859, and it was followed by a string of new associates: 'platformism' (1866), 'platformally' (1870), 'platformistic' (1892), 'platformish' (1892). By the 1880s, miniature Houses of Parliament had sprung up in many areas of the country, modelling themselves on proceedings at Westminster. Blanchard Jerrold observed of this 'growth of bibulous discussion-assemblies' that 'there might be a member for High Street in each House'.[79] The transformation of high politics to the high street is a succinct marker of how a fascination with speaking places had changed the face of popular political reaction. This imagined participation in the government of the nation was not seen merely as an impotent echo of the voices at Westminster, but as a potential influence on those voices.

Such developments coincided with the steady erosion of parliamentary influence as the century drew to a close. Changes in parliamentary procedure allowed party leaders to dictate discussions in the House. Nights set aside for government business rose from two to four, and the implementation of the *clôture* (or 'closure') meant that debates could be brought to an end with the consent of the Speaker.[80] Henry Maine gravely predicted that the closure 'will probably lead to a constitutional revolution, the House of Commons abandoning the greatest part of its legislative authority to a Cabinet of Executive Ministers'.[81] Such predictions proved true. As parliamentary supremacy finally gave way to Cabinet government, so the demand for press coverage of discussions on the floor of the House petered out. By 1905, Alfred Kinnear could observe: 'It may be said that verbatim reports are now uncalled for. They are as dead as the Dodo.'[82] The era of government by talk was coming to an end.

The vexed, intimate relations between oratory and literature are not peculiar to the nineteenth century, but they are, then, particularly relevant to it (the

[78] John Wodehouse, quoted in J. Powell (ed.), *Liberal by Principle: The Politics of John Wodehouse, 1st Earl of Kimberley, 1843–1902* (London: Historians' Press, 1996), 167.

[79] Blanchard Jerrold, 'On the Manufacture of Public Opinion', *Nineteenth Century*, 13 (June 1883), 1080–92, p. 1092.

[80] See Edward Hughes, 'The Changes in Parliamentary Procedure, 1880–1882', in Richard Pares and A. J. P. Taylor (eds.), *Essays Presented to Sir Lewis Namier* (London: Macmillan, 1956), 289–319.

[81] Henry Maine, *Popular Government: 4 Essays* (London: Murray, 1885), 95.

[82] Alfred Kinnear, 'Parliamentary Reporting', *Contemporary Review*, 87 (Mar. 1905), 369–75, p. 369.

prominence of religious and barristerial public speakers are other landmarks of the age).[83] Recent literary criticism has tended to concentrate on what might be termed 'the politics of form' in order to chart the relations between literary and political realms, but this approach can be enriched by dwelling on the political languages most widely disseminated and discussed during the period itself—supplementing work on the politics of form with a concurrent attentiveness to the forms of politics. This study involves deliberately varying approaches to the material: local engagements of writers with rhetorical *topoi* (such as paralipsis, *circumlocutio*, litotes, *restrictio*), political orators, and styles stand alongside more general considerations of how various types of concession might operate in vocal and printed addresses, or of the ways in which the responsibilities of a writer to his audience can be aligned with those of a politician to his constituents. Public speaking is, therefore, conceived and studied as a spoken and a written phenomenon. Indeed, around the beginning of the nineteenth century, 'volume' came to refer to something you could hear as well as to something you could see (the *OED* gives 1801 for the first citation of 'volume' as 'the compass of a voice'). Two other examples from the mid-century hint at crossovers between the visual and the aural; 1850 sees the first recorded instance of the verb 'voice' applied to 'writings', while 1855 witnessed the word 'audience' being used to refer to 'readers of a book'.

These developments suggest that grand narratives of the century as breaking with an oral past, instituting a decisive shift to print culture, stand in need of revision.[84] A brief survey of some intersections between speech and print reveals the protean culture in which writers were located. While the diction and cadences of political speeches were pored over on the printed page, written texts were read aloud. As MPs took to the platform to influence their audiences, writers embarked on reading and lecture tours to disseminate their work.[85] Ruskin may have been appalled by 'this age of lecturers', but he also claimed that *Modern Painters* was 'itself a lecture with no conclusion', and he soon mounted the platform to provide a spoken rendition and extension of his printed

[83] See Robert H. Ellison, *The Victorian Pulpit: Spoken and Written Sermons in Nineteenth-Century Britain* (Selinsgrove: Susquehanna University Press, 1998); Jan-Melissa Schramm, *Testimony and Advocacy in Victorian Law, Literature, and Theology?* (Cambridge: Cambridge University Press, 2000); and Joseph S. Meisel, *Public Speech and the Culture of Public Life in the Age of Gladstone* (New York: Columbia University Press, 2001).

[84] See Walter Ong, *Orality and Literacy: The Technologizing of the Word* (London: Methuen, 1982). For a revisionary argument, see John M. Picker, *Victorian Soundscapes* (Oxford: Oxford University Press, 2003).

[85] See Philip Collins, *Reading Aloud: A Victorian Métier* (Lincoln: Tennyson Society, 1972); Philip Waller, *Writers, Readers, and Reputations: Literary Life in Britain, 1870–1918* (Oxford: Oxford University Press, 2006), 575–614.

words.[86] Readers were also keen to get in on the act. Reading and speaking manuals flooded the market, urging people to recite works of literature aloud.[87] One manual aimed to help 'every one engaged in *speaking* or *writing* for the public', as if both types of eloquence required the same skills.[88] Another begins by insisting that 'you must learn to think aloud' in the act of reading if you are to learn to be a proficient public speaker, and, with the assistance of Lord Brougham, Edward Cox founded a Public Reading Association that invited members of the public to read literature to an audience.[89]

The public vocalization of literature was encouraged as a way of integrating an increasingly literate community into responsible citizenship. A monthly journal devoted to elocution and oratory was set up, announcing that public speaking was 'an accomplishment without which no man or woman can be considered to have received a proper education'.[90] To better your speech was to better your station, and literature was often enrolled in the cause. *Live and Learn*, for example, a manual that went through twenty-eight editions in seventeen years, encouraged readers to 'Take, every morning, some passage from a good writer, poetry or prose; mark every letter and syllable with respect to which a mistake is likely to occur, using a good dictionary in the case of the slightest uncertainty; pronounce each word several times by itself'.[91] 'Taking' literature every morning, perhaps along with the paper, and reading the former aloud before then reading voices on the pages of the latter, underlines how the permeable boundaries between speech and print were related to those between politics and literature.

The presence of literary culture in political life is highlighted by the practice of politicians, many of whom made frequent allusion to literary texts during debate. Disraeli noted that, not only were MPs quoting 'Byron & Tennyson' (poets, at least), 'But Bright & Cobden, & all those sort of people, are always quoting Dickens & *Punch*, &c'.[92] Notwithstanding Disraeli's sneer, the

[86] John Ruskin, *The Library Edition of the Works of John Ruskin*, ed. E. T. Cook and Alexander Wedderburn, 39 vols. (London: George Allen, 1903–12), xii. 387, xxii. 511.

[87] See Donald C. Stewart, 'The Nineteenth Century', in Winifred Horner (ed.), *The Present State of Scholarship in Historical and Contemporary Rhetoric* (Columbia: University of Missouri Press, 1990), 151–85.

[88] Chauncey Goodrich, *Select British Eloquence* (London: Sampson Low, 1852), p. iii; my emphasis.

[89] Edward Cox, *The Arts of Writing, Reading and Speaking* (London: Crockford, 1863), 2.

[90] Anon., *Speech*, 1/1 (Oct. 1889), 1. On the gendered aspects of public speaking in the period, see the essays in *Nineteenth-Century Prose*, 29 (Spring 2002).

[91] Anon., *Live and Learn: A Guide for All Who Wish to Speak and Write Correctly*, 28th edn.. (London: Shaw, 1872), 160–1. See Lynda Mugglestone, *'Talking Proper': The Rise of Accent as Social Symbol* (Oxford: Clarendon Press, 1995).

[92] Benjamin Disraeli, *Disraeli's Reminiscences*, ed. Helen M. Swartz and Marvin Swartz (New York: Stein and Day, 1976), 98.

fact that politicians even quoted such texts suggests that they were still felt to carry political weight and authority even as the 'literary' was becoming increasingly defined as a realm apart from such debate. John Bright highlights the suppleness of the technique; in Birmingham in 1858 he observed the plight of 'the poor half-starved farm-labourer' before saying:

You know what a Peer is. He is one of those fortunate individuals who are described as coming into the world 'with a silver spoon in their mouths'. Or, to use a more polished and elaborate phraseology of the poet, it may be said of him—

> 'Fortune came smiling to his youth and woo'd it,
> And purpled greatness met his ripened years'.[93]

The poet's written words are enlisted into what 'may be said' against the Lord through the pressure of Bright's appositions. The 'silver spoon', when polished up, exerts a pressure on '*purpled* greatness' and '*ripened* years' that pushes the figurative into the literal, for the excessive wining and dining of the Peer points to a constitution which allows others to starve. Such rhetorical flights of fancy led many to conceive oratory itself as a form of literary endeavour. T. H. Escott looked back over his career as a reporter and said that in the 1870s 'parliamentary speaking was still studied and practised as a fine art, not merely as a civic function'.[94] Bright's speeches were published as models of oratory and literature in the 'popular-classical' Everyman's Library until 1907, and, in his preface to the collected edition of the speeches James Rogers was impressed by 'the artistic value of these compositions, which will give them now, and will give them hereafter, so high a place in English Literature'.[95]

In this environment, Parliament was seen as a form of literary entertainment. William White noted that 'the mania outside the House to hear a speech is stronger even than the mania inside to make one', and called Parliament 'the theatre of St. Stephen;'[96] while *The Times* exclaimed: 'They say that we have lost as a nation our theatrical taste, but the truth is Parliament is our theatre.'[97] The drama of politics continued outside Westminster, and Bulwer-Lytton's observation that 'The man who writes a play for Covent Garden ought to remember that the Theatre is but a few paces from the Hustings' carried extra

[93] John Bright, *Speeches on Questions of Public Policy by John Bright, M.P.*, ed. J. E. T. Rogers, 2 vols. (London: Macmillan, 1868), ii. 9, 15.

[94] T. H. Escott, *Platform, Press, Politics and Play* (Bristol: Arrowsmith, 1895), 325.

[95] Bright, *Speeches*, i. p. vi. See also the section on 'Political Orators' in A. W. Ward and A. R. Waller (eds.), *The Cambridge History of English Literature*, xiv: *The Nineteenth Century* (Cambridge: Cambridge University Press, 1916), 119–37.

[96] William Hale White, *The Inner Life of the House of Commons*, ed. Justin McCarthy, 2 vols. (London: Unwin, 1897), i. 157, ii. 156.

[97] *The Times*, 4 Feb. 1859, 2c.

weight in an age where political rallies were held in the theatre.[98] 'A few paces' was an exaggeration in this instance; in Covent Garden, politics and theatre shared the same stage. *The Times* observed of the Anti-Corn Law meetings held at the venue that 'maids and matrons flock to the theatres, as if it were but a new "translation from the French" '.[99]

The political orator was a celebrity.[100] *The Times* observed that readers 'expect to be told not only what [he] said, but how he looked when he said it, how he took the answer of the other side, and how he looked when he replied to it'.[101] The allure of a seat in the Lords or the Commons also brought literary and cultural figures into the fray: as well as the poet-lords (Byron and Tennyson) and novelists-turned-MPs (Disraeli, Bulwer-Lytton), John Stuart Mill, Trollope, Dickens, Thackeray, Bagehot, Arnold, and Conan Doyle were either asked to stand, or did stand for Parliament. Literary-political crossovers were further highlighted by an irreverent supplement to *The Times*—referred to by one Chancellor of the Exchequer as 'that publication so familiarly known to all Members of this House'[102]—*Punch*. The journal forged a political satire that drew frequent analogies between literary sources and political speeches and events. In the 1840s Peel appeared in its pages in the guise of various Dickens characters, including Nicholas Nickleby, Joseph Bowley, and Oliver Twist: 'We have heard that MR. CHARLES DICKENS is about to apply to the Court of Chancery for an injunction to prevent SIR ROBERT PEEL continuing any longer, in his capacity as Premier, the character of MR. PECKSNIFF, as delineated in *Martin Chuzzlewit*, that character being copyright.'[103] David Vincent's sense of a contemporary audience accustomed to moving from 'politics as reasoned arguments to politics as entertainment to entertainment alongside politics' is clear from such sprightly examples.[104]

Oratorical and literary realms, then, met and parted company in many ways throughout the period, and a sustained focus on four authors writing between the early nineteenth and twentieth centuries stands in need of some explanation. The writers are chosen partly because of their popularity and influence; they are representatives as well as focal points, and might stand as synecdoches for the larger history of relations between writers and speakers in

[98] Edward Bulwer-Lytton, 'On Art in Fiction', *The Monthly Chronicle*, 1 (Apr. 1838), 138–49, p. 146.

[99] Quoted in Donald Read, *Cobden & Bright: A Victorian Political Partnership* (London: Camelot, 1967), 54.

[100] See Stefan Collini, *Public Moralists: Political Thought and Intellectual Life in Britain, 1850–1930* (Oxford: Oxford University Press, 1991), 33–4.

[101] *The Times*, 7 Feb. 1874, 9b.   [102] *Hansard*, cxxxvii. 781 (19 Mar. 1855).

[103] *Punch* (London: Bradbury & Evans, 1844), vii. 25.

[104] David Vincent, *Literacy and Popular Culture: England, 1750–1914* (Cambridge: Cambridge University Press, 1989), 210.

the period. They also sought, in varying ways, to create a printed speech that could offer indirect resistance to the terms of evolving political debate. The focus is on novels and poems, not on plays, because a recurrent concern of this book is to show how printed words and private scenes of reading might form reflective yet engaged counterpoints to fast-paced vocal utterances and immediate crowd responses.[105] The opening sections of each chapter situate the writer in relation to his peers, but these peers are given cameo roles rather than lead parts because one of my central contentions is that oratorical culture was not a sporadic influence, but a formative principle across the whole span of these prominent literary careers. Each chapter claims that, in order to shed new light on each author's socio-political engagements, we need to remain attentive—as he did—to political oratory throughout his early and late writings.

Byron was born in the year in which *The Times* came into existence (1788), and he was an avid reader of the oratory that commanded unprecedented space in early nineteenth-century newspapers. He was also the first popular writer in these new historical circumstances to have trained for and begun a career in Parliament, and thus provides a valuable starting-point. Chapter 1 examines his engagements with Whig, Tory, and radical oratory in his speeches and poetry, and ends by looking in detail at the biggest-selling literary work of the Romantic period, *Don Juan* (1818–24). Dickens provides the most varied body of spoken and written engagements with Liberal reform rhetoric in the nineteenth century, and—as Davis notes—he reaches 'further down and further across the social scale than any of his contemporaries'.[106] His novelistic debut, *The Pickwick Papers* (1836–7), takes its bearings from his apprenticeship as a parliamentary reporter, and was published in volume form a few months before *Hansard* first went on sale to the general public. Chapter 2 considers how his diverse careers as shorthand writer, journalist, speaker, and public reader informed his attempts to shape the Victorian periodical novel into a mode of civic eloquence.

Chapter 3 aims to offer new insight into perhaps the most significant poetic development of the age—the dramatic monologue—by looking at how the printed voices of Tennyson's early poems were shaped by orators at the Cambridge Union and beyond. It then charts the ways in which the Laureateship asked the poet to speak *for* as well as *to* his public, exploring how Tennyson's reading of imperialist oratory (and his long-standing relationship with the most famous orator of the age, William Gladstone) influenced

---

[105] On the theatre, see Julia Swindells, *Glorious Causes: The Grand Theatre of Political Change, 1789 to 1833* (Oxford: Oxford University Press, 2001).

[106] Davis, *Victorians*, 205.

the rhetorical structures of *Maud* (1855) and *Idylls of the King* (1859–85). Chapter 4 focuses on Joyce and 'the Irish question'. The aims of Irish eloquence were recurring features of political debate, partly as a result of the Act of Union that saw Irish politicians enter Westminster in 1801. Born in the year that *clôture* was implemented (1882), Joyce is the last writer who had persistent recourse to the styles of Victorian oratory in his work. Indeed, the closure was itself instituted to combat Irish obstructionism in the Commons, and the loquacious tactics had a key part to play in the erosion of parliamentary autonomy at the end of the century. The chapter considers Joyce's early work, and ends with a sustained focus on *Ulysses* (1922), thinking through the implications of the writer's choice to structure his masterpiece around the figure of the most renowned orator in the classical literary tradition.

This book is primarily concerned to chart how writers envisaged their work in relation to contemporary political voices, but it also considers how modern debates about relations between poetics and rhetoric are inflected by classical forbears. Three of the four authors studied were classically trained, and Dickens's early years as a parliamentary reporter involved prolonged exposure to the voices of those who were educated in the same tradition. This tradition acknowledged that poetics could inform and enrich political debate—Aristotle, Cicero, and Quintilian all recommended the study of poetry as part of a sound rhetorical training and quoted poets as examples of procedure to be emulated. As Jeffrey Walker has recently shown, even as distinctions were made between poetics and rhetoric, epideictic 'literaturized' forms of rhetoric (concerned with the 'forming' of opinions) were also seen as the foundation of pragmatic modes of persuasion in parliaments or courts (concerned with making decisions). That is, civic eloquence was descended from poetic discourse—epideictic modes were formative influences rather than ornamental afterthoughts.[107] The emergence of the categories of the 'literary' and the 'aesthetic' in the nineteenth century is informed by this heritage. Post-Romantic discussions are full of oppositions—as Walker puts it, ' "Rhetoric" and "poetry" align with the practical and the aesthetic, the mundane and the ineffable, manipulation and truth, constraint and freedom, and so forth.'[108] However, these oppositions are constantly being tested by writers who sense the value of forms of literary eloquence that may seek to shape opinion by offering something more than the clear statement of an opinion.

When Aristotle defended the central ideal of classical rhetoric, he observed: 'One should be able to argue persuasively on either side of a question . . . in

---

[107] Jeffrey Walker, *Rhetoric and Poetics in Antiquity* (Oxford: Oxford University Press, 2000).
[108] Ibid. 329.

order that it may not escape our notice what the real state of the case is.'[109] Like Arnold and his contemporaries, Aristotle had concerns about the ethical and socio-political dangers of such reflexive and reflective powers, but considered that—if rhetoric was to be an 'art'—it would need to face these dangers rather than to avoid them by abandoning the ideal. A commitment to arguing on both sides is an acknowledgement of the inescapability of conflicting attachments and callings: rhetoric 'is concerned with the sort of things we debate . . . And we debate about things that seem to be capable of admitting two possibilities.'[110]

The art of modern literary eloquence shares this perspective, and is founded on an appreciation of literary style as a form of conduct as well as a mode of persuasion. Eugene Garver writes:

An art of rhetoric never stops being a capacity for arguing both sides of a question . . . despite this ethically troubling status, rhetorical activity . . . is itself valuable, even if not all its products are valuable . . . An art which proves opposites creates mistrust. Today we don't need to be reminded of this mistrust. But we do need to know about its nobility.[111]

Literary eloquence can embody this nobility, for it offers us a form of expression that stands by what it says in two senses: we 'stand by' our utterances when we commit ourselves to them; but we also 'stand by' such utterances when we reconsider them, stand back to survey them from a more disinterested perspective, acknowledging and incorporating counter-claims. As Empson once wrote, such an imagining 'combines breadth of sympathy with energy of judgment; it can keep its balance among all the materials for judging'.[112] This is the poised conviction that a literary persuasion may carry.

---

[109] Aristotle, *On Rhetoric*, I. i. 12.   [110] Ibid.

[111] Eugene Garver, *Aristotle's Rhetoric: An Art of Character* (Chicago: University of Chicago Press, 1994), 180, 212, 248.

[112] William Empson, *Some Versions of Pastoral* (1935; repr. New York: New Directions, 1974), 64.

1

Byron's Hearing

QUESTION, QUESTION

Byron was alert to alliteration. The poet was quick to admonish those who allowed such acoustic licence into their writing. Reviewing William Spencer's poems, he asked, 'Why is "horse and horseman *pant* for breath" changed to "*heave* for breath," unless for the alliteration of the too tempting aspirate?'[1] Good question, although the poet was not immune to the temptation himself; in the first stanza of the work that made him a literary celebrity, *Childe Harold's Pilgrimage*, we encounter 'Hellas' deemed of 'heavenly birth', a Muse 'formed or fabled' and 'since shamed' by 'later lyres', along with a 'feeble fountain' and a 'lowly lay'.[2] When William Gifford suggested that Byron revise a line from Canto IV, the poet replied: 'but the Alliteration—I cannot part with it—I like it so'.[3] Byron had a weakness for such effects, but he also felt that they might betoken a kind of strength. They were reminders that his poetry was to be heard as well as seen, and to be conceived as a form of public speech.

At another moment in *Childe Harold's Pilgrimage*, the narrator considers the importance of George Washington:

> Can *t*yrants *b*ut *b*y *t*yrants conquer'd *b*e,
> And Freedom *f*ind *n*o champion and *n*o child
> Such as Columbia saw arise when she
> Sprung forth a Pallas, arm'd and undefiled?
>
> (IV, 856–9; my emphasis)

The alliterative display in the first two lines is a raising of the poet's voice, and this emphasis is present so that Byron might respond to another speaker who haunts these lines. The poet observed that 'Mr. Pitt was liberal in his additions to our parliamentary tongue',[4] and one of Pitt's most celebrated additions came in a speech reported by Coleridge: the orator defended the war against

---

[1] *BCP*, 12.   [2] *BPW*, Canto I, 1–9.   [3] Ibid. ii. 338.   [4] Ibid. i. 432.

France, swore enmity to those who 'have profaned the name of liberty', and labelled Napoleon 'the child and the champion of Jacobinism'.[5] Byron's lines incorporate Pitt's coinage but invest it with a different kind of energy, for the 'champion' and 'child' now refer to Washington and those who might follow his example. The orator's assured jibe becomes part of an investigation into the nature of political power.

Joseph Priestley claimed that an interrogative appeal to an audience aimed to 'engage belief', for 'no person would seriously make such an appeal, who did not believe his course to be so clear that all the world, if they considered it, would concur with him in it'.[6] Like many of Byron's interrogatives, the question in *Childe Harold's Pilgrimage* does not quite seek to persuade or to engage belief, but instead asks the audience to reconsider an apparently 'clear' course from an unclear vantage-point. It is uncertain whether 'Can tyrants but by tyrants conquered be?' is a rhetorical question: the existence of a Washington would seem to imply that tyranny need not be self-replicating, and yet, mindful as the stanza is of the post-Waterloo restoration of the Bourbons that Pitt's policy helped to secure, the tone can also be heard as beleaguered, even desperate, rather than invigorating. The ambiguity of Byron's printed question-marks is part of their power; as Peter Robinson has observed of questions in verse, the reader cannot 'fix the cadence and pitch intonationally to make such an insinuated answer, as would need to be done in a politician's speech'.[7] Byron's lines are astir with multiple insinuations, for they also suggest that Pitt and his political descendants have themselves 'profaned' as well as fought for 'the name of liberty' in their war against 'the child and champion of Jacobinism'.

The poet's mixture of hope and hesitancy is to be found in many other Romantic questionings ('If winter comes, can spring be far behind?'). Such writing practises a Byronic ideal:

> If you can add a little, say, why not?
> As well as William Pitt and Walter Scott; . . .
> 'Tis then, and shall be, lawful to present
> Reforms in writing, as in Parliament.
>
> (*Hints from Horace*, 83–8)

---

[5] William Pitt, cited in *The Collected Works of Samuel Taylor Coleridge*, iii: *Essays on his Times in the Morning Post and the Courier*, ed. David V. Erdman, 3 vols. (Princeton: Princeton University Press, 1979), i. 185.

[6] Joseph Priestley, *A Course of Lectures on Oratory and Criticism* (London: Johnson, 1777), 108–10.

[7] Peter Robinson, *Poetry, Poets, Readers: Making Things Happen* (Oxford: Clarendon Press, 2002), 68.

Byron felt that readers were frequently 'auditors'.[8] Hearing as well as reading the first line, we catch the poet having his 'little say', and this defence
of the value of presenting reforms in writing comes from an awareness
of the alliances between literary and oratorical endeavour. Mark also the
speaker's absolute 'shall', whereby the poetic becomes performative, and
writing becomes legislation. As Byron observed when discussing the figures
of '*poet*' and '*Orator*': 'both *ancients* and *moderns*, have declared, that the
2 pursuits are so nearly similar . . . he who excels in the one, would on
application succeed in the other'.[9] Such declarations are made by Cicero
and Quintilian,[10] and the 'moderns' to whom Byron refers followed their
lead.[11] Yet, 'so *nearly* similar' carries a reservation. The poet's career would
also involve consideration of how 'reforms in writing' might ward off oratorical examples, and of how poetry could be conceived and practised as a
mode of eloquence that offered its own kind of political wisdom ('reforms
in writing' is fruitfully ambiguous; the writing might embody reform, rather
than just present it—an oblique template as well as an explicit petition).
Byron's willingness to 'add a little' to one of Pitt's 'additions to our parliamentary tongue' in *Childe Harold's Pilgrimage* is, after all, a peculiar type
of reform and reformulation—it does not offer a proposal for a specific
measure, but engages in a process of taking the measure of other political
standpoints.

Jerome McGann suggests of Byron's writing that 'The difference from
usual Romantic practice is crucial': 'His work assumes the presence of an
audience that listens . . . It is as if Byron . . . were declaring or even declaiming
his inmost thoughts out loud, and directly to others.'[12] The 'usual' Romantic
practice is more varied than this distinction suggests, for many contemporary
writers adopted declamatory and rhetorical stances in their work.[13] McGann
has in mind poets like Wordsworth and Coleridge, yet Wordsworth's homage
to Burke's 'most eloquent tongue' in *The Prelude*, and his recollection of
when his own 'breast had heaved | Under the weight of classic eloquence',
indicate the importance of his training in rhetoric for a vision of the poet

---

[8] *BCP*, 9.   [9] *BLJ*, i. 113.

[10] See Cicero, *De Oratore*, I xv. 70; Quintilian, *Institutio*, x. i. 27.

[11] See Hugh Blair, *Lectures on Rhetoric and Belles Lettres*, 3rd edn., 3 vols. (London: Strahan &
Cadell, 1783); George Campbell, *The Philosophy of Rhetoric* (Newbury Port: Wait and Whipple,
1809).

[12] Jerome McGann, *Byron and Romanticism*, ed. James Soderholm (Cambridge: Cambridge
University Press, 2002), 96, 117–18, 120.

[13] See e.g. *The Anti-Jacobin* (1797–8), in John Strachan and Graham Stones (eds.), *Parodies
of the Romantic Age*, 5 vols. (London: Pickering & Chatto, 1999), and John Strachan and Steven
Jones (eds.), *British Satire, 1785–1840*, 5 vols. (London: Pickering & Chatto, 2003).

who must '*address* himself' to his audience as 'a man *speaking* to men' (my emphasis).[14] Coleridge felt that 'Fears in Solitude' was also a search for ears in solitude—'perhaps not poetry, but rather a sort of Middle thing between Poetry & Oratory'[15]—and his reporting of contemporary oratory, meditations on his own talk and lecturing styles, and awareness of the political engagements of his 'conversation' poems kept him attuned to what written and spoken forms of utterance might have in common. Shelley's defence of the poet as unacknowledged legislator is also indebted to a sense of the writer as speaker: Lord Bacon's writings show him to be a 'poet', for 'All the authors of revolutions in opinion are necessarily poets', and Bacon's language 'bursts the circumference of the *hearer's* mind' (my emphasis).[16] Byron's work is the most sustained poetic engagement with oratorical culture in the period, but it is by no means alone or idiosyncratic; many other writers assume 'the presence of an audience that listens'. As David Wellbery has suggested, 'the relationship of Romanticism to rhetoric should be conceived less as the abandonment of a tradition than as its transformation'.[17]

Byron's search for a blend of declarative and deliberative utterances began with a study of the orators themselves, and of two Whig speakers in particular: Richard Sheridan and Edmund Burke. A crucial debate on the French Revolution highlights the socio-political charges of their styles. Burke's denunciation of the Revolution draws on literary sources—he cites Tacitus, Virgil, and Ovid[18]—and such quotation seeks to lend a temporal amplitude and authority to his arguments (after quoting Virgil, Burke notes of the Revolution that 'he was astonished at it—he was alarmed at it—he trembled at the uncertainty of all human greatness').[19] These quotations, given without reference to the authors from whom they are taken and without translation into English, are appeals to the educated honourable gentlemen in the audience, those

---

[14] William Wordsworth, *The Prelude* (1850), in *The Prelude: A Parallel Text*, ed. J. C. Maxwell (Harmondsworth: Penguin, 1984), Book VII, 517, 541–2, and 'Preface to *Lyrical Ballads*' (1802), in *William Wordsworth: The Major Works*, ed. Stephen Gill (Oxford: Oxford University Press, 2000), 603.

[15] Samuel Taylor Coleridge, cited in *The Collected Works of Samuel Taylor Coleridge*: xvi: *Poetical Works*, Part 1, ed. J. C. C. Mays (Princeton: Princeton University Press, 2001), 469.

[16] Percy Bysshe Shelley, 'Defence of Poetry' (written 1819, pub. 1840), in *Shelley's Poetry and Prose*, ed. Donald H. Reiman and Sharon B. Powers (New York: Norton, 1977), 485.

[17] David Wellbery, 'The Transformation of Rhetoric', in Marshall Brown (ed.), *The Cambridge History of Literary Criticism*, v: *Romanticism* (Cambridge: Cambridge University Press, 2000), 185–202, p. 186. See also Don H. Bialostosky and Lawrence D. Needham (eds.), *Rhetorical Traditions and British Romantic Literature* (Indianapolis: Indiana University Press, 1995), and James Mulvihill, *Upstart Talents: Rhetoric and the Career of Reason in English Romantic Discourse, 1790–1820* (Newark: University of Delaware Press, 2004).

[18] *PH*, xxxviii. 353, 355, 356, 363 (4 Mar. 1790).   [19] Ibid. 354.

whose classical learning will, Burke hopes, help them to resist 'the excesses of an irrational, unprincipled, proscribing, confiscating, plundering, ferocious, bloody, and tyrannical democracy'.[20]

For the Foxite Whigs, as for Byron, the Revolution was not 'unprincipled', and it was left to Sheridan to take up the gauntlet, employing the strategic re-quotation and sardonic wit for which he had become famous: 'What action of theirs [the French National Assembly] authorized the appellation of a "bloody, ferocious, and tyrannical democracy?" . . . Mr. Sheridan next attacked Mr. Burke's declaration, that the French might have received a good constitution from their monarch. What! was it preparing for them in the camp of marshal Broglio? or were they to search for it in the ruins of the Bastile?'[21] Rousing stuff, but the speech also misrepresents Burke's argument. As he pointed out in his rejoinder, he had not used the words Sheridan quoted in reference to the National Assembly, and he also answered Sheridan's rhetorical questions by offering his own: 'Was that a fair and candid mode of treating his argument? . . . [Sheridan's] argument was chiefly an argument *ad invidium*, and that all the applause for which he could hope from clubs, was scarcely worth the sacrifice which he had chosen to make for so insignificant an acquisition.'[22] The philosophical flourish ('*ad invidium*') is coupled with the dig at Sheridan's interest in applause from 'clubs', implying that Sheridan is addressing himself more to the populace outside the House than to the gentlemen inside. For Sheridan, Burke's lofty classicism bespeaks a lack of concern for the lower orders; for Burke, Sheridan's lowering of the tone points to an unwillingness to rise above the seductions of popular applause. For both, oratorical styles were intimately linked to political principles.

This was a pivotal moment in the relations between the two men (Burke lamented that 'henceforth, his hon. friend and he were separated in politics'),[23] and it underlined the fractures in the Whig Party that would dominate its fortunes for the next forty years. Byron began to find his own voice by listening to these voices: he claimed that Burke was 'the nearest approach to Oratory in England'; but he observed that Sheridan 'was the only one I ever wished to hear at greater length'.[24] Although the poet was delighted at Lord Grenville's response to his maiden speech ('[he] remarked that the construction of some of my periods are very like *Burke's*!!'),[25] he had also asserted that Sheridan was a 'great name' whom he would attempt to 'imitate' but 'never equal' in the House.[26] The two orators spoke to different aspects of the poet's temperament. David Erdman's description of Byron as a man with 'puzzling inner tensions between radical aristocrat and aristocratic radical'[27] is apt, and these tensions were first explored in the agile movements of his parliamentary speeches.

On turning 21, the poet bought Cobbett's *Parliamentary Debates* and *Parliamentary History of England*.[28] From the start, Byron was reluctant to be seen as a party man, and took up a seat on the cross-benches.[29] Lord Holland, Byron's mentor and leader of the Whigs in the Upper House, helped the poet to prepare his maiden speech, and was pleased to find that his young charge was 'anxious to learn the forms' of parliamentary etiquette.[30] But this learning of the forms was achieved in order that Byron might more effectively decline to be on good form. After his speech, a perturbed Holland complained that Byron's oratory was 'full of fancy, wit, and invective, but not at all suited to our common notions of Parliamentary eloquence'.[31] The poet put it more bluntly: he spoke 'with a sort of modest impudence'.[32] The speeches are peppered with literary quotations, and include references to sources of which Burke would have approved (Virgil, Publilius Syrus, Quintilian, and Seneca), but also to works closer to home, and closer to Sheridan's tastes (Swift, Prior, Pope, and Smollett). The modest impudence was an effort to blend Burke's attentiveness to authoritative forms with Sheridan's gift for the artful insinuation as a challenge to the limits of such forms.

His maiden speech highlights this mixture of tones and sympathies. The Frame Work Bill set out the case for the death penalty for frame-breakers, and Byron's brief from Lord Holland was to follow the moderate party line by asking for a Committee of Inquiry into recent disturbances. The poet had other ideas:

But whilst these outrages must be admitted to exist to an alarming extent, it cannot be denied that they have arisen from circumstances of the most unparalleled distress . . . Frames of this construction tend materially to aggravate the distress & discontents of the disappointed sufferers.—But the real cause of these distresses & consequent disturbances lies deeper.—When we are told that these men are leagued together not only for the destruction of their own comfort but their very means of subsistence, can we forget that it is the bitter policy, the destructive warfare of the last eighteen years which has destroyed their comfort, your comfort, all men's comfort [?] . . . You call these men a mob, desperate, dangerous & ignorant, & seem to think

---

[27] David. V. Erdman, 'Lord Byron', in Kenneth Neill Cameron (ed.), *Romantic Rebels: Essays on Shelley and his Circle* (Cambridge, Mass.: Harvard University Press, 1973), 161–202, p. 163.

[28] Leslie A. Marchand, *Byron: A Biography*, 3 vols. (London: John Murray, 1957), i. 168. The poet had already read 'Parliamentary Debates from the Revolution to the year 1742'; see *BCP*, 6, 233.

[29] Marchand, *Byron*, i. 164.

[30] Henry Richard Vassall, *Further Memoirs of the Whig Party, 1807–1821, With Some Miscellaneous Reminiscences*, ed. Lord Stavordale (London: John Murray, 1905), 123.

[31] Ibid.   [32] *BLJ*, ii. 167.

that the only way to quiet the "Bellua multorum capitum" is to lop off a few of it's superfluous heads.—But even a mob may be better reduced to reason by a mixture of conciliation and firmness, than by additional irritation & redoubled penalties.—Are we aware of our obligations to a *Mob*?—It is the Mob, that labour in your fields & serve in your houses, that man your navy and recruit your army, that have enabled you to defy all the world, & can also defy you, when Neglect & Calamity have driven them to despair.—You may call the people a Mob, but do not forget, that a Mob too often speaks the sentiments of the People.[33]

Those Burkean 'periods' can be heard in Byron's attempts to widen the temporal perspective of the debate by going 'deeper' into the causes of the issue (from 'these outrages' to more generalized 'circumstances'; from 'these men are leagued together' to 'the destructive warfare of the last eighteen years'), and in his borrowing from Horace's *Epistulae* that refers to 'the many-headed monster' of the populace (a Burkean distaste for the 'swinish multitude'). But Burke's speech-tics are not translated into Burkean positions: the widening of the time-frame asks that the ministers acknowledge that unrest at home is a corollary of the war against France, while the show of classical learning is immediately followed by Byron's calculated veering into colloquialism ('lop off') and a defence of the people's cause. The archly dextrous syntax of 'You call these men a mob, desperate, dangerous & ignorant' allows the speaker to mean two things at once: 'you call these men desperate, dangerous and ignorant', or 'your act of calling these men a mob is itself desperate, dangerous and ignorant'.

The speech also gestures towards the voice that Sheridan had cultivated in Parliament, whereby the speaker's forms of address mirror his political point by extending beyond those in Westminster. Cobbett had complained that Sheridan was the first to introduce '*low-banter*' into debate, aiming at 'falling in with the humour of the common people',[34] and one contemporary noted that both Whigs and Tories considered Byron's speech 'a sarcastic discourse, adapted rather to the taste of a popular meeting than to the business of a legislative assembly'.[35] Byron once wrote that he 'thought rather of the *public without* than the persons within'[36] when speaking in the Lords, and this train of thought can be heard in his oscillation between first- and second-person plural pronouns, themselves a 'mixture of conciliation and firmness': 'Can *we* forget . . . destroyed *your* comfort . . . *You* call these men . . . Are *we* aware . . . labour in *your* fields.' These shiftings between implicated and aloof

[33] *BCP*, 22, 23, 25.

[34] William Cobbett, *The Political Proteus: A View of the Public Character and Conduct of R. B. Sheridan, Esq.* (London: Cox and Baylis, 1804), 201.

[35] Horace Twiss, *The Public and Private Life of Lord Eldon*, 3 vols. (London: John Murray, 1844), ii. 190.

[36] *BLJ*, ix. 17.

stances announce a speaker who sees himself as a part of and apart from the
Lords. The 'we' speaks as one of the Peers on the subject of the disgruntled
people, while the 'your' speaks in the voice of the people to the Lords who
should legislate in their name.

The tussle of political registers in Byron's speech is encapsulated in his final
chiasmus: 'You may call the people a Mob, but do not forget, that a Mob
too often speaks the sentiments of the People.' The drift seen on the page
from 'people' to 'People' is something that an attentive ear would have heard.
Byron is deliberately invoking a contested word in contemporary political
discussion; 'the People' might refer to the traditional Whig sense of that term,
which signifies the political nation, defined as those whose property grants
them the privilege of representation; or it might carry a more democratic
slant, referring to all members of the nation, who have the right to have their
demands addressed.[37] Burke was a defender of the former sense, Sheridan
flirted with the latter, and Byron is treading a fine line between the two.
His phrasing would suggest that he is using the term in a predominantly
Whig sense (his 'often' implies that 'a Mob' should not be conflated with 'the
People'). However, because it arrives on the back of another reference to 'the
people' in general, the sense shades towards a populist line of argument: 'those
who you deem to be beneath your attention, and beneath the privilege of
representation, are a part of the political community to which you owe your
allegiance and your deference'.

Byron's speech hovers between deference and provocation in order that he
might push at the limits of the sayable in this arena, and that he might give voice
to his diverse sympathies. These sympathies are often sensed in one of the poet's
most cherished words: '*But* whilst these outrages . . . *But* the real cause . . . *But*
even a mob . . . *but* do not forget' (my emphasis). Whilst acknowledging the
'paltering' potential of 'but', Christopher Ricks writes: 'Byron's greatness is his
various insistence upon the word and upon the thousand ways in which it is
urgent . . . "But" is the vocable for a profound and generous sceptic . . . "But"
is also a word that recognizes conflicting impulses, and conflicting impulses
are at the heart of Byron's feat.'[38] The 'but's that animate Byron's speech are
principled rather than paltering; they urge the Lords to reflect on the causes of
the disturbances as a way of enlarging their deliberations on how to deal with
their effects. Byron conceded that he was 'not famous for decision' and that he
was drawn to 'a Spirit of contradiction',[39] but he also felt that a willingness to
entertain contradiction in both print and speech could foster the grounds for a

[37] See Leslie. G. Mitchell, *Charles James Fox* (Oxford: Oxford University Press, 1992), 141.
[38] Christopher Ricks, *Allusion to the Poets* (Oxford: Oxford University Press, 2002), 143, 146.
[39] *BLJ*, x. 157, xi. 137.

more measured process of decision making. This commitment was embodied in one of his most renowned recourses to the word 'but': 'but I was born for opposition' (*Don Juan*, XV, 176).

Byron's constitutional feeling for opposition is indebted to the Whig view of the ideal constitution. The party's defence of the need for a balanced government, and its emphasis on the importance of curtailing the growing powers of the executive that had taken place under George III, were major influences on Byron's speeches and poems. Indeed, Whig political culture might be seen as a formative influence on Romantic poetics more generally: when Coleridge writes that the poet's imaginative power 'reveals itself in the balance or reconciliation of opposite or discordant qualities',[40] his language recalls Burke's on the recommended Whig form of government; for the politician's ideal state involves 'the reciprocal struggle of discordant powers' that 'we reconcile, we balance'. Such balancing is 'an excellence in composition', and when Burke describes the constitution as 'that great work, a combination of opposing forces, "a work of labour long, and endless praise"', his quotation from Spenser again underlines how poetic and public forms of government might be considered alongside each other.[41]

Byron's 'but' is an axis on which 'opposing forces' might turn, and another marker of this oppositional rhetoric, itself frequently accompanied by a 'but', is the question. MPs shouted 'question, question' to urge that debates be brought to a close, whereby the Speaker would put the question to the House and then move to a taking of 'Ayes' and 'Noes'. However, the actual questioning of ministers during debate was subject to strict rules; it was prohibited to ask them 'for an expression of their opinion upon matters of policy'.[42] The Whig Party increasingly tried to get round these proscriptions, and the historical growth of questions during debate coincided with the development of sustained Whig opposition at the end of the eighteenth century.[43] The poet's own interrogative mode in the House would often tread a fine line between being a question and a rhetorical question (the latter might not constitute a direct breaking of the rules): 'can we forget that it is the bitter policy, the destructive warfare of the last eighteen years, which has destroyed their comfort [?] . . . Are we aware of our obligations to a *Mob*?'

---

[40] Samuel Taylor Coleridge, *Biographia Literaria: Or Biographical Sketches of My Literary Life and Opinions*, ed. George Watson (London: Dent, 1980), 174.

[41] Edmund Burke, *Reflections on the Revolution in France*, ed. Leslie G. Mitchell (Oxford: Oxford University Press, 1999), 35, 170, 289.

[42] See Thomas Erskine May, *A Treatise on the Law, Privilege, Proceedings and Usage of Parliament* ([1844]; repr. London: Clowes, 1893), 236–40.

[43] See Patrick Howarth, *Questions in the House: The History of a Unique British Institution* (London: Bodley Head, 1956), 55.

Leigh Hunt finely noted that the poet's observations were frequently uttered 'in an under-tone between question and no-question'.[44] Such an undertone is heard in the poet's maiden speech, and in the question 'Can tyrants but by tyrants conquer'd be?' with which this chapter began. For the orator, this vocal tremor combines tact and temerity: the questions above are meant to compel assent, yet they are both structured around 'we' rather than 'you'. That is, Byron creates a form of address that carries the incredulous urgency of 'Surely you would agree that . . .', whilst also softening the antagonistic blow by retaining a sense that he is somehow implicated in his own line of questioning: 'I, too, would have to admit that . . .'. For the poet, the undertone between question and no-question was something more than an astute political strategy ('Can tyrants but by tyrants conquer'd be?' does not have the calculated swagger of Byron's spoken questions). It was also an investment in interrogative acts that were to be considered valuable for their commitment to balanced constitutions, whether personal or political. Hence, a month before his maiden speech in the Lords, he could write consecutive letters that take slightly different stances on questions: one announced the politician's dutiful decisiveness ('a division is expected in the house, & I must be present during the question'), the other defended the poet's more personal sense of his own circumspection ('it would be very unfair, and very contrary to my disposition, not to hear both sides of the question').[45]

Critics have often envisaged Byron as Whig Party spokesman. Richard Cronin suggests that 'Byron's inconsistencies are at least as characteristic of his party as they are of himself: he is never more truly a Whig than in his bewilderment . . . he remained happy until the end of his life to "retain", as he puts it in the Dedication of *Don Juan*, his "buff and blue" '.[46] Malcolm Kellsall claims that Byron is often to be found 'conforming' to a Whig 'paradigm', and notes that his poems and speeches do not produce 'a coherent, practical and effective strategy for resolving the problem with which they were faced'.[47] Byron owed much to the party, but from his early position on the cross-benches to his later work he was anxious to point out that 'I belong to *no* party—and claim the independence of saying what I please of *any* according to their acts'.[48] As the narrator of *Don Juan* also explains: 'being of no party | I

---

[44] Leigh Hunt, cited in Ernest J. Lovell (ed.), *His Very Self and Voice: Collected Conversations of Lord Byron* (New York: Macmillan, 1954), 310.

[45] *BLJ*, ii. 158.

[46] Richard Cronin, *The Politics of Romantic Poetry: In Search of the Pure Commonwealth* (London: Macmillan, 2000), 142, 157.

[47] Malcolm Kellsall, *Byron's Politics* (Brighton: Harvester Press, 1987), 32, 52.

[48] *BLJ*, x. 166.

shall offend all parties' (IX, 201–2).[49] Moreover, there is the danger that an exclusive focus on Byron's political commitments will merely conceive the poems as failed polemics, and assume that they *should* aim to 'resolve' the political issues they diagnose or discuss (Kellsall notes that some passages of Byron's poetry are 'akin to oratory' before again bemoaning their lack of 'practical effect').[50] It depends on how one measures 'effect': recall Hazlitt's astute observation that Burke's 'poetic' speeches often furnished audiences 'with *reasons* for action which might have little effect upon them at the time, but for which they would be wiser and better all their lives after'.

Byron was excited by the idea that poetry is 'akin' to oratory, but he was also insistent that 'politics and poetry are different things'.[51] One difference, to be valued with caution, was that poems might raise rather than settle questions. To ask a *reader* a question is, in some sense, to preclude an answer, or perhaps to suggest that no simple answer can be given. The gravitation towards the question-mark in Byron's work is evidence of an abiding attraction towards what John Hollander has termed the 'poetic' rather than the 'rhetorical question'. These questions 'may suppose not the usual empty answer (for example, "Yes" or "No" or "Nobody" or "Everybody" or the like), but rather some hedged response, like "You may well ask! There are great problems implicit in putting it that way. Let's see what they are." '[52] In such a realm, the call of 'question, question' does not necessarily serve as a prelude to the counting of Ayes and Noes. Nor does what Cronin refers to as 'bewilderment' signify only an inert 'inconsistency', for the hedged response may mediate between contradictions rather than succumb to them. Like his 'but', Byron's question-mark is often a herald of the potential richness and responsibility of unsettled thinking.

FORMS OF ADDRESS

The earliest known use of the word 'apostrophic', meaning 'of, pertaining to, or addicted to the use of rhetorical apostrophe', has been traced to Byron: 'Mrs. Hemans is . . . too stiltified and apostrophic' (*OED*). Byron's early

[49] On Byron's critical engagement with Whiggism, see Michael Foot, *The Politics of Paradise: A Vindication of Byron* (London: Collins, 1988).

[50] Malcolm Kellsall, 'Lord Byron', in David Pirie (ed.), *The Romantic Period* (Harmondsworth: Penguin, 1994), 289–310, pp. 291, 295.

[51] *BLJ*, i. 159.

[52] John Hollander, *Melodious Guile: Fictive Patterning in Poetic Language* (New Haven: Yale University Press, 1988), 22.

poetry is shot through with forms of address even as it considers the potential limitations of such forms. *Childe Harold's Pilgrimage* (Cantos I and II; 1812) is insistently apostrophic: the first lines of both cantos contain a call to a 'thou'. Anne Barton has noted that the word 'reader' is absent from the poem,[53] and a possible reason for this is suggested by a line in manuscript: 'Listen, readers, to the man of ink.'[54] To call for readers to 'listen' is to reconceive isolated scenes of writing and reading as shared arenas of vocal address and reception. Harold's own pronouncements are often staged as solitary musings, before then being recast as forms of invocation. His first song in the poem comes 'when deem'd he no strange ear was listening' (I, 112), but this cherished lyrical isolation soon shifts to a needy address: 'Come hither, hither, my staunch yeoman, | Why dost thou look so pale? | Or dost thou dread a French foeman? (I, 158–60). Question, question: this voice is anxious to remain within earshot, and the reference to the 'French foeman' reminds us that, even in his most lonesome musings, Harold frequently has contemporary politics on the tip of his tongue. As Stuart Curran has noted of the genre within which Byron was working: 'with Napoleon's invasion of Spain in 1807 and the introduction of British armies onto the Peninsula, the storied land of romance was enveloped in modern reality'.[55]

The poem was composed as Byron prepared for his career in Parliament. He attended the House of Lords in 1809, and he took volumes of parliamentary debates with him when he left for his Grand Tour later that year.[56] Once back in England, he described both his maiden speech and his poem as 'experiments',[57] and felt that his speech gave 'the best advertisement for Childe Harold's Pilgrimage'.[58] Yet the work is not merely an oration in literary form; it is also a space in which Byron considers how poetry might interrogate as well as imitate rhetorical procedures. Richard Cronin observes that the poem is 'designed as a calculated affront to any demand that the individual surrender to a national "unanimity"'.[59] It is therefore fitting that Byron has very little recourse to collective pronouns in his addresses: 'we' appears only twice in the main narrative of Canto I (ll. 610, 908), while 'our' makes three appearances (ll. 255, 311, 908), and 'us' just one (l. 664). Indeed, the only appearance of the word 'address' in the poem hints at a contrapuntal rhythm that challenges its gravitation towards apostrophe: 'It came to pass, that when

---

[53] Anne Barton, *Byron: Don Juan* (Cambridge: Cambridge University Press, 1992), 79.

[54] *BPW*, ii. 41.

[55] Stuart Curran, *Poetic Form and British Romanticism* (Oxford: Oxford University Press, 1986), 131.

[56] Marchand, *Byron*, i. 314.   [57] *BLJ*, ii. 167; *BPW*, ii. 3.

[58] Robert Dallas, *Recollections of the Life of Lord Byron* (London: Knight, 1824), 203–4.

[59] Cronin, *Politics*, 133.

he did address | Himself to quit' (II, 613–14). At the line-end we expect that Harold is about to address someone else, but the enjambment translates public invocation into private communing. It's as if the speaker suddenly loses his voice. This movement from stridency to hesitancy is also characteristic of the poem's political enquiries; it does not quite manage to inspire conviction, but one reason for this is that Byron is searching for a form of address that can unsettle convictions.

Michael Broers points out that the British troops defending Spain against Napoleon's army were also guilty of brutality against Spanish cities and civilians: 'Both armies despised the deeply Catholic culture they encountered, and the British desecrated churches just as the French had done ... An abhorrence of bullfighting did not, it seemed, preclude visiting far worse horrors on humans.'[60] Byron is often drawn to an exploration of political issues through a consideration of bestial and belligerent actions, and his oratorical researches had a bearing on this rhetorical manœuvre. In the last parliamentary debate he attended before he left for the Continent, one of the most renowned Whig apologists, Thomas Erskine, presented his Cruelty to Animals Bill in the Lords. The speech focused on acts of cruelty to horses and on the 'barbarous sport' of 'Bull-Baiting'.[61] The former, in particular, led to an outburst at Londoners for their offences against God's creatures:

Observe what we all of us are obliged to see every day in our lives—horses panting—what do I say! literally dying under the scourge . . . on looking into the chaises, we see them carrying to and from London men and women . . . More than half the post-horses that die from abuse in harness, are killed by people . . . galloping over our roads for neither good nor evil, but to fill up the dreary blank in unoccupied life. I can see no reason why all such travellers should not endeavour to overcome the *ennui* of their lives without killing poor animals, more innocent and more useful than themselves.[62]

These words stayed with the poet. Ruskin once acutely perceived in 'the most violet-bedded bits of [Byron's] work...a strange taint...London air'.[63] Lyricism inhales civic air—the air of the speakers inside and outside the House. In the first Canto the narrator is embarking on his description of the bullfight and 'the spouting gore | Of man and steed' (ll. 688–9) as a way of criticizing the 'day of blessed rest' on the 'Christian shore' (ll. 684–5) in Spain, when he suddenly checks himself and casts his searching eye back to his homeland. Erskine's voice is mingled with the cries of the London streets:

---

[60] Michael Broers, *Europe under Napoleon, 1799–1815* (London: Arnold, 1996), 246.

[61] *PD*, xiv. 559 (15 May 1809).   [62] Ibid. 562.

[63] John Ruskin, *Fiction, Fair and Foul* (1880–1); cited in Andrew Rutherford (ed.), *Byron: The Critical Heritage* (London: Routledge & Kegan Paul, 1970), 435.

The seventh day this; the jubilee of man.
London! right well thou know'st the day of prayer:
Then thy spruce citizen, wash'd artisan,
And smug apprentice gulp their weekly air:
Thy coach of Hackney, whiskey, one-horse chair,
And humblest gig through sundry suburbs whirl,
To Hampstead, Brentford, Harrow make repair;
Till the tir'd jade the wheel forgets to hurl,
Provoking envious gibe from each pedestrian Churl.

Some o'er thy Thamis row the ribbon'd fair,
Others along the safer Turnpike fly;
Some Richmond-hill ascend, some scud to Ware,
And many to the steep of Highgate hie.
Ask ye, Boeotian shades! the reason why?
'Tis to the worship of the solemn Horn,
Grasp'd in the holy hand of Mystery,
In whose dread name both men and maids are sworn,
And consecrate the oath with draught, and dance till morn.

(ll. 693–710)

In contrast to Erskine's apostrophe, there is no appeal to a 'we' in these snarling lines. Although the specificity of the scene is founded on an insider's knowledge, the 'thou' in the second line puts the speaker at a distance from the society he anatomizes. The additional creation of an address at an even further remove ('Ask ye, Boeotian shades! the reason why?') underlines the narrator's intimacy with a foreign perspective, and his overhearings of his countrymen's voices hint at a divided as well as united nation (with space for the 'envious jibe' of the churl as well as the 'oath' that unites the drinkers). The tussle between linguistic registers (from the earthy 'gulp' to the ethereal 'Thamis') also intimates a voice at war with itself as well as with others. The whole passage generates an eerily arresting effect—audible in much of the poem—of a disoriented yet discerning speaker who is allowing his countrymen to eavesdrop on his address while he talks behind their backs.

Such lines are a retort to those Englishmen who prided themselves both on their united front and on their superiority to their foreign allies. Byron's complication of the structure of Erskine's address creates a sense that something more than the treatment of 'the tir'd jade' is at stake, and he extends the remit of the orator's speech by following up Erskine's brief reference to domestic bull baiting with an extended look at the Spanish bullfight. The description's close proximity to the vision of London asks readers to consider the similarities as well as the differences between the two nations, for we now hear about the matadore and his 'tortur'd horse' (l. 766): 'His gory chest unveils life's

panting source, . . . Staggering, but stemming all, his lord unharm'd he bears'
(ll. 771–3). Erskine's vision of 'horses panting. . . literally dying under the
scourge' is present here, and the 'tortur'd horse' in Cadiz brings to mind the
'tir'd jade' in London, again suggesting that the British should not see themselves as above such cruelty even as they find it reprehensible. To emphasize
the point, the description of the bullfight is also carefully modelled on the
poem's description of the savagery of the British troops at Talavera.[64]

Talk of cruelty to animals may seem a far remove from the complexities
of international politics, but Byron is shaping a language that can enlarge
his readers' political considerations by indirect means. Arousing their disgust
at the 'hideous sight' of the bullfight, the poem's verbal echoes ask them to
reconsider their alternate support and disregard of other forms of violence and
ill-treatment. This analogic mode was itself employed by Erskine: answering
those who thought that the subject was of negligible interest in such pressing
times, the orator claimed that the law would awaken 'the moral sense': 'the
humanity you shall extend to the lower creation will come abundantly round
in its consequences to the whole human race'.[65] Such appeals are based on
one of the three traditional resources of the classical orator: *pathos* (the appeal
to the emotions). Byron's poem frequently draws on such resources, aiming
to cultivate 'the moral sense' by drawing attention to the way in which acts of
oppression might replicate themselves on an ever-increasing scale.

Childe Harold aims to move us, yet his pilgrimage is wary of single-minded
movements, as if fearful of where the orator's calling (*movere*) might lead.
While Byron's mentor, Lord Holland, was demanding unconditional support
for the Spanish fight for freedom,[66] the poet was shaping a less strident rhythm:

> Nor yet, alas! the dreadful work is done,
> Fresh legions pour adown the Pyrenees;
> It deepens still, the work is scarce begun,
> Nor mortal eye the distant end foresees.
> Fall'n nations gaze on Spain; if freed, she frees
> More than her fell Pizarros once enchain'd:
> Strange retribution! now Columbia's ease
> Repairs the wrongs that Quito's sons sustain'd
> While o'er the parent clime prowls Murder unrestrain'd.
>
> (I, 909–17)

A perceptive reviewer felt that the poem's stanza-form housed a vocal address
that had taken a wrong turn: 'as to the suspension of the sense . . . no man reads

---

[64] Compare e.g. ll. 436–7 with 691; 434 and 443 with 733 and 738; 422–7 with 751–6.
[65] *PD*, xiv. 556.
[66] See Leslie. G. Mitchell, *Holland House* (London: Duckworth, 1980), 228–30.

a single stanza without feeling a sort of strain upon the intellect and lungs—a kind of suffocation of mind and body, before he can either discover the lingering meaning, or pronounce nine lines'.[67] It is apposite that a hesitantly oratorical poem which frequently draws our attention to shortness of breath (the citizens of London who 'gulp their weekly air', the 'panting' horses) should also stage these strainings in its form. Throughout *Childe Harold's Pilgrimage*, the difficulty of vocal pronouncing is intimately related to the difficulties of political pronouncement.

The strain is felt here, particularly at the stanza's mid-point, where the sense blurs at the line-end 'if freed, she frees'. For a moment, intellect and lungs read 'frees' as an intransitive verb: Spain's fight is seen as an inspiration for other nations looking to secure their liberty against the imperial French (the Spanish resistance was followed by revolts in Austria, Germany, and Italy). And yet, there is another outlook on this situation, for as 'frees' turns transitive over the enjambed line, so we hear a reminder that Spain is also an enslaver. Quito, one of the provinces in Peru that Pizarro had conquered in the sixteenth century, is recalled alongside American independence, for one corollary of the continued struggle against Napoleon was Spain's inability to hold on to its own colonies: the war precipitated the collapse of the Spanish empire in Latin America, and the eventual rise of independent nations there.[68] While the first half of the stanza laments the cost of Spain's war against an imperial power, the second half sees this war as part of another region's gain of its own 'well asserted right' (I, 921), a gain secured against Spain's territorial ambitions. The shift of emphasis is also heard in the modulation from '*Fall'n* nations' to '*fell* Pizarros'; Spain is both the potential champion of the fallen and the fell opponent of others who are trying to raise themselves. The 'suspension of the sense' and 'lingering meaning' in this stanza are calculated waverings, a poetic bating of breath. The strain on the intellect and lungs is brought about by acoustic tremors and echoes that give voice to something other than rhetorical confidence.

Childe Harold's Pilgrimage is drawn to speakers who raise awkward or unexpected questions. On the opening of Parliament in 1812, as Byron was revising his poem for publication, Lord Holland was asking ministers to acknowledge that they would preserve 'the integrity of the Spanish colonies'.[69] The poet would have cast a quizzical eye at this reference to 'integrity' (a defence of the Spanish empire does not sit easily alongside Holland's plea for

---

[67] Anon., 'Review of *Childe Harold's Pilgrimage*', *Christian Observer*, 11 (June 1812), 376–86, p. 382.

[68] See Jan Read, *War in the Peninsula* (London: Faber & Faber, 1977), 231.

[69] *PD*, xxi. 15–16.

Spain's right to be free from the French imperial aggressor). On the same day in the Commons, the radical Sir Francis Burdett asked for another form of integrity. His speech was a sensation (it was subsequently published and sold 30,000 copies).[70] Turning his attention to the complexities of the Spanish situation, Burdett said:

We never once heard mention of that word, as the spring of our exertions, the word 'freedom'... we now found ourselves engaged in another seemingly endless contest; and he did not believe that any one of the persons who defended it, could say what we were fighting for... the victories they had achieved were barren... The cause of this failure was the radically vicious principle of supporting despotism in this instance, as we did all over the world,—the attempt to support desperate, falling, and not to be supported, states... It was a serious fact, that the Inquisition remained in existence in those parts only of the country of which the English had possession.[71]

When the narrator of Byron's poem observes that 'Nor mortal eye the distant *end* foresees', he suggests not only that the war seems interminable, but also that it is not clear from public pronouncements what end it is meant to secure, and Burdett's reference to a 'seemingly endless contest' is similarly probing. The orator's sense that Britain's support of the Spanish was at odds with some of its own constitutional principles was percipient: when the contest ended in 1813, Britain oversaw a return to the despotic rule of Ferdinand VII.[72]

Burdett's demand that discussions of 'freedom' enter political debate is echoed in the edgily apostrophic form of Byron's poem:

> Not all the blood at Talavera shed,
> Not all the marvels of Barossa's fight,
> Not Albuera lavish of the dead,
> Have won for Spain her well asserted right.
> When shall her Olive-Branch be free from blight?
> When shall she breathe her from the blushing toil?
> How many a doubtful day shall sink in night,
> Ere the Frank robber turn him from his spoil,
> And Freedom's stranger-tree grow native of the soil.
>
> (I, 918–26)

The narrator finally allows 'Freedom' to escape his lips, but the word comes within a stanza whose tone is drained of Burdett's indignant cadences. The beleaguered eloquence that is so characteristic of *Childe Harold's Pilgrimage*

---

[70] Byron and Burdett were mutual admirers of one another's oratory; see Lovell (ed.), *His Very Self and Voice*, 545; *BLJ*, ix. 14, ii. 167.

[71] *PD*, xxi. 18–20 (7 Jan. 1812).

[72] See Alexander Grab, *Napoleon and the Transformation of Europe* (Basingstoke: Palgrave Macmillan, 2003), 143.

is heard in the not-quite-completed triadic structures: 'Not all . . . Not all' shifts to 'Not Albuera'; 'When shall . . . When shall' drifts into slight metrical ripple of 'How many'; 'free from . . . breathe her from' veers into 'shall sink in'. The stanza would seem to end on a third question, although its inability to summon up the energy for a third question-mark turns the query into a half-hearted assertion. It is as if the speaker does not have the appetite for the fight. The sighing of the rhymes suggests as much, moving from combative righteousness ('fight/right') to a wearied loss of bearings ('blight/night').

Swinburne had little patience with such disquiet, and suggested that one should read *Childe Harold's Pilgrimage* in translation: 'Stumbling stanzas, transmuted into prose and transfigured into grammar, reveal the real and latent rhetorical energy that is in them: the gasping, ranting, wheezing, broken-winded verse has been transformed into really effective and fluent oratory . . . He rants no longer out of tune.'[73] To translate: 'When shall the poem breathe her from the blushing toil?'. From this perspective, *Childe Harold's Pilgrimage* suffers from a unconsummated flirtation with oratory; Swinburne's sense of the verse as 'broken-winded' recalls the earlier reviewer's feeling that the stanzas were 'a strain on the lungs'. And yet, the value of the poem may lie in its troubled floundering rather than its assured fluency. The moment at which the verse is heard to be 'out of tune' in the stanza above is a particularly well-timed stumble: after the even tread of the first seven lines, we hear the first strong metrical substitution in the penultimate line as pyrrhic precedes spondee: 'Ere the *Frank robber*'. The broken-winded movement is not without cutting edge: readers would have been expecting the speaker to berate the 'French' rather than the 'Frank' robber on Spanish soil, but the metre buckles at the very moment when the narrator shifts the terms of the debate.

Byron uses 'Frank' elsewhere in the first two Cantos to refer to the Europeans in general and to his own countrymen.[74] The poet's reference to 'Freedom's stranger-tree' is a particular criticism of the British (when his countrymen conquered French territory after 1793, they pulled up the liberty trees that the French had planted). 'The blushing toil' of war can be—like a blush itself—a sign of virtue or shame, and the government's support of Spain's cause is a mixture of both (a defence of a country against an imperial aggressor, and a protection of Britain's own aggressive imperial interests). The war against the French led to the greatest expansion of British imperial control since the seventeenth century. Like Burdett's speech, Byron's poem refuses

---

[73] Swinburne, 'Wordsworth and Byron' (1884); cited in Rutherford (ed.), *Byron: The Critical Heritage*, 468–9.

[74] See Canto II, 602, 732, and *BPW*, ii. 202, 204, 206, 210.

to let such things go unsaid, and his reference to the Frank robber's spoil throws the spotlight on what one commentator has called Britain's 'dual-faced system': 'absolutist and monopolistic in the outside world, and oligarchy tempered with liberalism in Europe'.[75] When the poet penned this stanza, every colonial possession of France and her dependants was in British hands.[76] For those statesmen who constantly warned against the towering ambitions of the French empire, and for those countrymen who prided themselves on the British defence of Spain, the poet's frank use of the word 'Frank' is a considered form of heckling. The term appears in a 'broken-winded' stanza, and in a line that is metrically 'out of tune', because Byron wanted his words to stick in the throat.

In his schooldays, Byron was a budding orator: 'My qualities were much more oratorical and martial—than poetical.'[77] The apposition of the 'oratorical' and 'martial' in contrast to the 'poetical' is striking, particularly in relation to *Childe Harold's Pilgrimage*, a work frequently sceptical about the value of martial achievements. Even though Byron's poem is a form of fighting talk, the poet's distrust of the probity and efficacy of contemporary military conquests leads him to shy away from verbal conquest in his analysis of them—hence the mixture of 'latent rhetorical energy' and 'stumbling' in his stanzas. Like Harold's pilgrimage, Byron's poem never quite has an end in sight: literary circumspection and oratorical commitment stand in uneasy relation to one another, and the 'poetical' becomes, to adopt a phrase from Canto II, a kind of 'baffled zeal' (l. 201).

This baffled zeal was noted by reviewers. When expressing their admiration for the poem, they also paused to express concern about its lack of one particular ingredient: 'enthusiasm'.[78] The word carried with it an oratorical inflection for Byron and his contemporaries. Timothy Clark explains that 'enthusiasm' and its cognates fed into debates about demagoguery and 'such issues as the nature of the social bond, the political responsibility of the poet, the ethics of communication';[79] while John Mee points out that 'both the fleshly seeing of the crowd and the highest flights of poetic inspiration were

---

[75] C. A. Bayly, *Imperial Meridian: The British Empire and the World, 1780–1830* (London: Longman, 1989), 228.

[76] See Michael Duffy, 'World-Wide War and British Expansion, 1793–1815', in P. J. Marshall (ed.), *The Oxford History of the British Empire: The Eighteenth Century* (Oxford: Oxford University Press, 1998), 184–207.

[77] *BLJ*, ix. 42–3.

[78] See Donald H. Reiman (ed.), *The Romantics Reviewed: Contemporary Reviews of British Romantic Writers*, 5 vols. (New York and London: Garland, 1972), 'Part B: Byron and Regency Society Poets', ii. 837, v. 2113.

[79] Timothy Clark, *The Theory of Inspiration: Composition as a Crisis of Subjectivity in Romantic and Post-Romantic Writing* (Manchester: Manchester University Press, 1997), 164.

identified with the word' and suggests that although many 'poets came to view the enthusiasm that reached beyond the self as integral to their art', they also 'wished to quarantine it from the vile bodies of the crowd'.[80] Byron's varying perspectives on enthusiasm help to account for the attenuated eloquence of *Childe Harold's Pilgrimage*: he often designated it *'entusymusy'*, and the appellation was sometimes used to rib those with pretensions to warm feeling and sometimes to give a name to ardour of his own attachments.[81] He once wrote of those whose 'opinions, without enthusiasm or appeal to the passions, can never gain proselytes';[82] yet his poem is trying to gain perspective as well as proselytes, and as a result its forms of address and appeals to the passions are frequently shorn of their enthusiastic credentials. The poem becomes a form of eloquence in which enthusiasm is both raised and curbed.

Although the poem's narrator figures himself as a speaker, his relations with 'the crowd' and the public are at once intimate and antagonistic. The provocations of Canto I find their way into the poem's most frequently cited lines:

> I have not loved the world, nor the world me; . . .
> Nor coin'd my cheek to smiles,—nor cried aloud
> In worship of an echo; in the crowd
> They could not deem me one of such; I stood
> Among them, but not of them.

> (III, 1049–55)

The loneliness that the narrator both laments and cherishes should not preclude an awareness of how his voice takes its bearings from other public orators as he searches for listeners amid the crowd. 'Nor cried aloud': the hesitation at the line-end again allows for a whispered ambiguity, for the phrase initially seems to mean that this narrator is no speaker, that he has stayed silent, before we then realize that he might be seen as a certain kind of speaker (one who *has* cried aloud, but not in order to pander to the crowd's enthusiasms).

'Among' but not 'of': the words point to an oscillating stance continually seen and heard in the poem's bereft forms of address, from the enthusiasms of the public speaker to the uncertainties of the isolated writer. As the poem draws to a close, the narrator is still unsure, sometimes announcing a defiant resistance to vocal apostrophe—'in this page a record will I seek. | Not in

---

[80] John Mee, *Romanticism, Enthusiasm, and Regulation: Poetics and the Policing of Culture in the Romantic Period* (Oxford: Oxford University Press, 2003), 2, 295–6.

[81] For instances of Byron's mockery, see *BCP*, 156, and *BLJ*, iv. 263; for more positive examples, see *BLJ*, iii. 209, v. 218.

[82] *BPW*, vi. 224.

the air shall these my words disperse' (IV, 1202–3)—and sometimes hearing his utterance as an impassioned voice—'My voice sounds much' (IV, 1276). *Childe Harold's Pilgrimage* ends as a 'song' and 'echo' (IV, 1657–8), and also as something 'writ' (IV, 1661). 'Sounds much' is a nicely judged pun: despite its cultivated interiority, the poem continually asks that we hear the sounds of contemporary oratory within it, and that we also pay attention to the sounding out of those voices in the calculated hesitancies of the printed page.

THE ELOQUENCE OF ACTION

Byron's last performance in the House of Lords did not go well. He presented a petition; but parliamentary rules required that petitions be accompanied by a 'prayer', in which 'the particular object of the petitioner is expressed . . . Without a prayer, a document . . . will not be received.'[83] The poet tried his luck: 'What was the necessity of a prayer? If that word were to be used in its proper sense, their lordships could not expect that any man should pray to others.'[84] The Lords were not swayed by this ingenious haggling over semantics, and the petition was refused. Four days after this embarrassing parliamentary swan-song, Byron's first 'Eastern Tale', *The Giaour* (1813), was published. Like many Byronic heroes, the Giaour refuses to countenance 'the necessity of a prayer'; yet now such refusals are not awkward pleadings, but defiant stands against received opinion. Byron made a late addition to the tale; his hero snaps back to a monk: 'Waste not thine orison—despair | Is mightier than thy pious prayer' (ll. 1267–8). The poet's impotence in Parliament is translated into a strange kind of assertive power in print, as the tale gives him space for a flourish that was not available to him in the House.

Rebellious words and actions are the driving force of Byron's 'Eastern Tales', even as the poet frames these gestures in narratives that weigh the implications of such force in the balance. Criticism of the tales has drawn attention to their divided political charges,[85] but they need to be considered as a particular kind of reaction to the parliamentary process and to certain forms of public speech. In 1812, the Prince Regent dropped his Whig alliances; he was predicted to invite the party to take up office as the Regency began, but instead turned to the Tories to form an administration. Consecutive entries

---

[83] May, *Treatise*, 496.   [84] *BCP*, 45.

[85] See Peter Manning, *Reading Romantics* (Oxford: Oxford University Press, 1990), 195–237; Nigel Leask, *British Romantic Writers and the East: Anxieties of Empire* (Cambridge: Cambridge University Press, 1992), 13–67; and Susan Wolfson, *Formal Charges: The Shaping of Poetry in British Romanticism* (Stanford, Calif.: Stanford University Press, 1997), 133–63.

in John Hobhouse's diary offer a comically condensed version of the shifting tone of Byron's letters in this period: '[27 May] Whigs coming in at last. [2 June] Whigs not coming in.'[86] This defining moment helped to foster the poet's growing sense of disillusionment with the parliamentary process, and poetry becomes increasingly associated in Byron's mind with a critical stance towards the procedures at Westminster.[87]

In December 1813 Castlereagh announced that the government was to adjourn Parliament until March 1814. Many Whigs protested, including Lord Holland, seeing the measure as more evidence of the Tories' lack of concern for parliamentary authority: 'Why then adjourn? Are ministers afraid of being harassed by any motions?'[88] Byron began *The Corsair* the day after Castlereagh's announcement, and had finished writing most of it within ten days.[89] It was rushed through the press within a month and published on 1 February 1814, selling 10,000 copies on the day of publication. Rather than using the recess to gather himself for more speech making, Byron had chosen another form of expression, another kind of 'motion', in order to take issue with what was occurring in the parliamentary arena. His antipathy towards 'parliamentary mummeries'[90] led him to proclaim: 'Give me a republic, or a despotism of one, rather than the mixed government of one, two, three . . . it is the same who are in or out;—we want something more than a change of ministers, and some day we will have it.'[91] Such battle-cries bring us closer to a despotic republican figure at the forefront of political debate, a figure who played a vital role in the creation of the Byronic hero's audacious accents.

Napoleon Bonaparte's preferences for a one-man executive were clearly demonstrated by his rejection of parliamentary supremacy in France.[92] Byron attempted to be what he termed 'impartial and discriminative' when considering 'the incredible antitheses' of such absolutism.[93] A couple of months before he began *The Corsair*, the Empress of France delivered a speech to the senate, expressing fears about the English enemy: 'Acquainted . . . with the most intimate thoughts of my spouse, I know with what sentiments he would be agitated on a degraded throne, and under a crown without glory.'[94] In November, George Canning replied in the Commons:

[86] John Cam Hobhouse, *Recollections of a Long Life*, ed. Lady Dorchester, 6 vols. (London: John Murray, 1909–11), i. 40.

[87] See *BLJ*, iii. 32, 206; iv. 146.   [88] *Hansard*, xxvii. 297.   [89] *BLJ*, iv. 14.

[90] Ibid. iii. 206.   [91] Ibid. 218.

[92] Irene Collins, *Napoleon and his Parliaments, 1800–1815* (London: Edward Arnold, 1979), 8–27.

[93] See *BPW*, v. 683, and James Hogg, 'Byron's Vacillating Attitude towards Napoleon', in Erwin A Stürzl and James Hogg (eds.), *Byron: Poetry and Politics* (Salzburg: Salzburg University, Press, 1981), 380–427.

[94] *The Times*, 14 Oct. 1813, 3c.

The Empress of France most probably was not conscious, when she delivered the speech of Bonaparte from his throne, of the sentiments of that speech which our great epic poet had put into the mouth of the first rebel and usurper. Satan said, speaking of those who suffered from his ambition and his promises,

> 'Ah, me! they little know
> How dearly I abide that boast so vain,
> Under what torments inwardly I groan,
> When they adore me on the throne of hell.'

But the personal glory, as it was called, of Buonaparte, and the maintenance of his usurpations, formed the policy on which it was fit to call on France to make her sacrifices of treasure and of blood. Great Britain ought to conduct herself as the provident guardian of the liberty of Europe, and the disinterested spectatress of the blessings she had been, under Providence, the instrument of restoring.[95]

Canning is harnessing the power of a popular analogy (the demonization of Napoleon was becoming increasingly common).[96] The Empress is of the devil's party without knowing it; by linking Satan as 'usurper' with Napoleon's 'usurpations', the orator aligns the Allies' cause with the providential one, wrestles the call to 'liberty' out of the hands of the opponent, and implies that Napoleon's project is doomed. 'Our great epic poet' and 'Great Britain' speak the same language; poetic and patriotic endeavour would seem to stand in firm alliance.

Canning was not, however, a 'disinterested' spectator.[97] Byron once described him as 'a genius, almost a universal one; an orator, a poet, and a statesman',[98] but he was also increasingly aware that the talents of the 'poet' and the 'orator' might not always sit easily alongside one another. The two men read each other's work, and dined together a few days after Canning's oration.[99] Two weeks later Byron wrote a skit, 'The Devil's Drive', in which he played devil's advocate by having Satan visit Westminster—'they say he stood pretty near the throne' (l. 140)—and listen to a speech by 'Canning for War' (l. 163). The devil was distinctly unimpressed by proceedings in the House, and *The Corsair* followed his lead. Canning had employed poetry to take issue with an oration, and Byron paid him the compliment of adopting his method. When the narrator pauses to consider why Conrad inspires such loyalty from his troops, the contours of Canning's speech

---

[95] *Hansard*, xxvii. 151.

[96] Simon Bainbridge, *Napoleon and English Romanticism* (Cambridge: Cambridge University Press, 1995), 95–133.

[97] The Whigs saw the speech as Canning's attempt to 'bid for office by declamation' by endorsing the 'warlike and Bourbon notions' favoured by the court; see R. G. Thorne (ed.), *The House of Commons, 1790–1820*, 5 vols. (London: Secker & Warburg, 1986), iii. 399.

[98] Lovell (ed.), *His Very Self and Voice*, 545.   [99] See *BLJ*, iii. 80, 170, 173.

are viewed from an answering perspective with one of Byron's well-placed
'but's:

> —but let the wretch who toils
> Accuse not, hate not *him* who wears the spoils.
> Oh! if he knew the weight of splendid chains,
> How light the balance of his humbler pains!
>
> (I, 189–92)

Canning had quoted Satan's 'Ah, me! they little know' to emphasize Napoleon's
duplicity. Byron's 'Oh! if he knew' revises the devil's soliloquy into omniscient
commentary in order to stress the heroic aspect of such pains. The passage
is at once lament and eulogy; tied as he is to a cause which is as 'splendid'
as it is costly, Conrad's inward torments are no reason to gloat. His people,
like the people of France and the other countries in which Napoleon's liberal
reforms were disseminated, gained as well as suffered 'from his ambition and
his promises'. Moreover, Conrad's enemy (like Napoleon's) is not merely
what Canning terms 'a provident guardian of liberty', but also an aggressive
power with its eye on 'merchant's gains' (II, 69).

The reviewer for the Canning-inspired *Antijacobin Review* picked up on the
similarities between Byron's aspiring Corsair and the ambitious Corsican.[100]
The poet's defence of his unparliamentary hero through an engagement
with words uttered in Parliament suggests that his tale is an attempt to
weigh up the claims of differing forms of governance as well as different
political positions within governments. Byron once observed: 'The great error
of Napoleon . . . was a continued obtrusion on mankind of his want of all
community feeling for, or with them; perhaps more offensive to human vanity
than the active cruelty of more trembling and suspicious tyranny. Such were
his speeches to public assemblies as well as individuals.'[101]

This hints at the shortcomings of political systems through a consideration of
the kinds of public speech to which they give rise. Napoleon's '*great* error' (both
an aspect of his greatness and something that compromises it), can be heard in
his address to the Legislative Body, spoken as Byron was writing *The Corsair*:

Twice have 24,000,000 of French called me to the throne: which of you durst undertake
such a burden? . . . All authority is in the Throne; and what is the Throne? this wooden
frame covered with velvet?—no, I am the Throne! . . . You advise! how dare you debate

---

[100] Anon., 'Review of *The Bride of Abydos* and *The Corsair*', *Antijacobin Review*, 46 (Mar.
1814), 209–37, p. 225.
[101] *BPW*, ii. 304.

of such high matters!... I am above your miserable declarations... my victories shall crush your clamours![102]

The rhetorical questions themselves invert and subvert the impulse to 'debate'. Byron investigated his hesitant attraction to such eloquence as he ushered *The Corsair*'s daring hero into being. Like most Byronic heroes, Conrad does not say much—'Few are his words, but keen his eye and hand' (I, 634)—and by the time *Childe Harold's Pilgrimage* went to press, the poet had begun to express concern that Harold was all talk and no action, admitting that he might 'do more and express less'.[103] Announcing his shift to heroic couplets in *The Corsair*, Byron wrote: 'the stanza of Spenser is perhaps too slow and dignified for narrative'.[104] The 'Eastern Tales' embody a new sense of speed: all were written quickly, their narratives progressed at lightning pace, and their couplet forms accentuated fast movement. In addition, Byron's anti-parliamentary snipings during this period are full of Napoleonic insistences on one particular impulse: action.

' "Action—action—action"—said Demosthenes: "Actions—Actions," I say.'[105] Demosthenes was referring to *actio*, the part of classical rhetoric dealing with delivery (including vocal emphasis and physical gestures), and Byron recalls his claim that this was the most important part of oratory from his reading of Cicero and Quintilian.[106] The elocutionary movement in which the poet was trained had made *actio* central to its studies,[107] and he had read manuals by Thomas Sheridan, William Enfield, and Gilbert Austin,[108] all of which emphasized the need to cultivate what Austin termed 'corporal eloquence'.[109] Byron deemed himself 'a Critic in Elocution',[110] and his training for his parliamentary career centred on the 'eloquence of action'.[111] His participation in speech-days at Harrow gained him a reputation: Dr Drury predicted 'that I should turn out an Orator—from my fluency—my turbulence—my voice—my copiousness of declamation—and my action'.[112] Byron's relish for turbulence gave him a sense not only of the way in which

---

[102] Cited in Louis Antoine Fauvelet de Bourrienne, *Memoirs of Napoleon Bonaparte*, ed. R. W. Phipps, 3 vols. (London: Bentley, 1885), iii. 83–4.

[103] *BPW*, ii. 6.   [104] Ibid. iii. 149.   [105] *BLJ*, iii. 220. See also *BLJ*, iii. 179.

[106] See Cicero, *De Oratore*, iii. lvi. 213, and Quintilian, *Institutio*, xi. iii. 6.

[107] See Wilbur Samuel Howell, *Eighteenth-Century British Logic and Rhetoric* (Princeton: Princeton University Press, 1971), 145–258.

[108] *BCP*, 6.

[109] Gilbert Austin, *Chironomia; or, a Treatise on Rhetorical Delivery* (London: Davies, 1806), 1.

[110] *BLJ*, i. 164.   [111] Ibid. iv. 231.

[112] Ibid. ix. 43. See also Paul Elledge, *Lord Byron at Harrow School: Speaking Out, Talking Back, Acting Up, Bowing Out* (Baltimore and London: Johns Hopkins University Press, 2000).

speakers might persuade audiences through recourse to body language, but also of how a watcher/listener might analyse or resist a speaker's blandishments by attending to their delivery. Austin had advised the budding orator that 'it is more particularly important to attend to the mouth, than even to the eyes themselves'.[113] This perhaps suggests why Byron 'often hides his mouth with his hand when speaking'.[114] The poet once claimed: 'I can recognize any one by the teeth, with whom I have talked. I always watch the lips and mouth: they tell what the tongue and eyes try to conceal.'[115]

In *The Corsair*, body language is conceived as an index to, and influence on, the body politic. What the narrator of the tale suggestively terms Conrad's 'governed aspect' (I, 232) is a key to a mode of governance, and the hero is well read in the arts of corporeal eloquence. He has learned 'to curb the crowd, | By arts that veil, and oft preserve the proud; | His was the lofty port, the distant mien' (I, 539–41). His 'statelier step' (I, 537) becomes an embodiment and enforcement of his vision of state.[116] Conrad's ability to 'command assent' (I, 545) is reminiscent of that regal forcefulness in Napoleon that Byron saw as a potential force for good, and this force energizes the dashing syntactical verve of the tale:

> 'Steer to that shore!'—they sail. 'Do this!'—'tis done.
> 'Now form and follow me!'—the spoil is won.
> Thus prompt his accents and his actions still,
> And all obey and few enquire his will.
>
> (I, 77–80)

Saying effects doing ('"Steer to that shore!"—they sail'), but it also feels as if saying *is* doing ('"Do this!"—'tis done'). The dash between utterance and narration seems to mark the temporal distance between cause and effect, whilst also suggesting that there is no pause between saying and doing: it is 'done' as Conrad says 'Do this!'. Similarly, the order to 'form and follow me!' seems to win the spoil in the act of utterance. Such effects are gained as a result of Byron's passive verbal structures ('tis done', 'is won'), which make it hard to locate the agency of the actions; things were not only done or won because Conrad spoke, but also as he spoke. Conrad's movement from perlocutionary to illocutionary speech acts is effected by the command of 'his accents and his actions' (what the classical rhetorical authorities referred to as *pronunciatio* and *actio*) and—just as for Napoleon—'victories crush

---

[113] Austin, *Chironomia*, 122.

[114] Anne Isabella Milbanke, cited in Lovell (ed.), *His Very Self and Voice*, 50.

[115] Ibid. 305.

[116] For other instances of people reading each other's body language in order to gauge political allegiances, see I, 149–50; II, 45–6, 51, 300–1; III, 182–3.

clamours'. The enterprising Byronic pun on 'prompt' (which stands primarily as a verb, but which also hovers in the line as an adjective) embodies the power of *actio* as action: 'prompt' at once describes an attribute of Conrad's eloquence, and signifies the active force it has on his world.

The Corsair's vigorous grammatical shorthand frequently emphasizes how forms of delivery can embody and exercise power: Gulnare marks how Conrad's 'red hand's wild gesture waved, a law!' (II, 285), and when she says to the hero that 'a single word of mine removes that chain' (III, 314), the syntax encourages the reader to feel that utterance itself performs the act. The 'eloquence of *action*' is often foregrounded in the tale at moments when the rebel will takes control of its own destiny in an act of resistance against tyranny. Yet, the narrator's attentiveness to body language is often a warning about the provenance and probity of decisive *actio*—a warning akin to Byron's sense that Napoleon was in 'error' when adopting modes of address and action that refused to foster 'community feeling'. Performative utterances preclude debate—they are themselves their own answer—and the hypnotic appeal of the rebel hero is investigated as well as admired when we watch him in action:

> And oft perforce his rising lip reveals
> The haughtier thought it curbs, but scarce conceals . . .
> Too close enquiry his stern glance would quell.
> There breathe but few whose aspect might defy
> The full encounter of his searching eye.
>
> (I, 205–16)

The awestruck writing testifies to Conrad's power, but it also gently resists it by placing us in a position beyond that of the put-upon spectator in the crowd. There 'breathe but few' who might watch the leader closely, but we are allowed to become one of those few as the act of reading gives us breathing space to observe Conrad's 'rising lip' without the threat of his being able to see us ('I always watch the lips and mouth: they tell what the tongue and eyes try to conceal'). Our 'aspect', then, might be considered a subtle form of defiance, as we are given time to see things that Conrad's subjects might only half glimpse. In fact, it is not clear from 'Too close enquiry his stern glance would quell' which act of observation is quelling which (our enquiry may quell *him*). The acoustics of the line whisper of Conrad's wish 'to close' enquiry, but its syntax breathes a more enquiring spirit. Austin noted that 'the reserve and dark consciousness of an unworthy heart do not willingly expose themselves to be penetrated by the beam of a searching eye',[117] and although

---

[117] Austin, *Chironomia*, 107.

the 'searching eye' in this passage belongs to Conrad, the implication is that his suspicious gaze is a reflex of his own sense of unworthiness.

The elocutionary tradition through which the Byronic hero is filtered and represented is itself wary of political and oratorical despotism. Peter de Bolla suggests that 'public elocution . . . designates the proper bounds allowed to the individual, his or her space in and for representation'.[118] From this perspective, the frequent insistence of the elocution manuals upon 'moderation' and 'temperance' in *actio* suggests that their advice is given with parliamentary society and speakers in mind.[119] Orators are to understand themselves as located within an arena shaped by vocal exchange and by certain kinds of auditory expectation to which they should adhere. The Byronic hero's *actio* points to a very different form of government; Conrad's first spoken words in the main narrative of *The Corsair* are imperatives that tell his subjects to stop talking: ' "Peace, peace!" — He cuts their prating short' (I, 146). Byron's admiration of Napoleon informs this line, as does his impatience with Parliament (he once quipped of Westminster's procedures: 'there is no good in so much prating—since "certain issues strokes should arbitrate" ').[120] But his tale is shadowed by a feeling that commitment to such verbal laceration portends war, not peace. Conrad's eloquence of action is not only a needful source of power in the fight against the despotic rule of Seyd; it also contains within itself the potential to become the double of such tyranny. Significantly, the narrator's first descriptions of the body language of Conrad and Seyd echo each other: Conrad 'spake not—but a sign expressed assent' (I, 140) and more than 500 lines later, a slave 'took the sign from Seyd's assenting eye' (II, 51). Conrad's *actio* and actions are linked to Seyd's, and therefore envisaged both as a threat to freedom and as a spur to it. Such moments point to the hero's potential implication in forms of tyranny against which he is fighting. As Byron once claimed of Napoleon, 'he was a glorious tyrant'.[121]

In *The Corsair*, then, Byron explores the potential consequences of his own fascination with the French Revolutionary resistance that fostered and helped to maintain Napoleon's rule. Many critics have seen Gulnare's murder of Seyd as the pivotal moment in the tale,[122] but this moment is itself indebted to Byron's parliamentary heritage. The most renowned instance of *actio* in

---

[118] Peter de Bolla, *The Discourse of the Sublime: Readings in History, Aesthetics and the Subject* (Oxford: Blackwell, 1989), 180.

[119] See Austin, *Chironomia*, 93, 70, 441; William Enfield, *The Speaker* (London: Johnson, 1774), p. xxix; Thomas Sheridan, *A Course of Lectures on Elocution* (London: Strahan, 1762), 19.

[120] *BLJ*, iv. 146.

[121] See Thomas Medwin, *Medwin's Conversations of Lord Byron* (1824), ed. Ernest J. Lovell (Princeton: Princeton University Press, 1966), 184–5.

[122] See Caroline Franklin, *Byron's Heroines* (Oxford: Clarendon Press, 1992), 79.

parliamentary history was provided by Burke, in a speech on the Revolution.[123] On 28 December 1792, he took a dagger into the House of Commons. According to one source, 'the dagger had been sent from France to a manufacturer in Birmingham, with an order for a large number to be made like it':[124]

[Here Mr. Burke drew out a dagger which he had kept concealed, and with much vehemence of action threw it on the floor.] This, said he, pointing to the dagger, is what you are to gain by an alliance with France . . . He then held the dagger up to public view, which he said never could have been intended for fair and open war, but solely for murderous purposes. It is my object, said he, to keep the French infection from this country; their principles from our minds, and their daggers from our hearts . . . When they smile, I see blood trickling down their faces; I see their insidious purposes; I see that the object of all their cajoling is—blood! [125]

Holding the dagger up to 'public view', the orator's body language becomes a signifier of '*fair* and *open* war' (my emphasis). 'When they smile' refers to some members of the Whig opposition, who laughed when Burke threw the dagger to the floor, some even 'asking where the fork was'. His rejoinder quieted them, and his next recourse to *actio* silenced them: Burke chose this moment to break with the Whigs—impervious to Fox's tears, he left his place, crossed the floor to the Treasury bench, and seated himself next to Pitt.[126]

When Gulnare tells Conrad of her plan to stab Seyd to death with a dagger while he sleeps, the hero objects, defending the use of 'the open hand' in 'war': 'To smite the smiter with the scimitar; | Such is my weapon—not the secret knife' (III, 361–4). The diction recalls Burke's concealed weapon and his defence of an 'open war', but Gulnare ignores this advice. When she returns to Conrad, *actio* again speaks louder than words. As one reviewer put it, 'a spot of blood is all eloquence':[127]

They meet—upon her brow—unknown—forgot—
Her hurrying hand had left—'twas but a spot—
Its hue was all he saw, and scarce withstood—
Oh! slight but certain pledge of crime—'tis blood!

(III, 414–17)

Burke's 'eloquence of *action*' is transposed into Byron's narrative, as Conrad—the man of action—finds himself appalled by revolutionary *actio*. The

---

[123] Byron's friends often referred to the speech. See John Cam Hobhouse, *Byron's Bulldog: The Letters of John Cam Hobhouse to Lord Byron*, ed. Peter Graham (Columbus: Ohio State University Press, 1984), 247.

[124] George Henry Jennings, *An Anecdotal History of the British Parliament* (London: Cox, 1899), 169.

[125] *PH*, xxx. 189.   [126] See Thorne (ed.), *The House of Commons*, iii. 324.

[127] Anon., 'Review of *The Corsair*', *Critical Review*, 5 (Feb. 1814), 144–55, p. 152.

Byronic hero shares Burke's horror at bloody faces; yet the story in which he appears also asks readers to consider causes alongside effects. Seyd's rule seems to have left Gulnare few alternatives, and when the narrator notes that 'She was a slave—from such may captives claim | A fellow-feeling, differing but in name' (III, 202–3), he asks us to see the heroine as a representative of other oppressed peoples as well as a dangerous revolutionary. Indeed, her recourse to violence might even be seen as a lesson learnt from Burke's *actio*, as his own brandishing of the weapon insisted that there were some causes worth fighting for. More disturbingly, though, the tale intimates that forms of governance which refuse to address the plight of those like Gulnare risk the loss of their own freedoms by eroding the respect for liberty in the subjects they oppress. Byron not only felt that 'there is *no* freedom—even for *Masters*—in the midst of slaves', but also sensed that 'there is no tyrant like a Slave'.[128]

Walter Scott suggested that Byron's poetry was 'like the oratory which hurries the hearers along without permitting them to pause on its solecisms or singularities'.[129] This is half of the truth, and Leigh Hunt hits on the other half when he refers to 'an air between hesitation and hurry' in Byron's voice.[130] His print has a similar air: the stuttering speed of the passage above crystallizes and embodies this rhythm, and in so doing bespeaks the divided political allegiances of the poet's 'Eastern Tales'. The typographical dash that cuts such a dashing figure in the tales both speeds up and slows down the narrative, accentuating a quickening revolutionary pulse and marking those moments when the trepidatory heart might skip a beat. From one perspective, the shift in the lines just quoted from ' — *'twas* but a spot' to ' — *'tis* blood!' (my emphasis) moves from past narration to present re-enactment, while the 'Oh!' feels more like Conrad's gasp than the narrator's recollection. Print verges on the condition of broken speech, and the dashes seem to turn sequential events into simultaneous impressions. And yet, we read and reread these lines, in part resisting their momentum as we hear voices like Burke's running through them. We too 'see' a 'hue', and in doing so, we are asked to stand back from the hue and cry to consider both gains and losses of such *actio*.

The 'hurrying hand' that composes *The Corsair* is not without its hesitancies. A writer for the *Monthly Review* noted Byron's frequent use of the '*dash*' and pointed out that the tale had 'an air of declamation'.[131] This air is heard clearly in Gulnare's central Byronic contention: 'I *felt*—I *feel*—love dwells with—with the *free*' (II, 502; my emphasis). In addition to the alliterative

[128] *BLJ*, ix. 41; *BCP*, 193. On his dispassionate appraisal of the atrocities and the value of the French Revolution, see Lovell (ed.), *His Very Self and Voice*, 147; *BLJ*, xi. 38; *BPW*, vi. 223.

[129] Cited in Rutherford (ed.), *Byron: The Critical Heritage*, 143.

[130] Cited in Lovell (ed.), *His Very Self and Voice*, 330.

[131] John Hodgson, 'Review of *The Corsair*', *Monthly Review*, 73 (Feb. 1814), 189–200, p. 199.

bindings, 'felt' chimes with 'dwells' and 'feel' modulates into 'free'. The poet's sonic cohesions lend a vocal assurance to a speaker who is stuttering her way towards a new realization; yet the dashes also capture the disorientation and the instability of such a voice. George Wilson Knight once suggested that 'Byron's revolutionary thinking is grafted on to as keen an awareness of and feeling for tradition . . . as any in English literature'.[132] In *The Corsair*, the poet's sympathy for the revolutionary impulses displayed by the Napoleonic Conrad and the rebellious Gulnare is conducted through a feeling for the parliamentary tradition of which the poet was both an admirer and an antagonist. The tale's reworkings of Byron's elocutionary training, and its critical engagements with Canning and Burke, demonstrate how the style through which the poet examines the limits of the British parliamentary process is itself richly indebted to that process.

Leigh Hunt shrewdly commented that 'Lord Byron will never be skilful in addresses, nor in any other oratorical part of poetry . . . His talent does not lie so much in appealing to others, as in expressing himself. He does not make you so much a party as a witness.'[133] Byron's poetic expressiveness can be an appeal to others, and his poetry does have its 'oratorical parts', but his distinctive talent lies in his ability to enrich such parts with an eloquence that calls for reflection as well as persuasion. *Childe Harold's Pilgrimage* is the wary prelude to his parliamentary career, *The Corsair* is its enquiring epilogue; Harold is the talker who desires yet fears action, the Byronic hero is the man of action haunted by oratorical ghosts. *Don Juan* (1818–24) would move beyond these voices; the poem is the most enduring witness to Byron's parliamentary heritage, not least because it acts as a witness for what that heritage overlooks.

POETIC JUSTICE

Thomas Moore recalled Byron's breezy account of his final parliamentary speech:

He spouted forth for me, in a sort of mock-heroic voice, detached sentences of the speech he had just been delivering. 'I told them,' he said, 'that it was the most flagrant violation of the Constitution—that, if such things were permitted, there was an end of English freedom, and that—' 'But what was the dreadful grievance?' I asked,

---

[132] George Wilson Knight, *The Burning Oracle: Studies in the Poetry of Action* (Oxford: Oxford University Press, 1939), 286.
[133] Hunt, *Examiner*, 22 Sept. 1816, 603.

interrupting him in his eloquence.—'The grievance?' he replied, pausing as if to consider—'Oh, *that* I forget.'[134]

This is characteristic of Byron's shrewd levity, for it winningly highlights and checks his indulgence in his own eloquence, pointing to the poet's awareness of himself as at once immersed in, and distanced from, the terms of contemporary political enthusiasm. Byron often expressed his antipathy towards 'the pettier factions and contests for power among parliamentary men', but when he tells Medwin that 'I am not made for what you call a politician',[135] his phrasing snatches a critical engagement from a pride in critical distance: 'what *you* call a politician' implies that Byron considers himself a certain kind of politician, rather than removed from politics altogether.

The 'mock-heroic voice' with which the poet revisited his vocal efforts in Parliament is similar to the tone of his *ottava rima* poems. Drawing on *Don Juan*'s sense that one can 'Sound . . . heroic syllables both ways' (IX, 2), William Keach asserts that 'no writer in English raises more pointedly the question of whether sounding the syllables both ways is an act of evasive political cynicism or provocative political integrity'.[136] This question is raised when Byron is sounding out the voices in Parliament. In *Beppo* (1818), the studied nonchalance of the outsider is often combined with the snappy impatience of someone who refuses to let things go:

> 'England! with all thy faults I love thee still,'
>   I said at Calais, and have not forgot it;
> I like to speak and lucubrate my fill;
>   I like the government (but that is not it);
> I like the freedom of the press and quill;
>   I like the Habeas Corpus (when we've got it);
> I like a parliamentary debate,
> Particularly when 'tis not too late.
>
>   (ll. 369–76)

The last line sounds the syllables two ways: the speaker either likes a parliamentary debate when it is not 'too late' because he is anxious to get home, or because he is angry that debates frequently come 'too late' for anything to be done about the grievances they are meant to be redressing. Or, perhaps the line offers a combination of both options: protracted debate in Parliament is often the symptom of a disreputable temporizing, so the narrator's aversion to talk going on late into the night is both personal and political. The line can

---

[134] Byron, cited in Lovell (ed.), *His Very Self and Voice*, 68.

[135] Medwin, *Medwin's Conversations*, 228.

[136] William Keach, 'Political Inflections in Byron's *Ottava Rima*', *Studies in Romanticism*, 27 (Winter 1988), 551–62, p. 562.

be heard as indulgent and indignant, and the mobility of the couplet makes it unclear what tone one is meant to take when reading the political engagements of the preceding lines.

Empson observed that 'a metrical scheme imposes a sort of intensity of interpretation upon the grammar', and that 'rhythm allows one, by playing off the possible prose rhythms against the super-imposed verse rhythms, to combine a variety of statements in one order'.[137] This stanza embodies such order, and makes the narrator's defence of English constitutional freedoms seem at once languid and impassioned. The relaxed prose rhythms of 'but that is not it' suggest that the narrator cannot find exactly the right words to describe his love of England, but the verse rhythms hint that 'the government' he admires is not at present available in his homeland under the Tories. The metrical form acts as a kind of heckling menace behind the more immediate sense of conversational chit-chat, so that we are alerted to an angry finger pointing beneath apparent ease; he likes the government, 'but *that* is *not* it'.

For Keach, such equivocal syllables might be heard as evidence *either* of 'evasive political cynicism' *or* of 'provocative political integrity', but Empson's sense of a combination of statements in one order outlines another possibility: what these lines register is not so much an evasion of a particular political commitment, but a suspension of it. Byron was fascinated by how rhetorical arguments could sometimes become unconvincing to audiences as a result of the very force of a speaker's convictions, and also by how such forcefulness could itself generate the oversights and intolerance against which the speaker might be fighting. The richly compacted tones of his *ottava rima* poems aim to offer a model of balanced political conduct through a carefully crafted language—both as a means to a more effective form of persuasion and as a defence against those who would wish to hear only one side of the argument. When the narrator of *Beppo* says, ' "England! with all thy faults I love thee still" ', his irony is not self-satisfied sarcasm, but an attempt to acknowledge diverse political sympathies. The narrator's later comment, 'I'd preach on this till Wilberforce and Romilly | Should quote in their next speeches from my homily' (ll.543–4) is reminiscent of Byron's 'mock-heroic' spouting of his speech to Moore, but this sending up of his own penchant for speechifying also includes a certain urgency. The orators in the House might learn something from this speaker's ability to acknowledge the limitations of his own rhetoric.

Don Juan develops *Beppo*'s balancing act into a sustained investigation into the sounds of the age. Critics have tended to see the poem's closeness to forms

---

137 William Empson, *Seven Types of Ambiguity* (1930; repr. London: Hogarth, 1991), 28, 30.

of speech as a marker of a predominantly declarative, rhetorical style, and as a sign of its alliance with Whig rhetoric.[138] But the poem frequently attempts to foster a form of expression that can contain more than meets the ear. In *Heaven and Earth*, one of Byron's characters refers to 'silent books, which, in their silence, say | More to the mind than thunder to the ear' (III, 276–7). This sense of how the pregnant silence of the page might speak volumes often jostles for room alongside the poet's need to set his audience by the ears: 'when I once take pen in hand—I *must* say what comes uppermost . . . I have not . . . the temper (as it is called) to keep always from saying—what may not be pleasing to the hearer—or reader'.[139] This language points to a rhetorical cast of mind, as taking a pen in hand leads to the poet's feeling that he is 'saying' something rather than merely writing it. And yet, the shift back from 'hearer' to 'reader' hints at a counter-movement, one that itself revisits what 'comes uppermost'. The afterthought is apt for a writer who asks that we see through voices as well as listen to them—perhaps this is why the narrator of *Beppo* takes care to note that he likes to 'lucubrate' as well as 'speak'. *Don Juan* is not all talk; it is talk transcribed, transfigured, and finessed.

Byron was an avid reader of newspapers and journals—both Whig and Tory—after he left England,[140] while his association with Leigh Hunt also kept him in touch with *The Examiner*'s 'radical politics'.[141] When the poet mentions the papers in his letters, the most common notice is to political oratory (his friends John Hobhouse and Douglas Kinnaird were orators): 'I read your various speeches in The Times', 'The papers tell me your "whereabouts" in politics—and also give a "sheet of speech" '.[142] Byron pored over sheets of speech while composing *Don Juan*, and the work was begun in 1818 as the Tory government's repressive domestic policies gathered force. That year, Hunt designated most MPs as 'a very dull, interested, and contented set', claimed that Parliament was 'inferior to the growing intellect out of doors', and advised that 'it is hopeless to expect a Reform from *within* the House, as now constituted'.[143] The emphasis on those 'within' is meant as a spur to those 'without', and the rise of the extra-parliamentary platform at this time was a crucial part of the post-Waterloo reaction against the Tories.[144] The *OED* traces the first use of the word 'platform' in its modern political sense to the same year in which *Don Juan*'s first cantos were published; the poem was the

---

[138] See e.g. Jerome McGann, *Don Juan in Context* (London: John Murray, 1976), 79, 109, 134, and Kellsall, *Byron's Politics*, 169, 179, 191.

[139] *BLJ*, ix. 168.

[140] See Jane Stabler, *Byron, Poetics and History* (Cambridge: Cambridge University Press, 2002), 137.

[141] *BLJ*, v. 185, vii. 205.   [142] Ibid. x. 188, ix. 124.

[143] *Examiner*, 8 Feb. 1818, 81; 1 Mar. 1818, 129, 130.   [144] Jephson, *The Platform*, i. 477.

biggest-selling literary work of the Romantic period, and it was also conceived as a form of extra-parliamentary eloquence.[145]

The Dedication announces the poem's oratorical as well as its literary leanings. It was written during the week that Castlereagh gave a speech to placate those opponents of the government legislation that was curtailing freedoms of speech and the press.[146] Byron was frequently angered by Castlereagh's blithe complacency—in his complaint about 'evil tongues' (l. 73), the narrator labels the politician as 'an orator of such set trash of phrase' (l. 97). His first stanza homes in on another Tory who supported Castlereagh's policies, labelling Robert Southey 'an epic renegade' (l. 5). The epithet has a parliamentary precedent. A year earlier William Smith had denounced the Seditious Meetings Bill brought forward by Castlereagh; the bill was designed to curb the power of the extra-parliamentary platform, and the demagogues who were apparently—as Canning put it—'employing every kind of artifice and irritation, to excite them [the people] to riot and rebellion'.[147] Smith created a stir when he alluded to Southey as a 'renegado' who was now supported by the Tories.[148] Byron's stanza takes up a similar position and phrasing; from this perspective, it might be seen to be in tune with the Whig parliamentary opposition for which Smith speaks.

However, the stanza also takes a liberty that announces the poem's departure from parliamentary form. 'In order to guard against all appearance of personality in debate, it is a rule, in both houses, that no member shall refer to another by name.'[149] Although Southey was not an MP, Smith did not refer to him by name in the House in an attempt to keep the debate above the 'appearance of personality', but the first words of Byron's poem refuse to stand on ceremony. The epic opens with a capitalized shout, and even reduces Robert Southey to 'BOB SOUTHEY!' (l. 1) as a further provocation. So while the lines borrow something from a parliamentary speaker, they also take on an extra-parliamentary tone, forging a voice that captures the cadences of those 'within' and 'without'. When the narrator says that his opponents are 'A nest of *tuneful* persons *to my eye*' (l. 7; my emphasis), his phrasing hints at another aspect of the poem's eloquence: he watches, rather than just listens to, the voices of the age. The verse is not only an echo chamber in which they can be heard, but also a microscope under which their contours can be seen more clearly.

---

[145] See William St Clair, *The Reading Nation in the Romantic Period* (Cambridge: Cambridge University Press, 2004), 333. St Clair also notes: '*Don Juan* was read by more people in its first twenty years than any previous work of English literature.'
[146] See *Examiner*, 12 July 1818, 438.   [147] *Hansard*, xxxv. 1116 (14 Mar. 1817).
[148] Ibid. 1091.   [149] May, *Treatise*, 317.

The dedication deliberately speaks out of turn, and out of tune, recalling Byron's earlier endeavours in Parliament; some politicians 'told me that my manner of speaking was not dignified enough . . . I believe it was a Don Juan kind of speech'.[150] *Don Juan* is that kind of speech where undignified things might finally get said. The domestic spats in the poem are often permeated by a sense that they betoken more public principles and utterances, for the characters do not merely talk *with* one another; they deliver speeches *to* one another. In Canto I, Don Alfonso's opening of his mouth is rendered as 'the anvil of his speech' (l. 1299), the maid's reply becomes 'the oration of the trusty maid' (l. 1378), and Alfonso's final comments are glossed: 'His speech was a fine sample, on the whole, | Of rhetoric' (ll. 1391–2). 'On the whole': the phrase comes from a listener who is not wholly convinced, from a political intelligence that refuses to be completely swayed by the claims of any one voice or moment.

Byron took more care with the first Canto than with any other,[151] and the poem gains momentum by returning to the two most important oratorical influences on his work: Burke and Sheridan. The cause over which the two speakers united was the most celebrated trial of the eighteenth century: the impeachment of Warren Hastings (Governor-General of India) before the House of Lords from 1788 to 1795. The impeachment was part of the long-standing Whig campaign against despotic executive power; when, in his opening speech for the prosecution, Burke referred to the 'desolating consequences of arbitrary power', he was taking aim at George III as well as Hastings, referring to the fortunes of the Whig Party and to those of the subjects in India.[152] The defining speech on the subject was Sheridan's. Burke, Pitt, and Fox pronounced the oration the most distinguished they had ever come across, and Byron claimed that it was 'the very best Oration . . . ever conceived or heard in this country'.[153] A polished-up, enlarged version was delivered in 1788 at the trial in Westminster Hall, and—as Byron observed—'this Speech he [Burke] called always "the grand desideratum"—which was neither poetry nor eloquence—but something *better* than both'.[154] The poet was not uncritical of this version,[155] but his 'Monody on the Death of The Right Honourable R. B. Sheridan' (1816) had contained a call to 'Bards' to 'emulate him' for

[150] Medwin, *Medwin's Conversations*, 229.

[151] See Truman Guy Steffan, *Byron's Don Juan: The Making of a Masterpiece*, 2nd edn., 4 vols. (Austin: University of Texas Press, 1971), i. 107.

[152] See Conor Cruise O'Brien, *The Great Melody: A Thematic Biography and Commentated Anthology of Edmund Burke* (London: Sinclair-Stevenson, 1992), 369.

[153] See Linda Kelly, *Richard Brinsley Sheridan: A Life* (London: Sinclair-Stevenson, 1997), 141; *BLJ*, iii. 239.

[154] Ibid. ix. 13.   [155] Ibid.

his blend of 'eloquence' and 'Poesy' (ll. 106, 111). The first canto of *Don Juan* attempts such a blend.[156]

One of the charges against Hastings was the spoliation of the Begums (or Princesses) of Oudh, and the unlawful obtaining of their treasury through force. Sheridan summed up:

> They had also proved . . . how sacred was the residence of women in India. A threat, therefore, to force that residence, and violate its purity, by sending men armed into it, was a species of torture . . . What, he asked, would their lordships think of the man who could threaten to profane and violate the sanctuary of the highest description of ladies in Oude, by saying that he would storm it with his troops, and remove the inhabitants from it by force?[157]

Such flourishes bring us closer to *Don Juan*. Don Alfonso, who senses that his wife Julia may be having an affair, decides to storm the room in which two ladies (Julia and her maid) are meant to be sleeping. He brings 'lackeys, arm'd with fire and sword' (l. 1111), but Sheridan's enraged advocacy is mingled with, and tempered by, another tone:

> I can't tell how, or why, or what suspicion
> Could enter into Don Alfonso's head;
> But for a cavalier of his condition
> It surely was exceedingly ill-bred,
>
> (1105–8)

'Surely'? Sheridan's rhetorical question was calculated to raise indignation; Byron's tactful broaching of questions is designed to raise eyebrows. The stanza's coy balance between surprise and surmise is neatly captured in its opening phrase: 'I can't tell how' primarily means 'I don't know how', but could also mean 'I may not tell how'. Swinburne's comment on the mixture of tones in Byron's *The Vision of Judgment* is appropriate here: 'those who read it . . . not too gravely and not too lightly, will understand more than can be set down'.[158] The co-presence of gravity and lightness in this stanza is characteristic of *Don Juan*, and is hard to capture when reading it aloud. The poem's dual cadence deftly resists a straightforward oratorical rendering, and requires that we hear more than one voice as we read. When Julia goes on to note her husband's disreputable eagerness to locate 'the secret cavern of this lurking *treasure*' (l. 1223; my emphasis), we are again alerted to the subject of

---

[156] Sheridan was on Byron's mind as he began the first canto; see *BLJ*, vi. 67–8.

[157] Richard Sheridan, *Speeches of the Late Right Honourable Richard Brinsley Sheridan*, ed. 'A Constitutional Friend', 3 vols. (London: Bohn, 1842), i. 375.

[158] Charles Algernon Swinburne, *Essays and Studies* (London: Chatto & Windus, 1875), repr. in Rutherford (ed.), *Byron: The Critical Heritage*, 380.

Sheridan's speech (he kept referring to the Begums' 'treasure'), only now the 'ill-bred' nature of the aggressor is framed within a narrative that asks us to see things from more than one perspective. Julia, after all, is not above suspicion.

The poised recasting of the scene and style of Sheridan's oration touches on the contentious issue of whether the Begums had a right to the treasury.[159] Julia's right to her own treasure (Juan) is also a tricky case, but this does not stop her remonstrances. Consider first the protest of the Begum:

> Mr. Sheridan next read the letter of the Begum to Mr. Hastings . . . 'I request you will not place implicit confidence in my accusers; but weighing in the scale of justice *their falsehoods* and *my representations,* you will exert your influence in putting a period to the misfortunes with which I am overwhelmed.' Here Mr. Sheridan remarked, that the plain and simple language of truth gave to the representations of the Begum an Herculean force—her complaints were eloquence, her supplications persuasion, and her remonstrances conviction.[160]

Sheridan's closing triadic structure is canny. The rhythm of the orator's voice is meant to persuade listeners that 'eloquence' is to be allied with 'persuasion' and 'conviction', as if the style of the Begum's complaint—and, by extension, Sheridan's—is in itself enough to guarantee her veracity. Invigorating the printed word through vocal rendition, Sheridan lends his voice to the cause.

Byron crafts voices into print so that we might take time to dwell on how causes need a more thorough 'weighing in the scale of justice'. Towards the end of his speech, Sheridan had said, 'If I dare to use the figure,—we shall constitute Heaven itself our proxy.'[161] Julia takes a similar liberty, but her daring is matched by an auditor's response:

> Now Julia found at length a voice, and cried,
>   'In heaven's name, Don Alfonso, what d'ye mean?
> Has madness seized you? would that I had died
>   Ere such a monster's victim I had been!
> What may this midnight violence betide,
>   A sudden fit of drunkenness or spleen?
> Dare you suspect me, whom the thought would kill?
> Search then the room!'—Alfonso said, 'I will.'
>
>   (ll. 1129–36)

All Julia's sentences end with either '?' or '!'—the gesticular emphases of a voice that is going on 'at length'. Our enjoyment of these lines comes from the

---

[159] Kelly says that Hastings's opponents, 'probably incorrectly, insisted that it [the treasure] was the Begums' personal property' (*Richard Brinsley Sheridan,* 139); while C. C. O'Brien says that Hastings's own claim was 'false', *Great Melody,* 286.
[160] Sheridan, *Speeches,* i. 390.   [161] Kelly, *Richard Brinsley Sheridan,* 143.

justice as well as the terseness of Alfonso's rejoinder, even while we admire and sympathize with Julia's gutsy performance. It is significant that his voice rhymes with hers; the couplet announces a knowing couple, for it takes one to know one (we are told by the narrator that 'Alfonso's loves with Inez were well known' (ll. 1402)). Byron's stanza allows room for 'remonstrances' that don't quite lead to 'conviction'. His narrator asks that, rather than confusing 'supplication' with 'persuasion', we acknowledge the importance of competing claims.

Sheridan ended his speech with 'My Lords, I have done', before fainting into the arms of Burke ('A good actor', Gibbon wryly noted when recalling Sheridan's peroration).[162] Julia is similarly impressive, rounding off her speech with a customary minding of p's and q's, proclaiming 'sir, I have done' (l. 1249), before falling to her bed and sobbing into her pillow. Knowing as we do that Juan is hidden in her bed, Julia's *actio* is a canny course of action, a remonstration that seeks to avoid 'conviction' by asking that the auditor read her body language as a sign of innocence. Unlike Alfonso, however, readers of *Don Juan* are frequently encouraged to imagine what lies beneath surfaces (and bed sheets). Byron observed of his poem that 'its real qualities are not on the *surface*—but still if people will dive a little—I think it will reward them for their trouble'.[163]

Diving a little deeper, we might recall the only date that Byron mentions in all seventeen cantos of the poem, the fateful 6 June when Julia gives in to temptation with Juan (I, 817). This date has a particular significance for Byron. 'Sheridan told me . . . I should make an Orator if I would but take to speaking and grow a parliament man—he never ceased harping upon this to me . . . my old tutor Dr. Drury had the same notion when I was a *boy*.'[164] It is noteworthy that Byron should remember the two men alongside one another: the main part of Sheridan's speech on the Begums was delivered on 6 June 1788; Byron spoke at a Harrow speech-day on 6 June 1805. The date registers a confluence of two voices—the poet's and the politician's. Despite Sheridan's wishes, Byron would never 'grow a parliament man'. But, by allowing the cadences of Sheridan's much-loved voice to hover in the margins of *Don Juan* (and by allowing this date into his poem), he registered his commitment to a voice in print that might contribute to public debate through its willingness to take issue with, as well as taking its bearings from, the most cherished of Whig causes. The canto admires the ardour of Sheridan's voice at the same as it tests its limits through the figure of Julia, suggesting that there was something potentially suspect in Sheridan's defence speech.[165] Byron's engagement with

---

[162] Sheridan, *Speeches*, i. 425; Kelly, *Richard Brinsley Sheridan*, 149. [163] *BLJ*, ix. 55.
[164] Ibid. 16.
[165] Some contemporaries had mocked Sheridan's 'theatricals', which threatened to transform the House of Lords from 'a vast stage of justice . . . into a theatre of pleasure'; cited in Anna

a central strand of Whig oppositional rhetoric (what Burke referred to as 'the desolating consequences of arbitrary power') makes readers aware that Don Alfonso (whether one has a sense of him as a kind of nebulous stand-in for Hastings or for George III) is not the only guilty party in the story.

Julia almost lost her voice on 6 June in *Don Juan*: 'A little still she strove, and much repented, | And whispering "I will ne'er consent"—consented' (ll. 935–6). The date enshrines a moment in which spoken words are not the only things that should be taken into account, one in which eloquent avowals are qualified by a narratorial voice that is wise after the event. The acoustic allusiveness of Byron's poem is not only a retrospective enquiry into his Whig heritage; it is also a contemporary engagement with where that heritage has led. Commentators have observed that the poem intermingles three time schemes: the time of Byron's youth (the 1780s and 1790s), the period of his engagement with Regency society (1809–16), and the time of the poem's composition and reception (1818–24).[166] As Jerome Christensen puts it, *Don Juan* 'stretches the contemporary from the 1790s until tomorrow'.[167] This stretching employs the past as a way of providing a commentary on the present and a glance towards the future, seeking to speak to the moment by seeing beyond it. In 1819, readers confronted by the story of an unfaithful wife, a powerful husband who was not himself beyond reproach, and talk of 'a divorce' that would get 'into the English newspapers, of course' (ll. 1503–4), would have thought of another Whig cause also built on a critique of arbitrary power: the party's denunciation of the Prince Regent for his attempts to divorce Princess Caroline. When *Don Juan*'s narrator archly informs us that the best newspaper report of 'the whole proceedings' (l. 1505) is 'that in shorthand ta'en by Gurney' (l. 1511), he is alerting readers to the parliamentary inflections of his tale (Gurney was the official shorthand clerk to the Houses of Parliament). By extension, then, *Don Juan* goes beyond parliamentary forms, for it includes the longhand version of events that official proceedings will not always disclose.

In 1813, a report seeking to prove Caroline's adultery was published, and that year saw the Whigs take up her cause in Parliament (Byron corresponded and met with the Princess).[168] The poet was sympathetic yet circumspect: 'I by no means consider myself as an *attaché* to her, or any party; though I certainly

Clark, *Scandal: The Sexual Politics of the British Constitution* (Princeton: Princeton University Press, 2004), 106.

[166] See *BPW*, v. pp. xxiii–xxiv.

[167] Jerome Christensen, *Lord Byron's Strength: Romantic Writing and Commercial Society* (Baltimore: Johns Hopkins University Press, 1993), 311.

[168] See David V. Erdman, 'Lord Byron and the Genteel Reformers', *PMLA*, 56 (1941), 1065–94, and Andrew Nicholson, 'The Princess of Wales and Byron in 1813', *Byron Journal*, 30 (2002), 54–66.

should support her interest in Parliament if brought forward.'[169] The interest was again brought forward when *Don Juan*'s early cantos were being written and published. On his ascent to the throne in 1820, the King brought a Bill of Pains and Penalties against his wife. The Queen's cause was taken up by the Whigs as part of their fight against the executive, and by the radical platform orators outside Westminster who aligned Caroline's predicament with those of the politically excluded.[170] On 6 June 1820 she returned to London to proclaim her innocence, and thousands of people turned out to cheer her: *The Times* explained that 'The Queen of England is at present every thing with every body'.[171]

Byron perhaps allowed himself a smile at this support of the wronged maiden (and at the date of her momentous march through the capital). The messy, tangled story of Alfonso and Julia had offered the public a template for a more balanced view of the 'affairs' of state. Reading proceedings of the trial, he purred: 'Was there ever such evidence published? Why it is worse than . . . "Don Juan".'[172] Hobhouse became one of the Queen's most ardent defenders, claiming that her trial was a 'mock form of justice',[173] and his maiden speech questioned whether Parliament 'should meddle with the criminal jurisdiction of the courts of law', lamenting that 'there are many precedents for this interference'.[174] One precedent was the Hastings trial; outlining the case against the Queen, the Attorney-General noted that 'Their lordships would remember that that of Mr. Warren Hastings . . . went upon the same principle.'[175] Byron was as suspicious as Hobhouse of the mock forms of justice embodied in Westminster (he approved of the maiden speech),[176] for if the parliamentary chamber had been misused by the Whigs in the Hastings affair, it was now being misused by the Crown. Still, when he wrote to Kinnaird 'what trash your parliament is',[177] he was objecting not merely to the King's attempt to besmirch the Queen's reputation, but also to how the defence of that reputation by Whig orators was impoverishing public debate by refusing to acknowledge the complexities of the issue.

As the trial drew to a close, Byron began to pen the episode in which Juan visits a Turkish court (Cantos V and VI). Here readers are treated to talk of a 'Princess' and her 'pleasure' (V, 579), a 'masquerading mood' (V, 581), and cross-dressing in Turkish clothing. Many contemporaries would

---

[169] Cited in Erdman, 'Lord Byron and the Genteel Reformers', 1085.

[170] See Anna Clark, 'Queen Caroline and the Sexual Politics of Popular Culture in London, 1820', *Representations*, 31 (Summer 1990), 47–68, and Nicholas Rogers, *Crowds, Culture, and Politics in Georgian Britain* (Oxford: Clarendon Press, 1998), 272.

[171] *The Times*, 7 June 1820, 2 f.   [172] *BLJ*, vii. 207.

[173] *Hansard*, i. 1388 (26 June 1820).   [174] Ibid. 255 (9 May 1820).

[175] Ibid. ii. 732 (19 Aug. 1820).   [176] See *BLJ*, vii. 154.   [177] Ibid. 191.

have taken the hint; the Lords trial had featured debate about Caroline's enjoyments of 'masqued balls' with her lover, their dressing up as Turks, and the Queen's penchant for wearing men's clothing.[178] A witness for the Queen's defence pleaded that the 'Turkish trowsers' in question were 'very much like a common petticoat',[179] and Byron's narrator glances in this direction when he notes that part of Juan's dress comprised a 'petticoat' (V, 613), but also—it should be said—'a pair of trowsers of flesh-colour'd silk' (V, 610). The orators on both sides of the House were dressing up the issue as one exclusively concerning female propriety. As a corrective to such oversights, *Don Juan* is more intent on dressing down some of the other players in the drama.

It was a rule of parliamentary debate that 'reflections must not be cast... upon the conduct of the sovereign'.[180] Still, rules might be bent rather than broken, as Hobhouse demonstrated in the Commons:

The lives of sovereigns should not be scrutinized so nearly. If they are, I know not where the example may stop. Suppose that at some future period this country should be governed by a prince, not an absolute tyrant nor a subverter of the laws of the land, but steeped to the lips in sloth and voluptuousness, neglectful of his duty, of his character, of his honour, of the interests of the people and the dignity of the Crown.[181]

Just suppose. The name cannot pass the orator's lips, but everybody present would have known to whose lips he was referring.[182] Byron employs a similar art of insinuation, but pushes the limits of parliamentary forms further by exploring the relationship between the Sultan and his Queen, Gulbeyaz, as a means of considering the sexual politics of the relationship between George IV and Queen Caroline. Indeed, the radical platform-speakers outside Parliament had been making explicit links between the King and the figure of an 'absolute tyrant' at this time, seeing him as a 'Grand Turk' and labelling him as 'Sultan Sham'.[183] Byron combines these oratorical emphases: just as Hobhouse drew attention to the monarch's neglect of his civic duty and to his interest in more voluptuous activities, so we learn that the Sultan 'left to his vizier all state affairs' (V, 1179) and concentrated instead on his 'twice five hundred maids' (V, 1183). Mentioning no names, Byron mentions numbers instead: the Sultan, we learn, 'had fifty-nine | Years' (VI, 63–4). The adulterous George IV was the same age when the poet penned these lines.

Gulbeyaz is both victim and victimizer, a slave to the Sultan and a tyrant who is willing to trample on others should they not bow to her desires; sympathy

---

[178] *Hansard*, ii. 1111–55 (30 Aug. 1820).   [179] Ibid. iii. 363 (6 Oct. 1820).

[180] May, *Treatise*, 316.   [181] *Hansard*, i. 1388 (26 June 1820).

[182] Byron was in the House in 1812 for a debate about the propriety of using the Prince Regent's name during parliamentary proceedings (*PD*, xxii. 55–8).

[183] See Clark, *Scandal*, 194–5.

for her abject state is frequently mingled with a sense of her powerful status. Much attention had been given to the sleeping arrangements of the Queen and her alleged lover, Pergami (witnesses were asked whether beds had been slept in by one or two members, and whether sheets were stained or clean).[184] Byron's narrator instead prefers to dwell on the bedside manners of the royal couple. While the Sultan sleeps, Gulbeyaz is kept awake by her longing for another bedfellow:

> These are beneath the canopy of heaven,
>   Also beneath the canopy of beds
> Four-posted and silk curtained, which are given
>   For rich men and their brides to lay their heads
> Upon, in sheets white as what bards call 'driven
>   Snow.' Well! 'tis all hap-hazard when one weds.
> Gulbeyaz was an empress, but had been
> Perhaps as wretched if a *peasant's quean*.
>
> (VI, 193–200)

During the trial, Tory speakers focused on the class inflections of the Queen's conduct; she had dressed as a 'peasant' for the ball, and Pergami was referred to as a 'menial servant' (the original bill against Caroline had referred to Pergami's 'low station').[185] The Whig speakers, on the other hand, made continual protestations of the Queen's dignity and innocence, and Murray's 1832 edition contained a note to this stanza: 'The *bards* of Queen Caroline, in the Times newspaper, were continually, during the period of her trial, ringing the changes on the "driven snow" of her purity.'[186] The source of this allusion was one of the most quoted phrases of the trial, when Thomas Denman claimed that Caroline was 'pure as unsunned snow'.[187]

Byron's disinterested stanza moves beyond the snobbery of the Tory rhetoric and the artifice of the Whig speakers by creating a form of eloquence that manages to cast aspersions on the Queen without casting her off. 'I sometimes almost think that eyes have ears' (XV, 601), our narrator later admits, and this is what our eyes need when reading *Don Juan*. After finishing the Turkish cantos, Shelley wrote to Byron to express his admiration of its language: 'a sort of c[h]ameleon under the changing sky of the spirit that kindles it, such as these lisping days could not have expected . . . One can hardly judge from recitation and it was not until I read it in print that I have been able to do it justice.'[188]

---

[184] See Roger Fulford, *The Trial of Queen Caroline* (London: Batsford, 1967), 91.
[185] *Hansard*, ii. 1116; Fulford, *Trial*, 235, 244.   [186] *BPW*, v. 721.
[187] Cited in Fulford, *Trial*, 51.
[188] Shelley, cited in Rutherford (ed.), *Byron: The Critical Heritage*, 197.

Shelley rightly senses that Byron's achievement is not quite oratorical because it owes much to his ability to infuse more than one vocal charge into his written words. In the stanza above, the beautifully poised 'Well!' might be heard as a sidelong snipe ('well. . . really?') or as a tolerant sigh ('oh well'). The stanza's couplet also takes the measure of both Tory and Whig rhetoric by forging two co-present voices in its own measure. 'One can hardly judge from recitation': the narrator's reference to the Queen as '*quean*'—'a bold, impudent, or ill-behaved woman; a jade, hussy' (*OED*)—is more frank than the Whigs cared to be about the Queen's behaviour. But then, the word is to be heard as well as seen; as a peasant's 'queen' she and the lower orders with whom she is associated are also deemed worthy of respect. As so often in the poem, an ability to view things more than one way is related to the possibility of giving such matters a more equitable hearing.

Gulbeyaz's circumstances are at once privileged and pitiful. Unlike the Tories, the narrator does not associate her royal highness with the peasantry in order to scoff, but to suggest a tentative alliance between her sufferings and those of the people. The extra-parliamentary radical orators had made frequent analogies between Caroline's predicament and the people's cause (as one observer noted, 'radicalism has taken the shape of affection for the Queen').[189] Yet, she is only 'perhaps' as wretched as the lower orders. The qualification does not allow us to forget that her circumstances are 'rich' as well as 'wretched', and that it would be disingenuous of the narrator to claim that her situation should be viewed as wholly analogous with that of the people. This self-checking eloquence is meant as a riposte to that of the most prominent orator in the Lords; reading the early cantos, John Croker thought he could detect the voice of Henry Brougham. Referring to the style of Brougham's speeches—which he saw as 'poor from their richness, and dull from their infinite variety'—he noted that 'the Protean style of *Don Juan*' was similar, and that 'something of the same kind, and with something of the same effect, is Lord Byron's wonderful fertility of thought and facility of expression'.[190] 'Something of the same kind', yes, but with a distinction, for Byron himself had complained about Brougham's infinite variety in some draft stanzas: 'Tory by nurture | Whig by circumstance, | A Democrat some once or twice a year | Wheneer it suits his purpose . . . the Adulterer's advocate when duly feed'.[191] That is, Brougham's eloquence is an unequivocal advocacy of either this or that position, rather than a weighing up of the pros and

---

[189] Cited in C. N. New, *The Life of Henry Brougham to 1830* (Oxford: Clarendon Press, 1961), 261.

[190] Samuel Smiles, *A Publisher and his Friends: Memoir and Correspondence of the Late John Murray*, 2 vols. (London: John Murray, 1891), i. 413–14.

[191] *BPW*, v. 85–7.

cons of each position he takes. What looks like purposive mobility is in fact unprincipled expediency. Brougham's eloquence changes its tune; Byron's insists on taking more than one tune into account.

Byron was right about Brougham's sustained oratorical duplicity and deceit in the Caroline affair,[192] but he rightly cut the sharp-tongued lines from his poem because he was searching for a tone that might carry more weight by offering less stringent judgements. Brougham's two-day closing speech for the defence became the most renowned oration of the trial, and ended by succumbing to the temptation that Byron's poem resists—disingenuously eliding the Queen's cause with that of 'the people': 'she has . . . the heartfelt prayers of the people . . . I do here pour forth my supplications at the Throne of Mercy, that that mercy may be poured down upon the people . . . and that your hearts may be turned to justice.'[193] The poet would have demurred at the closing word, for *Don Juan* is tight-lipped when it comes to 'justice', allowing space for the word only twice throughout its seventeen cantos, once to point out that he 'ne'er saw justice done' to the 'bust' of an Irish lady he knew (II, 948), and once in the Turkish cantos when referring to Gulbeyaz's beauty: 'it would strike you blind | Could I do justice to the full detail; | So, luckily for both, my phrases fail' (V, 774–6). These winning, urbane shrugs of the shoulders are frequent in the poem, testimony to its refusal to get carried away by its own eloquence. Byron's phrases don't quite *do* justice—or rather, they do so only by intimating the ways in which readers might begin to consider *how* justice is done.

Brougham's stance—a glib summation of the Whig position—is the quintessence of the poet's most frequent target in *Don Juan*: cant. Both Hazlitt and Shelley referred to 'cant' as the predominant aspect of the trial,[194] and Byron's appended Preface to his poem (sandwiched between the two Turkish cantos) also drew attention to 'the *Cant* which is the crying sin of this double-dealing and false-speaking time'.[195] The eloquence of *Don Juan*, which expresses what the orators deem unsayable, attempts to translate the hypocrisy of cant into a mobile irony that can remain double-jointed without becoming double-dealing. After the case was thrown out of the Lords, Byron defended the virtues of equivocation in matters at once private and political: 'it was a business with which I should have been sorry to have had anything to do; in which they who voted her guilty cut but a dirty figure and those who

[192] See Robert Stewart, *Henry Brougham, 1778–1868: His Public Career* (London: Bodley Head, 1986), 146–51.

[193] *Hansard*, iii. 210 (4 Oct. 1820).

[194] Hazlitt, *Complete Works*, xx. 136; Percy Bysshe Shelley, *The Letters of Percy Bysshe Shelley*, ed. Frederick L. Jones, 2 vols. (Oxford: Clarendon Press, 1964), ii. 207.

[195] *BPW*, v. 297.

call her innocent not a very clean one'.[196] The outsider stance should not be mistaken for lack of engagement: Byron's backing off from the parliamentary debate and its accompanying forms is itself a form of political critique and enquiry, and his poem had involved itself in the 'business' by offering readers a model of the tone that should be taken in such matters. For the Whigs, justice was desired in the form of a full acquittal; for the Tories, in a complete conviction. Byron's poem cuts a different figure, and embodies another type of just procedure, one more interested in forging discriminating judgements than final sentences.

ON SECOND THOUGHTS

'And now I think on't' (I, 494). *Don Juan* is full of second thoughts about first impressions, a movement often captured in the sportive concessions of its couplets—'They grieved for those who perish'd with the cutter, | And also for the biscuit casks and butter' (II, 487–8). The later cantos are particularly rich in these swervings, incorporating the voice of the second-guesser into their structure and encouraging readers to be on their guard. It is as though we are permitted to hear an orator's doubts *as* he speaks, as Byron allows what the ancients referred to as *correctio* and *restrictio* into the structure of his writing: 'whene'er I have expressed | Opinions two, which at first sight may look | Twin opposites, the second is the best' (XV, 690–2). The second opinion? Or the second look at the 'first sight' that originally saw the opinions as opposites? 'Perhaps I have a third too in a nook, | Or none at all—' (XV, 693–4), the next lines suggest. These playful accretions enact a political principle to which the English cantos are committed: a search for a way beyond mere opposition by seeking out productive combinations (less emphasis on the 'opposites', more on the 'twin'). In addition, the voice that addresses us admits that the primary concern here is not just the adoption and holding of 'opinions'; rather, the reader is being invited to take part in a process of entertaining them.

Byron wrote the English cantos as the radical platform began to challenge Whig ideology by demanding annual parliaments, an extension of the franchise, and the abolition of the country's borough-mongering oligarchy. Hobhouse's attempts to become MP for Westminster, the largest constituency in the country and the centre of the radical movement, drew him into this tussle of political vocabularies. Prior to his election, he was jailed for issuing a pamphlet that enquired: 'What prevents the people from walking down to the

---

[196] *BLJ*, vii. 253.

House, and pulling out the members by the ears, locking up their doors, and flinging the key into the Thames?'[197] Byron's attraction to the provocations of questions that might or might not be rhetorical, and his support of the eloquence of *Don Juan* as something that 'must set us all by the ears',[198] made him cautiously supportive of Hobhouse's turbulent progress, and he read his friend's pronouncements very closely.[199] Yet his admiration of the orator's reformist fervour was matched by criticisms of the duplicity of some of his public utterances and actions.[200] Hobhouse's unprincipled oscillation between Whig and radical utterances on the election platform, and his subsequent rejoining of the Whig rank and file on entering Parliament, proved the shrewdness of Byron's initial judgements.[201]

As Juan becomes involved in the English political scene, the content and style of the poem modulate into a sustained engagement with the political drama unfolding at Westminster. One of the stylistic delights of *Don Juan*—digression—shows a marked increase in the English cantos.[202] Digressions were prohibited in parliamentary debate ('when a member wanders from the question, the Speaker reminds him that he must speak to the question . . . A member who resorts to persistent irrelevance may . . . be directed by the Speaker or the chairman to discontinue his speech').[203] Digressions, then, are distinctly unparliamentary forms of speech. Early in *Don Juan*, the narrator explains to us that 'If I have any fault, it is digression . . . But these are my addresses from the throne, | Which put off business to the ensuing session' (III, 858–62). The implication is that if digressions are seen as asides from the parliamentary session, then the main narrative of the poem is conceived as something akin to an extended parliamentary debate. The narrator's growing indulgence of this 'fault' in the very cantos in which Juan visits Parliament, listens to speeches, and dines with orators suggests that Byron's poetic form is offering itself as an increasingly open breach of parliamentary form.

Hobhouse had also pushed his luck after arriving at Westminster. On 18 September 1820 he drew attention to proceedings in the Lords (another breach of parliamentary etiquette) and was called to order for wandering from licensed parameters of debate. Byron congratulated his friend on his plucky impropriety ('you were called to order—but I think you had the best of it'), and Hobhouse replied: 'As to the being called to order—you know it

[197] John Cam Hobhouse, *A Trifling Mistake* (London: Stoddart, 1819), 49.
[198] *BLJ*, vi. 123.　　[199] See e.g. ibid. vi. 89, vii. 123.　　[200] See *BPW*, iv. 286–8.
[201] See William Thomas, *The Philosophic Radicals: Nine Studies in Theory and Practice, 1817–1841* (Oxford: Clarendon Press, 1979), 66–94, and Robert E. Zegger, *John Cam Hobhouse: A Political Life, 1819–1852* (Columbia: University of Missouri Press, 1973), 63–79.
[202] See M. K. Joseph, *Byron the Poet* (London: Gollancz, 1964), 334.
[203] May, *Treatise*, 299–300.

is nothing . . . for I pursued the same line afterwards, though I pretended to have dropt it.'[204] Byron adopts a similar approach in *Don Juan*, as digressions become a way of prompting readers to extend their consideration of the question before them even as the narrator pretends 'to have dropt it'. When the narrator pleads, 'Oh, pardon me digression—or at least | Peruse! 'Tis always with a moral end | That I dissert' (XII, 305–7), the acoustics of his print develop Hobhouse's point: 'dissert' might also be heard as 'desert', as the narrator's moral dissertation also becomes a form of desertion from the rules of parliamentary procedure.

Descriptions of what Juan sees when he visits the House veer into reflections that would have been called to order if uttered in Parliament. A subsidiary rule regarding digression was that 'a debate must not stray from the question before the house to matters which have been decided during the current session, nor anticipate a matter appointed for the consideration of the house'.[205] The peculiar blend of retrospective anticipation that is an effect of *Don Juan*'s multiple time schemes refuses to bow to this ruling:

> He saw however at the closing session,
>   That noble sight, when *really* free the nation,
> A king in constitutional possession
>   Of such a throne as is the proudest station,
> Though despots know it not—till the progession
>   Of freedom shall complete their education.
> 'Tis not mere splendour makes the show august
> To eye or heart—it is the people's trust.
>
> (XII, 657–64)

One matter that had been decided during the 'current session' (Byron wrote the stanza in 1822) was that the bill for parliamentary reform was shelved. In keeping with *Don Juan*'s dextrous rhythms, the stanza looks back as a way of looking forward: the narrator's asides suggest that the nation under George IV is losing the freedoms it once enjoyed, while his 'till' constitutes not only an 'anticipation' of 'a matter appointed for the consideration of the house', but a prediction that progress outside the House will eventually force the issue. The stanza's defence of 'the people', and its suggestion that they educate their leaders rather than the other way round, carries that radical emphasis that Hobhouse and others had been cultivating in their speeches (during the Westminster elections, Hobhouse had claimed that he was the people's 'pupil').[206] Yet, the closing reference to the people's 'trust' might complement

[204] *BLJ*, vii. 204; Hobhouse, *Byron's Bulldog*, 302.   [205] May, *Treatise*, 299.
[206] *Examiner*, 22 Nov. 1818, 748.

this political outlook ('trust' as 'an estate committed to the charge of trustees' (*OED*)), but also complicate it, by suggesting that the people should, despite the political victimization to which they are subject, trust those in power who should know better. Like many of Byron's couplets, this one is delivered not as a punch-line, but as a double-take.

Digressions in *Don Juan* act as pauses for second thoughts that would have been difficult to deliver in the House. Another rule stipulated that 'a member is not permitted to read his speech . . . his own language must be delivered *bona fide*, in the form of an unwritten composition. Any other rule would be at once inconvenient and repugnant to the true theory of debate.'[207] This implied that 'true' debate was an improvised, spur-of-the moment exchange of ideas, as if *bona fide* spoken language was reliable as a result of its spontaneity. The poet's oratorical heroes did not subscribe to this view, and frequently got round the rule (as did Byron) by writing out speeches and learning them by rote before they entered the House. Burke was particularly impressed by those speeches that displayed 'a spirited air of *impromptu*'[208] even though they had been carefully crafted, and Moore noted of Sheridan's speeches that often 'he prepared the miracle of the moment beforehand'.[209]

Christopher Reid suggests that such techniques preserved 'an action of the written and premeditated on the spoken and momentary . . . the discipline of writing is infused with the immediacy and sociality of speech'.[210] For literary speakers like Burke and Sheridan, debate was to be enriched rather than impoverished by the 'premeditated', and the narrator of *Don Juan* spryly acknowledges his indebtedness to this form of prepared improvisation when indulging in his digressions:

> I ne'er decide what I shall say, and this I call
> Much too poetical. Men should know why
> They write, and for what end; but, note or text,
> I never know the word which will come next.
>
> (IX, 325–8)

'Say . . . write': part of the pleasure of reading such lines is owing to our feeling that they stage 'a spirited air of *impromptu*' even as we sense the poet's premeditations behind such an air (the poem's rhymes are themselves

---

[207] May, *Treatise*, 295.

[208] Edmund Burke, *The Correspondence of Edmund Burke*, ed. Thomas W. Copeland *et al.*, 10 vols. (Cambridge: Cambridge University Press, 1960–78), viii. 244.

[209] Thomas Moore, *Memoirs of the Life of the Right Honourable Richard Brinsley Sheridan* (London: Longman, 1825), 703.

[210] Christopher Reid, *Edmund Burke and the Practice of Political Writing* (Dublin: Gill & Macmillan, 1985), 116, 133.

a frequent clue to the 'text' which will come 'next'). Indeed, half the lines in this stanza were revised from initial manuscript versions before they made it to their final form (over half the closing couplets in *Don Juan* were changed at least once from Byron's original versions).[211] When readers learn that 'I write what's uppermost, without delay' (XIV, 53), or that 'I rattle on exactly as I'd talk' (XV, 151), we are aware that the demands of the *ottava rima* form in which these rattlings find expression help to create a mode of speech that is, in the words of the narrator, 'at once adventurous and contemplative' (IV, 850).

Such eloquence is a model of political conduct, for while it involves an immersion in the present, it also attempts to stand back from immediate commitment in order to offer a more disinterested survey of the scene. Erik Gray has suggested that 'every aspect of *Don Juan* . . . contributes to our sense that the stanza is to be read hurriedly' and that such hurry 'forbids all backtracking' and 'encourages a similar hurry and a similar carelessness in the reader'.[212] *Heard* hurriedly, perhaps, but not *read* so, for there is care in Byron's carelessness. Just as the action of the poem frequently allows for a critical engagement with the first impressions left by political orators, so its style is founded upon Byron's willingness to take a second look at his own utterances. Pondering his 'conversational facility' (XV, 155), he suggests:

> Of this I'm sure at least, there's no servility
>   In mine irregularity of chime,
> Which rings what's uppermost of new or hoary,
> Just as I feel the 'Improvisatore'.

> (XV, 157–60)

Byron spoke of sending manuscript versions of his poems to his publisher in their 'most republican and uncorrected state'.[213] This association of the 'republican' with the 'uncorrected' implies that the poet felt that his more radical political sympathies stood in need of revision; as he composes himself, he senses the need to recompose parts of his work. The first line of this closing couplet originally read: 'Which never flatters either whig or tory'.[214] 'Never' is intemperate and 'either . . . or' is disingenuous—not wholly true to Byron's support of certain aspects of political order that both Whigs and Tories defended. The poet's preferred accent is much more in tune with the language of 'both/and', as he acknowledges elsewhere:

---

[211] See Steffan, *Byron's Don Juan*, 313.

[212] Erik Gray, *The Poetry of Indifference from the Romantics to the Rubáiyát* (Amherst and Boston: University of Massachusetts Press, 2005), 59.

[213] *BLJ*, x. 26.   [214] *BPW*, v. 594.

> And if I had to give a casting voice,
>> For both sides I could many reasons show,
> And then decide, without great wrong to either,
> It were much better to have both than neither.

(IV, 197–200)

A casting voice, not vote: the final form of the stanza on improvisation breathes, rather than merely utters, a lack of 'servility', and it does so because the poet resists the 'improvisatore' feeling. His irregularity of chime is a rhetorical emotion recollected in tranquillity, a speech becalmed to print, which rings true because it rings with something more than the 'uppermost'.

Don Juan's shiftings between 'adventurous' improvisation and 'contemplative' revision mirror the larger play between narration and digression, and these negotiations embody a Byronic yearning for both vigorous progress and studied pause. Byron felt that a 'debater' was 'as different from an Orator as an Improvisatore or a versifier from a poet'.[215] The alignment suggests that poets and orators are to be ranked above their peers because they aspire to an utterance beyond the heat of momentary battle. He did not undervalue 'extempore talents',[216] but he rightly sensed that this was not where his own talents lay; advising Hobhouse on how to be a successful speaker, he wrote: 'above all don't *diffide* in yourself. . . leave that to poets and such fellows—& don't be afraid of your own talents'.[217] Poetic diffidence might be considered an expressive disposition that, though it would be unsuccessful in the House, could offer itself as a supplement to the necessary yet limited art of the extempore. The last cantos of *Don Juan* offer themselves as such a supplement. They are founded not on an attempt to avoid flattering 'either whig or tory', but on a desire to combine what Byron perceived as the mixed blessings of such voices with other, more radical utterances that could responsibly resist them.

The post-war tussle between radical and conservative agendas was foregrounded in Hobhouse's prolonged engagement with Canning. A disciple of Pitt, a constant antagonist of parliamentary reform, and one of the best speakers in the Commons, Canning stood as the most prominent defender of the unreformed borough system.[218] The clash between political vocabularies was particularly apparent in a skirmish between Canning and Hobhouse in 1821. Canning once noted that he knew of 'no pleasure (*sensual* pleasure I had almost said)' equal to that of delivering a pointed, persuasive speech.[219] In a discussion on 'the danger to arise from the return of demagogues to parliament', Canning took pleasure in defending the borough system against the

---

[215] *BLJ*, ix. 14.   [216] Ibid. vii. 205   [217] Ibid. vi. 93.
[218] See Wendy Hinde, *George Canning* (London: Collins, 1973), 283.   [219] Ibid. 34.

radicals, and then glanced at Hobhouse: 'He had never known a demagogue who, when elected to a seat in that House, did not in the course of six months shrink to his proper dimensions... Although they [demagogues] had been qualified in palace-yard. "Here," he would say "Let the demagogue appear; and let him do his worst".'[220] This insinuates that the small group of radicals is no threat to the large consensus in the House, but it is also a personal allusion to Hobhouse, a short man whose 'dimensions' were no match for Canning's imposing stature (the latter was described by Byron as 'the tall wit').[221] Size mattered (mention of 'shrinking' suggests his opponent's ill-preparedness for '*sensual* pleasures' at once oratorical and sexual), and Hobhouse squirmed in his seat: 'The House laughed and looked at me.'[222]

Hobhouse spent a month composing his reply, and in April delivered a speech against the 'systematically vicious and ruinous' process of borough-mongering. Quoting Canning's words on demagogic shrinking, he then offered up a 'portrait' of his own, turning the embarrassment of the diminutive newcomer into the bite of the underdog by revising his antagonist's sexual innuendos:

A smart sixth-form boy, the little hero of a little world, matures his precocious parts at college... A minister or some borough-holder of the day thinks him worth saving from his democratic associates... The hopeful youth yields at once; and, placed in the true line of promotion, he takes his beat with the more veteran prostitutes of parliament... Such a man does not find his level, he does not shrink to his proper dimensions in the unreformed House; on the contrary, he is the true House of Commons hero. Despised and detected as he may be without doors, he finds shelter in the bosom of the senate... Such a man, I say, Sir, would have no place in a reformed parliament.[223]

Canning's gentleman's club becomes a brothel. Talk of 'precocious parts' and youthful 'associates', a 'yielding' to the 'prostitutes of parliament', and the 'bosom' of the senate would seem to imply that, while Canning does not suffer from 'shrinkage', the very potency of the system he represents is something of which he should not be so proud. This vignette of the prostitution of the constitution caused a stir in the House. Canning turned 'all colours', pulled his hat over his eyes and did not reply to the speech; William Smith said to Hobhouse: 'if you are nothing else, I must say you are the boldest man in parliament'.[224] Byron's response to such boldness was congratulatory and cagey; he felt the speech was 'quite a piece of *permanent* Oratory'[225] but also suggested that his views 'might have differed' slightly from those of his

---

[220] *Hansard*, iv. 1313 (16 Mar. 1821).   [221] *BPW*, iv. 163.
[222] Hobhouse, *Recollections*, ii. 143.   [223] *Hansard*, v. 403, 424–6.
[224] Hobhouse, *Recollections*, ii. 147–8.   [225] *BLJ*, ix. 138.

friend.[226] *Don Juan* returns to the matter through the only complete political oration that is allowed into its pages (Lord Henry's speech).

The very form in which the last cantos of Byron's poem appeared tells us something of the writer's resistance to the aristocratic political culture that is their subject. The shift from the Tory (John Murray) to the radical (John Hunt) as the publisher of *Don Juan* led to a new form of publishing venture, as the poem was issued in three sizes, including one version sold for a shilling.[227] For the first time in English literary history, 'a great new work of literature was designed, manufactured, and priced, so as to be able to address the whole reading nation simultaneously'.[228] This 'address' was seized upon as a breach of political form: one reviewer complained that 'these little one-shilling duodecimos' are 'very un-aristocratic company' and that 'the writer appears aware that he has *lost caste*, and yet he will proceed'.[229] The 'proceedings' are extra-parliamentary; the company the poem keeps is very different from the company its characters keep, and when readers were introduced to Lord Henry, Lady Adeline, and their circle at Norman Abbey, they would have been alert to the scepticism that bristles beneath the surface of the narrator's civility. Lord Henry stands as the epitome of the unreformed borough system and the influence of property on elections; he is engaged in 'a lawsuit upon tenures burgage' (XVI, 523), and such boroughs contained some of the worst abuses of the system.[230]

Don Juan is frequently aspiring towards a form of verbal conduct that can be politically agile without being what Lord Henry claims to be: 'all things to all men' (XVI, 610). Aware of how a tactful dexterity might shade into an expedient lack of principle, yet seeking a mobility that could mediate between 'twin opposites', the poet's creative transcription of Lord Henry's electioneering speech takes the measure of both conservative and radical political agendas. Though Lord Henry speaks Canning's language, that language is nestled in a form that has been influenced by Hobhouse's boldness in the House:

> A friend to freedom and freeholders—yet
> No less a friend to government—he held,
> That he exactly the just medium hit
> 'Twixt place and patriotism—albeit compelled,

[226] Ibid. 101.
[227] See William St Clair, 'The Impact of Byron's Writings: An Evaluative Approach', in Andrew Rutherford (ed.), *Byron: Augustan and Romantic* (Basingstoke: Macmillan, 1990), 1–25.
[228] St Clair, *Reading Nation*, 327.
[229] Anon., 'Review of *Don Juan*, XII–XIV', *Monthly Review*, 103 (Feb. 1824), 212–15, p. 212.
[230] See Frank O'Gorman, *Voters, Patrons and Parties: The Unreformed Electoral System of Hanoverian England, 1734–1832* (Oxford: Clarendon Press, 1989), 32–3.

Such was his Sovereign's pleasure (though unfit,
    He added modestly, when rebels railed)
To hold some sinecures he wished abolished,
But that with them all law would be demolished.

He was 'free to confess'—(whence comes this phrase?
    Is't English? No—'tis only parliamentary)
That innovation's spirit now-a-days
    Had made more progress than for the last century . . .

He was as independent—aye, much more—
    Than those who were not paid for independence,
As common soldiers, or a common—Shore,
    Have in their several arts or parts ascendence
O'er the irregulars in lust or gore, . . .

All this (save the last stanza) Henry said,
    And thought. I say no more—I've said too much;
For all of us have either heard or read
    Of—or *upon* the hustings—some slight such
Hints from the independent heart or head
    Of the official candidate. I'll touch
No more on this—the dinner bell hath rung,
And grace is said; the grace I *should* have *sung*—

                                            (XVI, 617–64)

Lord Henry's spouting of the rhetoric of 'independence' in 1791 means little
to him, but it is meant by Byron to spur an enquiry into the contemporary
situation in post-war England, for the emphasis on 'freedom and freeholders',
the concerns about 'place', and the defence of 'progress' had been handed
down to nineteenth-century radicals as a bequest from those who defended
independence some thirty years earlier.[231] Indeed, when the narrator suggests
that 'all of us have either heard or read' such rhetoric, he is pointing out how
little change Lord Henry's words have effected.

    George Ridenour noted the 'fruitful tension between octave and the con-
versational flow' of *Don Juan*, and finely observed that 'much of the peculiar
effect of the poem as a whole is a function of the interaction of forces pushing
us onward and forces compelling us to linger'.[232] Such fruitful tension is a
particular source of strength for a poet who is interested in holding speech
steady so that we might take a closer look at it. In the first stanza, the form
engages critically with Lord Henry's fluency. When we arrive at 'Such was

---

[231] See O'Gorman, *Voters, Patrons and Parties*, 265–316.
[232] George Ridenour, *The Style of Don Juan* (New Haven: Yale University Press, 1960), 142.

his Sovereign's pleasure (though unfit, | He added modestly, when rebels railed)' we see that Henry smilingly means: 'Oh, I really don't deserve these sinecures, you know—they're just too, too much.' But the printed word resists oratorical seduction, for the stanza holds Henry's speech in check and gestures towards another meaning: 'though unfit' hovers at the line-ending, and we read backwards as well as forwards, sensing that the 'Sovereign's pleasure' may itself be 'unfit' at a time when voices are raised against his rule. Similarly, while Lord Henry moves forward to sing the praises of 'progress', the parenthetical aside (at once a heckle and a hesitation) asks that readers do not progress too quickly: '(whence comes this phrase? | Is't English? No—'tis only parliamentary)'. 'Only' has its glint: one might hear the offhand Lord Henry in it ('oh, don't worry about the phrase—it's only a form of speech—the important thing for you to note is that . . . '), but we can also hear the discerning narrator behind the utterance ('it's only parliamentary, this language, and it needs to be so much more').

The third stanza recalls and engages with the tussle between Canning and Hobhouse. We have been told earlier that Lord Henry was 'a great debater, | So that few members kept the House up later' (XIII, 159–60). Keeping 'members' up in Houses ('house'; 'house of ill repute; a brothel' (*OED*)) late at night would seem, like Canning, to suggest that the speaker's persuasiveness may be a reflection of his sexual potency.[233] A way with figures of speech hints at a way with other figures, and when Lord Henry adopts Canning's position in his criticism of 'demagogues' (XVI, 637), we are to imagine that he too would not 'shrink' from a task. However, when the stanza above turns to the 'ascendence' of 'parts', it employs Hobhouse's figure (the politician as prostitute) to interrogate what Henry's vaunted independence actually means in practice. The third line of the stanza had originally ended 'or a w—re'; the shift to 'Shore' is one of Byron's politic yet forceful second thoughts, for Jane Shore was the infamous mistress of Edward IV. After he died, her political influence and connections made the future Richard III her antagonist; she was accused of sorcery and imprisoned, later dying in poverty and disgrace. The allusive structure of the stanza implies not only that Lord Henry's independence is a sham, but that his position is not a wholly secure one. Just as Hobhouse had issued a threat in the form of a prediction ('Such a man, I say, Sir, would have no place in a reformed parliament'), so this stanza

---

[233] Byron used the same pun on '*standing* for a *member*' in a letter to Hobhouse about the speeches at the Westminster election (*BLJ*, vi. 107). The poet often toyed with sexual and political vocabularies in this way; Southey's attempts to 'soar too high' make him 'quite adry, Bob!' (*Don Juan*, 'Dedication', 23–4), while Castlereagh's 'trash of phrase' renders him 'an intellectual eunuch' ('Dedication', 97, 88). Parliamentary 'motions', 'maiden' speeches, and 'parts' of speech are similar figures of fun (see 'Dedication', 104; *BLJ*, v. 168; *Don Juan*, IX, 388).

implies that too close an alliance with the King is fraught with danger. Such prostitution means that Lord Henry and others like him may not be wholly removed from the threat of beggary in future.

'The dinner bell hath rung': in 1791, the ring signals the continuance of the political culture that Byron criticizes in these digressive stanzas, but in 1824 it also tentatively sounds its death-knell. While protestations of independence like Lord Henry's continued to ring in contemporary ears, the sound of voices like Byron's meant that they were not so readily granted a hearing. The movement from repetition to critical reflection—'All this (save the last stanza) Henry said'—is a microcosm of the poem's larger patterning: a measured respect for high Whig political culture (Lord Henry is described as 'a cold, good, honourable man' (XIV, 553)) is weighed against the sense that such culture stands in need of revision and reform ('But there was something wanting on the whole' (XIV, 561)). The narrator's own oratorical flourishes—his modes of address when he too feels 'free to confess'—embody such revisions, and usually occur just moments after he has called himself to order with comments like 'I say no more' or 'No more on this' (but then, 'As to the being called to order—you know it is nothing . . . for I pursued the same line afterwards, though I pretended to have dropt it'). For instance: 'For all of us have either heard or read | Of—or *upon* the hustings—some slight such | Hints'. For a moment, 'slight' is heard as a noun before then being read as an adjective (Henry's speech is a 'slight' to his audience). In such moments, the audience is no longer succumbing to oratory, but resisting its blandishments; for 'all of us' elaborates a knowing community that has probing questions to ask of such 'friends to freedom'.

Finally, just after the narrator decides to dwell 'No more on this', talk of the missed 'grace' brings in a ghost of a 'parliamentary phrase' only to resist it, for an 'act of grace' may be '*spec.* a free and general pardon, granted by Act of Parliament' (*OED*). The poet should have been singing this—and, indeed, cultivating his airs and graces at Lord Henry's table—but he, like Juan, is an outsider in the in-crowd, not fully beholden to those in the House and therefore not willing to confer either fulsome approbation or full pardon. He would seem to be minding his p's and q's in this last stanza, but he also takes care to see to it that propriety does not swallow up his anger at the corrupt use of Lord Henry's property. As so often with Byron, a form of address speaks volumes: at the beginning of this speech, the narrator refers to 'Lord Henry' (XVI, 601); by the end of it, he names him merely 'Henry'—the dropping of the title is the dropping of a hint.

Byron once pointed out that 'I have always been a friend to and a Voter for reform . . . I cannot but approve of a Constitutional amelioration of long abuses'.[234] This is Whig politics (although not necessarily Whig Party politics). Yet, for Byron, the search for a language that could defend the 'constitutional' whilst also subjecting it to criticism often involved a critique of Whig culture. The poet was attracted to the political wisdom that might be enshrined in opposed impulses, but he was also attentive to how oppositions could be devalued by a rhetoric that lurched from one position to another (such lurching is heard in the first stanza above, in the dithering of Lord Henry's shifts from 'yet' to 'albeit' to 'But'). Lord Henry claims that he has hit on 'exactly the just medium', but this language is not the kind of middle ground towards which Byron's poetry aspires, for Lord Henry is prevaricating rather than mediating. *Don Juan*'s creative attentiveness to such voices is a template for a more just medium—a kind of 'hear, hear' that is valuably difficult to read in just one tone: '*hear! hear!* . . . the regular form of cheering in the House of Commons, and expresses, according to intonation, admiration, acquiescence, indignation, derision, etc.' (*OED*). *Don Juan* brings speeches to book, and its intonational ambiguities require us to look out for the ways in which eloquent voices might stand in need of a second glance, as well as of a second hearing.

[234] *BLJ*, vii. 44.

2

An Audience with Dickens

ADDRESSING THE TIMES

'Dickens once declared to me that every word said by his characters was distinctly *heard* by him.'[1] The author was not the only person to hear voices at his writing-desk: his gardener at Gad's Hill 'used to hear what sounded like someone making a speech. I wondered what it was at first, and I found out it was Mr. Dickens composing his writing out loud.'[2] Such a composer, 'making a speech' as he makes characters' speeches, is an orator of sorts. His daughter remembered him mouthing the words of his creations in front of a mirror, before beginning to write while 'talking rapidly in a low voice'.[3] There is frequently the sense of an audience in Dickens (he imagines himself *as* an audience while he composes), a sense of words being heard as well as read. Remarking to one correspondent how he found it difficult to compose for sustained periods in silent places, he longed for the London streets and crowds: 'I want these . . . *My* figures seem disposed to stagnate without crowds about them.'[4] Those 'figures' are the characters in his novels, but they are also his figures of speech—revitalized amid company, energized by publicity.

Dickens's sensitivity to sound often carries a political charge. His pulse is quickened when there is a debate in view, and this quickening is part of the rhythm of his age. Silver-fork novels traded on tales of political networking and electioneering, and the governing forces of Disraeli's early works are speakers who address themselves to developments at Westminster. As Joseph Childers has suggested, Disraeli 'calls Parliamentary politics to account in terms of a competing interpretative enterprise, the novel . . . it

---

[1] G. H. Lewes, cited in Philip Collins (ed.), *Dickens: Interviews and Recollections*, 2 vols. (London: Macmillan, 1981), i. 25.

[2] George Woolley, ibid. ii. 272.

[3] Mamie Dickens, *My Father as I Recall Him* (London: Roxburghe, 1897), 47.

[4] *DL*, iv. 612–13.

can comment upon, interpret, *think* politics in ways politics cannot think or know itself'.[5] Trollope also frequently attempts to forge a speech-pattern to answer back to the voices in the Commons: Plantagenet Palliser's careful vocal tread is placed in opposition to the fluency of other public speakers: 'He had taught himself to believe that oratory, as oratory, was a sin against that honesty in politics by which he strove to guide himself.'[6] Following his experiences of election corruption during his parliamentary candidacy for Beverley, Trollope conceived his novels as extensions of, and as steadily sceptical objections to, oratorical procedures: 'as I have not been able to speak from the benches of the House of Commons, or to thunder from platforms . . . they [my novels] have served me as safety-valves by which to deliver my soul'.[7]

Delivering souls through the deliverance of printed orations, such novels become a parliamentary forum and also something more—a debating chamber where some unpalatable truths about parliamentary democracy can be said. When the protagonist gets into the Commons in *Phineas Finn* (1867–9), his nerves get the better of him when he rises to speak, but Trollope's narrator is on hand to make sure that the tongue-tied hero finds a voice: 'He could not explain his idea that the people out of the House had as much right to express their opinion in favour of the ballot as members in the House had to express theirs against it.'[8] Writing brings the unsaid into earshot. In *Phineas Redux* (1873–4), the following sentence is a microcosm of the procedure of the Victorian parliamentary novel: 'The House was bound to let the outside world know that all corrupt practices at elections were held to be abominable by the House; but Members of the House, as individuals, knew very well what had taken place at their own elections, and were aware of the cheques they had drawn.'[9] The sentence hinges on a 'but' that shifts from public rhetoric to interior consciousness, from a transcription of speech to an appreciation of the silences that inhabit and surround it. 'The outside world' is encouraged not just to listen, but to listen in.

Even those novelists who are unwilling or unable to enter the House are captivated by the sounds of politics. George Meredith explained in *Beauchamp's Career* (1875) that 'It is not possible to gather up in one volume of sound the

[5] Joseph W. Childers, *Novel Possibilities: Fiction and the Formation of Early Victorian Culture* (Philadelphia: University of Pennsylvania Press, 1995), 39–40.

[6] Anthony Trollope, *Can You Forgive Her?* (1876), ed. Andrew Swarbrick (Oxford: Oxford World's Classics, 1982), 246–7.

[7] Anthony Trollope, *An Autobiography* (1883; repr. London: Williams & Norgate, 1946), 166.

[8] Anthony Trollope, *Phineas Finn*, ed. David Skilton and Hugh Osborne (London: Dent, 1997), 226.

[9] Anthony Trollope, *Phineas Redux*, ed. John C. Whale, 2 vols. (Oxford: Oxford World's Classics, 1983), ii. 28.

rattle of the knocks at Englishmen's castle-gates during election days',[10] but his novel makes a good stab at it, giving readers the longest continuous narrative of a day's canvassing in Victorian fiction.[11] The 'volume of sound' is heard throughout the period. When composing *Felix Holt: The Radical* (1866) and *Middlemarch* (1871–2), George Eliot ploughed through *Times* reports of the political oratory and riots surrounding the 1832 Reform Bill for her material.[12] *Adam Bede* (1859) had been quoted during parliamentary debate,[13] and G. H. Lewes expressed the same hopes for *Felix Holt* in relation to the 1867 Reform Bill: 'just in the thick of the reform discussion so many good quotable "bits" would be furnished to M.P.'s'.[14] Like his creator, Felix often displays a desire to rise above the clash of political voices even as he finds himself unable to stay impervious to sound: 'To tell you the truth, I had shut myself up, and tried to be as indifferent to the election as if I'd been one of the fishes in the Lapp, till the noises got too strong for me.'[15] To shut oneself up is to remain silent as well as sequestered, but the noises exert an insistent pressure throughout Eliot's work. Recall Mr Brooke delivering his speech to the Middlemarch electors:

there had arisen, apparently in the air, like the note of the cuckoo, a parrot-like, Punch-voiced echo of his words. Everybody looked up at the open windows in the houses at the opposite angles of the converging streets; but they were either blank, or filled by laughing listeners. The most innocent echo has an impish mockery in it when it follows a gravely persistent speaker, and this echo was not at all innocent; if it did not follow with the precision of a natural echo, it had a wicked choice of the words it overtook.[16]

Eliot's reportage shares the impish mockery of that Punch-voiced echo (the laughing listeners *in* the novel are meant to spur on the readers *of* the novel). Accompanied by an omniscient commentary that is itself an interruption and a form of heckling, the novelist's description of Brooke's speech is at once affectionate and antagonistic. This narrative voice—an echo of an echo—is a compressed version of the dual accent that resonates throughout Victorian fiction, in which we hear both a fascination with oratorical endeavour and a need to resist the orators.

[10] George Meredith, *Beauchamp's Career*, 2 vols. (London: Constable, 1910), i. 180.

[11] On elections in fiction, see Richard D. Altick, *The Presence of the Present: Topics of the Day in the Victorian Novel* (Columbus: Ohio State University Press, 1991), 668–758.

[12] Rosemary Ashton, *George Eliot: A Life* (London: Penguin, 1996), 284.

[13] *Hansard*, clii. 1508.

[14] Cited in *The George Eliot Letters*, ed. Gordon Haight, 9 vols. (New Haven and London: Yale University Press, 1954–78), viii. 373–4.

[15] George Eliot, *Felix Holt: The Radical*, ed. Lynda Mugglestone (London: Penguin, 1995), 308.

[16] Eliot, *Middlemarch*, 474.

Dickens declines to write parliamentary or electioneering novels, yet his ear is always close to this ground. As parliamentary reporter, political journalist and correspondent, platform speaker, and public reader of his own work, the novelist is often drawn to making noise as well as to recording it in and out-of-doors. From the beginning, the precocious reporter acknowledges a rhythm of immersion and resistance. In *Sketches by Boz* (1836) the figure of *paralipsis* (drawing attention to something in the act of passing it over—'not to mention x, y and z . . . ') is envisaged as the 'celebrated negative style' and the quintessence of 'the parliamentary style' against which Boz pits his wits. The writer homes in on the figure again in 'Public Dinners', mocking the chairman who, 'after stating that he feels it quite unnecessary to preface the toast he is about to propose, with any observations whatever, wanders into a maze of sentences'.[17] Yet Dickens's farewell to *Bentley's* includes its own maze of a sentence (more than 200 words long) in which a refusal to talk shop is housed in the oratorical figure, as he imagines himself as editor/parent to his magazine/child and refuses 'to dilate on the steadiness with which I have prevented your annoying any company by talking politics . . . to expatiate, in short, upon my own assiduity as a parent, is beside my present purpose'.[18] The *paralipsis* is a wink to the reader, for it concedes that Dickens is often talking politically even when he is not directly talking about politics.

The job of the parliamentary/newspaper reporter was itself an apprenticeship in the art of constructing echoes that were complimentary as well as critical—or, in Eliot's terms, both 'natural' and 'Punch-voiced'. When Thomas Hansard was summoned before the Select Committee investigating the standard of parliamentary reports and asked, 'So it might happen that you put into a Member's mouth what he ought to have said, rather than what he said?', his canny reply was: 'That would not be a very great evil.'[19] He then pointed out that reporters' reshaping of speeches should not be seen as disreputable, but as 'literary work'.[20] Dickens began reporting at a time when this literary work was under scrutiny: debates about how the medium for the dissemination of political speech could act as a filter in which that speech could be condensed, altered, or even silenced were widespread.[21] The dangers inherent in this mixture of impartial support and partial report were noted by *Fraser's* when it observed that 'Reporting is certainly not *sine arte*,

---

[17] *DJ*, i. 24, 166.   [18] Ibid. 552.
[19] *Parliamentary Papers* (1878), xvii. 20.   [20] Ibid. 32.
[21] See H. C. G. Matthew, 'Rhetoric and Politics in Britain, 1860–1950', in P. J. Waller (ed.), *Politics and Social Change in Modern Britain: Essays Presented to A. F. Thompson* (Brighton: Harvester Press, 1987), 34–58; J. M. Robson, *What Did He Say? Editing Nineteenth-Century Speeches from* Hansard *and the Newspapers* (Lethbridge: University of Lethbridge Press, 1988).

but for the rest a young beginner must frequently be scrupulous as to truth'.[22]
Moreover, as the dexterity of the reporter shaded into the inventiveness of the
sketch-writer, parliamentary speech was transposed to print in another form
that attempted to criticize as well as to transcribe.[23]

Dickens's early piece 'A Parliamentary Sketch' (1836) is a glimpse into how
the 'literary work' of his reporting days exerts a formative pressure on his imaginative writing. Here we meet the notorious Colonel Sibthorp, renowned for his
ultra-Tory antipathy to reform.[24] The assiduous reporter notes that 'He is very
punctual in his attendance at the House, and his self-satisfied "He-ar-He-ar"
is not infrequently the signal for a general titter'.[25] This graphic representation
of the speaker's tone ('He-ar-He-ar') and the tittering coda take their bearings
from reporting techniques: Sibthorp had complained that Whig papers were
misrepresenting how his words were received by the House by breaking up his
speeches, erroneously inserting 'laughter' and 'Cries of "oh, oh" and "question,
question"' into the reports.[26] Here as elsewhere, Dickens's jaunty prose style
would seem to be at once complicit and critical, for the 'titter' might be heard
as indulgent as well as enquiring. 'A Parliamentary Sketch': the title, like the
sketch, playfully worries about whether it can resist the procedures by which its
author is captivated—we may be reading 'A sketch whose style is parliamentary' or 'A sketch about Parliament', or both. The mixture of cheeriness and
sassiness in much of Dickens's early work is permeated by the concerns raised
in the title's ambiguous shorthand. These concerns would prompt him to consider how he might negotiate between the topicality of party-political animus
and a voice that looked beyond these immediate political commitments.

Searching for a way to address the times, Dickens is often drawn to consider
the temporal emphases of the politicians' addresses. The debate over the
1832 Reform Bill was centrally concerned with timing, as Tories and Whigs
discussed whether reform was undesirable because it was an affront to the past
and an uncertain bequest to posterity, or necessary because of the exigencies of
the moment.[27] Such discussions take their bearings from a classical emphasis
on *kairos* (the opportune occasion for speech), in which a speaker takes into

[22] [William Maginn], 'Place-Men, Parliament-Men, Penny-a-Liners, and Parliamentary
Reporters', *Fraser's Magazine*, 2 (Oct. 1830), 282–94, p. 293.

[23] See Christopher Silvester (ed.), *The Literary Companion to Parliament* (London: Sinclair-
Stevenson, 1996), pp. xxii–xxvi.

[24] See Richard Altick, ' "Our Gallant Colonel" in *Punch* and Parliament', in *Writers, Readers
and Occasions: Selected Essays on Victorian Literature and Life* (Columbus: Ohio State University
Press, 1989), 267–95.

[25] *DJ*, i. 154.   [26] *Hansard*, vi. 1307–12.

[27] The temporal slant to these debates was informed by Bentham; see his 'Essay on the
Influence of Time and Place in Matters of Legislation' (1789), in *The Works of Jeremy Bentham*,
ed. John Bowring, 11 vols. (Edinburgh: Tait, 1843), i. 192–3.

account the contingencies of a given place or time—what Hazlitt refers to as 'the one thing needful in public speaking...not to say what is best, but the best that can be said in a given time, place and circumstance'.[28] Calls for timely circumspection might be heard either as contemplation raised or as commitment parried: Peel's future-oriented anti-reform polemic involved the cry 'others will outbid you, not now, but at no remote period', while Macaulay's defence of the Bill emphasized that 'The danger is terrible. The time is short'.[29] The diverging emphases of these voices sound concurrently in the rhetoric of John Russell, the man of whom Dickens once said, 'there is no man in England whom I more respect in his public capacity'.[30] Russell's emphasis on clear and present danger did not preclude a consideration of other times, for although 'policy and expediency speak loudly for reform...I maintain, that in departing from the letter, we preserve the spirit of those institutions'.[31] Time-serving, then, but also bequeathing his services to time.

Scribbling down such voices in the press gallery, Dickens's attentive ears picked up on these disquisitions regarding the temporalities of reform, and when his own literary voices dwelt on politics, it was to these timings that they recurred.[32] One figure, in particular, loomed large. According to Macaulay, in the early 1830s Brougham was, next to the King, the most popular man in England, constantly featured in the press as an advocate of law reform, the abolition of slavery, the extension of education, and, most prominently, the Reform Bill.[33] He delivered the most famous speech of the reform crisis, rising to a House so full that the thermometer read 85 degrees. The speech (the longest ever delivered in the Lords at that time) defended the bill and denounced the Tories, and the speaker perorated thus:

> As your friend, as the friend of my order, as the friend of my country, as the faithful servant of my Sovereign, I counsel you to assist with your uttermost efforts in preserving the peace, and upholding and perpetuating the Constitution. Therefore, I pray and I exhort you not to reject this measure. By all that you hold most dear—by all the ties that bind every one of us to our common order and our common country, I solemnly adjure you—I warn you—I implore you—yea, on my bended knees, I supplicate you—Reject not this Bill![34]

Like Russell, Brougham combines the timings of Peel and Macaulay. By drawing attention to the need for 'preserving the peace' alongside the vision of 'perpetuating the Constitution', he conspires to point out the danger presented

[28] William Hazlitt, 'On the Present State of Parliamentary Eloquence', *London Magazine*, 2 (Oct. 1820), 373–84, p. 381.

[29] *Hansard*, ii. 1353, 1205.   [30] *DS*, 288.   [31] *Hansard*, ii. 1065, 1085.

[32] Dickens began reporting in early 1831; see *DL*, i. 2.

[33] See R. Stewart, *Henry Brougham*, 230–84.   [34] *Hansard*, viii. 275.

by a disgruntled populace if the Lords should reject the bill, and also to see the bill itself as a continuation of the past rather than as a break from it. The train of verbs carries an artful mixture of intimidation and entreaty: 'counsel, adjure, warn, implore, supplicate'. The periodic structure of the last sentence encourages the audience to hear the verbs as synonyms while we anticipate the completion of the sense, but a warning is not a supplication, and Brougham's audience may have noted the premeditated menace within the apparently spontaneous enthusiasm. The speaker is minding his manners, but we might also hear a dark whisper: 'Pass this bill, or else . . . '.

Notwithstanding the comedy of the peroration (a drunken Brougham had to be picked up off his knees—Dickens recalled that the orator had polished off four bottles of port during the speech),[35] the author admired this well-timed voice. What Dickens esteemed most in public speaking was a balance between temporalities, a balance of present needs with the need for more than the present: 'Brougham in his prime was by far the greatest speaker he had ever heard. Nobody rivalled him in sarcasm, in invective, and in spirit-stirring eloquence. He was the man, too, he said, who of all others seemed, when he was speaking, to see the longest way before him.'[36] For Dickens, to be 'by far' the greatest speaker is to be both far-seeing and short-sighted, and the extent to which the timings of his own prose could develop and test what he so admired in this version of parliamentary speech was to become a vital concern of his early career. Indeed, the desire for a balance between short- and long-term considerations, a need to steer a way between obstructionist gradualism and hasty reform, was particularly visible both in emergent liberal rhetoric and in Dickens's early novels.[37]

The Pickwick Papers (1836–7), like Mr Pickwick himself, displays a relish for 'oratorising'.[38] The novel marks not just an explosive Dickensian entrance on to the Victorian scene, but also the inauguration of the serial novel and the age's first publishing phenomenon—John Sutherland calls it 'the most important single novel of the Victorian era'.[39] The novelist was going places,

---

[35] Cited in Collins (ed.), *Dickens: Interviews*, ii. 291.

[36] Recorded by the Revd. Whitwell Elwin, in Warwick Elwin (ed.), *Some XVIII. Century Men of Letters*, 2 vols. (London: John Murray, 1902), i. 249.

[37] Dickens, although averse to the irresponsible hesitancy of many politicians, was also a political gradualist in many respects, especially in regard to the franchise. See Philip Collins, 'Dickens the Citizen', in *Politics in Literature in the Nineteenth Century* (Lille: Editions Universitaires, 1974), 61–82.

[38] Charles Dickens, *The Pickwick Papers*, ed. Malcolm Andrews (London: Dent, 1998), 332. Subsequent page references are given parenthetically in the text.

[39] John Sutherland, *The Longman Companion to Victorian Fiction* (Harlow: Longman, 1988), 506.

but his novel often throws out oblique hints about where he has come from:

'The word politics, sir,' said Mr Pickwick, 'comprises, in itself, a difficult study of no inconsiderable magnitude.'

'Ah!' said the Count, drawing out the tablets again, 'ver good—fine words to begin a chapter. Chapter forty-seven. Poltics. The word poltic surprises by himself—' And down went Mr Pickwick's remark, in Count Smorltork's tablets, with such variations and additions as the Count's exuberant fancy suggested, or his imperfect knowledge of the language, occasioned. (p. 205)

This vignette casts Pickwick as political speaker and Smorltork as press reporter, for the latter's 'variations and additions' are akin to the art in which Dickens had schooled himself. Dickens is sending up that art, but also setting it to work, for the 'exuberant fancy' of his writing is making use of sounds to create its own kind of sense: the reporter's name tells us not only that he is making 'small talk', but also that the artist who creates him breathes life into him through a form of small talk, an acoustic shorthand. Pickwick's 'sir' and 'comprises' are joyously squashed into 'surprises': the novel is full of political surprises, and is itself founded upon Dickens's unwillingness to take things as read. *The Pickwick Papers*, as the title suggests, contain within them that mixture of the imaginative and the documentary already observed in the selective newspaper report ('certainly not *sine arte*, but . . . scrupulous as to truth'). The political implications of this mixture can be seen in its opening chapter, for the 'entry' from the Transactions of the Pickwick Club is, as contemporary reviewers observed, an entry into the House of Commons. The *Morning Post* noted that 'Dickens's imitations of Parliamentary eloquence and etiquette in the proceedings of the Pickwick Club are particularly good'.[40]

Pickwick's oration and the subsequent debate 'bear a strong affinity to the discussions of other celebrated bodies; and, as it is always interesting to trace a resemblance between the proceedings of great men, we transfer the entry to these pages' (p. 5). The transference is a report and something more, and the author returns to Brougham for the cadences of the debate. The temporal focus of the scene is at once circumscribed and far-seeing: the Pickwick meeting takes place on 'May 12, 1827' (p. 3), but it takes its bearings from a renowned discussion in the Commons between Brougham and Canning on 17 April 1823, and is aligned with the voices of those 'celebrated bodies' at the time of publication (April 1836). The 1823 debate revolved around Catholic Emancipation, but before considering the relevance of this debate to

[40] *Morning Post*, 11 May 1836.

the mid-1830s, we should consider what caught Dickens's ear and imagination in the exchanges of the two men.[41] As so often, Brougham was quick to adapt temporal considerations to his own ends. Defending the Catholic claims, he incredulously ventured 'whether there should be an end now, at once, and for ever, to the—(Cries of "No, no," interrupted the hon. and learned gentleman before he concluded his sentence.) He confessed that he was much cheered then by the negative which had just been, in something of an irregular manner, administered to him (laughter).'[42] Brougham's tripartite 'now, at once, and for ever' invites the 'interruptions' that he then turns to his advantage. It also accentuates the gravity of the reform question by making 'now' lead to a consideration of 'for ever', as if to give up the present debate is to give up the possibility of its ever being broached in the future. When Brougham went on to allude to Canning and to accuse him of 'monstrous truckling for the purpose of gaining office', the accused interrupted the speaker with 'I rise to say that is false'.[43] Brougham was striving for the tone that Dickens admired, blending 'invective' with attention to 'the longest way' through the allegation of 'truckling'. The political reality of the situation was, however, more stirring than 'spirit-stirring'. As Machin has observed of the April exchange: 'the debate became merely an opportunity for the pro-catholics who were "out" to charge with treachery those who were "in" . . . They [the Tories] became targets for the abuse of the Whigs who, sharing the same pro-catholic views, remained free and uncommitted.'[44] In this instance, what looks like a principled attack on opportunism is itself opportunistic.

   In the opening scene of *The Pickwick Papers*, Dickens implements the licence of the report-form in order to mock such disingenuously principled stands. With Pickwick and Blotton in place of Brougham and Canning, the author engages with the political subtext of the Catholic debate by having his 'reporting' narrative voice recast parliamentary interruptions into new shapes:

He (Mr Pickwick) would not deny that he was influenced by human passions, and human feelings (cheers)—possibly by human weaknesses—(loud cries of 'No') . . . Let them look abroad . . . boats were overturning, and boilers were bursting. (Cheers—a voice 'No.') No! (Cheers.) Let the honourable Pickwickian who cried 'No' so loudly come forward and deny it, if he could. (Cheers.) Who was it that cried 'No?' (pp. 5–7)

Pickwick's triple clause structure (like Brougham's 'now, at once, and for ever') invites and is received by loud cries of 'No', but his artful magnanimity then

---

[41] The debate was reported in *The Times* and reprinted with a discussion in the *Annual Register* (1823), 79. Dickens often consulted the *Register* as well as the papers; see J. H. Stonehouse (ed.), *The Catalogue of the Library of Charles Dickens* (London: Picadilly, 1935).

[42] *The Times*, 18 Apr. 1823, 2e.   [43] Ibid. 2f.

[44] G. I. T. Machin, *The Catholic Question in English Politics, 1820 to 1830* (Oxford: Clarendon Press, 1964), 40–1. See also R. Stewart, *Henry Brougham*, 205, 212.

grants the audience an opportunity that threatens his authority, as the two separate reports '(cheers)' and ('No') are combined '(Cheers—a voice 'No.')'. The whimsical vigour of the prose allows commemoration and criticism to blend in order to satirize each type of spoken interruption by suggesting their similarities: where the first 'No' is too quick for circumspection, the second is too eager for an argument, and the ardent haste of both interjections raises a smile.

An argument ensues, but Dickens's satire on the Pickwickian debate becomes curiously divided between mocking the pettiness of the discussion itself and the rapidity with which the discussion is dropped. In 1823, both MPs refused to take back their words, until Robert Wilson suggested that Canning make a conditional retraction, so as to enable Brougham to disavow any purpose of personal offence. Canning agreed, and Brougham followed suit by claiming that his allusion to his adversary was meant in a 'political' and not a 'personal' sense.[45] In Dickens's scene, Blotton is asked if he had called Pickwick a 'humbug' in 'a common sense'; he finally decides that he meant it only 'in a Pickwickian point of view', and Pickwick then notes that 'his own observations had been merely intended to bear a Pickwickian construction' (p. 8). To divide the 'personal' from the 'Pickwickian' or the 'political' is to sign away responsibility for what is said in public, and yet, a latitude has to be given to the speaker in order for the debates to proceed. Our amusement at this scene is caught between a sense that the debate isn't worth having and the need for a genuine debate once it has begun.

Dickens's satire would seem to have affected conduct. After the publication of novel, *Fraser's* observed a remark by an MP that 'since the appearance of the first number of the *Pickwick Papers* . . . we had not been treated with a single scene of this kind, formerly so common, in which honourable Members, after accusing each other of falsehood, swindling, or some other little irregularities of a similar kind, ended the affair amicably, at last, by declaring that these terms were only meant to apply "in a *parliamentary* sense".'[46] The writer suggests that the accusations from one MP to another are no more, but the question arises as to what has taken the place of these arguments. In Dickens's scene, the shift from the 'angry' to the 'amicable' is a mixed blessing, for the point at which discussion of 'little irregularities' is given up is sometimes the point at which a necessary antagonism is eschewed for the easy life. Parliament suffers from too much and from too little arguing.

Dickens's attention to the cadences of the Brougham–Canning exchange included a concern for other times and other reform debates. As the writer

45 *The Times*, 18 Apr. 1823, 3b.
46 Anon., 'Loose Thoughts', *Fraser's Magazine*, 18 (Oct. 1838), 495–504, p. 500.

for *Fraser's* notes, such back sliding was 'common', and Dickens's scene carries a further political charge when we remember that the past dispute was envisaged as an analogy for the 'celebrated bodies' and 'great men' (p. 5) at Westminster at the time of publication (April 1836). Catholic Emancipation and political reform were often seen as part of the same process,[47] so the dual timing of Dickens's scene pointed towards the suggestion that contemporary politics were still stuck in the unreformed past. In 1836, the writer was one of many previous supporters of the Great Reform Act who were becoming disillusioned with the Whigs' professed commitment to liberal reforms. After 1832, the government had brought in the reviled new Poor Law, and Brougham's reputation as the beneficent Whig champion of reform had become tarnished by his successful guiding of the bill through Parliament. Dickens's satire on the past debate in *The Pickwick Papers*, then, aimed to highlight how apparently principled calls for reform could forget themselves in party-political skirmishes, and how the Gentleman's club at Parliament had promised more in earlier years. It is in the timings of the prose where we once again catch a hint of his political engagement.

Brougham founded and was elected chairman of The Society for the Diffusion of Useful Knowledge in 1826. Nearly half the members of the first Committee were Whig MPs, and so when we learn from the first page of Dickens's novel that the Pickwick meeting takes place on 'May 12, 1827', and that Pickwick's speech is said to help 'the advancement of *knowledge*, and the *diffusion* of learning' (p. 3; my emphasis), we need to consider the muddled precision of the scene anew. A Whig-led reform movement is here envisaged as a newly founded Corresponding Society that organizes rambles around the countryside: the temporal flash-back of the prose is there to jog the memory of the Whigs and their supporters in 1836, telling them what their former high-flown rhetoric has been reduced to. Dickens's double timings again answer back to the two-timing politicians, and while the tone of the novel's opening is often light-hearted, the Pickwickian point of view still carries within it the Whig apostasy that angered its creator.[48]

Raymond Williams asserts that, when reading Dickens, we 'often feel that we are reading an *account* of a debate by a passionately committed and polemical reporter'.[49] This is not quite true to the feel of Dickens's writing: in the first

---

[47] See John Cannon, *Parliamentary Reform, 1640–1832* (Aldershot: Gregg Revivals, 1994), 191.

[48] See Dickens's arch noticing: 'I see honourable mention of myself, and Mr. Pickwick's politics, in Fraser this month. They consider Mr. P. a decided Whig' (*DL*, i. 161). Dickens himself was far from 'decided'.

[49] Raymond Williams, 'Dickens and Social Ideas', in Michael Slater (ed.), *Dickens 1970: Centenary Essays* (London: Chapman & Hall, 1970), 77–98, p. 82.

chapter of *The Pickwick Papers* the cadences of political oratory are matched not by polemical report, but by a mixture of amusement and impatience. The transposition of report techniques into fiction to create an address to time that goes beyond immediate party-political debate is evident when we are welcomed into Eatanswill, for the word Williams chooses to italicize, Dickens chooses to qualify: the headnote to the chapter promises us 'Some Account of Eatanswill' (p. 161). '*Some* account': the balance between the exactitude of a report and the selectiveness of a narrative is a balance that tempers the 'passionately committed and polemical' with other concerns.

In his reports for the Whig *Morning Chronicle* during the election campaign of 1834–5, Dickens is intent on taking sides: Liberals display 'perfect order',[50] others are denounced for 'the trammels of Toryism'.[51] Such embellishments to the report-form make it clear whose side the writing is on, but commitment to the party cause is permeated by another tone when Dickens comes to describe the Eatanswill election. As so often with Dickens, an attenuated form of *paralipsis* marks a self-conscious refusal to play by the rules of the game: 'it is almost superfluous to say that everything in Eatanswill was made a party question' (p. 162). The reporter's earlier immersion in the contemporary political scene is now offset by the novelist's willingness to laugh at both 'Blues' and 'Buffs'. Press-forms are both courted and mocked, and this ambivalence is carried through to the jostling styles of the prose timings.

During the election, we are often allowed to hear the timely diligence and topical engagement of the reporter: a 'burst of mirth' is 'of about quarter of an hour's duration' (p. 175), one speech is 'of half an hour's length' (p. 175), a quarrel between voters lasts 'for three-quarters of an hour' (p. 176), and victory is secured for the Blues 'one hour before the close of the poll' (p. 178). However, passages of time in this chapter are subtly overdetermined as well as meticulously documented. A month before Dickens wrote the election scene, the Bribery at Elections Bill had been debated in Parliament, and an earlier report on the Northampton by-election had seen the writer blame the 'Tory Party' for having 'driven up' electors to the polls 'like herds of swine'.[52] Given the climate, when readers arrived at the following sentence they may have noticed how the Pickwickian reporter's earlier temporal precision is met by a deft ambiguity: 'A small body of electors remained unpolled on the very last day. They were calculating and reflecting persons, who had not yet been convinced by the arguments of either party, although they had had frequent conferences with each' (p. 178). In the novel, the object of this satirical 'report' is not merely this or that party, but also those who vote for them. There is

---

[50] *Morning Chronicle*, 1 Dec. 1834.   [51] *Morning Chronicle*, 14 Jan. 1835.
[52] *DJ*, ii. 28.

a suggestion here that time is not all that these voters are taking, as their 'calculating' natures may perhaps be working out the largest bribe they can get for their political commitment.

This suggestiveness is borrowing and departing from the animus of Dickens's press-reports, and it highlights a characteristic of the novelist's early work. Lewes finely observed that 'His language, even on the most trivial points, has, from a peculiar collocation of the words, or some happy expression, a drollery which is spoiled by repeating or reading loud, because this drollery arises from so fine an association of idea that the sound of the voice destroys it.'[53] One can read aloud the passage on the 'small body of electors' so as to defend or incriminate them, but to lend the sound of the voice to the passage would be either to confirm or to deny what the narrator's prose voice so exquisitely intimates; the 'fine association' conveyed by the politic reticence of the printed page would be lost to the spoken polemic. In *The Pickwick Papers*, Dickens's satire frequently returns to the political topicality of his reporting days, but his prose contains more than meets the ear because it is intent on seeing things from more than one perspective.

Dickens's fictional beginnings mark an attentiveness to oratorical endeavour even as they seek a distance from it, and this is one reason why—despite the author's comic tilts at the Parliament and the election process—he dedicated his first novel to an MP. The author praised Serjeant Talfourd for his Copyright Bill, and for 'the inestimable services you are rendering to the literature of your country, and of the lasting benefits you will confer upon authors of this and succeeding generations' (p. xxxv). Dickens's concern that literature be of the moment but not only for it is mirrored, as he sees it, by Talfourd's own efforts in Parliament, and what Talfourd had actually said in the House when presenting the bill offers us similar pause for thought about the possible reciprocities and differences between spoken and written addresses to time. Of authors he observed: 'While I believe that their claims to some share in the Legislature will not be denied ... the interest of their case is not of that stirring kind which belongs to the busy present, but reflects back on the past, of which the passions are now silent, and stretches forward with speculation into the visionary future.'[54] Talfourd's tentatively formed 'some share' speaks of literature's bearing on politics and its distance from it through temporal analogy. While Dickens admired such claims for literature's indebtedness to the past and its bequests to the future—as his dedication

---

[53] George H. Lewes, cited in *Versatile Victorian: Selected Writings of George Henry Lewes*, ed. Rosemary Ashton (London: Bristol Classical Press, 1992), 60.

[54] *Hansard*, xxxviii. 867.

makes clear—his need to see the moment as an indexical part of other times (rather than merely separate from them) also insists upon a 'belonging' that Talfourd's defence of authors has not fully supported. For Dickens, the corollary of this insistence is that the legislature should also look beyond 'the busy present'.

Ten years after the publication of *Pickwick*, in the Preface to the Cheap edition, Dickens looked back over the period and expressed his pleasure that 'legal reforms have pared the claws of Messrs Dodson and Fogg'. Nevertheless, 'an improvement in the mode of conducting Parliamentary Elections (especially for counties) is still within the bounds of possibility... With such a retrospect, extending through so short a period, I shall cherish the hope that every volume of this Edition will afford me an opportunity of recording the extermination of some wrong or abuse set forth in it.'[55] By expressing the hope that the representations in his work will become anachronisms, Dickens attests to the continuing timeliness of his original. Just as the first edition of *The Pickwick Papers* contained a sketch of a pre-reform constituency whose abuses spread into the post-reform time of its publication, so the 'extending retrospect' here speaks of how the book's occasions do not tie it to the date of its first reception by the public. The Preface in 1867 (the year of another important reform bill) made the point even more strongly: 'an improvement in the mode of conducting Parliamentary Elections (and even Parliaments too, perhaps) is still within the bounds of possibility' (p. xli). The 'still' is still there, and the parentheses now contain a political concern that embraces and goes beyond the aside in the 1847 edition.[56] The 1847 Preface had addressed itself to 'Posterity'[57] as well as to the present; *The Pickwick Papers* continued to be at once timely and, as the full title of the novel indicated, '*posthumous*', continued to re-anchor itself in and out of specific times and places. This founding Victorian novel was itself founded on the timely art of speech-making and speech-taking, but its own commitment to *kairos* seeks a larger temporal ambit in which to work its influence. Pickwickian politics is not a programme, but an encouragement towards a disinterested mode of political enquiry and expression—an address to time that is at once urgent and enduring.

[55] Repr. in Charles Dickens, *The Posthumous Papers of the Pickwick Club*, ed. Robert Patten (London: Penguin, 1986), 46.

[56] 'If anything, corruption was on the increase after 1832 and it was probably more widespread in 1880, eight years after the passage of the Ballot Act, than at any other time' (H. J. Hanham, *The Nineteenth Century Constitution, 1815–1914* (Cambridge: Cambridge University Press, 1969), 257).

[57] Patten (ed.), *Pickwick*, 43.

PLOTTING TALK

Dickens's acoustic imagination led him to conceive his novels not only as printed forms within which public speeches could be represented and revised, but also as forms of public speaking themselves, models of linguistic conduct that might enact as well as represent politics. Indeed, the political negotiation between short- and long-term perspectives that he attempts in his early fiction is also a formal concern. The first Preface to *The Pickwick Papers* explains the difficulty of publishing in monthly numbers: 'In short, it was necessary—or it appeared so to the author—that every number should be, to a certain extent, complete in itself, and yet that the whole twenty numbers, when collected, should form one tolerably harmonious whole, each leading to the other by a gentle and not unnatural progress of adventure' (p. xxxvii). The need to turn sketches into plot competes with a desire to hold off such harmonies in favour of 'detached and desultory' serial parts: 'it was necessary, *or it appeared so*, to a *certain* extent, *and yet, tolerably* harmonious, *not un*natural'. The prose is walking a tightrope, attempting to stay true to a vision of the present moment as infiltrated by past and future concerns. Furthermore, 'a gentle and not unnatural progress' might define a political as well as an aesthetic ideal. As Dickens turned his attentions to how his stories might best progress, he also thought about how the nation might do the same.

Contemporary debates about Dickens's novels involved consideration of the closeness of their serial form to that of the newspapers. *Fraser's* complained that the novels were 'stuffed "with passages that lead to nothing" merely to fill the necessary room' and asked: 'The habits of the reporter break out—the copy is to be given in—and what shall we write of but what we know? How fill the paper but by reports of debates[?].'[58] Such criticism sees too much journalistic 'copy' and not enough innovation. Carlyle lent his fierce, awkward eloquence to this issue by considering the political implications of such developments. In one of the most widely discussed studies of the art of the novel in the 1830s, he denounced the all-too-contemporary 'perfection of extemporaneous writing': 'Print the *talk* of any man, and there will be a thick octavo volume daily . . . If once Printing have grown to be as Talk, then DEMOCRACY (if we will look into the roots of things) is not a bugbear and probability, but a certainty, and event as good as come!'[59] Printing had grown to be as talk in *Hansard* and

[58] Anon., 'Charles Dickens and his Works', *Fraser's Magazine*, 21 (Apr. 1840), 381–400, p. 400.

[59] Thomas Carlyle, 'Lockhart's *Life of Scott*', *London and Westminster Review*, 28 (Jan. 1838), 293–345, pp. 340–1.

the newspapers, and this outburst of pages inspires the prophet's growling (*Hansard* first went on sale to the public in the year in which Carlyle's piece was published).

Kathryn Chittick has observed 'a kind of commercial symbiosis' operating in Dickens's early novels: 'the newspapers cannibalized Dickens's stories to fill up their columns, and Dickens in turn thickened his own narratives with newspaperish daily matter . . . They [were] above all political entities, in their subject matter, in their audience, and in their publishing ephemerality . . . What was wanted was news. In particular, parliamentary news.'[60] Yet, the author was not always willing to participate in 'symbiosis', for while he was struggling to be responsive to public demands he was also attempting to forge a responsible public voice, one that could take the measure of the 'talk' Carlyle feared. This political mediation finds expression in the plotting of talk, and in the tussle between isolated periodical installments and the 'progress of adventure' that Dickens was searching for in a plot. The full title of his next novel suggests as much, as it splices Dickens's phrase in two: *The Adventures of Oliver Twist; or, The Parish Boy's Progress* (1837–9). Plural 'adventures' or singular 'progress'? The novelist's '*or*' does not yet undertake to decide.

The opening numbers of *Oliver Twist* carry a comedic fury of appeal and indignation against the New Poor Law.[61] Although Oliver starts out as an orphan in a 'baby-farm', and his situation is not that of a supposedly lazy pauper denied outdoor relief, the elimination of relief in 1834 encouraged many unmarried mothers to place their children in baby-farms in return for a weekly allowance; Oliver is, therefore, meant to symbolize the effects of the act, and the way it stigmatized poverty.[62] As Ruskin once observed, 'let us not lose the use of Dickens's wit and insight, because he chooses to speak in a circle of stage fire'.[63] The chapters 'speak' in response to a much more excited and excitable voice that hovers in their wings: the voice of Brougham, who had became one of the bill's most renowned supporters while Dickens was reporting the Poor Law debates for the *Morning Chronicle*.[64] In July 1834, he

---

[60] Kathryn Chittick, *Dickens and the 1830s* (Cambridge: Cambridge University Press, 1991), 131, 40.

[61] The new law eliminated 'outdoor relief' and encouraged 'able-bodied' paupers to seek work in the free market; if they needed help, they would have to enter the workhouse, where conditions were designed to be 'less eligible' than those outside; see Anthony Brundage, *The Making of the New Poor Law: The Politics of Inquiry, Enactment, and Implementation, 1832–39* (London: Hutchinson, 1978).

[62] See David Paroissien, *The Companion to Oliver Twist* (Edinburgh: Edinburgh University Press, 1992), 42.

[63] John Ruskin, 'Unto this Last', *Cornhill Magazine*, Aug. 1860, repr. in Philip Collins (ed.), *Dickens: The Critical Heritage* (London: Routledge & Kegan Paul, 1971), 314.

[64] On Dickens's reporting, see Edgar Johnson, *Charles Dickens: His Tragedy and Triumph*, 2 vols. (New York: Simon & Schuster, 1952), i. 88.

delivered his last great oration in the House, breaking his personal best in a four-hour extravaganza of bombast. Defending the new measure against the existing Poor Law, Brougham drew a vignette of the 'pampered' pauper:

Industry . . . sweetens the coarsest morsel, and softens the hardest pillow;—but not under the Poor-law! Look to that volume, and you will find the pauper tormented with the worst ills of wealth—listless and unsettled—wearing away the hours, restless and half awake, and sleepless all the night that closes his slumbering day—needy, yet pampered—ill-fed, yet irritable and nervous. Oh! monstrous progeny of this unnatural system, which has matured, in the squalid recesses of the workhouse, the worst ills that haunt the palace, and made the pauper a victim of those imaginary maladies which render wealthy idleness less happy than laborious poverty! Industry, the safeguard against impure desires—the true preventive of crimes;—but not under the Poor-law![65]

This is the epitome of the 'Westminster view of benevolence' and the 'grim alliance between Malthusianism and Nonconformity' that Humphry House so well anatomized and glossed in his study of Dickens: 'Let the poor live hard lives, sober, celibate, and unamused; let them eat the plainest food, pinch to save, and save to lower the rates—then "civilization" might win through.'[66] Brougham had never been inside a workhouse, and his rhetoric papers over the cracks of those 'squalid recesses' by turning real 'maladies' into mental delusions—'The poor? They've never had it so good, and that's what's making them so miserable.'

Dickens was rightly angered by the self-satisfied floridity of this speech, and in *Oliver Twist* he revised Brougham's vision of the worker whose indolence apparently created a 'slumbering' day and 'sleepless' night. In place of Brougham, we have Bumble, a man who 'had a great idea of his oratorical powers' and is esteemed by Mrs Mann for his 'literary character'.[67] Bumble transports Oliver to the workhouse, where the child's request for more food leads to punishment:

He only cried bitterly all day; and, when the long, dismal night came on, spread his little hands before his eyes to shut out the darkness, and crouching in the corner, tried to sleep: ever and anon waking with a start and tremble, and drawing himself closer and closer to the wall, as if to feel even its cold hard surface were a protection in the gloom and loneliness which surrounded him. (p. 16)

---

[65] *Hansard*, xxv. 231.

[66] Humphry House, *The Dickens World*, 2nd edn. (Oxford: Oxford University Press, 1942), 73–6.

[67] Charles Dickens, *Oliver Twist*, ed. Steven Connor (London: Dent, 1994), 8–9. Subsequent page references are given parenthetically in the text.

The orator's images are tested here within an altered perspective, as the sleepless night is not so much the product of ill-fed irritability, but of the starving desperation of a day in which Oliver does not have the luxury even to be 'half-asleep'. The boy's huddling up to a 'cold hard surface' answers to Brougham's 'hardest pillow' by making the pauper grateful where the MP saw him as spoilt. The narrator does not presume to speak for the boy's internal state; the tactful reticence of Dickens's 'as if' in the final sentence keeps its distance, refusing the encroachment that Brougham makes when he takes the liberty of telling the poor how they feel.

Brougham had also envisaged the poor man's domineering over the ratepayer in the following terms: 'He comes with a sturdy gait and a masterful air . . . He demands his allowance not as a man, but as a master; his tone is imperative, for he knows he must be obeyed.'[68] The only sentence of direct speech attributed to any child at the orphanage, and perhaps the most famous sentence ever spoken by a Dickens character, deliberately takes up Brougham's language while refusing to take up his tone: 'He rose from the table; and advancing to the master, basin and spoon in hand, said: somewhat alarmed at his own temerity: "Please, sir, I want some more"' (p. 13). To imagine someone alarmed at his own temerity is to imagine a tone that partakes of the downtrodden and the purposeful. Advancing to the master, but not speaking 'as a master', Oliver's manner is less than imperative, and yet not quite subservient. He does not, after all, shape his desire as a question ('Please, sir, can I have some more?'), but nor does he drop the deferential 'sir', nor forget to mind his p's and q's. The suggestion that Oliver's address had Brougham in mind was picked up by *Punch* in the early 1840s. In one of the first *Punch* illustrations to be based on a Dickens novel, Leech parodied Cruikshank's engraving of this scene in '"Henry" Asking for More', with Brougham as Oliver holding out his bowl ('£5,000') to an angry John Bull.[69] The politician's angling for a bonus now speaks out from, and takes precedence over, the needs of the parish boy.

Benedict Anderson has examined the 'novelistic format of the newspaper' and shown how these two periodical forms are stylistically aligned and politically analogous.[70] The opening of *Oliver Twist* supports this view to a certain extent: informed by contemporary oratory, and by the journalistic heritage of Dickens's novelistic form, it is a heckling voice plotted alongside (and plotting against) the voices of the MPs in the newspapers. That said, Dickens is also striving for another type of civic engagement, and a comment Anderson relegates to a footnote should be pursued: 'reading a newspaper is

---

[68] *Hansard*, xxv. 223.   [69] *Punch*, vi. 141.

[70] Benedict Anderson, *Imagined Communities: Reflections on the Origins and Spread of Nationalism* (London: Verso, 1991), 22–36.

like reading a novel whose author has abandoned any thought of a coherent plot'.[71] Dickens's early novels are searching for this coherence, and plotting for 'a not unnatural progress' also brings with it an awareness of how the novelist might need to shape an expression that is meditative as well as mobilizing. Reading for the plot, as Peter Brooks reminds us, it itself an action that blends foresight and hindsight as a way of making sense of the moment: 'Perhaps we would do best to speak of the *anticipation of retrospection* as our chief tool in making sense of narrative, the master trope of its strange language.'[72] When, in the Preface to *The Pickwick Papers*, Dickens indulged in 'such a retrospect, extending through so short a period' as he considered the future import of his tale, he was adopting this master trope as a cautionary political rhythm—reform without revolution.

The rise of another form of public speech in the 1830s helps to account for *Oliver Twist*'s movement away from a certain kind of political interventionism. By the time the fifteenth number came out in July 1838, the anti-Poor Law agitation was gaining momentum. Feargus O'Connor was travelling the country to speak against the Whig legislation, and against Brougham in particular.[73] In June, O'Connor repeated one of his favourite set-pieces on 'Harry' Brougham, in which the politician is packed off to the workhouse after being refused what he considers to be his due (an increase in his pension): 'if the people had their rights they would no longer pay his salary'.[74] The time was ripe for Dickens to join in with this gleeful bating of 'Harry' in order to further the anti-Poor Law cause, but in his July 1838 number the author was intent upon creating another kind of civic voice.

Chapter 36, the middle chapter of three (emphasizing its status as neither beginning nor end, but serial link), has a headnote that tells us not *what* we will read, but *how* we should read: '*Chapter 36* is a very short one, and may appear of no great importance in its place. But it should be read, not withstanding, as a sequel to the last, and a key to one that will follow when its time arrives' (p. 255). This formal anticipation of retrospection is mirrored in the plot, for, unlike O'Connor's Harry, Dickens's character Harry Maylie is part of a debate that goes beyond parliamentary issues. Harry has just proposed to Rose and been rejected, for she feels that her own status as orphan would be a 'blight',

---

[71] Benedict Anderson, *Imagined Communities: Reflections on the Origins and Spread of Nationalism*, 33.

[72] Peter Brooks, *Reading for the Plot: Design and Intention in Narrative* (Oxford: Clarendon Press, 1984), 23.

[73] See James Epstein, *The Lion of Freedom: Feargus O'Connor and the Chartist Movement, 1832–1842* (London: Croom Helm, 1982), 94–101.

[74] Repr. in R. G. Gammage, *History of the Chartist Movement, 1837–1854* (London: Truslove & Hanson, 1894), 26.

'stain', and 'great obstacle' to his 'progress in the world' (pp. 253–4). Harry now plans to go away, and the doctor mocks him—much as the critics had mocked Dickens's newspaper-novels—for his lack of consistency over time: ' "Why, you are not in the same mind or intention two half-hours together!" "You will tell me a different tale one of these days," said Harry, colouring without any perceptible reason' (p. 255). Telling a different kind of tale is what the plot is attempting to do. Harry's 'one of these days' echoes Dickens's 'one that will follow when its time arrives', and, in doing so, hints at a solidity over time that the doctor has not yet fathomed.

Harry's stance has political implications, for his apparently mercurial nature is then posited as sound parliamentary acumen by the doctor:

'Well,' said the doctor, 'you are a queer fellow. But of course they will get you into parliament at the election before Christmas, and these sudden shiftings and changes are no bad preparation for political life. There's something in that. Good training is always desirable, whether the race be for place, cup, or sweepstakes.'

Harry Maylie looked as if he could have followed up this short dialogue by one or two remarks that would have staggered the doctor not a little; but he contented himself with saying, 'We shall see,' and pursued the subject no further. (p. 256)

Harry could easily have been the vehicle for a Dickensian offensive on parliamentary procedures and legislation at this point, or on the 'sudden shiftings and changes' of other Harrys, but 'one or two remarks' unspoken hold back the political animus for the sake of good form. Contrary to the doctor's wager, neither Harry nor Dickens's prose is gambling here: the character will not in fact enter Parliament, but will bide his time until chapter 51 (the readers must wait eight months until *after* Christmas for this episode in March 1839), where he will reject the 'political life' in order to obtain Rose's hand in marriage (p. 386). The 'We shall see' here sounds out the foresight of the novel's form and contents, as the present unwillingness to 'pursue the subject' becomes the beginning rather than the end of a narrative. Tales of political networking are being given up for the more intricate networks of Dickens's plot.

The timings and significances of this chapter cannot find their way into the newspapers as isolated set-pieces; nor can they be said to carry the polemical charge of the early chapters, for Harry's identity and the novel's seriality are built on choices that move the plotting of speech away from direct political engagement. Dickens's unwillingness to replicate the tone of O'Connor's attacks on Brougham at this point in the novel is in tension with his own earlier satire on the cadences of Brougham's rhetoric, but by the time the author was writing these numbers O'Connor had openly identified himself with the lawless side of anti-Poor Law protest as the spokesman for

Chartist demands.[75] The Poor Law Amendment Act had led directly to the Chartist movement, and during 1838 the country was flooded with speaking tours that cultivated a rhetoric of menace.[76] Chartism was becoming seen as an alloy of political oratory and violence (O'Connor on the platform 'with a petition in one hand, and a musket in the other');[77] the 'right to arm' was a key refrain of early Chartist speeches.[78] Dickens was wary of these developments: his response to O'Connor's battle-cry of 'if the people had their rights' was attentive to the sounds behind the 'talk': 'When we talk of "rights of labour", do we picture to ourselves a hideous phantom whispering discontent . . . sharpening the Chartist pike by stealth?'[79]

The People's Charter was published a month before Dickens wrote chapter 36, and its calls for universal suffrage were premised on the belief that all legislative reforms would be negligible without an overhaul of the system. Chartist rhetoric was 'a totalizing critique . . . not suited to the discrimination between one legislative measure and another'; further, a central tenet of Chartism was 'the attribution of evil and misery to a political source'.[80] However, this heady combination of militancy, totalizing critique, and political determinism was, for the novelist, a dark and dangerous exaggeration of elements in his own satirical style. Dickens, like Harry, was not altogether sure that involvement in political life was always the surest or only guarantee of social progress, and this uncertainty informs the 'progress' of his plot in *Oliver Twist*, turning it away from an emphasis on direct political intervention and towards a focus on the indirect power of social attitudes. Harry's long-standing refusal to countenance the views of those who would denounce his wish to marry a woman 'on whose name there is a stain' (p. 242), for instance, is meant to be appreciated as a socio-political act, a template for a more enlightened attitude to those on the outskirts of respectability.

Rose, like Oliver, is to be seen not merely as a victim, but as a tutelary spirit that might be taken to heart by readers—another 'Principle of Good surviving through every adverse circumstance, and triumphing at last' (p. xxxviii). On one level, the entanglement of the novel's earlier reformist satire in the machinations of the plot bespeaks Dickens's divided mind: the magic wand that waves the happy endings of the orphans into existence would

[75] Epstein, *Lion of Freedom*, 96.

[76] See Dorothy Thompson, *The Chartists: Popular Politics in the Industrial Revolution* (Aldershot: Wildwood, 1986), 28, 62.

[77] Fergus O'Connor, paraphrased in *Northern Star*, 6 July 1839.

[78] See James Epstein, 'The Constitutional Idiom: Radical Reasoning, Rhetoric and Action in Early Nineteenth-Century England', *Journal of Social History*, 23/3 (1990), 553–74.

[79] *DL*, iii. 282.

[80] Gareth Stedman Jones, *Languages of Class: Studies in English Working Class History, 1832–1982* (Cambridge: Cambridge University Press, 1983), 177, 105.

seem to pull against the earlier vision (akin to the Chartist critique) of the constitutive power of the state over the lives of the poor. And yet, the parish boy's progress has always been a nightmare as well as a fairy-tale, and Dickens does not renege on the urgency of his reformist anger merely because he sets it alongside other considerations towards the end of his novel; for a refusal to succumb to politico-economic determinism is not to be equated with a complacency about the pressures of circumstance.

This complexity is illustrated in the chapter that so speedily ties up all the loose ends, restoring Oliver's fortune and marrying off Rose to Harry. Oliver travels back with Rose towards his birthplace and thinks of his childhood friend at the workhouse, Dick, whom readers had last seen almost two years earlier as Oliver waved him goodbye with the prediction, 'You will be well and happy!' (p. 50). The plotting of talk across this arch of time sees the prediction return in March 1839, as Oliver, like Harry, attempts to remain consistent and to keep his word: 'we'll take him away from here, and have him clothed and taught, and send him to some quiet country place where he may grow strong and well' (p. 377). This desire for a domesticated happy-ever-after, for a way in which Oliver's pastoral progress can serve as a synecdoche for all others in his position, receives its answer at the very moment that we learn that Rose has accepted Harry's hand in marriage. Oliver comes into the room crying, is asked what the matter is, and the narrator—as if unwilling to make Oliver say the words—sympathetically takes the words out of his mouth by moving to indirect report for the closing words of the chapter: 'It is a world of disappointment; often to the hopes we most cherish, and hopes that do our nature the greatest honour. Poor Dick was dead!' (p. 387). The sudden narrative address to the reader, the shift to the present tense, the call to our better nature, is both an oratorical appeal and a sigh of beleaguered acceptance—a voice that insists on what still remains to be done as well as one that acknowledges the limits of its own ability to act.

The potential effects of Oliver's voice haunted Dickens. Our last glimpse of Dick in *Oliver Twist* comes when the 'little speaker' (p. 121) decides to follow Oliver's vocal lead by confronting Bumble. His demands inspire the following response from the exasperated beadle: 'They're all in one story, Mrs Mann. That out-dacious Oliver has demogalized them all!' (p. 121). This plotting of speech involves an apt series of Dickensian twists: Oliver is 'audacious' and an 'out'-of-doors speaker, for he not only 'demoralizes' the boys, he also 'demagoguizes' them. Oliver's cry on behalf of the oppressed might be seen as a tentative analogue for the Chartist leaders and crowds out-of-doors that were beginning to answer back to the voices of the parliamentary in-crowd. Yet, this voice does not aim to incite rebellion, and is plotted in a 'story' that resists some emphases of the radical orators.

John Plotz has shown how the rise of the Victorian mass platform and its attendant crowd culture emerged as an alternative source of order and as a 'potent rival to the claims of literary texts themselves'.[81] Carlyle's *Chartism* (1839) is the pivotal text in response to this situation, and shares Dickens's dual concern about the injustices of parliamentary talk and the dangers of excess inspired by the talk on the extra-parliamentary platforms. As Plotz demonstrates, Carlyle seeks to contain the ill-disciplined voices of the crowd even as he harnesses their rhetorical power, 'borrowing their energy and hence their modes of speech' to go beneath the surface clamour in search of a more profound political diagnosis.[82] That is, Carlyle translates the platform-talk into a need for a plot, as he explains in *Chartism* when listening to the orators: '*in*articulate cries as of a dumb creature in rage and pain; to the ear of wisdom they are inarticulate prayers: "Guide me, govern me! I am mad and miserable, and cannot guide myself" '.[83] Carlyle's printed speech offers itself as one such form of guidance and governance—a template for a leadership beyond the specious seductions of the Chartist demagogues.

Chartism casts its shadow over Victorian aesthetics. Ivan Kreilkamp has explored how writers in the 1840s, fearful of the way in which Chartist speech could shade into physical violence, also attempted to shape a novelistic craft that could absorb and subdue oratorical power: 'If Chartist practices had transformed rational speech and oratory into dissident and threatening utterance, then novels could redeem this degraded orality . . . political speech is defused as it is translated into written texts and introduced into the national sphere.'[84] Dickens's wrestlings with the wayward forces of his early fiction are part of such developments. Chesterton enthusiastically observed that he was 'a demagogue of fiction',[85] that his rise was 'like the rising of a vast mob', and that 'a deep, confused clamour of comradeship and insurrection fills all his narrative'.[86] There is also an attempt to rein in an appetite for insurrection in Dickens's early prose; words are continually threatening to riot, and sentences have the potentially unruly energy of demagogic utterance, but from within such portents of linguistic crowd trouble one can sense a talent for plotting, shaping, and managing linguistic exuberance—the assiduous reporter's ability to take down and translate voices into print,

[81] John Plotz, *The Crowd: British Literature and Public Politics* (Berkeley: University of California Press, 2000), 2.

[82] Ibid. 143.

[83] Carlyle, cited in *Carlyle: Selected Writings*, ed. Alan Shelston (London: Penguin, 1971), 184.

[84] Ivan Kreilkamp, *Voice and the Victorian Storyteller* (Cambridge: Cambridge University Press, 2005), 38, 66.

[85] G. K. Chesterton, *Criticisms and Appreciations of the Works of Charles Dickens* (1911) (London: Stratus, 2001), 98, 121.

[86] G. K. Chesterton, *The Victorian Age in Literature* (1913) (Denton: Edgeways, 2001), 50–1.

blended with the aspiring novelist's search for an enduring fictional and political order.

These aesthetic and political allegiances are channelled into a controlled ferocity of expression in *Barnaby Rudge: A Tale of the Riots of 'Eighty* (1841), an oblique yet sustained engagement with Chartism and with the contemporary political scene.[87] The novel's ordering of its own narrative voice is revealing in this respect, for temporal analogue is marked out by the first and last words of the novel: '*In the year 1775*, there stood upon the borders of Epping Forest . . . he has very probably gone on talking to *the present time*.'[88] The arch of the novel's duration draws the past into the present by linking the internal action to the time of reading, and it is within the parameters of such bindings that the fiction hints to its readers that it is newsworthy. Yet, placed within the contours of *Barnaby Rudge*'s fearful, fascinated attentiveness to mass discontent, Dickens's desire for an urgent action jostles alongside a suspicion of an insurgent people.

When describing the crowd that hunts down Fagin in *Oliver Twist*, the narrator spoke of how 'word was passed among the crowd . . . intelligence ran from mouth to mouth' (pp. 373–4) as the people incited themselves into escalating fury. This sense of Chinese whispers, of what loose tongues might let loose through echo, repetition, and insinuation, becomes increasingly common in Dickens's work—the figure of an unruly spoken energy from which the printed narrative voice often attempts to distinguish itself. *Barnaby Rudge* is full of such images: from Solomon Daisy's 'relating the story very often, and ornamenting it . . . with a few flourishes suggested by the various hearers from time to time' (p. 17), to Gabriel Varden thinking of the 'flaming terms in which to relate his adventure' (p. 28), to the 'constant restlessness, and flitting to and fro' that 'gave rise to strange stories' (p. 127), to 'the air' that is 'filled with whispers of a confederacy' (p. 280) as the political discontent takes shape. Dickens composes the scenes of rioting and crowd trouble with a demagogic relish ('I think I can make a better riot than Lord George Gordon did')[89] and warms to his task with a gleeful ferocity: 'the object is . . . to select the striking points and beat them into the page with a sledge-hammer . . . to convey an idea of multitudes, violence, and fury'.[90] However, from within the violence and fury of his own verbal energy there is an insistent equation of the crowd with energies that his novels are setting themselves to withstand.

[87] See Iain McCalman, 'Controlling the Riots: Dickens, *Barnaby Rudge* and the Romantic Revolution', *History*, 84 (July 1999), 458–76, for a critique of readings that see the novel as merely 'anti-Chartist' and 'counter-revolutionary'.

[88] Charles Dickens, *Barnaby Rudge*, ed. Donald Hawes (London: Dent, 1996), 3, 635 (my emphasis). Subsequent page references are given parenthetically in the text.

[89] *DL*, ii. 337.   [90] Ibid. 417–18.

Plotz suggests that the novel-form 'can aspire to provide depth that the newspaper never can' and offers 'an analogy that elucidates the nature of contests for public sphere legitimacy in the era: as Chartist crowds are to Carlyle's "profound" politics, so newspapers are to the novel'.[91] This analogy is suggestive, for Dickens's descriptions of crowds often echo the terms in which his early reviewers conceived the ephemeral aspects of his newspaper-novels. In *Barnaby Rudge*, the narrator observes how the mob 'had no definite purpose or design' (p. 396). In the crowd, 'every symptom of order or preconcerted arrangement' vanishes, with people reacting only 'on the spontaneous suggestion of the moment': 'Each tumult took shape and form from the circumstances of the moment . . . In a word, a moral plague ran through the city' (p. 403). Dickens's novels had also been questioned for the effervescent comings and goings of characters; the crowd has 'new faces and figures presenting themselves every instant' while others disappear into 'chasms of passages' (p. 415; recall *Fraser's* complaint about 'passages that lead to nothing' in Dickens's work). The figure of the crowd, like that of the newspaper, lacks a sense of temporal amplitude; unplotted and unchecked, its immersion in the excitement of the moment is both enjoyed and endured by a narrative commentary that seeks to rise above its all-consuming rhythms.

Chesterton claimed that Dickens had much in common 'with Wat Tyler and Wilkes; for the man led a mob. He did what no English statesman, perhaps, has really done; he called out the people.'[92] But the Gordon riots saw Lord George Gordon take advantage of a Wilkite precedent for an intolerant anti-Catholic crusade, even as that crusade was itself informed by radical sympathies for American revolutionaries.[93] Dickens's choice of subject-matter for his novel in the early 1840s was, therefore, a deliberately challenging case, one that would involve the author in a qualified defence of radical principles alongside a consideration of where radical fervour might lead. His prose calls the mob into being, but it does not call it out, and the following sentences are a microcosm of the political rhythms of the early work: 'The air was filled with execrations, hoots, and howlings. The mob raged and roared, like a mad monster, as it was, unceasingly, and each new outrage served to swell its fury' (p. 376). While the alliterative buzz ('hoots, howlings, raged, roared, mad monster, served, swell') joins and revels in the clamour, the stuttering syntax of the final sentence also attempts to frame and to curb the crowd's enthusiasm. It is as though

[91] Plotz, *The Crowd*, 153.

[92] G. K. Chesterton, *Charles Dickens* (1906; repr. London: Methuen, 1956), 79.

[93] See Charles Tilly, *Popular Contention in Great Britain, 1758–1834* (Cambridge, Mass.: Harvard University Press, 1995), 159, and Dickens's chief historical source for the novel: Robert Watson, *The Life of Lord George Gordon* (London: Symonds, 1795), 9–10.

the narrator is weighing up the value of two kinds of calling—that of the rabble-rouser and that of the man called in to read the riot act.

Dickens never quite sees fit to 'call out the people'; Gordon's public speaking and popularity outside Parliament is a Dickensian ideal that becomes fraught with difficulties and dangers. Repeatedly in the novel, the reporter's art of speech selection is transposed into a novelistic medium that compromises Gordon's enthusiasm: ' "It's a proud thing to lead the people, Gashford," he added as he made a sudden halt' (p. 272). The rallying cry meets with 'a sudden halt', and that halt testifies to the reticence of the early work even as it admires and sometimes appeals for a proud radical stand. Dickens's print was to be listened to as well as read, and when sentences like these were read aloud in homes and meeting-places across the country, audiences would have heard enthusiastic voices intermingled with monitory epilogues. Documenting the mix of political and literary culture that the newspapers had helped to foster, Bulwer-Lytton observed: 'Fiction, with its graphic delineation and appeals to the familiar emotions, is adapted to the crowd—for it is the oratory of literature.'[94] Dickens's work gives partial assent to such a claim; but it also resists mere adaptation to 'the crowd', turning voices into a '*graphic delineation*' and insisting that literature's close relations with oratory, like its relations with the newspapers, are open to qualification.

HONOURABLE GENTLEMEN

While writing *Barnaby Rudge*, Dickens was asked to stand as MP for Reading. Lacking funds, he replied: 'I cannot satisfy myself that to enter Parliament under such circumstances would enable me to pursue that honourable independence without which I could neither preserve my own respect nor that of my constituents.'[95] Twenty years later, he was asked to stand for Finsbury: 'nothing would induce me to offer myself as a Parliamentary representative of that place, or any other under the sun'.[96] From 'I would if I could' to 'I can't and I *won't*', the shift in tone highlights the author's growing antipathy towards Parliament, as he increasingly associates the pursuit of 'honourable independence' with expression outside the Commons.

Dickens became increasingly vocal in the 1850s—on the platform and in his journalism—about the political mismanagement of the country, and

---

[94] Edward Bulwer-Lytton, *England and the English* (1833), ed. Standish Meacham (Chicago: University of Chicago Press, 1970), 298.
[95] *DL*, ii. 301.   [96] Ibid. ix. 511.

Household Words became a central forum for criticism of the words in
other Houses. In feisty mood, he said that the journal's aim was 'to have
made every man in England feel something of the contempt for the House
of Commons that I have'.[97] Such comments have generally been taken on
trust; Eric Evans's claim is representative: 'Dickens has little time either for
politicians or for the forms of politics practised in 19th-century Britain.'[98]
But the author dedicated his last three completed novels to MPs, and while
he had 'little time' for certain styles of political debate, he spent much time
thinking about these styles and imagining possible alternatives to them in
speech and in print. The figure of the 'honourable gentleman' in *Bleak
House*, *Hard Times*, and *Little Dorrit* evinces something more than contempt,
and the representation of the politician's voice is housed in an increasingly
experimental 'vocal' prose style that takes the author and his audience in
unexpected directions.

In 1850, Carlyle denounced 'platforms and public palaverings', insisting that
they succeeded only in 'drowning for the moment all reflection whatsoever'.[99]
This lack of circumspection was exemplified in the free-trade speakers of the
Anti-Corn Law League, those 'whole trade-winds of chaff' who spoke out for a
liberal politico-economic programme of which Carlyle was so wary.[100] Dickens
was a supporter of the League, and by the 1852 election—six years after the
repeal of the Corn Laws—discussions about the need for free trade and free
speech were at the centre of political debate.[101] Such developments would see
Dickens's belief in the emerging debating publics as a welcome corrective to
the eloquence of honourable gentlemen tested against his inheritance from
Carlyle. In 1851, David Masson claimed that 'Mr Dickens's opinions . . . are to
be found explicitly affirmed and argued in his novels', before complaining that
'we are entitled to expect something that shall, in both reason and expression,
have a finish and a beauty beyond the art of the mere platform speaker'.[102]
However, the author's sense of his work as an expression of dutiful citizenship
often complicated his commitment to it as a form of opinionated persuasion.
As he noted in 1848: 'teaching, to last, must be fairly conducted. It must not
all be on one side.'[103] In the 1850s, his need for fair conduct and a lasting

[97] Cited in John Forster, *The Life of Charles Dickens*, 3 vols. (London: Chapman & Hall, 1872–4), iii. 458.
[98] Cited in Paul Schlicke (ed.), *Oxford Reader's Companion to Dickens* (Oxford: Oxford University Press, 1999), 456.
[99] Carlyle, *Latter-Day Pamphlets*, 41, 263.   [100] Ibid. 263.
[101] See Anthony Howe, *Free Trade and Liberal England, 1846–1946* (Oxford: Clarendon Press, 1997), 28–37.
[102] David Masson, '*Pendennis* and *Copperfield*: Thackeray and Dickens', *North British Review*, 15 (1851), 57–89, p. 66.
[103] *DJ*, ii. 104.

achievement would involve the cultivation of a public voice that attempted to take stock as well as sides.

As the press began to voice concern over the Tories' possible return to protectionist policies, Dickens published 'Our Honourable Friend' (it was widely quoted in the papers; Dickens noted: 'It seems to be making a great noise').[104] This noise was generated by the attack of many newspapers on the Conservative Party's electioneering rhetoric, which ruled neither in nor out a return to protectionist policies in order to conciliate the upper classes. The oratorical strategy was deliberately ambiguous or even inconsistent across different areas of the country.[105] *The Times* quoted from Dickens's impersonation of the honourable gentleman's Tory 'pledges' and added its approval:

'His principles were these—concurrently with the general revision of something, speaking generally, and a possible re-adjustment of something else, not to be mentioned more particularly.' Can jest come so near earnest and the playful irony of a political satirist so closely resemble the high-wrought enthusiasm of a thick and thin partisan? We rather incline to think the Honourable member for Verbosity the more explicit of the two: for 'revision' and 're-adjustment' have a meaning.[106]

The meaning of 're-adjustment' is the reintroduction of sliding-scale taxes on corn, and the close resemblance of Dickens's prose to the political speech he is questioning is praised for its ability to mimic the rhetoric while at the same time drawing attention to its hidden assumptions. Nevertheless, the question this reporter asks would preoccupy Dickens for much of his later career. The writer was wary of fostering a close alliance between the 'political satirist' and the 'thick and thin partisan', and in *Bleak House* (1852–3) the self-assurance of his 'playful irony' was translated into a more searching kind of address.

In his election address, Disraeli observed:

The times are favourable to such an undertaking; juster notions of taxation are more prevalent than heretofore, powerful agencies are stirring, which have introduced new phenomena into finance and altered the complexion of the fiscal world: and the possibility of greatly relieving the burdens of the community, both by adjustment and reduction *seems to loom in the future*.[107]

Disraeli's language is particularly cagey: a 'possibility' is already speculative, even before we are told that it 'seems' to be a future option. Dickens remembered Disraeli's oblique reference to the 'possibility' of 'adjustment and reduction' when he had the MP for Verbosity envisage 'the general revision

---

[104] *DL*, vi. 729.
[105] See Robert Blake, *Disraeli* (London: Eyre & Spottiswoode, 1966), 322.
[106] *The Times*, 31 July 1852, 4f.   [107] *The Times*, 7 June 1852, 4c.

of something, speaking generally, and a possible re-adjustment of something else'. However, what stayed with the novelist was the phrase *The Times* reported in italics: 'I foresee (I think) some very good things in Bleak House. I shouldn't wonder if they were the identical things that D'Israeli sees looming in the distance. I behold them in the months ahead, and weep.'[108] Dickens's own form of 'speaking generally' has a new tone here. What *The Times* had seen as 'playful irony' in the sketch is forgone for something more troubling, as a resemblance between the writer and the orator whom he distrusts turns into a vision of 'identical things'. Weeping at what he is about to create, Dickens now sees his blurred perspective as a part of that which it condemns. In his novel, the author was concerned not merely to mock the Conservatives, but to examine his own guarded attraction to certain impulses in their rhetoric.

Bleak House is continually haunted by the voices of those in and around Parliament, just as the house parties at Sir Leicester Dedlock's Lincolnshire estate are full of chatter about the state of the parties in the House. Sir Leicester is introduced as a 'gentleman', but also as something more and less than honourable: 'He is an honourable, obstinate, truthful, high-spirited, intensely prejudiced, perfectly unreasonable man.'[109] This is characteristic of the narrator's mercurial tone, for the voice of the 'thick and thin partisan' is both thickened and thinned by the rush of adjectives. Sir Leicester is a target for Dickens's satire against the ruling classes, but also a figure to whom we are meant to warm: 'Sir Leicester feels it to be right and fitting that the housekeeper of Chesney Wold should be a remarkable person. Apart from that, he has a real regard for Mrs Rouncewell, and likes to hear her praised' (p. 449). We move from narrow-minded snobbery to tender-hearted generosity over the space of two sentences—it's as though the sitter refuses to remain still for his portrait as a symbol of upper-class complacency. Sir Leicester keeps turning human.

Dickens's return to the 1852 election in his March 1853 installment of the novel ('National and Domestic') furthers the political implications of this technique. On one level, the narrator is quick to seize on the disingenuous nature of Sir Leicester's rhetoric. Widespread reports of corrupt practices at the election led to the Derby administration being nicknamed 'The Bribery Parliament', and Dickens delivered a speech in the same month as 'National and Domestic' was published in which he alluded to the public petitions against bribery at elections.[110] When Sir Leicester refers to the 'necessary expenses'

---

[108] *DL*, vi. 721. See also ibid. 756.

[109] Charles Dickens, *Bleak House*, ed. Nicola Bradbury (London: Penguin, 1996), 22. Subsequent page references are given parenthetically in the text.

[110] *DS*, 162.

(p. 645) of an election, the narrator/reporter follows up with a sidelong glance at his phrasing: 'these necessary expenses will, in some two hundred election petitions, be unpleasantly connected with the word bribery' (p. 645).

As the chapter proceeds, though, other tones begin to make themselves heard. When Tulkinghorn informs Sir Leicester that Mr Rouncewell (a figure for the up-and-coming manufacturing interest) has made several 'plain and emphatic' speeches denouncing him, the great man's portentous response to this news is as grand and as general as was Disraeli's prophecy:

'Then upon my honour,' says Sir Leicester, after a terrific pause, during which he has been heard to snort and felt to stare; 'then upon my honour, upon my life, upon my reputation and principles, the floodgates of society are burst open, and the waters have—a—obliterated the landmarks of the framework of the cohesion by which things are held together!' (p. 648)

Mark Lambert has noticed the frequency of what he terms 'the catch-word suspended quotation' in Dickens's fiction (seen here in ' "Then upon my honour," says Sir Leicester . . . "then upon my honour" '). Envisaging this suspended quotation as a form of 'hostility' from a 'jealous author' towards his characters, Lambert remembers Dickens's early career as a professional reporter of speech: 'How nice, after that self training to keep up with public blather, after the waiting for speakers in inconvenient places, after the humiliations inflicted by crack speakers—how nice to be able to interrupt the speaker at will and be able, with the catchword suspension, to force the crack speaker to start over again.'[111] In the instance above, though, it is hard to tell whether the crack speaker is 'forced' to start over again (the 'terrific' pause is as much Sir Leicester's as it is his creator's), or whether he repeats himself. That is, the speech-form in which Sir Leicester's voice is presented could be a faithful transcription of an exasperated stutter ('Then upon my honour . . . then upon my honour'), or Dickens's contribution of his own antagonistic style to the character's Conservative rhetoric.

Alongside Lambert's emphasis on Dickensian hostility, we should place Chesterton's characteristically astute awareness of the character's charm as a result of his author's artistry: he grants that he is 'an effective condemnation of oligarchy', but adds that 'It is very hard not to like Sir Leicester Dedlock, not to applaud his silly old speeches, so foolish, so manly, so genuinely English, so disastrous to England'.[112] Indeed, at this point in the novel, our enjoyment of Dedlock's exaggerated sense of the threat of 'plain' rhetoric to 'the landmarks of the framework of the cohesion by which things are held together' holds any

---

[111] Mark Lambert, *Dickens and the Suspended Quotation* (New Haven: Yale University Press, 1981), 35, 90.

[112] Chesterton, *Charles Dickens*, 153.

political animus toward oligarchy in check, for we are encouraged to laugh at
the ridiculous tautology of his phrasing, rather than to attend to the political
alternative towards which these phrases point.

If our liking of Sir Leicester turns the scene into something more than party-
political point scoring, the overlap between 'National' and 'Domestic' further
contributes to its intricacy. We now learn about Mr Tulkinghorn's knowledge
of Lady Dedlock's secret (her illegitimate child); the lawyer introduces his
threat to Lady Dedlock under cover of an anecdote that he relates to Sir
Leicester: 'A townsman of this Mr Rouncewell, a man in exactly parallel
circumstances as I am told, had the good fortune to have a daughter who
attracted the notice of a great lady. I speak of a really great lady; not merely
great to him, but married to a gentleman of your condition, Sir Leicester' (p.
650). In the 'national' focus of Dickens's chapter, Rouncewell's 'circumstances'
and his benevolent oratorical force against the Conservatives were casually
supported by Dickens's satire on Dedlock's foolish political stand. Here in the
'domestic' plot, though, Rouncewell's 'exact parallel' and social equivalent is a
threat to Lady Dedlock, a threat that the narrative does not invite us to enjoy.
Leicester's apparently ridiculous fear of the lower orders—encapsulated in his
'upon my honour . . . upon my reputation'—is invested with a seriousness
now as Lady Dedlock's honour and reputation are endangered by the revealing
of an involvement with those classes that Dickens had supported.

Robert Garis has noted of the writer's later narrative style that 'it is something
like oratory . . . Our response to Dickens's presence in his prose takes the form
of an impulse to applaud.'[113] '*Something like* oratory', perhaps, although in
'National and Domestic' the interplay between reported speech and narrative
commentary blends an appetite for performance with a sense of what Graham
Greene once described as 'the tone of Dickens's secret prose, that sense of
a mind speaking to itself with no one there to listen'.[114] When examined
in their immaculately constructed surroundings, the phrases and images of
Sir Leicester's 'silly old speeches' take on new dimensions, for the narrator's
sombre, foreboding tone quietly takes on and dignifies certain aspects of
the honourable gentleman's voice. Sir Leicester's heated oratory, evidenced
by his 'own particular fire in the evening' (p. 644), infuses the twilight of
the scene: 'but the fire of the sun is dying . . . bringing the Dedlocks down
like age and death' (p. 641); where Sir Leicester obsessively worries about
'dangerous hands' in the political world (p. 649), the narrator's voice imagines

---

[113] Robert Garis, *The Dickens Theatre: A Reassessment of the Novels* (Oxford: Clarendon Press, 1965), 9.

[114] Graham Greene, from 'The Young Dickens', in *The Lost Childhood and Other Essays* (London: Eyre & Spottiswoode, 1954), 53.

the shadows in Chesney Wold as 'threatening hands raised up' (p. 642); the humour of his obtuse pleasure at Tulkinghorn's 'footing of equality with the highest society' (p. 647) is encroached upon by a darkness in which 'every downward step [is] a pit' (p. 641). Finally, the rhetoric that announces that 'the *flood*gates of society are burst open, and the *waters* have—a—obliterated the landmarks' is revised in the constrained terror of Lady Dedlock as she leaves the room, fearful that her secret will out: 'the *stream* of moonlight has swelled into a *lake*, and then Lady Dedlock for the first time moves, and rises, and comes forward to the table for a glass of *water*' (p. 651; my emphasis). The stream swelling into a lake recalls the floodgates of society bursting open; but here Lady Dedlock's domestic predicament, a predicament intimately associated with her husband's political one, inspires our sympathy as the hyperbolic reference to 'waters' evaporates into the need for just 'a glass of water'.

Dedlock's oratorical fervour becomes infused with new, more disturbing life as a result of the artistry with which the novelist mingles spoken and written languages in this scene. Behind this artistry is Dickens's imaginative engagement with Disraeli and Conservative rhetoric: 'I shouldn't wonder if they were the identical things that D'Israeli sees looming in the distance. I behold them in the months ahead, and weep.' The MP's 'looming in the distance' is echoed in the narrator's reference to the 'distant phantom' and 'gloom' of the Dedlocks' place (p. 641), as the narrative begins to register a concern about threats to landed estates from the lower orders. The progress of *Bleak House* will also see those 'suspended quotations' revisited and revised: fourteen chapters later, Sir Leicester is told his wife's secret by Inspector Bucket, and the earlier interruption to his speech—'says Sir Leicester, after a terrific pause, during which he has been heard to snort and felt to stare'—is now reworked into the heartbreak of 'Sir Leicester, who has covered his face with his hands, uttering a single groan, requests him to pause for a moment' (p. 821). The 'pause' and the oratorical actions of mouth and eyes—recalling the earlier snorts and stares—are returned to at the end of the chapter, 'Then he stops; and, with more of those inarticulate sounds, lifts up his eyes and seems to stare at something' (p. 838), and again in a later scene as his health fails and we hear his 'stertorous breathing' and see his 'fixed eyes' (p. 857).

As Sir Leicester loses his voice, his pity for Lady Dedlock becomes an occasion for speech from a narrator who is anxious that we see beyond party politics and class antagonism to a larger view of the situation. After Dedlock's expression of forgiveness, the narrator is in no mood to poke fun at Conservative downfalls:

His formal array of words might have at any other time, as it has often had, something ludicrous in it; but this time it is serious and affecting . . . his generous conquest of his own wrong and his own pride for her sake, are simply *honourable*, manly, and true. Nothing less worthy can be seen through the lustre of such qualities in the commonest mechanic, nothing less worthy can be seen in the best-born *gentleman*. In such a light both aspire alike, both rise alike, both children of the dust shine equally. (p. 895; my emphasis)

This formal array of words insists on referring to Sir Leicester as both 'honourable' and as a 'gentleman', even as it embeds such testimony in a comparison that puts mechanic and baronet on an equal footing. The shift to the present tense makes the narrative voice feel 'something like oratory'; and yet, by taking part of its tone from the Conservative rhetoric that Dickens had so often parodied, and by mingling it with an emphasis on forms of equality, the prose acknowledges the widening of its own sympathies in the hope of extending ours.

Bleak House owes much to another honourable gentleman whom the author admired: Bulwer-Lytton, who had also made his political name in Lincolnshire when he served as an MP in the 1830s and 1840s. Dickens's collaborations and friendship with Lytton stood behind the achievement of *Bleak House*, for the novel was dedicated to 'my companions in the Guild of Literature and Art' (p. 4), a Guild co-founded by the two men in 1851. Lytton was returned as a Conservative MP in the 1852 general election, and his career as a playwright, novelist, and politician led many to comment on the excellence of his parliamentary addresses even while they complained about his unfortunately stuttering, inaudible manner of speaking: 'whatever criticism and satire might have said' about his manner, 'As compositions [they] are not excelled by anything that the House listens to'.[115] Something similar may be said of Dedlock's manner and matter, and the character may well have been based on Lytton.[116] Just as the measured narrative voice of *Bleak House* asks us to hear something composed within the discomposure of Dedlock's stuttering premonitions, so Dickens's response to his friend's unfortunate oratorical style was a mixture of the satirical and the sympathetic: one person recalled him impersonating Lytton ('his deaf manner of speaking he represents exactly'), and noted the author's comment that Lytton 'knows everything [but] lacks a kind of confidence in his own powers which is necessary in a good speaker'.[117]

---

[115] White, *Inner Life of the House of Commons*, i. 40.

[116] See Dickens's note to Forster in 1850: '*Alluding to a common friend*, a dreadful thought occurs to me! How brilliant in a book!'; the editors suggest that this is 'possibly Lytton' (*DL*, vi. 252).

[117] M. A. De Wolfe Howe, *Memories of a Hostess* (London: Unwin, 1923), 176–7.

Lytton was not deaf, then, to competing points of view. Dickens admired his friend's politics and his willingness to bring what one commentator called 'a literary style' into political debate.[118] During the composition of *Bleak House* the MP had defended the Derby ministry that Dickens satirized in 'Our Honourable Friend', pointing out that the Conservatives—contrary to many predictions—*had* abandoned protectionist policies since taking power in 1852. In November, Lytton asked Members of the House to 'lay aside upon this occasion all party feeling and political jealousies', and a month later he requested 'a fair and cordial trial' to be given to a government that 'did not come into office as the exclusive advocates of a single class, or the supporters of a retrograde policy [protectionism]'.[119] Such words would have stung Dickens's ears, and at the founding meeting of the Guild of Literature (Dickens was present) the final words of Lytton's speech would have been heard as pertinent to his writing of *Bleak House*: 'Perhaps more and more, with advancing time, we may find that in men of books are the wise conciliators and gentle arbiters in the strifes and contests of the men of action.'[120]

Dickens once remarked that Lytton was often 'saying the subtlest and finest things',[121] and his emphasis on 'advancing time' would have suggested to the writer that advances might be made through arbitration as well as agitation. The novel is cognizant of such voices, and its conciliations should not be seen either as an avoidance of political critique or as a retreat to a reactionary politics. Nancy Armstrong feels that in the hands of 'Dickens in particular, domestic fiction carried the process of suppressing political resistance into the domain of popular literature';[122] yet the author's intertwining of 'National' and 'Domestic' concerns in this novel (and throughout his fiction) takes continual pains to remind readers that home life is influenced by, and can in turn influence, socio-political and economic realms. D. A. Miller's emphasis on *Bleak House*'s place in a grand narrative of the novel's embodiment of the disciplinary, policing power it would seem to criticize is similarly reductive: 'what is promoted in the process [of reading] is a paternalism that, despite the dim view the novel takes of the power structures of the British state, can only be useful in maintaining such structures'.[123] 'Only'? Such comments unhelpfully narrow down the potentially progressive effects of the reading

---

[118] See E. M. Whitty, *History of the Session, 1852–3: A Parliamentary Retrospect* (London: Chapman, 1854), 10.

[119] *The Times*, 26 Nov. 1852, 2e; 11 Dec. 1852, 2d.   [120] *The Times*, 2 Sept. 1852, 6f.

[121] *DL*, ix. 433.

[122] Nancy Armstrong, *Desire and Domestic Fiction: A Political History of the Novel* (Oxford: Oxford University Press, 1987), 163.

[123] D. A. Miller, *The Novel and the Police* (Berkeley: University of California Press, 1988), 92.

process, making it sound as though 'maintaining' something could not also include altering or improving it.[124]

The mobility of the narrative voice in *Bleak House*—the way it finds room to sympathize with as well to scold Sir Leicester, taking on his tone even as it takes issue with it—mirrors the larger patternings of the plot, and these unexpected imaginative leaps contain the seeds of socio-political change. Just as Sir Leicester is carried some way out of his own social prejudices through his pity for his wife, and just as we see him lose interest in the in-House politicking of 'Buffy and Boodle' (p. 983) as a result of his humbling of his own house, so readers are invited into a process of analogous self-examination—'National' as well as 'Domestic'. Philip Davis singles out the shift of Dedlock from the merely 'laughable' to the 'genuinely noble emotional centre of *Bleak House*' as one of the legacies of Victorian fiction; for 'It is then that people in these novels find themselves going beyond themselves in ways that also shake the reader's habitual orderings and prejudices'.[125] Talk of the 'suppression' of 'political resistance', or of 'maintenance' of 'policing structures', does not do justice to the potential for creative thinking and action that such writing can inspire. The novel's narrative does not only embody a 'paternalism'; it also offers a provocation to readers to think for themselves, and of their relations with others, in new ways.

Bleak House encourages reconsideration of the figure of the honourable gentleman by allowing its own narrative voice to be permeated by his accents. This movement towards free indirect style is an increasingly marked feature of Dickens's later novels,[126] and when outlining how 'diversity of voices' might constitute the ground of 'novelistic discourse', Mikhail Bakhtin chose *Little Dorrit* to show the 'double-accented, double-styled *hybrid construction*' at work.[127] As Dorrit Cohn suggests, superimposing two voices in this way implies the narrator's '*identification*—but not his *identity*—with the character's mentality',[128] and Dickens became fascinated by the political implications of this double accent. Free indirect style can be the linguistic embodiment of 'being in two minds', yet such double-mindedness need not be conceived

---

[124] For an excellent critique of such approaches, see Brigid Lowe, *Victorian Fiction and the Insights of Sympathy: An Alternative to the Hermeneutics of Suspicion* (London: Anthem Press, 2006).

[125] Davis, *Victorians*, 553.

[126] See Robert Golding, *Idiolects in Dickens: The Major Techniques and Chronological Development* (London: Macmillan, 1985), 62; Norman Page, *Speech in the English Novel*, 2nd edn. (London: Macmillan, 1988), 152.

[127] Mikhail Bakhtin, *The Dialogic Imagination: Four Essays*, ed. Michael Holquist, trans. Caryl Emerson and Michael Holquist (Austin: University of Texas Press, 1981), 302–8.

[128] Dorrit Cohn, *Transparent Minds: Narrative Modes for Presenting Consciousness in Fiction* (Princeton: Princeton University Press, 1984), 112.

as mere confusion, but as ethical and socio-political expansion—a way for a writer to seek out ways of speaking through and across political divides, acknowledging reciprocities as well as differences.

In *Hard Times* (1854), Gradgrind becomes an MP for Coketown, and the humanizing of the 'honourable gentleman' over the course of the novel is similar in some respects to the treatment of Sir Leicester (he moves from being the butt of a joke to the object of our concern). When he found out news of Lady Dedlock, we recall that Sir Leicester 'covered his face with his hands, uttering a single groan'; likewise Gradgrind as his world falls around him when he hears of his daughter's unhappiness: 'he bowed his head upon his hand and groaned aloud'.[129] The final pages envisage a return to the Commons as Gradgrind ponders his future as a reformed MP:

How much of futurity did *he* see? Did he see himself, a white-haired decrepit man . . . making his facts and figures subservient to Faith, Hope and Charity . . . Did he catch sight of himself, therefore much despised by his late political associates? Did he see them, in the era of its being quite settled that the national dustmen have only to do with one another, and owe no duty to an abstraction called a People, 'taunting the honourable gentleman' with this and with that and with what not . . . Probably he had that much foreknowledge, knowing his men. (p. 276)

This 'knowing' voice marks the moment at which Gradgrind and the narrator join forces, and marks out the radical change of which an individual is capable even as it admits to the limits of that individual's power. Free indirect style captures the dismissive tones of the MPs ('the People—pah! a mere abstraction!'), but it also hints at Gradgrind's redeeming voice within such phrases, turning his calculating utilitarian vocabulary to noble ends ('*abstraction*, yes, but to be taken into account nonetheless'). Strangely, the placing of 'honourable gentleman' in quotation-marks rescues the epithet here from the wholesale condemnation it had suffered earlier in the novel (p. 88); for in the very act of its being used sarcastically by Gradgrind's enemies, the reader is reminded that Gradgrind has indeed become both honourable and gentle, and—the novel whispers, almost despite itself—there *is* a place in parliament for such men. As Martha Nussbaum observes, 'the novel cannot describe its opposition without doing battle with it'.[130] When *Hard Times* ends on its own apostrophic abstraction, 'Dear reader! It rests with you and me, whether in our two fields of action, similar things shall be or not' (p. 277), it

[129] Charles Dickens, *Hard Times*, ed. Grahame Smith (London: Everyman, 1988), 201. Subsequent page references are given parenthetically in the text.

[130] Martha Nussbaum, *Poetic Justice: The Literary Imagination and Public Life* (Boston: Beacon Press, 1995), 43.

announces its commitment to the kind of address that Gradgrind is attempting to foster in the House.

The 'honourable gentleman's journey towards self-consciousness in *Bleak House* served as a warning about the oversights of aristocratic complacency, while the same journey in *Hard Times* aimed to foreground the limits of the economic ideology proclaimed by the self-made manufacturing men.[131] In keeping with Dickens's disinterested efforts to see things from more than 'one side', *Little Dorrit* (1855–7) extends the critique to include that 'abstraction called a People'. Justin McCarthy felt that Dickens had 'perverted the novel from a work of art to a platform', a platform, moreover, from which he neither offered an explanation of the causes of 'defects in the working of institutions', nor 'pointed out any remedy'.[132] But one of 'Fiction's highest uses', Dickens maintained, was 'to rouse the public soul to a compassionate or indignant feeling that it *must not be*—without obtruding any pet theory of cause or cure, and so throwing off allies as they spring up'.[133] The events of 1855 would see the author attempt to create political allies through recourse to discussions about causes and cures, whilst at the same time defending fiction's partial remove from such oratorical standards.

Dickens's letters testify to his growing despondency at the scene inside and outside Parliament.[134] Sick of a sycophantic public as well as corrupt officialdom, he characteristically searches for an individual figure in the crowd who might offer a model of conduct: once again, his eye lands on an 'honourable gentleman', Austen Henry Layard, MP. Layard led an attack in the Commons on the mismanagement of the Crimean War and the administrative incompetence of the civil service.[135] He was consequently mocked in Parliament, but this very isolation caught Dickens's attention and imagination.[136] The Administrative Reform Association (ARA), founded by Layard on 5 May, organized meetings and speeches in many towns, and it merits particular attention because it was the only political organization that Dickens ever joined. Olive Anderson observes that while the Association's function was to support Layard's efforts in the House, 'its loudest call was to the electorate': 'if they would only choose their representatives from merit alone, and then refrain from asking them for favours, they would set off

---

[131] On Dickens's criticisms of both aristocratic assumption and free-market capitalism, see Andrew Sanders, *Dickens and the Spirit of the Age* (Oxford: Clarendon Press, 1999), 132–44.

[132] Justin McCarthy, 'Modern Novelists: Charles Dickens', *Westminster Review*, Oct. 1864; cited in Collins (ed.), *Dickens: The Critical Heritage*, 447, 451–2.

[133] *DL*, vii. 405.   [134] Ibid. 523.

[135] See Emmeline W. Cohen, *The Growth of the British Civil Service, 1780–1939* (London: Cass, 1965), 87–116.

[136] See *DL*, vii. 583, 587–8.

a chain reaction which would transform the calibre of the men in public life'.[137] The ARA, then, was aiming at parliamentary as well as administrative reform, and addressing itself to those outside as well as inside Westminster. According to Dickens, this dual focus was exactly what a popular political organization should have, and—prior to the writing and publication of *Little Dorrit*—he lent his support to Layard's efforts through his journalism and speeches.

Dickens's pieces in *Household Words* focus mainly on the predilection for laughter in Parliament as a response to agitation for reform, and Palmerston's reputation for jokes becomes something of an obsession (the MP is named the 'First Lord of the Jokery').[138] Yet these articles often seem to imitate the jocularity they are attempting to castigate (Arthur Helps once revealingly observed that Dickens 'often put me in mind of Lord Palmerston . . . They had both a certain hearty bluffness of manner').[139] In May, Layard asked when the issue could be debated, and Palmerston quipped: 'I really, Sir, cannot undertake to find the hon. Gentleman a day; he must find one for himself.'[140] Layard's motion was later defeated amid loud jeering, with Palmerston again looking for laughs as he dismissed the ARA meetings at the Drury Lane Theatre with 'I shall say no more about the Drury Lane private theatricals. [*Renewed cheers, and laughter*]'.[141] A week after Layard's parliamentary defeat, Dickens finally found himself in 'speechifying circumstances' at a meeting of the ARA.[142] He also found himself in the not altogether comfortable position of making jokes about jokes.

Early in 1855, when Palmerston had claimed that his opponents were 'making much ado about nothing', Bulwer-Lytton had wittily replied that '*Much Ado* came after *The Comedy of Errors*' in the Shakespearean corpus.[143] In his speech, Dickens took his lead from the jovial chaff of the House by noting that 'We have seen the *Comedy of Errors* played so dismally like a tragedy that we cannot bear it'.[144] But his own relish for making comedy out of errors was also met by a tone that went beyond such quips. It is as if, with an audience actually in front of him, Dickens starts to become discomfited by his listeners' laughing at his jokes, as if their laughter and approbation come too freely for his liking. At one moment in the speech he refers to the 'gloomy

---

[137] Olive Anderson,'The Administrative Reform Association, 1855–1857', in Patricia Hollis (ed.), *Pressure from Without in Early Victorian England* (London: Arnold, 1974), 262–88, pp. 266, 277.

[138] *DJ*, iii. 363. See also 291, 295, 298.

[139] Arthur Helps, 'In Memoriam', *Macmillan's Magazine*, 22 (1870), 236–40, p. 239.

[140] *Hansard*, cxxxviii. 184.   [141] Ibid. 2209.   [142] *DL*, vii. 620.

[143] Bulwer-Lytton, cited in Asa Briggs, *Victorian People: A Reassessment of Persons and Themes, 1851–67* (New York: Harper & Row, 1955), 71.

[144] *DS*, 200.

silence' of 'the people', and his observation is met by '*cheers*'.[145] Agreement with the speaker's diagnosis begins to sound ominously like an approval of the present state of affairs.

For Dickens, such reactions were not wholly appropriate, but his complicity in fostering these reactions alerted him to the need for another type of eloquence. The following passages are taken from the beginning and the end of the speech:

[That noble lord] turned an airy period with reference to the private theatricals at Drury Lane Theatre. [*Cheers and laughter.*] I have some slight acquaintance with theatricals, private and public, and I will accept that figure of the noble lord. I will say that if I wanted to form a company of Her Majesty's servants, I think I should know where to put my hand on 'the comic old gentleman' [*roars of laughter*] . . . Said the noble lord at the head of the Government, when Mr. Layard asked him for a day for his motion, Let the hon. gentleman find a day for himself. [*Shame, shame.*] . . . Name you the day, First Lord; make the day; work for a day beyond your little time, Lord Palmerston.[146]

George Gissing observed of Dickens's humour that 'Only because they laughed with him so heartily, did multitudes of people turn to discussing the question his page suggested'.[147] Humour often becomes a social force in Dickens as it is intermingled with more serious tones (recall the movement from the comic to the sober treatment of Sir Leicester and Gradgrind). The jokes let off steam, bringing writer and readers into a receptive harmony as well as encouraging them to see the vulnerability of the object of ridicule. That is, the audience is entertained into considering something more than entertainment, as Dickens's relish for the comedic touch acts as a needful prelude to a chastened and chastening 'But seriously, now . . .'.

This is what happens in this speech. Zeroing in on Palmerston's jokes, Dickens opts for two tones: first, the ironic voice of a political commentary that encourages an audience's laughter; and second, the address that refuses to make comic capital out of parliamentary failings. Alexander Southern reported this speech and noticed 'a jump in the voice and an archness of expression which showed Dickens to be a consummate actor . . . He was, however, gravely in earnest, and his voice changed greatly to suit the occasion when he denounced Palmerston for his heartlessness and for his *insouciance* of behaviour.'[148] The voice of the 'actor' is heard when Dickens mocks the 'theatricals' in the Commons—at one point he says that the Commons should be 'hustled and pinched in a friendly way'[149]—but the movement from 'the noble lord' to 'Lord Palmerston' is one that breaks the rules of parliamentary

---

[145] *DS*, 201.   [146] Ibid. 199–200, 206–7.
[147] George Gissing, *Charles Dickens: A Critical Study* (London: Blackie, 1898), 166.
[148] *DS*, 207–8.   [149] Ibid. 203.

speech by finally giving the Premier's name, a distinctly unfriendly licence that Dickens's journalism had not taken. '[W]ork for a day beyond your little time, Lord Palmerston' brings with it an intimation of mortality (Palmerston was 70 years old in 1855) and requires that the audience laugh no longer. The politician is translated from a stage fool, the timeless 'comic old gentleman', into an old man who should be attentive to the sound of the clock ticking.

Little Dorrit's expansion of these serio-comic rhythms is also a mode of political exploration. When Dickens says 'I will accept that figure of the noble lord', he does so because he senses that burrowing from within the logic of the opponent's language can offer an opportunity for a more convincing and searching political critique. This acceptance of an opponent's tone, metaphor, or speech-tic as a prelude to an enlargement of its potential through revision is similar to the contours of free indirect style, the form that allows the voice of another into its structure even as it insists on keeping a critical distance from that voice. Critics have often referred to the image and language of imprisonment as the controlling metaphor of *Little Dorrit*; but there is another figure that structures the tale and which comes directly from Dickens's attentiveness to the language of the honourable gentlemen: *circumlocutio* ('talking around'). In his ARA speech Dickens denounced Parliament and 'the machinery of the Government and legislation going round and round'.[150] When brooding over *Little Dorrit* and the political scene, he moaned, 'I am sick and sour to think of such things . . . I am in the first stage of a new book, which consists in going round and round the idea'; and a few weeks later he snarled: '[I] go on turning upon the same wheel round and round over and over again until it may begin to roll me towards my end.'[151] Angry at parliamentary circumlocution, and yet committed to a similar process of creative circumnavigation as he plans his own words for *Little Dorrit*, Dickens is sick 'to think of such things', yet not quite sick of thinking about them.

The narrator's sharp eye is drawn to circular motion: Young John turns his hat 'round and round upon his left hand', the wind rushes 'round and round' the graveyard, Mr Flintwinch shakes the sediment in his tea-cup 'round and round', Arthur's mother in her wheelchair 'turned the same unvarying round of life'.[152] Phrases and words continually 'circulate' (p. 131) in the novel, as do people's lives: 'the debtor was a very different man from the doctor, but had already begun to travel, by his opposite segment of the circle, to the same point' (p. 68). And, of course, the most vicious circle is presented in chapter 10

---

[150] Ibid. 201.   [151] *DL*, vii. 571–2, 609.

[152] Charles Dickens, *Little Dorrit*, ed. Angus Easson (London: Dent, 1999), 220, 350, 363, 345. Subsequent page references are given parenthetically in the text.

of *Little Dorrit*—'Containing the whole Science of Government'—which revolves the 'all-sufficient wheel of statesmanship' (p. 109) for our delectation. Barnacle Junior is constantly 'feeling all round himself' (p. 112) for his eye-glass, while Mr Barnacle winds red tape 'round the neck of the country' (p. 115). The chapter's opening and closing words hint at the circular nature of the problem: '*The Circumlocution Office* was . . . if she overdid *the Circumlocution Office*' (pp. 109, 127; my emphasis)

Dickens's novel is plagued by the figures of the right honourable gentlemen, but the early satire on the Circumlocution Office also attempts to translate the motions of the ARA speakers into the movements of his prose. Glad-stone—himself a supporter of civil service reform—had complained about the 'general, abstract' language of the reformers who had no 'definite and clear view, either of the evils which they meant to assail, or the remedies they proposed to apply'.[153] Dickens's defence of ARA rhetoric echoes his defence of his novelistic art: they may not diagnose either 'cause or cure' at this stage, but rousing the people into concern was a necessary prelude to such diagnosis: 'I quite agree with you that they [the ARA speakers] hardly know what to be at; but it is an immensely difficult subject to start, and they must have every allowance.'[154]

These allowances are made in *Little Dorrit*. We are told of the '*all*-sufficient wheel of statesmanship' and that 'How not to do it' was the 'study and object of *all* public departments and professional politicians *all* round the Circumlocution Office' (pp. 108–9; my emphasis). All these 'alls' finally arrive at the narrator's assertion that 'All this is true' (p. 109). All this was not true, but this chapter claims a certain latitude for itself by virtue of the fact that so much time was being taken up in parliamentary deliberations. The novel often recommends its own simplicity as a heuristic principle and as a prescript for action; where one reviewer stresses the need for 'seeing every possible side of any one measure',[155] in contrast to Dickens's hasty oratorical fervour, chapter 10 questions those in government who are concerned with 'looking at it from various points of view' (p. 124). The risk of Dickens's caricature is a calculated one in this instance, and asks for risks to be taken in a political world in which time is often the one thing that reform hasn't got.

Chesterton saw Dickens's melodramatic style as an appeal to the moral sense in a simplified state, with 'the object of gaining a resounding rapidity of action which subtleties would obstruct'.[156] From this perspective, satirical writing

[153] *Hansard*, cxxxviii. 2079, 2100–3.   [154] *DL*, vii. 661.

[155] Anon., from *Dublin Review*, Apr. 1880, cited in Collins (ed.), *Dickens: The Critical Heritage*, 597.

[156] Chesterton, *Charles Dickens*, 139.

might be responsibly defended and appreciated because it can reveal the truth by stretching it. But the satire in chapter 10 also raises the question of whether the political end justifies the artistic means, and whether an exaggeration could be deemed an ill-considered liberty rather than encouraging a melioristic rapidity. The prose does have a certain vague simplicity in its allusion to the debates between Layard and Palmerston in the Commons:

> Sometimes, angry spirits attacked the Circumlocution Office. Sometimes, parliamentary questions were asked about it, and even parliamentary motions made or threatened about it by demagogues so low and ignorant as to hold that the real recipe of government was, How to do it. Then would the noble lord, or right honourable gentleman, in whose department it was to defend the Circumlocution Office, put his orange in his pocket, and make a regular field-day of the occasion . . . The Circumlocution Office was always voted immaculate by an accommodating majority. (p. 110)

We hear that 'jump in the voice' and 'archness of expression' that Southern heard in Dickens's speech, for when free indirect style is employed here ('demagogues so low and ignorant'), it has a bluntness that insists on the writer having things all his own way. The irony is meant to defend Layard's motion in the Commons, but the motion of Dickens's style is itself reminiscent of what Gladstone had called the 'general, abstract' language used by Layard himself. The real recipe may indeed be 'How to do it', yet the exact content of the 'how' and the 'it' is not broached by the satirical intent. In fact, the level of generality in this passage is heightened as it progresses, for certain instances become infallible rules: 'sometimes, regular, always'. The exaggerated, enjoyable forcefulness of the writing weakens the force of the political statement.

However, the movement observed in Dickens's ARA speech from 'archness of expression' to being 'gravely in earnest', from satirical pyrotechnics to sobering reflection, is echoed in his novel. There is a narrative perspective within the chapter on the Circumlocution Office that gestures towards the act of looking at the object from all angles which so interests and disturbs Dickens. Daniel Doyce, the inventor, is encountered as we take 'a *turn* in the Park' (p. 121; my emphasis) with Meagles and Arthur. He too suffers under circumlocutory tyranny, but his own way of going round and round seems to imply a more measured approach to the situation: 'He had a spectacle case in his hand, which he turned over and over . . . with a certain free use of the thumb that is never seen but in a hand accustomed to tools' (p. 122). He speaks in an 'undertone, which is often observable in mechanics who consider and adjust with great nicety . . . as if he were contemplating some half-finished work of his hand, and thinking about it' (p. 125). Until now, this chapter has been orotund rather than rotund—tending towards the viciously circular rather than the fully rounded. Doyce—like Dickens—is contemplating the half-finished work of his hand; his 'undertone' and act of turning things 'over and over' become incorporated into the novel as a model of conduct as it progresses.

This model of conduct can be seen in Dickens's increasingly deft handling of free indirect style, and in his portrayal of one of his most enigmatic 'honourable gentlemen', Mr Merdle MP, another who is committed to circularity—'evasively rolling his eyes round' (p. 566). The character was based on John Sadleir, Junior Lord of the Treasury in 1853 and a director of the Tipperary Joint Stock Bank. He committed suicide in February 1856, and a history of fraudulent share dealing was soon revealed. His suicide, like Merdle's, caused a sensation.[157] John Carey feels that we miss Dickens's 'real greatness if we persist in regarding him primarily as a critic of society', and insists that his creativity is 'essentially amoral and unprincipled'; accordingly, he focuses not on Dickens's 'morals' or 'social criticism', but on 'the workings of his imagination'.[158] This segregation of morals from the workings of the imagination is fundamentally misplaced with regard to Dickens (the two realms may be distinct, but they are not dissociated). Carey puts his general theory into practice in his discussion of Merdle: 'He was "simply", Dickens asserts, "the greatest Forger and the greatest Thief that ever cheated the gallows". The word "simply" is, however, quite false to the presentation of Merdle in the novel, and Dickens' sudden descent into blame is out of key with the humorous sympathy with which he has encouraged us to follow Merdle's fortunes.'[159]

This is false to the presentation of Dickens's words. It is not the author who 'asserts' of Merdle that he was 'simply the greatest Forger and the greatest Thief that ever cheated the gallows'; indeed, it is not even the narrator who asserts this. We need to view the words in their context to see how Dickens brings the workings of his imagination to bear on his socio-political enquiries:

appalling whispers began to circulate, east, west, north and south . . . the whispers became louder . . . He had sprung from nothing, by no natural growth or process that any one could account for; he had been, after all, a low, ignorant fellow . . . he had been taken up by all sorts of people . . . In steady progression, as the day declined, the talk rose in sound and purpose . . . Numbers of men in every profession and trade would be blighted by his insolvency . . . every servile worshipper of riches who had helped to set him on his pedestal, would have done better to worship the Devil point-blank . . . So,

---

[157] Regarding the Sadleir affair, Dickens wrote: 'I shaped Mr. Merdle himself out of that precious rascality' (*DL*, viii. 79).

[158] John Carey, *The Violent Effigy: A Study of Dickens' Imagination*, 2nd edn. (London: Faber & Faber, 1991), 8, 10.

[159] Ibid. 197.

the talk, lashed louder and higher by confirmation on confirmation, and by edition after edition of the evening papers, swelled into such a roar . . . he, the shining wonder, the new constellation to be followed by the wise men bringing gifts, until it stopped over a certain carrion at the bottom of a bath and disappeared—was simply the greatest Forger and the greatest Thief that ever cheated the gallows. (pp. 722–3)

The writing partakes of the exaggerated rhythms of Dickens's earlier satire on Parliament (the earlier attraction to the word 'all' comes back here—it is repeated six times in two paragraphs); but now the attack on the 'honourable gentleman' is figured through the voice of that public whose 'talk' Carlyle had so feared—a public outside Parliament that seems to be the instigator of the corruption which it affects to despise and by which it is captivated. The imaginative workings of Dickens's free indirect style at this moment have far-reaching implications for the political animus of *Little Dorrit*, for in such a form collusion and criticism are not easily separated. Here the style through which the author chooses to envisage the public voice creates a prose that both mocks and participates in the spoken exaggerations of the political gossip ('sprung from *nothing, no* natural growth, *any* one, *after all, every* profession and trade, *simply* the *greatest*, that *ever*'). In this atmosphere, 'simply' is infused with complex significance, surrounded by extremes of which we are suspicious (like many of Dickens's 'honourable gentlemen', Merdle is guilty, but he is not 'simply' this). The closeness of the public's 'circulating' whispers to an appalling circumlocution is not so much 'a desperate attempt to cancel, at the last moment, the sympathy and humour of Merdle's presentation',[160] but an attempt to give voice to Dickens's dual sense of the MP's corruption and the public's contaminating influence. It was precisely this point, it should be noted, that the ARA had been making when it sought to address itself to the irresponsible public voters as well as to those inside Parliament.

Such writing practises a reflective and potentially enabling politics from within the very exaggerations of its style. Garrett Stewart observes *Little Dorrit*'s 'habit of threefold modification' and its fondness for adjectival triads (a common technique of orators), and explains that, although these triple clusters mimic the feeling in the novel that there is no breathing room outside a suffocating political prison, Dickens also tries 'to moderate and rectify' these structures through 'curative tripling'.[161] Free indirect style attempts a similar process of renovation from within, for while it can share with *circumlocutio* an obliquity of approach (a freely indirect way of talking around something

---

[160] Ibid. 200.
[161] Garrett Stewart, 'Dickens and Language', in John O. Jordon (ed.), *The Cambridge Companion to Dickens* (Cambridge: Cambridge University Press, 2001), 136–51, pp. 144–7.

without stating it), it also asks readers to see and hear their own implication in the targets of their ridicule as a necessary precursor to socio-political change.

In his ARA speech Dickens conceded that 'My trade and calling is not politics', but went on to add: 'Within my sphere of action . . . the circle of my own pursuits . . . I have, for some years, tried to understand the heavier social grievances and to help to set them right.'[162] The circlings of fictional forms may, then, include consideration of 'causes and cures', but they do so through a discriminating concern to show varying political perspectives. *Little Dorrit* becomes a '*sphere* of action' in which immediate action is not always the primary concern, and its achievement rests on Dickens's appreciation that the '*circle* of his own pursuits' may eventually prepare the grounds for a better political praxis by asking its readers to revolve for consideration where different actions might lead. The novelist was aware that, if not watched carefully, this enabling circumspection can degenerate into passive circumlocution, but it is precisely this difficult, valuable negotiation between analysis and activism that his novels frequently bring to our attention.

BRINGING THE HOUSE DOWN

As *Little Dorrit* reached the end of its serial publication, Dickens found himself attracted to the idea of being able '*to write a book in company* instead of in my own solitary room, and to feel its effect coming freshly back upon me from the reader'.[163] Writing a book in company—with the literary orator addressing the reader as listener—was an ideal that informed much of Dickens's writing career, and his late public readings were an extension of his passion for performance. Philip Collins suggests that they 'were not the occasion for social criticism',[164] yet one contemporary enthusiastically claimed that 'a modern reading' recalled those times 'when the stage, in its social influences, was at its highest',[165] and a reporter at a performance of *A Christmas Carol* observed that Dickens read 'so effectively that, at one point, a philanthropic legislator, carried away by his feelings, gave forth a vigorous "Hear, hear!" that echoed through the hall'.[166] The performances were meant to entertain, but the author was often seeking ways to connect the pleasures of reading and

---

[162] *DS*, 200–1.   [163] *DL*, viii. 367.

[164] Charles Dickens, *Charles Dickens: The Public Readings*, ed. Philip Collins (Oxford: Clarendon Press, 1975), p. lxv.

[165] Charles Kent, *Charles Dickens as a Reader* (London: Chapman & Hall, 1872), 11.

[166] *Leader*, 4 July 1857, 640.

listening to philanthropic action. In the full sense of the phrase, Dickens read for effect.[167]

In 1858, one reporter observed that 'All our literati seem inclined to become "oral instructors"',[168] and such instruction led to comparisons between political oratory and other types of public address. Dickens's immersion in 'these days of lecturings and readings'[169] encouraged him to raise his own voice; but the question of what spoken style would be appropriate ('lecturings' or 'readings') was not quite settled. 'Lecturings' were predominant in the Mechanics' Institutes, set up during the 1830s as educational organizations for the lower classes;[170] but by 1860 Dickens complained that the lecturers had a 'custom of putting the natural demand for amusement out of sight' as they continually spoke down to their audience in 'a pretence of dreariness'.[171]

An antidote to such dreariness was provided by the rise of penny 'readings'. Here the emphasis was on entertainment; there were no reserved seats, and the working classes were themselves encouraged to take to the platform to read passages of literary works aloud.[172] Such activities provided a challenge to the spirit of patronage at the Mechanics' Institutes.[173] Edward Cox, co-founder of the Public Reading Association, explained: 'Your manner upon the platform should be *deferential*.'[174] Whether Dickens was to associate performances of his work with the formality of 'lecturings' or the ease of 'readings' carried political implications, and the author wasn't always sure where he stood; he refers to his new form of public speaking both as 'my Reading' and as 'my lecture'.[175] His performances were ticketed (with the lowest prices often around a shilling rather than a penny), but seats were also reserved for the lower classes on some occasions, and the speaker's attitude to these audiences was not consistent. Dickens insisted that 'a mixed audience was absolutely necessary'[176] for success, but expressed no particular concern about attempts

---

[167] The fullest account of the readings is by Malcolm Andrews, *Charles Dickens and His Performing Selves: Dickens and the Public Readings* (Oxford: Oxford University Press, 2006). I am grateful to Professor Andrews for allowing me to read his book in manuscript.

[168] *Illustrated News*, 15 May 1858, 487.   [169] *DL*, iv. 631.

[170] See G. W. Roderick and M. D. Stephens, 'Mechanics' Institutes and the State', in Ian Inkster (ed.), *The Steam Intellect Societies: Essays on Culture, Education and Industry, c. 1820–1914* (Nottingham: Nottingham University Press, 1985), 60–72.

[171] Charles Dickens, 'The Uncommercial Traveller', *All the Year Round*, 30 June 1860, 274–8, pp. 276–7.

[172] See Evelyn Sivier, 'Penny Readings: Popular Elocution in Late Nineteenth-Century England', in David Thompson (ed.), *Performance of Literature in Historical Perspectives* (Lanham, Md.: University Press of America, 1983), 223–30.

[173] H. P. Smith, *Literature and Adult Education a Century Ago: Pantopragmatics and Penny Readings* (Oxford: Smith, 1960), 7.

[174] Cox, *Arts of Writing*, 284.   [175] *DL*, x. 89.

[176] George Dolby, *Charles Dickens as I Knew Him* (London: Unwin, 1885), 456.

to keep the crowd respectable: 'Wills is to do the genteel tonight at the Stalls, and Dolby is to stem the shilling tide, *if* he can.'[177]

The tide of people saw Dickens's performances as a form of instruction and as an opportunity for entertainment—authoritative as well as deferential. The *Critic* referred to the readings as 'elocutionary illustrations' that provided 'running critical commentaries upon his own works'.[178] But while Dickens was concerned about how far his 'lumpish'[179] audiences were capable of appreciating the finer points of his prose, he was also aware that the reactions of listeners helped to shape the style of the readings. This form of public eloquence was interactive, and he wrote gleefully that he had done 'new things' with *A Christmas Carol* as a result of his audience's enthusiasm: 'I wish you could have seen them—firstly, for my effect upon them—secondly, for their effect upon me!'[180]

Dickens's readings, by turns imperious and intimate, and his shifting attitudes to his audiences, find an analogue in the emerging political style of Liberalism. Helen Small observes a tension in franchise debates 'between the desire to incorporate men of judgement, and the concern to ensure that their judgement would only be exercised in acknowledging the authority of others', and asserts that 'the political ideals of liberal reform have their cultural realization in these Readings'.[181] Although many of Dickens's texts were adapted from work written before the 1860s, the author's revisions of his fiction for performance reveal how the style of the readings became a reaction to, as well as a 'realization' of, contemporary Liberal rhetoric.

Around the mid-century, the elector and not the representative became the focal point of the parliamentary reform question as Liberalism ousted radical vocabularies: 'debates about democracy in Britain would be centred around the franchise. The independent MP made way for the intelligent artisan . . . The idea of virtual representation—parliament as a form of trust or devolved authority—disappeared. Progressive MPs increasingly became the focal point of mandates.'[182] With emphasis placed on the 'respectability' of the elector, the MP himself was to be seen as a voice for local interests rather than as the guardian of national concerns. Gladstone and Bright moved towards a 'rhetoric of moral entitlement' that saw a steadily 'improving' public

---

[177] *DL*, xi. 185.   [178] Anon., 'Charles Dickens as a Reader', *Critic* (4 Sept. 1858), 537.
[179] *DL*, ix. 532.   [180] Ibid. x. 210–11.
[181] Helen Small, 'A Pulse of 124: Charles Dickens and a Pathology of the Mid-Victorian Reading Public', in James Raven, Helen Small, and Naomi Tadmor (eds.), *The Practice and Representation of Reading in England* (Cambridge: Cambridge University Press, 1996), 263–90, p. 267.
[182] Miles Taylor, *The Decline of British Radicalism, 1847–1860* (Oxford: Clarendon Press, 1995), 335, 342.

as the legitimate source of political power.[183] Bright's speech at Birmingham in October 1858 highlighted this change: 'I do not believe that Parliament, as at present constituted, does represent the people.'[184] For him, merely to praise them was not enough:

We have members of the aristocracy of this country exhibiting themselves frequently upon platforms on various occasions. They tell the people how wonderfully education has advanced: how much Parliament grants every year, and how much voluntary effort does; what a great step the people have taken forward. I wish they would come to the legitimate conclusion after all this praise of the people.[185]

That is, 'the people' should have a share of political power. The aristocracy's stress on how much 'voluntary effort' achieves merely masks the injustice of the present system. Bright sees such rhetorical manœuvres as disingenuous temporizing: Parliament is still being envisaged as a 'virtual' rather than a direct representation of the people.

Dickens's early public readings are supportive and suspicious of this Liberal critique of Parliament as a form of devolved authority. Many of the texts he chose to turn into readings tended to lay less stress on what was wrong with political institutions than on how the efforts of individuals might bring about social reform. While they proved particularly adaptable to the Liberal interest in the 'intelligent artisan' outside Parliament, rather than the honourable gentlemen in it, they did not envisage any change in the structure of political power as a result of the fictional characters' efforts. When, in *A Christmas Carol*, Scrooge's nephew waxes lyrical about how Christmas offers people a chance 'to think of people below them', the old man replies sarcastically: 'You're quite a powerful speaker, sir . . . I wonder you don't go into parliament' (p. 7). The plot of Dickens's tale, however, is not hostile to Scrooge's sarcasm, for the story ends with his change of heart rather than with any suggestion of change at Westminster. The reading version furthers this emphasis by omitting reference to institutional corruption; in the original printed version, we learn that 'phantoms . . . wore chains like Marley's Ghost; some few (they might be guilty governments) were linked together'.[186] There is no mention of 'guilty governments' when Dickens reads his story on the platform; it is Scrooge's own repentance and 'voluntary effort' that makes the world of the Cratchits a better place. Similarly, in his reading of *The Chimes* Dickens excised Will Fern's

---

[183] See John Belchem and James Epstein, 'The Nineteenth-Century Gentleman Leader Revisited', *Social History*, 22 (May 1997), 174–93, pp. 188–93; Peter Mandler, *Aristocratic Government in the Age of Reform: Whigs and Liberals, 1830–52* (Oxford: Clarendon Press, 1990), 279.

[184] *The Times*, 28 Oct. 1858, 7b.   [185] Bright, *Speeches*, i. 46–7.

[186] Charles Dickens, *The Christmas Books*, ed. Sally Ledger (London: Dent, 1999), 23.

speech against those in power. The labourer had originally complained to the MPs that 'your laws are made to trap and hunt us'.[187] The reading omits this complaint, and concentrates on the importance of individual, ameliorative endeavour rather than on collective, legislative entrapment.

The differences between Dickens's written and spoken versions of *Nicholas Nickleby* show how the author's political focus was reconsidered and revised when he came to address the public as a reader. For his reading Dickens adapted one of his most renowned pieces of social criticism, the account of Squeers's Yorkshire School. In the reading, Dickens's enjoyment in impersonating that which he criticized brought out the comic potential of the story, and with it, a different political inflection. Admitting to Nicholas that he has lied in his advertisement about the conditions at Dotheboys, Squeers adds: 'there's no act of Parliament against that, I believe?'[188] Audiences were not always sure how to respond: 'one scarcely knows whether to take Mr. Squeers for a mere ruffian or a humorist in disguise'.[189] Kate Field insisted that the reading was both 'satirical and funny': 'from beginning to end he [Squeers] is the brutal, cunning, diabolically funny beast the author's fancy paints him'.[190] Dickens himself was uncertain whether the mixture of the 'brutal' and the 'funny' was honourable, and his need to stress the brutality of Squeers to his audience often jostled uneasily alongside his relish for the fun of the scene: 'The people in the stalls set the example of laughing in the most curiously unreserved way; and they really laughed when Squeers read the boys' letters, with such cordial enjoyment, that the contagion extended to me. For one couldn't hear them without laughing too.'[191] Dickens's sense that the 'contagion' originates from the people in the stalls makes their laughter sound like something he'd rather not catch. Yet, while the author claims that he was only following their example, his own gruesome enjoyment of Squeers's voice would seem to be what leads them astray.

The scene in which Dotheboys Hall is described for the first time is heavily revised in the reading version. Chapter 8 of *Nicholas Nickleby* dwells on the 'horrible endurance of cruelty and neglect' at the school, on the 'sullen, dogged suffering' of the boys, and on the way in which 'an incipient Hell was breeding' amid such squalor (p. 83). In the reading text, however, these details are cut, and the stress is upon Squeers's impressive manipulation of the boys' letters

---

[187] Charles Dickens, *The Christmas Books*, 151.
[188] Charles Dickens, *Nicholas Nickleby*, ed. David Parker (London: Dent, 1994), 256. Subsequent page references are given parenthetically in the text.
[189] Cited in Dickens, *Public Readings*, 275.
[190] Kate Field, *Pen Photographs of Charles Dickens's Readings: Taken From Life* (1868; repr. New York: Whitston, 1998), 34–5.
[191] *DL*, ix. 500.

to suit his own ends. When we come to Bolder's letter, we hear only that Squeers 'caned him soundly' (p. 261); in the novel, Dickens had prolonged this punishment with 'not leaving off, indeed, until his arm was tired out' (p. 88). For Dickens to read the letter to Cobbey so as to inspire 'cordial enjoyment' and 'laughter' in both himself and his listeners—the letter starts: 'Cobbey's grandmother is dead, and his uncle John is took to drinking' (p. 261)—he has to tone down the novel's sense of outrage.

These revisions seem to reduce the novel's social earnestness, so that a critical interrogation becomes a comic interlude, but Dickens was also concerned in the reading text to show how the ills of society could be overcome by the reforming efforts of honourable citizens outside Parliament. In the novel, when the young Smike tells Nicholas of his sufferings at the hands of Squeers, we find: ' "There is always hope," said Nicholas; *he knew not what to say*' (p. 91; my emphasis). The reading version drops the italicized phrase. As a result, Nicholas's need to say something in the face of such anguish loses some of its desperation: he now believes what he says. Moreover, when Nicholas finally beats Squeers to the ground in front of the school, an addition in the reading text insists upon the value of such individual action: 'Then such a cheer arose as the walls of Dotheboys Hall had never echoed before, and would never respond to again. When the sound had died away, the school was empty; and of the crowd of boys, *not one remained*' (p. 275). Dickens underlined the last phrase three times in his prompt-copy, and it is here where he wanted the emphasis to lie. It is as if we are now listening to a fairy-tale; the boys are not seen to run away from the school as Smike did, but to vanish as the magical result of Nicholas's actions. Many audiences heard the reference to the word 'cheer' as a cue to join in with their own; Charles Kent observed that 'it was for all the world like assisting in person at that sacred and refreshing rite'.[192]

In *Nicholas Nickleby* itself, however, Dickens had not been so sure that one man could effect so much, nor that the enthusiasm of a crowd was to be encouraged. There are no cheers after Squeers's beating (p. 145), leaving the school to hover in the back of our minds for another fifteen monthly parts of the novel. When we finally return to Dotheboys Hall in chapter 64, we find that 'rebellion had just broken out', and that the 'malicious crowd, whose faces were clustered together in every variety of lank and half-starved ugliness', are intent on committing 'acts of outrage' by torturing Mrs Squeers (p. 756). It is no longer Nicholas who has secured their freedom; nor are the effects of the boys' continued squalor and deprivation allowed to go unnoticed.

Accounting for the popularity of his reading version, Dickens noted: 'I am inclined to suspect that the impression of protection and hope, derived from

---

[192] Kent, *Charles Dickens as a Reader*, 149.

Nickleby's going away protecting Smike, is exactly the impression . . . that an
Audience most likes to be left with.'[193] Giving the audience what they most
liked meant toning down Squeers's cruelty and stressing the importance of
Nicholas's efforts against it. In this sense, Dickens's platform eloquence has
something in common with what Bright saw as the misleading conservative
emphasis on 'how much voluntary effort does'. The author was himself alert
to this danger; in the past he had often become tetchy with those who focused
only on the efforts of 'the people'. In a review of Cruikshank he observed the
stress on the people's responsibility for their 'crimes and faults', but added
that the artist 'is bound to help us to glance at that other side on which
the government that forms the people, with all *its* faults and vices, is no
less plainly impressed' (again, note Dickens's association of 'artistry' with a
commitment to the study of the 'other side' of the question).[194] But if Dickens
(like many speakers in the newly formed Liberal Party) was unsure about
whether such efforts could always spur political reform, he was also becoming
increasingly concerned that the new language of Liberalism was itself both
disingenuous and ill-conceived. In 1864, he began *Our Mutual Friend*, a novel
that returned to the institutional and political framework in which 'voluntary
effort' was meant to take place. A comparison of the political allusiveness of
this novel with that of 'Dr Marigold's Prescriptions' (one of the most popular
of Dickens's later readings) elucidates how the writer/speaker's attitude to
Liberal rhetoric becomes more probing during the 1860s.

When the October 1864 episode of *Our Mutual Friend* came out (describing Veneering's election to Parliament), the first Liberal ministry had been in
power for five years. Nevertheless, franchise reform had been pushed to the bottom of the parliamentary agenda; the Liberal emphasis on the elector had not
changed the closed shop at Westminster.[195] In May, Gladstone cagily defended the extension of the franchise with what was to become one of his most
renowned phrases, but he was himself surprised when his words were cheered
by the radicals in the House: 'Every man who is not presumably incapacitated
by some consideration of personal unfitness or of political danger is morally
entitled to come within the pale of the Constitution (*Cheers and Counter
cheers*).'[196] The expansive call to 'Every man' (immediately qualified by the
hazy reference to 'some consideration'), and the refusal to define what 'personal unfitness' or 'political danger' might mean, turn a moral entitlement into a
vague possibility. 'Presumably' also seems to presume too much: every man is in

---

[193] *DL*, ix. 490.   [194] *DJ*, ii. 104.
[195] See Theodore Hoppen, *The Mid-Victorian Generation, 1846–1886* (Oxford: Clarendon
Press, 1998), 212.
[196] *The Times*, 12 May 1864, 8f.

danger of being incapacitated before Gladstone even describes him. After hearing the cheers, Gladstone quickly added that 'Of course, the meaning of that is this (*laughter*), that sudden, violent, and intoxicating changes must be avoided', and then redefined 'every man' as 'a select portion of the working classes'.[197]

Dickens had his concerns about a rhetoric of entitlement that viewed the vote as a right rather than a privilege, but he also feared that a temperate avoidance of intoxicating changes could provide cover for a temporizing opposition to any changes. Veneering's search for a parliamentary seat draws attention to the contemporary situation, and throughout the chapter (Book II, chapter 3) Dickens demonstrates that Liberal rhetoric fails to tell the whole story. Miles Taylor noted that during the 1860s 'the independent MP made way for the intelligent artisan' as the language of parliamentary reform became more democratic; but when Veneering speaks to the public he is meant to represent, he echoes these terms whilst also giving himself away. He may refer deferentially to 'any worthy and intelligent tradesman of your town—nay,—I will here be personal, and say Our town' (p. 252), but the calculated stutter betrays the candidate's distance from his audience:

[Veneering] issues an address to the independent electors of Pocket-Breaches, announcing that he is coming among them for their suffrages, as the mariner returns to the home of his early childhood: a phrase which is none the worse for his never having been near the place in his life, and not even now distinctly knowing where it is. (pp. 247–8)

'Independent electors' is a catch-phrase of 1860s liberalism; but here, when Veneering says that he comes 'for their suffrages', he unwittingly raises the question he is anxious to avoid. 'Suffrage(s)' could mean both 'the casting of a vote, voting' or 'the right or privilege of voting as a member of a body, state, etc.' (*OED*). Veneering neglects the latter meaning in favour of the former, twisting the Liberal ideal so that '*for* their suffrages' does not mean '*on behalf of* their rights', but '*in order to* gain their support'. In fact, such support is not even needed, as the deal for the seat is struck in clubland. This sketch of political networking was prescient: at the general election in July 1865 nearly half of all parliamentary seats remained uncontested, and in 1866 the buying up of seats was more widespread than ever.[198]

One reviewer complained that the 'sour and pithless account' of Pocket-Breaches did not come close to the 'genial and witty picture' of Eatanswill;[199]

---

[197] Ibid.

[198] See T. Lloyd, 'Uncontested Seats in British General Elections, 1852–1918', *Historical Journal*, 8/2 (1965), 260–5.

[199] Anon., in *Saturday Review*, Nov. 1865, cited in Collins (ed.), *Dickens: The Critical Heritage*, 462.

but by this time Dickens felt that being merely genial was a luxury he could not always afford. In contrast to the political slant of the earlier readings from *A Christmas Carol*, *The Chimes*, and *Nicholas Nickleby*, *Our Mutual Friend* is wary about entertaining the idea that the lower orders might effect beneficent change in public life. In one sense, then, its political satire (whilst drawing attention to the unpalatable reality behind Liberal rhetoric) could also be seen to carry conservative reservations embedded in early liberalism itself—as seen, for example, in Gladstone's reference to the 'personal unfitness' of the potential voter. George Bernard Shaw observed: '[Dickens] appeals again and again to the governing classes...Nowhere does he appeal to the working classes to take their fate into their own hands and try the democratic plan.'[200] *Our Mutual Friend* does not outline what such a 'plan' might involve, but the governing classes were not the only group to which Dickens felt he should be appealing in the mid-1860s. It was in his later public readings that he would search for a form of address that could accentuate *both* the importance of working-class effort *and* the need for the governing classes to help bring about change.

As the serial run of *Our Mutual Friend* came to an end, and as the debates over franchise reform gained momentum, Dickens turned to 'Dr Marigold'. His travelling cheap jack was hugely popular as both a written and a spoken phenomenon, selling more than 250,000 copies in the 1865 Christmas number of *All the Year Round* and becoming one of his most requested and performed public readings. The piece was written out of, and as a response to, the agonized atmosphere of *Our Mutual Friend*.[201] That novel seemed resistant to the kind of appeal to the lower classes that the earlier readings were full of, but 'Dr Marigold' has something to say about the strengths and weaknesses of both types of address. As the chirpy Doctor informs us at the beginning of his tale, his is a form of public speaking that imitates and innovates: 'I have measured myself against other public speakers, Members of Parliament, Platforms... and where I have found 'em good, I have took a bit of imitation from 'em, and where I have found 'em bad, I have let 'em alone.'[202] This is a quintessentially Dickensian rhythm—mimicry with a dash of revision (like his reporting style, or his use of free indirect style). Just as Veneering spoke to his constituency in 'a Market' (p. 251), so Marigold insists that he and the politicians speak 'in the same market-place' (p. 572), and the implications of this comparison are examined when Marigold conjures up an imaginary election.

[200] George Bernard Shaw, cited in *Shaw on Dickens*, ed. Dan H. Laurence and Martin Quinn (New York: Ungar, 1985), 34.

[201] See *DL*, xi. 105.

[202] Charles Dickens, *Christmas Stories*, ed. Ruth Glancy (London: Dent, 1996), 571.

He sets the scene thus: 'For look here! Say it's election time. I am on the footboard of my cart in the market-place on a Saturday night . . . I say: "Now here my free and independent woters . . . Now I'll show you what I'm going to do with you. Here's a pair of razors that'll shave you closer than the board of guardians, here's a flat-iron . . . here's a frying-pan," ' and so on (p. 382). When he comes to the voice of the parliamentary candidate, Marigold also has his patter off pat:

What does *he* say? 'Now my free and independent woters, I am going to give you such a chance' (he begins just like me) ' . . . Now I'll tell you what I'm going to do for you. Here's the interests of this magnificent town promoted above all the rest of the civilised and uncivilised earth . . . Here's uniwersal prosperity for you, repletion of animal food, golden cornfields, gladsome homesteads, and rounds of applause from your own heart, all in one lot, and that's myself. Will you take me as I stand? You won't? Well, then . . . I'll throw you in anything you ask for. There! Church-rates, abolition of church-rates, more malt tax, no malt tax . . . I'm of your opinion altogether, and the lot's yours on your own terms . . . You *are* such free and independent woters, and I *am* so proud of you—you *are* such a noble and enlightened constituency, and I *am* so ambitious of the honour and dignity of being your member . . . Take the lot on your own terms . . . You take it? Hooray! Sold again, and got the seat!' (pp. 383–4)

Marigold's satirical patter gently suggests to us that we might pursue more than one line of political enquiry as we listen to him. On the one hand, what is being mocked is the hypocrisy of a Liberal rhetoric that panders to the 'free and independent voter' in an attempt to secure the place of an MP, just as Veneering is ridiculed for his disingenuous address to the 'independent electors' of Pocket-Breaches. On the other hand, the fact that the people won't take him as he stands (Wright registered a pause after Dickens asked the question in the reading), the fact that they greedily demand their representative be of their opinion 'altogether', seems to poke fun at the emerging view of the MP as the people's delegate and a representative of their local interests ('this magnificent town'). The continual stress that the MP is parroting 'your own terms', that their 'lot' is 'myself', implicates the public in the sham by drawing attention to their insatiable and inconsistent demands.

The public readings had themselves brought home to Dickens the advantages of facing the people on their own terms. In the monologue as originally written, after his parliamentary impersonation Marigold added, 'These Dear Jacks soap the people shameful, but we Cheap Jacks don't. We tell 'em about themselves to their faces, and scorn to court 'em' (p. 573). As well as mocking those MPs who court 'the people' only to scorn them, this comment also refuses to see 'the people' as worthy of such sycophancy. With his own public physically in front of him, however, Dickens evidently judged that it was best not to push this point too far, and cut it from the reading-text. In the written version, Dr Marigold had neared the end of his story with: 'We were down at Lancaster, and I had done two nights' more than fair average business (*though I cannot in honour recommend them as a quick audience*) in the open square there' (p. 600; my emphasis). Again, Dickens cut the italicized phrase when reading aloud, unwilling to draw his audience's attention to how adversely they might be judged by the speaker addressing them. Such revisions highlight Dickens's tact, but they also show that his own readings could, on occasion, involve a degree of the flattery that he himself mocks in would-be MPs.

Dickens's shifting attitude towards his audience, and towards the politics of Liberal reform, can be heard in the accents of his speakers. Marigold's remark that the parliamentary candidate 'begins just like me' is no doubt inaccurate; the latter is likely to have said 'voters' rather than 'woters', for, as one contemporary remarked, 'a proper accent gives importance to what you say'.[203] Many of Dickens's readings were based on his renowned capacity for re-creating the accents of the lower classes. Like Sam Weller and Boots, Marigold often stole the show, and in allowing these characters to take centre-stage, Dickens seemed to be giving a voice to those who were not as yet 'free and independent woters' themselves. When Justin McCarthy tried to decide whether Dickens's impersonation of Sam Weller's cockneyisms was as good as the book, he remembered the heated contemporary arguments about such issues: 'We used to dispute over the point as if it were some great question of faith or politics.'[204]

However, giving a voice to what Kent called 'the lesser characters' did not mean that they were given equal status or allowed to speak for themselves.[205] One listener remembered Dickens's embarrassment at Sam Weller's licence: '[he] lowered his voice to the tones of one who was rather ashamed of what he was saying, and afraid of being reproved for the freedom of his utterances'.[206] Field observed that 'Dickens is never more gentlemanly than in dealing with passages that are capable of being vulgarly construed';[207] but if the writer has himself created such passages, what does it signify that he suddenly becomes 'ashamed' or 'gentlemanly' as he attempts to voice the words he has written? *The Times* report of the 'Marigold' reading noted how the cheap jack's accent and style hovered on the edge of the permissible, praising Dickens's 'mastery of a language which, in spite of offences against grammar, is prevented by the

[203] Anon., *Talking and Debating* (London: Groombridge, 1856), 15.

[204] Justin McCarthy, *Portraits of the Sixties* (London: Unwin, 1903), 24.

[205] Kent, *Charles Dickens as a Reader*, 33.

[206] W. P. Frith, *My Autobiography and Reminiscences*, 3 vols. (London: Bentley, 1887–8), i. 311–12.

[207] Field, *Pen Photographs*, 38.

honest dignity and good feeling of the man from becoming vulgar'.[208] The public reader's mastery of a language that is beneath him is inconsistent with the notion that what Marigold says is not 'vulgar' because it is 'honest'; accent is and is not important. Moreover, if 'the man' here refers to Dickens, then his mastery rescues his character from offence; if it refers to Marigold, then the character's dignity saves his author from vulgarity. Such relations between the speaker and the man for whom he speaks have different political implications, the first suggesting that Marigold needs a representative, and the second that he can represent himself.

The ambiguities of *The Times* report begin to outline the selectiveness of Dickens's representation of 'the people' in speech. Creating a form of public eloquence that mediates between the gentlemanly and the garrulous, the author/speaker is able to give poised expression to his political enquiries, and to ask that audiences follow his lead. With regard to such matters, Dickens was aware of the importance of how his character spoke as well as of what he had to say; he wrote of 'Marigold' that 'It is wonderfully like the real thing, of course a little refined and humoured'.[209] Deborah Vlock has recently examined the significances of street patter in Dickens, claiming that it was seen as 'a language of social undesirability' and that 'Dickens conflates verbal eccentricity with commercial fraudulence'.[210] But the tension between exact reproduction and artistic refinement, between the 'real' and the 'humoured', carries with it a more complicated series of judgements than Vlock suggests.

When, for example, Marigold talks of the confined living space of his family's caravan-home, he is obliged to admit to the audience that he has beaten his wife:

There's thousands of couples among you, getting on like sweet ile upon a whet-stone, in houses five and six pairs of stairs high, that would go to the Divorce court in a cart. Whether the jolting makes it worse, I don't undertake to decide, but in a cart it does come home to you and stick to you. Wiolence in a cart is *so* wiolent, and aggrawation in a cart is *so* aggrawating. (p. 385)

The initial focus is not so much upon Marigold's degrading conduct as upon the privilege of the 'thousands of couples among you' who are comfortably able to cast aspersions on the working classes as a result of contrastingly affluent circumstances. Dickens intensifies Marigold's accent at this point to lessen the shock of his confession; the 'wiolence' of the speaker becomes less violent, the 'aggrawation' less aggravating. Field said that 'no one but Dickens can endow the doleful confession with such unconscious humor. There never was

[208] *The Times*, 7 Oct. 1868, 10e.   [209] *DL*, xi. 99.

[210] Deborah Vlock, *Dickens, Novel Reading and the Victorian Popular Theatre* (Cambridge: Cambridge University Press, 1998), 98, 125.

so much good humor in so much bad humor,'[211] while the *Chester Chronicle* noted that the passage describing this temper in the cart 'fairly convulsed the audience with laughter'.[212]

Such laughter is unnerving as well as compassionate, for Dickens is playing to the audience as well as letting Marigold have a dig at them; the 'aggrawation' of the character and those like him becomes something that can be laughed off, as his family's plight becomes both a form of entertainment and a form of injustice. Charles Kent was aware of the fine line that the Dickens readings could tread: 'There is a point to which the passions must be raised to display that exhibition of them which scatters contagious tenderness through the whole theatre, but carried through but the breadth of a hair, beyond that point, the picture becomes an overcharged caricature, as likely to create laughter as diffuse distress.'[213] Yet, even if the shift from picture to caricature described here does on one level seem calculated to diffuse the distress of the audience rather than the character, Marigold's social commentary is not wholly jocular—he doesn't, after all, refer to the 'Diworce court'. Indeed, Dickens is not just looking for laughs, but asking audiences to become alert to the socio-political implications of their own laughter. Just as Marigold doesn't quite 'undertake to decide' the issues he raises, so Dickens creates a voice that amounts to something more politically searching than what Vlock would see as a conflation of 'verbal eccentricity' with 'social undesirability'.

Dr Marigold's prescriptions are not always meant to be taken with a grain of salt, but, as the title of the original written version reminds us, 'to be taken immediately' (p. 567). When Dickens has Marigold make his excursions into politics, he often tones down the accentual differences between the speaker and his audience, not so that the 'gentlemanly' accent might efface the 'vulgar' suggestion, but so that the audience may listen more attentively to *what* Marigold is saying. When comparing his trade with that of those who lead an itinerant life—the parliamentary candidates—Marigold demurs:

Why ain't we a profession? Why ain't we endowed with privileges? Why are we forced to take out a hawker's licence, when no such thing is expected of the political hawkers? Where's the difference betwixt us? Except that we are Cheap Jacks and they are Dear Jacks, I don't see any difference but what's in our favour. (p. 382)

No mention of 'priwileges' and 'fawour' here from the cockney who elsewhere talks about 'wiolence' and 'aggrawation'; not wanting to make light of this matter, Dickens lightens Marigold's accent instead. To ask for the same

---

[211] Field, *Pen Photographs*, 48.   [212] Quoted in Dickens, *Public Readings*, 385.
[213] Kent, *Charles Dickens as a Reader*, 30.

'privileges', to ask 'where's the difference betwixt us', is to pursue a line of demand and questioning analogous to the progressive side of that Liberal rhetoric that asked for an extension of the franchise and for MPs who were delegates from the people rather than guardians of them.

Even so, the refinement of Marigold's voice at such moments can cut both ways. Noting that Oliver Twist always speaks like a gentleman despite being brought up in an orphanage, Empson explains the compound politics of Dickens's refined accents: 'He meant that all the little boys in the orphanage were being robbed of their English heritage, and he thought that the best way to make his readers feel so was to make them imagine one of their own boys in such a place.'[214] However, after acknowledging 'the naturalness and force of the symbolic process', Empson points out an unintended side-effect and potential misreading: for some, 'the detail of the story is likely to offer a very soothing reflection. All you need to do, really, is go through these workhouses and pick out the little gentlemen, because all the other boys are just pigs.'[215] The oscillations of Marigold's accent point to a similar dilemma. Hearing his voice in its less 'vulgar' moments, the enfranchised part of Dickens's audience might feel that all one need do is pick out the gentlemen like Marigold and restrict voting privileges to them, because all the other cheap jacks are, in Gladstone's words, 'presumably incapacitated by some consideration of personal unfitness'. On the other hand, for those who were beginning to see the vote as part of an 'English heritage', Marigold's voice was an eloquent symbol of an oppressed class whose time had come.

Dickens inclined towards the latter of these two options, but he was not fully decided on such issues, and amid the genial, confident tones of his public readings one can hear this indecision. However, the author's abiding commitment to the exploration of different sides of the debate in his public eloquence is itself a valuable contribution to politics, and his best work embodies as well as depicts a mediation between the desire to persuade and the need to observe. Pondering the death of Dickens after the exertions of his reading tours, Ruskin's distaste for 'the pestiferous mob' led him to moan: 'I find the desire of audiences to be *audiences only* becoming an entirely pestilent character of the age. Everyone wants to *hear*—nobody to read—nobody to think; to be excited for an hour—and, if possible, amused.'[216] Dickens's gregarious appetite for the 'hour' included an enduring

---

[214] William Empson, 'The Symbolism of Dickens' (1962), in *Argufying*, 487.
[215] Ibid. 487–8. See Empson's spry footnote for an explanation of how Dickens took precautions against this misreading, 489.
[216] Ruskin, letter to the *Glasgow Herald* (1874), in *Works*, xxxiv. 517.

concern for 'the age', and his sense of his age's character also involved an appreciation of how amusement might be entwined with thought, and listening with reading. An audience with Dickens was an entertainment and a challenge; an 'audition', then, in both senses of the word—a critical engagement with the sounds of the era and a rehearsal for a politics of the future.

3

Tennyson and Sound Judgement

MEASURED LANGUAGE

Given the fineness of Tennyson's ear and his aptitude for ruminating, it is appropriate that the *OED*'s first recorded instance of the word 're-listen' should be traced to him ('The Brook' (1855)). Re-listening to a couple of his most celebrated lines, we hear more than one tune: 'But, for the unquiet heart and brain, | A use in measured language lies.'[1] Linguistic choreography assuages torment; and yet, the first line is not quite made to measure: 'unquiet' must be read as a disyllable (or 'the un' must become an elided syllable) if the line is to remain octosyllabic. The ripple in the metrical music hints at the limits of that music even as the balm is being administered. Re-listening again, 'But for' emerges from 'But, for': that is, '*If it wasn't for* the unquiet heart and brain, there would be a use in measured language'. The secondary meaning shadows the primary one: the unquiet heart and brain ward off as well as acknowledge the consolations of the melody. Tennyson had an ear for such complexities, and the acuity of his hearing has often been remarked—from Arthur Hallam's claim that 'his ear has a fairy fineness',[2] to T. S. Eliot's feeling that no poet 'in English has ever had a finer ear for a vowel sound',[3] to W. H. Auden's view that 'he had the finest ear, perhaps, of any English poet'.[4] Part of the fineness of this ear is its refusal to refine out of existence the unquiet aspects of life even as it seeks a way of quieting them. For Tennyson, a truly measured language needed to acknowledge its limitations as well as its potency.

---

[1] From 'In Memoriam' (1850), sec. V; *TP*, ii. 322. All quotations from Tennyson's poems are from this edition.

[2] Arthur Hallam, 'On Some of the Characteristics of Modern Poetry, and on the Lyrical Poems of Alfred Tennyson' (1831), in *The Writings of Arthur Hallam*, ed. T. H. Vail Motter (London: Oxford University Press, 1943), 191.

[3] T. S. Eliot, 'In Memoriam' (1936), in *Selected Essays*, 3rd edn. (London: Faber & Faber, 1951), 337.

[4] W. H. Auden, *Tennyson: An Introduction and a Selection* (London: Phoenix House, 1946), x.

The poet was especially sensitive to noises made by the public. He often grumbled about 'the publicities and gabblements of the 19th century', 'that wide-mouthed fool, society', 'these many tongued days', and 'these days of . . . multitudinous babble'.[5] The babble was heard most acutely in the newspapers—Tennyson was grimly amused by a description of the press as 'The whispering gallery of the world'.[6] But while he snaps that 'The Times is a fool', he also admits to reading it 'every day',[7] and when putting voices on paper, he often thought of the voices in the papers. William Allingham observed of his friend that 'prose often runs into rhyme', and that he 'treads newspaper into metre'[8] when talking. Although he was riled by an increasingly voluble public, it was 'the mouthability of poetry', as Christopher Ricks has noted, 'the urge to roll it aloud, which first caught Tennyson'.[9] The poet conceded: 'People sometimes say how "studiedly alliterative" Tennyson's verse is. Why, when I spout my lines first, they come out so alliteratively that I have sometimes no end of trouble to get rid of the alliteration.'[10] His life would involve the cultivation of an eloquence that could keep public voices at bay even as he sensed their proximity to, and claims on, his own forms of expressiveness.

Talk of the poet as 'spouter', and of his frequent awareness of his audience, seems a world away from the vision of poetic privacy that John Stuart Mill formulated at the beginning of the Victorian age: 'Poetry and eloquence are both alike the expression or uttering forth of feeling. But if we may be excused the seeming affectation of the antithesis, we should say that eloquence is *heard*, poetry is *over*heard. Eloquence supposes an audience; the peculiarity of poetry appears to us to lie in the poet's utter unconsciousness of a listener.'[11] Mill highlights the rhetorical nature of his own formulations by worrying over the seeming affectation of the 'antithesis'. The need to be excused suggests that the distinction is something of a *faux pas*, and Mill was right to be jittery, for the most vibrant poetic development of the age—the dramatic monologue—blurred the dividing lines between poetry and eloquence further by creating an internalized speaker–auditor relationship within the form itself. Moreover, Victorian poets were frequently concerned about how they might be heard as well as read.

Eric Griffiths's study of how poets explored the acoustic potential of the printed page, and of how such explorations entailed 'a vigilant and concrete

[5] *TL*, i. 275; ii. 9, 220, 298.

[6] Hallam Tennyson, *Alfred, Lord Tennyson: A Memoir by his Son*, 2 vols. (London: Macmillan, 1897), ii. 354.

[7] *TL*, ii. 23.   [8] Ibid. ii. 347, 474.

[9] Christopher Ricks, *Tennyson*, 2nd edn. (Basingstoke: Macmillan, 1989), 12.

[10] H. Tennyson, *Memoir*, ii. 15.

[11] John Stuart Mill, 'What is Poetry?' (1833), in *Collected Works of John Stuart Mill*, ed. J. M. Robson *et al.*, 33 vols. (1963–91; repr. London: Routledge & Kegan Paul, 1996), i. 348.

consciousness of the actual disparities in their public', is not primarily political in emphasis, but an aside suggests a further avenue of enquiry: 'In a parliamentary democracy, political and poetic changes meet at the level of voice . . . as the talking world expands, and new voices come into literary ear-shot, the perception of saliency itself is transformed, and the poet is tasked to make himself heard anew.'[12] Making oneself heard in this 'talking world' required a responsiveness to voices, and debate frequently centred on how—and how far—poets should take the call of their age into their own printed measures. In 1842, Francis Garden wrote: 'Call it [poetry] a fine art as much as you will,—it is discourse, it is utterance.'[13] This is strident, yet the phrase 'as much as you will' implies that the debate has not been settled. Alfred Austin complained that the weakness of 'the age and its worthy Laureate' was precisely this lack of emphasis on 'discourse': 'It hates rows. It regards a loudly avowed disbelief and discontent as disreputable . . . we may say of great poetry, what Demosthenes said of great oratory, that the soul of it is—action, action, action . . . Turn to see Mr Tennyson, and what do we see? Still life—almost uniform still life. There is a motion of a kind—but of what kind?'[14] Austin's desire for 'a motion' (not just 'motion') in poetry adopts parliamentary vocabulary to defend his own motion. Such emphases indicate that disagreements about whether poets should be rowing or retiring from the heat of battle often involved concerns about what poems should *sound* like.

Brief soundings from Tennyson's contemporaries give a sense of the 'consciousness' of a listener, one borne of the feeling that the poet was a speaker. R. H. Horne's 'A Political Oratorio' (1835) encapsulated the links between poetry and oratory that the *Monthly Repository*, led by W. J. Fox, was championing. Isobel Armstrong has highlighted the extended influence of this Utilitarian poetics, 'mounted through the polemic of the printed word in the cadences of political oratory . . . the reader is forced to hear, not overhear, a substantive and public poetry'.[15] The 'double poem' characteristic of the age (the dramatic monologue is Armstrong's main example) is 'inveterately political . . . because it is founded on debate and contest',[16] and although she does not look at particular speeches, consideration of how the cadences of political oratory might impinge upon and be revised by the printed word can shed further light on the 'debate and contest' within Victorian poetry.

[12] Eric Griffiths, *The Printed Voice of Victorian Poetry* (Oxford: Clarendon Press, 1989), 68, 79–80.

[13] Francis Garden, *Christian Remembrancer*, 4 (July 1842), 42–58, p. 49.

[14] Alfred Austin, *The Poetry of the Period* (1870) cited in Joseph Bristow (ed.), *The Victorian Poet: Poetics and Persona* (London: Croom Helm, 1987), 126, 123–4.

[15] Isobel Armstrong, *Victorian Poetry: Poetry, Poetics and Politics* (London: Routledge, 1993), 27, 147.

[16] Ibid. 13–14.

In the year in which Mill formulated his distinction between poetry and eloquence, Browning was developing a poetics that would seek to be 'heard'. The first word of his first published work, *Pauline* (1833), is an address—'Pauline, mine own, bend o'er me'[17]—and reviewers were quick to associate this poet's strange power of speech with that of the speakers in Parliament. William Maginn quipped: 'We have reasons for believing that *Pauline* is the production of one or all of the Whig ministers. The same folly, incoherence, and reckless assertion . . . is visible on each page of this book.'[18] Browning's relish for putting voices into print would continue to be informed by the voices of the ministers. His mornings were spent reading *The Times* before he retired to his study to write.[19] The links between his own pages and the speeches in the newspapers are sometimes made explicit—his speakers ask 'What's in the "Times"?' or comment on parliamentary discussion, 'Men meet gravely to-day | And debate, if abolishing Corn-laws | Be righteous and wise'[20]—but more often it is from within the vocal contours of his dramatic monologues that one can catch oblique engagements with politicians and speakers.[21]

Elizabeth Barrett Browning's work is frequently informed by what Matthew Arnold refers to as 'a rhetorical sense'.[22] The first part of *Casa Guidi Windows* (1851) complains about those who merely 'sigh' in poetry, 'Cooped up in music 'twixt and oh and ah',[23] and *Aurora Leigh* (1856) offers calculated disruptions to such music by running jolting speech rhythms across iambic metres. The poem announces a defence of 'The poet, speaker', a need to 'speak my verse', and a commitment to living life 'vocally, in books'.[24] Talk of 'speeches in the Commons and elsewhere | Upon the social question' (III, 593–4) flutters in and out of the narrative, and such talk permeates the sound of the verse. How, for instance, might one scan the line 'In Melbourne's poor-bills, Ashley's factory bills' (III, 549)? Such language is, as the narrator puts it, 'music interrupted' (VII, 882), a music that insists on allowing the cut and thrust of oratorical debate into its structure.

---

[17] Robert Browning, 'Pauline', in *Robert Browning: Poems*, i, ed. John Pettigrew (London: Penguin, 1981), 7.

[18] [William Maginn], 'Poets of the Day', *Fraser's Magazine*, 8 (Dec. 1833), 658–70, p. 670.

[19] William Grove, 'Robert Browning at Home: A Chat with a Former Servant of the Poet', *Pall Mall Budget*, 19 Dec. 1889, 1625.

[20] Browning, 'A Lover's Quarrel' (l.29), and 'The Englishman in Italy' (ll.288–90), in *Poems*, i. 530, 410.

[21] See Daniel Karlin and John Woolford, *Robert Browning* (Harlow: Longman, 1996), 165–71.

[22] Arnold, 'Preface to *Poems*', in *Poems*, 662.

[23] Elizabeth Barrett Browning, *Casa Guidi Windows*, ed. Julia Markus (New York: Browning Institute, 1977), I, 164.

[24] Elizabeth Barrett Browning, *Aurora Leigh*, ed. Margaret Reynolds (New York: Norton, 1996), I, 911; V, 24; II, 1183. Subsequent references are given parenthetically in the text.

Other Victorian poets display a sense of their work as a form of public speaking even as they seek a distance from the platform. We find Swinburne writing to Dante Gabriel Rossetti, asking him to make sure that *Songs Before Sunrise* (1871) 'is thoroughly pure of any prosaic or didactic taint, any touch of metrical stump-oratory or spread-eagleism, such as is so liable to affect and infect all but the highest political poetry. I will have nothing of the platform in it if possible—and yet if it is to be a success in its kind it must be practical, direct, actual in its bearing as Dante's politics and polemics.'[25] Metrical stump-oratory is seen as the norm, rather than the exception, and—so strong is the gravitational pull of the platform—the act of keeping a watchful eye on one's verse is no guarantee of its being safe from an appeal to the ears. Gerard Manley Hopkins echoes this dual rhythm of attraction and resistance, often evoking and qualifying the analogy between poetry and oratory in the same breath: 'My verse is less to be read than heard', for it is 'oratorical, that is the rhythm is so'; 'its performance is not reading with the eye but loud, leisurely, poetical (not rhetorical) recitation.'[26] 'That is' and '(not rhetorical)' announce hesitancies amid an enthusiasm for voicing.[27] From the conception to the reception of their work, Tennyson's contemporaries did not, as Mill put it, display an 'utter unconsciousness of the listener'. The listener might be resisted or ignored as well as courted or flattered, but the listener was present.

Tennyson was fascinated by the idea of poetry as a form of address. The first lines of two-thirds of the poems he contributed to *Poems by Two Brothers* (1827) include a vocative (either a 'thou' or a 'ye') or an appeal to collective concern (a 'we' or an 'our'). The nurturing and flowering of his talent in an oratorical environment was to have far-reaching effects on his later work. Armstrong sets the Utilitarian grouping of W. J. Fox against the 'opposite pole', the 'exclusive society' of Conservative Apostolic circles in which Tennyson moved at Cambridge: 'where the *Monthly Repository* circle find a public context for theorising consciousness the Apostles do not. Consciousness is necessarily concerned with the politics of privacy.'[28] The distinction is misleading, for Apostolic privacy maintained close links with a public, oratorical culture—signified most prominently at Cambridge by the Union debating society.

[25] Algernon Charles Swinburne, *The Swinburne Letters*, ed. Cecil Lang, 6 vols. (New Haven: Yale University Press, 1956–62), ii. 97.
[26] Gerard Manley Hopkins, *The Letters of Gerard Manley Hopkins to Robert Bridges*, ed. Claude Coller Abbott (London: Oxford University Press, 1935), 46, 246.
[27] On 'the drama of voicing' in Hopkins's work, see Griffiths, *Printed Voice*, 261–358. On the poet's rhetorical training, see Brian Vickers, 'Rhetoric and Functionality in Hopkins', in Anthony Mortimer (ed.), *The Authentic Cadence: Centennial Essays on Gerard Manley Hopkins* (Fribourg: Fribourg University Press, 1992), 73–142.
[28] I. Armstrong, *Victorian Poetry*, 27, 34.

In 1828, Arthur Hallam wrote to a close friend, William Gladstone, explaining the importance of the Union in university life: 'Its influence, as might be expected, is very much felt here, extending even among reading men, who actually have no share in it, but are modified in one way or another by its spirit... The ascendant politics are *Utilitarian*.'[29] The Apostles were not as 'exclusive' a society as Armstrong suggests; the four major speakers at the Union in the late 1820s and early 1830s were all members.[30] Subjects for Apostolic discussion were often political, and at Hallam's first attendance Thomas Sunderland spoke on the question 'Is the Study of Oratory desirable?' (all members voted 'Yes').[31] Nor was it only Union speakers who went off in search of honours through public speaking; of those elected to the Apostles between 1820 and 1859, nearly half progressed to the bar or to Parliament.[32] From his university days, then, Tennyson found himself in a world in which the cadences of political oratory were still studied and practised by 'reading men'.

Hallam was unnerved as well as excited by the links between literary and political discussion at Cambridge, and from within this environment he, like Mill, tried to delineate a firm division between political rhetoric and poetic achievement. As a prelude to his comments on Tennyson's *Poems, Chiefly Lyrical* (1830), he lamented that Wordsworth had written much which was 'powerful as rhetoric, but false as poetry', and complained that Leigh Hunt's poetic aspirations were threatened by his 'political habits of thought'. The writer who 'will pile his thoughts in a rhetorical battery, that they may convince, instead of letting them glow in the natural course of contemplation, that they may enrapture' had given himself over to the quotidian in the act of surrendering himself to the polemical, for 'half the fashionable poems in the world are mere rhetoric'.[33]

The word 'opinion' in Hallam's work is nearly always a pejorative term; this is why he points out that Tennyson 'comes before the public, unconnected with any political party, or peculiar system of opinions', and that 'elevated habits of thoughts' are 'implied' by Tennyson's poems, 'more impressive, to our minds, than if the author had drawn up a set of opinions in verse'.[34] Yet, Hallam's own opinionated voice betrays an uneasy sense that it is *because* poetry and

---

[29] Arthur Hallam, *The Letters of Arthur Henry Hallam*, ed. Jack Kolb (Columbus: Ohio State University Press, 1981), 244.

[30] Ibid. 241–2.

[31] See Peter Allen, *The Cambridge Apostles: The Early Years* (Cambridge: Cambridge University Press, 1978), 139.

[32] William C. Lubenow, *The Cambridge Apostles, 1820–1914: Liberalism, Imagination and Friendship in British Intellectual and Professional Life* (Cambridge: Cambridge University Press, 1998), 142–3.

[33] Hallam, *Writings*, 185.   [34] Ibid. 188, 192.

rhetoric are not wholly distinct forms of eloquence that he is trying so hard to make them so. Indeed, his letters are crammed with observations about parliamentary and Union orators alongside discussion of literary matters; he talks politics 'till I find my ears tingling', receives letters 'breathing politics at every pore', finds himself captivated by 'models of oratorical delivery' when he visits Parliament, and admits that, in the act of writing, his own 'elevated habits of thought' become quickly embroiled in arguments over opinion: 'I have forgotten I was writing a letter, not a speech.'[35]

Tennyson was writing poems, not speeches, but his early work gauges and offers 'opinions', testing out the limits of Hallam's counsel as well as taking it on board. Despite Hallam's claims that Tennyson was politically 'unconnected', early reviewers were quick to spot the political inflections of his writing.[36] Unpublished verses from around this time also give a clear sense of the poet's interest in the voices of the orators: 'The Wise, the Pure, the lights of our dull clime' complains about 'brass-mouthed demagogues, O'Connell, Hume, | And others whom the sacred Muse of rhyme | Disdains to name' (ll. 7–9). Such opinions are influenced by Tennyson's mixed feelings about the 1832 Reform Bill; he was pleased when it was passed, but worried that the 'instigating spirit of reform'—as opposed to the 'measure' itself—carried dangerous political consequences.[37] This 'spirit' was heard in the radical voices of Daniel O'Connell and Joseph Hume. That Tennyson should mention them in the same breath points to a contemporary anxiety in Apostolic circles; Hallam (himself vehemently opposed to the Reform Bill) wrote: 'If Dan carries it his own way, as is the general expectation, and if his pledged Repealers unite with the pledged Radicals of England, as is their obvious interest, they may, between them, govern the House.'[38]

Such a union implemented two rhetorical gestures: a hazily defined threat of violence should demands not be met and a reference to 'public opinion' as the source and authority of parliamentary deliberations. While O'Connell was persistently hinting at future outbreaks of violence in his extra-parliamentary addresses, Hume went so far as to intimate a future 'call to arms' when addressing the Commons.[39] In his poem, Tennyson disdains to name 'others' whose brash voices offend his delicate ear, but behind Hume and O'Connell there was another speaker whose voice struck closer to home: Charles D'Eyncourt Tennyson, the poet's uncle. D'Eyncourt was an ally of Hume and O'Connell

---

[35] Hallam, *Letters*, 74, 81, 140, 93.

[36] See Edgar F. Shannon, *Tennyson and the Reviewers* (Cambridge, Mass.: Harvard University Press, 1952), 21–6.

[37] See H. Tennyson, *Memoir*, i. 93; *TL*, i. 69.   [38] Hallam, *Letters*, 703.

[39] See Valerie Chancellor, *The Political Life of Joseph Hume, 1777–1855* (Stratford-on-Avon: Bloomfield, 1986), 75.

in the Commons,[40] and his language also hovered as close to the wire as was permissible when addressing honourable gentlemen: 'Public opinion would soon prevail over the decision of Parliament, and while he trusted that the Government would not precipitate the people into extreme measures, he confidently hoped that the people had too much good sense to precipitate themselves into anything like violence.'[41] Again, 'public opinion' is in close proximity to 'extreme measures'. The balanced clause structure betrays a threat: to 'trust' that something will not happen is a shade more confident than to 'hope' that it won't. D'Eyncourt denies a possibility of future violence only to formulate it, and his claim that public opinion would 'soon' prevail carries its own precipitate charge.

Tennyson's early work seeks to give voice to the people's desire for reform, whilst also modifying the language through which this desire is expressed by radical orators. In his review of the poet, Hallam felt that 'the people' was a collective that needed to be resisted: 'In the old times the poetic impulse went along with the general impulse of the nation; in these it is a reaction against it, a check acting for conservation against a propulsion towards change.'[42] A century later, when comparing Walt Whitman with Tennyson, T. S. Eliot astutely observed that 'both were conservative, rather than reactionary or revolutionary; that is to say, they believed explicitly in progress, and believed implicitly that progress consists in things remaining much as they are'.[43] The tussle between explicit and implicit feelings about what 'progress' might mean is explored throughout Tennyson's writing, but his search for a conservativism that was not mere quietism found early expression in the 1830s. It was in this period that he alighted on the stanza-form he was to adopt later for *In Memoriam*, a form that created a compound rhythm (an opposed to Hallam's reactionary 'check'), marrying 'propulsion' to 'conservation'.[44]

The first three poems he wrote in this form open with the lines, 'Hail Briton! In whatever zone', 'Love thou thy land, with love far-brought', and 'You ask me, why, though ill at ease'. All these hailings speak with assurance to an addressee who represents 'the people', but the poems display much less confidence than did the radical orators when they consider what this people represents (Tennyson had written to his uncle that 'the Public is a many-headed Monster').[45] Collective singulars turn plural: the hailed Briton is overwhelmed by

---

[40] O'Connell publicly commended D'Eyncourt's efforts; see *The Times*, 6 Mar. 1833, 3b, and the latter's motions were often seconded by Hume; see *The Times*, 9 Feb. 1833, 2f; 24 July 1833, 2a.

[41] *The Times*, 4 Nov. 1830, 1d.   [42] Hallam, *Writings*, 190.

[43] T. S. Eliot, in *The Nation and Athenaeum*, 18 Dec. 1926; cited in Ricks, *Tennyson*, 289.

[44] This is a frequent dual consideration of Tennyson's: 'Stagnation is more dangerous than revolution. But *sudden* change means a house on sand' (H. Tennyson, *Memoir*, ii. 339).

[45] *TL*, i. 7.

'babbling voices' (l. 45), the lover of his land is in the company of the 'dogs of Faction' (l. 85), and the asker-why is beset by 'banded unions' (l. 17). Mention of 'banded unions' is particularly important for a poet who was so often drawn to the idea of union; for many of Tennyson's contemporaries, the 'instigating spirit' of the Reform Bill was signalled by the rise of one of the first extra-parliamentary pressure groups of the era: the political Unions. Thomas Attwood founded the first organization in Birmingham in 1830, and within two years more than 100 similar groups were set up to agitate for the Whig government's Reform Bill. Radicals took the language of the Union platform into Parliament: O'Connell praised 'the brave and determined men of Birmingham'; Hume claimed that 'Political Unions ought to be formed in every parish'; and D'Eyncourt read out motions from the Birmingham Union with approval.[46]

Tennyson's 'Hail Briton!' is at once an oratorical endeavour and a resistance to such vocal exertion, an attempt to convince and a weighing of differing convictions in the balance. The poet's decision, for instance, to refer to 'Hampden' (l. 57) as an ideal example of the sagacious politician initially seems ill-chosen given the poet's political conservatism, for John Hampden's refusal to pay ship-money to Charles I in 1635 and his fatal wounding on Chalgrove Field during the Civil War had made him a popular revolutionary precedent in radical circles during the early nineteenth century. Hampden clubs had been set up in Birmingham, and *The Times* had claimed that they were 'notorious for inflaming the populace'.[47] Around the time Tennyson wrote his poem, Attwood stood up in Parliament to say: 'He had been an agitator . . . when he commenced his career, he expected to have to meet many dangers; but he expected to meet with no more in his small way, than Hampden had done in his large and extended career.'[48] *The Times* was disgruntled by such posturing from the Birmingham representative and ran a leader entitled 'The Brummagem Hampden', accusing Attwood of being 'a hair-on-end alarmist' and of making 'harangues in St. Stephen's'.[49]

The brummagem nature of contemporary speakers also informs 'Hail Briton!', but from within its own alarmist tones a new rhythm emerges, one that—in Austin's terms—portrays a need for both 'still life' and 'action'. After complaining about 'Men loud against all forms of power' who are 'voluble . . . windy tongues' (ll. 49–51), Tennyson shifts to a key more attuned to his own vocal strengths. We move from a single-minded complaint to a double-voiced measure of admiration and mourning:

---

[46] See Nancy LoPatin, *Political Unions, Popular Politics and the Great Reform Act of 1832* (Basingstoke: Macmillan, 1998), 4, 87; *The Times*, 12 Feb. 1830, 1a.
[47] *The Times*, 1 Nov. 1816, 3b. [48] *Hansard*, xvi. 919, 935 (21 Mar. 1833).
[49] *The Times*, 28 Mar. 1833, 5c.

> Not such was Hampden when he broke
>   Indignant from a silent life,
>   A single voice before the strife
> That, as it were a people, spoke:
>
> In whom the spirit of law prevailed
>   To war with edicts, and increased
>   By losing, but the mission ceased
> In Chalgrove, and the glory failed.
>
> (ll. 57–64)

Between the 'loud' and the 'silent', a use in measured language lies. The poet distances Hampden from the radical politics with which he has become associated, re-positioning the MP in a tradition in which 'war' with institutional abuses can still be seen (and heard) as 'law'-abiding.

Seamus Heaney has written sensitively about the enduring value of the poet's stanza-form: 'The *In Memoriam* stanza, with its unique combination of accelerating voice and metrical brake-lining, is still a potent chanter; it has wonderful tonal verity, capable of maintaining a purchase on the endured and a thrust into the desired.'[50] A purchase on the endured and a thrust into the desired are political as well as aesthetic ideals for Tennyson, and these qualities are heard here in the movement of 'Not such was Hampden when he broke | Indignant from a silent life'. The verb at the line-end pushes us quickly into the next line only for us to find that Hampden was not as pushy as we might have thought; the MP does not break *from* tradition, he breaks *into* it. Similarly, the succession of run-on lines in the last stanza allows the accelerating voice to become infused with Hampden's indignant reformist energy, but the acceleration is also held in check by the metrical brake-lining, as all the run-ons then receive the gentle resistance of mid-line caesurae.

Henry James once referred to the way in which, when Tennyson 'wishes to represent movement, the phrase always seems to me to pause and slowly pivot on itself', and added a similar observation after hearing the poet read his verses: 'With all the resonance of the chant, the whole thing was yet *still*, with all the long swing of its motion it remained where it was.'[51] Such language echoes the terms in which Eliot discusses Tennyson's politics (for James's 'movement' and 'motion', read Eliot's 'progress'; for James's 'remained where it was', read Eliot's 'things remaining much as they are'). This dual motion is captured in the rhythm of the lines above, and accentuated in the circular

---

[50] Seamus Heaney, 'A Hundred Years After', *Times Literary Supplement*, 2 Oct. 1992, 8.

[51] Henry James, *Views and Reviews* (1908) and *The Middle Years* (1917), cited in Matthew Bevis (ed.), *Alfred, Lord Tennyson: Lives of Victorian Literary Figures* (London: Pickering & Chatto, 2003), 229, 231.

movement of the stanza-form's rhyme-scheme. Indeed, the long vowels in the rhyme-words also ask that we do not pass over them too quickly. Hallam once referred to rhyme's ability to 'contain in itself a constant appeal to Memory and Hope',[52] and the sounds of Tennyson's rhymes often extrapolate a politics from within this twofold appeal. Here, they remind us of the potential costs of 'thrusts into the desired' or movements that seek to progress too quickly: 'increased' is heard alongside 'ceased', 'prevailed' takes into account 'failed'.

Tennyson's search for an inclusive national address was often conducted alongside his awareness of the oversights to which such an address might be susceptible. Hampden was one of Hallam's political heroes: 'Spirits of Hampden . . . animate my breast and nerve my arm for next session',[53] he enthused when gearing up for his speech making. This spirit animates Tennyson's poem, but he is characteristically less confident than his friend—altogether less 'rhetorical' about his 'opinions' even though more supportive of the movement for reform. His print accordingly breathes (and asks us to breathe) a more subdued spirit. The tentative admiration for 'A single voice before the strife | That, as it were a people, spoke' is embodied in the rhythm and phrasing; the second line's double caesura again asks us to go slow so that we might gather ourselves for the final assertive rhyme (the voice is encouraged to speak 'spoke' with the solid defiance of a Hampden). However, the act of slowing down also gives us opportunity to hear a syntactical tremor: 'as it were' might mean 'as *if* it were', not just 'because it was'. The poet was not sure how or whether single voices could bespeak and shape a people's best interests; this is why his poem draws on many voices, and why it allows callings for both propulsion and preservation to resonate within its form.

Tennyson did not publish 'Hail Briton!', but the poem's engagements with the orators cast their shadows over much of his future work, and he adapted many of its lines for later poems. In a lyric from *In Memoriam* that incorporated parts of 'Hail Briton', the poet paid tribute Hallam's 'potent voice' from within the contours of his own 'potent chanter'. Imagining what his friend would have achieved if he had lived, Tennyson envisages

> A life in civic action warm,
>   A soul on highest mission sent,
>   A potent voice of Parliament,
> A pillar steadfast in the storm,

(CXIII, 9–12)

The lines emulate the controlled potency of the voice they describe by harnessing that most Tennysonian of vocal temptations, alliteration, to measured

---

[52] Hallam, *Writings*, 222.   [53] Hallam, *Letters*, 69.

effect: 'civic action, soul, highest, sent, potent, Parliament, steadfast, storm'. The longer one listens, the more one sees: the *abba* rhyme-scheme is mirrored by the chiasmus of vowel sounds in the prepositions in each of the four lines: 'in, on, of, in'. What Eliot referred to as Tennyson's fine 'ear for a vowel sound' might be heard as part of the studied politics of such writing; each line opens with a long vowel before quickly shifting to a short version of that vowel, as though the speaker continually raises then reins in his own enthusiasm, moving from open-mouthed eulogy to a slightly more restrained vocal energy: 'life in, soul on, potent voice of, A pillar' (the effect is also echoed in the mid-line combination of 'highest mission'). The stanza is a miniature masterpiece of sonic cohesion, lending controlled literary support to a vision of oratorical endeavour.

Given Tennyson's admiration for reserve as well as enthusiasm in the highest forms of political speech, this stanza is not without its own reservations. The last two lines blend allusions to a poet (Milton) and an orator (Canning) who were close to Hallam's heart (Hallam had given a memorable speech defending Milton's political conduct at Eton, and had praised Canning as a 'man of genius').[54] 'Potent voice' is Adam's loving description of Raphael's voice in *Paradise Lost*, as he imagines how 'the great Light of Day yet wants to run | Much of his Race though steep, suspens in Heav'n | Held by thy voice, thy potent voice he heares, | And longer will delay to heare thee' (VII, 98–101). 'A pillar steadfast in the storm' is a reworking of Canning's tribute to Pitt in 1802, 'The Pilot that weathered the storm'. The Tory Prime Minister had resigned from his post a year earlier; Canning's poem also links the speaker to the sun, yet here he is 'admir'd in thy zenith, but lov'd in thy fall': 'When he sinks into twilight, with fondness we gaze, | And mark the mild lustre that gilds his decline.'[55] The combination of the allusions (the sun hanging on the words of the angel, the sun as symbol of a minister's decline) is characteristic of Tennyson's double-voiced craft when dealing with the 'warm' life of civic action, intimating a sense of a speaker's fragility alongside an awareness of his power. Although Hallam would have been a 'voice of Parliament' (not just a voice 'in' Parliament), an appreciation of such voices is usually accompanied by counter-rhythms in Tennyson's poetry. Indeed, the stanza is not self-enclosed; it runs on to consider 'cries' (l. 19) and 'undulations to and fro' (l. 20) which may resist spoken accents like Hallam's.

Tennyson's poised stanza offers its literary craft as complement and compliment to his friend's eloquence, and as an example of how 'undulations

[54] Hallam, *Letters*, 79–80, 161.
[55] George Canning, 'The Pilot that Weathered the Storm', in Leman Thomas Rede, *Memoir of the Right Honorable George Canning* (London: Virtue, 1827), 116–17.

to and fro' might be converted into a balanced synthesis of impulses. More enthusiastic about political reform than Hallam, yet less drawn to enthusiastic tones when discussing politics, the poet's tribute seeks to combine his friend's relish for direct political engagement with his view that poetry should maintain a respectful distance from such engagement. This writing is not divorced from 'rhetoric' as Hallam defined it, but then, nor is it merely 'a set of opinions in verse'. Tennyson would never quite give up on hailing Britons in this way, and his search for a style that could take the measure of civic voices in its own measure would see the flowering of his talent in the dramatic monologue.

TESTING VOICES

Mill's separation of poetry and eloquence was influenced by his fear of the influence of speech on writing. In his *System of Logic* (1843), he claimed:

Formerly if any one said, 'I am not alone responsible for this,' he was understood to mean, (what alone his words could mean in correct English), that he is not the sole person responsible; but if he now used such an expression, the reader would be confused between that and two other meanings; that he is not *only responsible* but something more; or that he is responsible not only for this but for something besides. The time is coming when Tennyson's Oenone could not say, 'I will not die alone', lest she should be supposed to mean that she would not only die but do something else.[56]

Mill's example foregrounds the ambiguity that he feels it is the privilege and duty of Tennyson's eloquence to fend off. Oenone says, 'I will not die alone, for fiery thoughts | Do shape themselves within me' (ll. 242–3), and 'I will not die alone . . . I will rise and go | Down into Troy' (ll. 253–7). Her 'alone' reaches for the community she had avoided earlier in the poem: she is saying 'I will not be alone when I die', and also 'I will not only die, I will do something else too'. Tennyson allows the vagaries of the spoken word to filter into his poem at the very moment when his speaker begins to look for a public that will no longer merely 'overhear'; for Oenone now wishes to be heard and to listen: 'I might speak my mind . . . Talk with the wild Cassandra' (ll. 223, 259). In fact, the whole poem is influenced by talk—in particular, by orations in the debating chamber of the Cambridge Union and by Apostolic speeches and debates about the merits of absolutist and constitutional governments.[57] 'The time is coming', Mill opines, but the time had already come: Tennyson's early

[56] Mill, *Collected Works*, viii. 690–1.
[57] See Richard Cronin, *Romantic Victorians: English Literature, 1824–1840* (Basingstoke: Palgrave, 2002), 147–65.

poems had begun to explore how the voice of the 'sole person' was forged amid community.

Mill's desire to keep 'alone' free from external influences (to keep 'alone' alone, as it were) is similar to his wish to keep the lyric 'I' unsullied by the need to acknowledge an audience. 'Oenone' is not a dramatic monologue, but it is heading in that direction, and the form—itself centrally concerned with public speaking—begins to flourish at around the same time that England was itself becoming seen, in the words of *The Times*, as 'a nation of public speakers'. In *The English Constitution* (1867), Walter Bagehot's discussion of the House of Commons included the flourish: 'The lyrical function of Parliament, if I may use such a phrase, is well done; it pours out in characteristic words the characteristic heart of the nation.'[58] But just as the lyrical voice of Parliament needed to find ways of addressing and accommodating new audiences out-of-doors, so the voice of lyric in the nineteenth century was developing its own sense of an audience. As Herbert Tucker puts it: 'Lyric, in the dramatic monologue, is what you cannot have and what you cannot forget.'[59] Tennyson's *Poems, Chiefly Lyrical* (1830) were precisely that: 'chiefly' lyrical, but also taking in other concerns.

A letter written by Mill suggests where these concerns might lead: 'Tennyson's poems—the best poems, in my estimation, which have appeared since the best days of Coleridge. Have you seen Peel's address to the electors of Tamworth? Was there ever such empty mouthing?'[60] Peel's address was described as 'a prodigious sensation . . . nobody talks of anything else',[61] for it marked a political sea-change. Jürgen Habermas observes: 'The conditions for the temporary era of government by public opinion became complete in 1834 with Peel's Tamworth Manifesto; for the first time a party published its election platform.'[62] The *Quarterly Review* fumed: 'When before did a Prime Minister think it expedient to announce to the *people*, not only his acceptance of office, but the principles, and even the details of the measures which he intended to produce?'[63] The fact that Peel addresses 'the *people*' implies that

---

[58] Walter Bagehot, *The English Constitution*, ed. Miles Taylor (Oxford: Oxford World's Classics, 2001), 123.

[59] Herbert Tucker, 'Dramatic Monologue and the Overhearing of Lyric', in Mary Ellis Gibson (ed.), *Critical Essays on Robert Browning* (New York: Hall, 1992), 21–38, p. 28. See also W. David Shaw, *Origins of the Monologue: The Hidden God* (Toronto: University of Toronto Press, 1999), 62–85.

[60] Mill, *Collected Works*, xii. 245.

[61] Lord Greville, cited in Stephen J. Lee, *Aspects of British Political History, 1815–1914* (London: Routledge, 1994), 78.

[62] Jürgen Habermas, *The Structural Transformation of the Public Sphere: An Inquiry into a Category of Bourgeois Society*, trans. Thomas Burger (Cambridge: Polity, 1989), 66.

[63] Quoted in Jephson, *The Platform*, ii. 173.

he is now beholden to them. His speech ended: 'I have the firm belief that the people of this country will so far maintain the prerogative of the King, as to give the Ministers of his choice, not an implicit confidence, but a fair trial.'[64] 'So far': the maintenance of the King's will now goes only so far and no further, while the shift from an 'implicit confidence' to 'a fair trial' is the shift to a judicial language whereby 'the people' are now the judge and jury—an audience before which ministers plead their cause. To put it another way: the parliamentary 'lyric' voice must no longer be merely 'overheard', but 'heard' and approved.

Mill's reference to Tennyson's poems in close proximity to Peel's speech is again meant to highlight a contrast between poetry and eloquence, but during the interval between the publication of the 'best poems' and Peel's speech Tennyson had been developing a form that incorporated addresses to 'the people'. While the speakers of his dramatic monologues are not always sure whom they are addressing (or, indeed, whether they are being listened to), they are asking for a hearing. The poetic form is more closely engaged with contemporary modes of public speaking than has been recognized, and consideration of two poems—'St Simeon Stylites' (often seen as the 'invention' of the form)[65] and 'Ulysses'—highlights their oratorical enquiries. Seamus Perry has observed that the writer's early political poems 'are only one example of Tennyson's argufying verse evading more straightforwardly single-minded attempts to persuade', and shrewdly notes that 'when resolute characters and men of action appear in the poems, their willed single-mindedness is typically regarded with the deepest misgivings, as though decisiveness were a sort of delusion or even madness'.[66] The single-minded is often equated with the simple-minded in Tennyson's work, and by setting himself to watch 'persuasion' in action in his monologues, he explores his own concerns about the perils of decisiveness. Both 'St Simeon Stylites' and 'Ulysses' were written in the immediate aftermath of Hallam's death, and in their margins one can hear his voice alongside the voices of others.

Richard Deacon draws attention to the Apostles' interest in the Saint-Simonians during the early 1830s, a group of French radicals who had just arrived in England to disseminate their plans for the political regeneration of modern society (Saint-Simon was the founder of French socialism). According to Deacon, 'it should be stressed that St Simeon Stylites had nothing whatsoever

[64] Robert Peel, 'The Tamworth Manifesto' (1835), repr. in G. M. Young and W. D. Handcock (eds.), *English Historical Documents, 1833–1874* (1956; repr. London: Routledge, 1996), 131.

[65] See Dorothy Mermin, *The Audience in the Poem: Five Victorian Poets* (New Brunswick, NJ: Rutgers University Press, 1983), 1; Herbert Tucker, *Tennyson and the Doom of Romanticism* (Cambridge, Mass.: Harvard University Press, 1988), 191.

[66] Seamus Perry, *Alfred Tennyson* (Tavistock: Northcote House, 2005), 58–9.

to do with the Saint-Simonians'.[67] He does not explain why this lack of connection should be stressed (presumably we should not be led astray by the sounds of words), but Tennyson's ear often seizes on fortuitous coincidences of sound and makes something out of them.[68]

The mix of religious and political vocabulary that characterized the rhetoric of Saint-Simon and his followers led to a heated debate in the journals. Moxon's liberal *Englishman's Magazine* (one of the earliest publishers of Tennyson's poetry) and the conservative *Quarterly* (one of its earliest critics) focused on the alleged sufferings of Saint-Simon, but disagreed about what such sufferings meant. The *Englishman's Magazine* informs us: 'He would often deprive himself of all but the bare necessities of life, take no other food than a scanty pittance of bread and water, consume no fuel, nay sell his very clothes, to provide for the expense of printing and distributing his works.'[69] This deprivation is seen as touching evidence of the reformer's profound concern for the poor, a concern that led him almost to his death, 'worn down as he was with long privation and physical suffering'.[70] In the *Quarterly*, Robert Southey took a dimmer view of such privation, quoting Saint-Simon's account of his sufferings ('For fifteen days I have lived upon bread and water; I have worked without fire, and I have even sold my clothes to defray the cost of copying my work') before aligning the man and his followers with pernicious radical MPs like the 'honourable member of the new parliament who may boast at an election dinner that he neither fears the clergy nor the devil'. Southey's gloss on Saint-Simon's long-sufferingness is curtly dismissive: 'he attempted to kill himself'.[71]

Like Saint-Simon, Tennyson's St Simeon is keen to wax lyrical on his suffering for a cause, and his self-mortification also borders upon the suicidal: 'In coughs, aches, stitches, ulcerous throes and cramps . . . Patient on this tall pillar I have borne | Rain, wind, frost, heat, hail, damp, and sleet, and snow' (ll. 13–16). Such relish for describing woes is at once amusing and disturbing. In the month that the *Quarterly* published its review of Saint-Simon's radicalism, *Fraser's* noted the peculiar pleasure that a listener could take from a speaker's tortured style when it discussed the oratory of the radical Joseph Hume: 'With all his defects, Joseph *Stylites*, alias Joseph of the "pillar," possesses an uncouth originality of sentiment, and a clumsy audacity of manner, which renders the most wearisome speaker in the House occasionally one of the most entertaining

---

[67] Richard Deacon, *The Cambridge Apostles* (London: Royce, 1985), 20.

[68] On Tennyson's knowledge of Saint-Simon, see John Killham, *Tennyson and The Princess: Reflections of An Age* (London: Athlone, 1958), 20–43.

[69] Anon., 'The School of Saint Simon', *Englishman's Magazine*, 1 (May 1831), 192–9, p. 194.

[70] Ibid.

[71] [Robert Southey], '*Doctrine de Saint Simon*; New Distribution of Property', *Quarterly Review*, 45 (July 1831), 407–50, pp. 423, 427, 425).

also.'[72] When Tennyson read out the voice of his own man on the pillar, he was also entertained by his speaker's wearisome cadences; FitzGerald recalled that 'this is one of the Poems A.T. would read with grotesque Grimness, especially at such passages as "Coughs, Aches, Stitches, etc.", laughing out loud at times'.[73] While the journals envisaged Saint-Simon's self-mortification as evidence of either virtuous or pernicious politics, the poet's grotesque grimness when reading his work aloud points to a less decided attitude towards such torment.

Before he died Saint-Simon became renowned in France for his oratory, and when his self-styled 'missionaries' arrived in London in 1832, they immediately hired the Lecture Rooms and began to speechify.[74] As Southey contemptuously put it: ' "the tongue", they say, "served them better than the press had done." '[75] Some Apostles went to London to listen, and discussions about the Saint-Simonians soon became the rage.[76] Hallam asked Tennyson: 'Have you considered them at all? The resemblance of their opinions in many points to Shelley is very striking; but they are much more practical.'[77] Lecturers who spoke like poets presented a danger and an opportunity. Tennyson had been considering them, and, like Hallam, was not quite sure about what their strange mix of political and religious rhetoric might portend.[78] In 'St Simeon Stylites', he transfered the rhetorical emphases of the lecturers into a form that tested their allegiance to the people.

The Saint-Simonist orators often took an anticlerical stance, emphasizing how the clergy had 'given to the faithful only a metaphysical object, a celestial paradise'. Religion, now apparently enlarged into 'a social bond', was to 'direct society towards the most rapid possible amelioration of the condition of the poorest class . . . to render men happy not only in heaven, but on earth'.[79] Saint-Simonist rhetoric also made comparisons between Christ and Saint-Simon himself. Christ was a noble political reformer, but he was no longer divine, relegated to a historical position in which Saint-Simon's own trials and sufferings took centre-stage. Southey drew attention to this, quoting with approval one observer who lamented: 'When I hear our Lord and Saviour spoken of . . . before three thousand persons, publicly and legally assembled,

---

[72] [William Phillips], 'Parliamentary Eloquence (No. II): House of Commons', *Fraser's Magazine*, 3 (July 1831), 744–57, p. 753.

[73] *TP*, i. 594.

[74] See Richard Pankhurst, 'Saint-Simonism in England', *Twentieth Century*, 152 (Dec. 1952), 499–512.

[75] [Southey], '*Doctrine de Saint Simon*, 429.

[76] See Melesina Trench (ed.), *Richard Chenevix Trench, Archbishop: Letters and Memorials*, 2 vols. (London: Kegan Paul, 1888) i. 103–4.

[77] Hallam, *Letters*, 522.   [78] See *TL*, i. 69.

[79] Henri de St Simon, *New Christianity by Henri de St Simon*, trans. Elimatet Smith (London: Effingham Wilson, 1834), 26, 7, 23. The main lecturers, Prati and Fontana, also stressed these points in *St Simonism in London* (London: Effingham Wilson, 1833).

as *a good man for his age*, but inferior to M de Saint-Simon by all the difference of eighteen centuries, I feel myself mortified in my inmost heart.'[80] When Simeon speaks of Christ before his audience, his overweening focus on his own mortification leads him to address the Saviour thus:

> O Jesus, if thou wilt not save my soul,
> Who may be saved? Who is it may be saved?
> Who may be made a saint, if I fail here?
> Show me the man hath suffered more than I.
>
> (ll. 45–8)

Was ever grief like his? Like many of Simeon's questions, these can't quite manage to be fully rhetorical. 'Who . . . may . . . Who . . . may . . . Who may': the oratorical triad is at once incredulous and anxious, and Simeon's implicit raising of his sufferings above those of Christ is undercut by his recourse to that man as the only one who could provide him with an authoritative answer. Reliant upon what he overlooks, St Simeon's questions capture a Saint-Simonian cadence, but they are in turn captured by the poet's interrogations of his speaker's position.

The loaded vagaries of address in Tennyson's monologue ask us to listen out for other potential sources of frustration for Simeon's projects. Although the Saint-Simonists dwelt on the emancipation of 'the poorest class', towards the end of the 1830s many supporters of such emancipation became disillusioned by the sect's rhetoric. Carlyle felt that the infusion of religious vocabulary into their politics carried with it 'superstition and deception'; Mill sensed a 'spiritual and temporal despotism' within the radicalism; and one working-class paper heard the tones of a 'new feudalism' in the 'New Christianity' that attempted to keep the lower orders in their place.[81] Tennyson's poem picks up on the unspoken despotism within an allegedly selfless public rhetoric. Simeon's view of 'the people' is an unstable one: sometimes they are 'silly' (l. 125), sometimes 'good' (l. 131), sometimes 'foolish' (l. 219). This indecision is developed by the varying targets of his address, for he does not seem certain whether he should be avoiding or listening to his public.

When the poem begins, it is not clear whether it is a dramatic monologue: Simeon's address to the 'Lord' (l. 8) is the first hint that he is talking, or perhaps praying; but when he says 'half-deaf I am | So that I scarce can hear the people hum | About the column's base' (ll. 34–6), another potential audience for his musings looms into view. We begin to suspect that Simeon is not so

---

[80] [Southey], '*Doctrine de Saint Simon*', 427.

[81] Quoted in Richard Pankhurst, 'Saint-Simonism in England: II', *Twentieth Century*, 153 (Jan. 1953), 47–58, pp. 56–8.

hard of hearing as he claims when he talks of his past: 'And they say then that I worked miracles' (l. 79). For the pious ascetic no longer interested in the voices at the base of the column, the appropriately unconcerned phrase would have been 'they *said* then'. Tennyson's sharp ear for speech rhythms allows 'then' to hover between being a past reference and a colloquial filler; this ambiguity hints at the possibility that while Simeon may be eyeful of a heavenly future, he also has an eye for the favour of the audience below.

Such an awareness of 'the people' may not have their best interests at heart. The political tenor of Simeon's voice is bound up with a consideration of whether he is 'heard' or 'overheard', and with how far he wants the people to be in on the act. Midway through his speech there comes a deliberation about where true authority lies:

> O Lord, thou knowest what a man I am;
> A sinful man, conceived and born in sin:
> 'Tis their own doing; this is none of mine;
> Lay it not to me. Am I to blame for this,
> That here come those that worship me? Ha! Ha!
> They think that I am somewhat. What am I?
> The silly people take me for a saint,
> And bring me offerings of fruit and flowers:
> And I, in truth (thou wilt bear witness here)
> Have all in all endured as much . . .
>   Good people, you do ill to kneel to me.
> What is it I can have done to merit this? . . .
> Yet do not rise; for you may look on me,
> And in your looking you may kneel to God.

> (ll. 119–39)

To 'bear witness here' is—as the words intimate—to look at and listen to the lines (to bear witness and to *hear*). Simeon's public serves to ratify and to threaten his visions of grandeur. The first part of this speech seems to be an address to God, but when we read '(thou wilt bear witness here)' we are prompted to consider why this phrase is presented as an aside. The parentheses make it sound as if this part of the speech is reserved for God's ear, and that the people can hear the rest of Simeon's musings. If so, Simeon's speaking of the 'silly people' takes on a new tone even before he comes to address them directly—the oily effacement of 'Oh, you *are* silly—but, yes, I am rather special, am I not?' By the time we arrive at 'What is it I can have done to merit this?', we are inclined to hear something disingenuous (there is one syllable too many in this line; Simeon's voice dwells for an extra moment on the thing he is pretending to pass over): 'Oh, good people, you really shouldn't have—you are just *too* good. No, no, I'm not a saint—but go on; how, exactly, do you think I'm like a saint?'

There is a growing sense that Simeon is trying to use public opinion in order to bully God into agreeing to his own self-estimation. At the same time, the shift from 'you do ill to kneel to me' to 'Yet do not rise' creates an opposing movement, as Simeon's alleged 'power with heaven' aims to coax the members of the audience into supporting him in order that they may get to God. This speaker's appeals to his audiences attempt to play one off against the other in order to further his own ends. When he goes on to claim excitedly, 'They shout, "Behold a saint!" | And lower voices saint me from above' (ll. 151–2), Tennyson ensures that his speaker gives away more than he intends: 'lower voices' are those whispers from heaven that Simeon thinks he can hear, but they may also be 'lower' in his estimation than the people whom he affects to scorn. The double-takes involved in the process of reading this poem invite us to hear the double-dealings of a voice that can claim to heal the maimed whilst also asking them to stay on their knees.

Another aspect of the Saint-Simonists' 'New Christianity'—its prophetic-political slant—is archly recalled at the end of the poem. Simeon's final act is to clutch his hands to his head as the visionary 'crown . . . is fitted on' (ll. 205–6), and his last words are:

> I prophesy that I shall die tonight,
> A quarter before twelve.
> > But thou, O Lord,
> Aid all this foolish people; let them take
> Example, pattern: lead them to thy light.
>
> > > (ll. 217–20)

The first two lines are characteristic of the way in which Tennyson blends sound judgement with the judgement of sound. The chipped, bathetic coda of 'A quarter before twelve' acquires its force partly from its contrast with the long vowels of the preceding line (most of which are metrically stressed), vowels that hint at the focus of Simeon's avowals: '*I* prophes*y* that *I* shall d*i*e ton*i*ght': 'I, I, I, I, I' (such egotism for a man preaching selflessness). As Ricks notes in his edition, the prophecy is not in Gibbon or Hone, two of the acknowledged sources for the poem. This mixture of the grand prophetic gesture, the specification of a time, and the dream of a foolish people's precarious future, is, however, captured in Saint-Simon's own last words: ' "Forty-eight hours after our second publication the party of workers will be formed: the future is ours". He lifted his hand to his head and died.'[82]

---

[82] *Globe*, 30 Dec. 1831; cited in Norman Cohn, 'The Saint-Simonian Portent', *Twentieth Century*, 152 (Oct. 1952), 330–40, p. 333.

Hallam regarded the Saint-Simonians as 'prophets of a false Future',[83] and Saint-Simon's reported last words would perhaps have been heard by the Apostle as an example of such falseness, raising expectations rather than addressing realities. The end of Simeon's life, though, like the ends of his speech, is never quite formulated in Tennyson's poem. It is open to debate whether Simeon thinks that the people should take their 'example' from God or from himself, and the final tremor between the singular and plural ('*this* foolish people, let *them*') points to the speaker's unsettled relations with the crowd below him. What Tennyson asks us to hear in this tremor is the varying conception of 'the people' in Saint-Simonist rhetoric, a people whose manifold sufferings demand attention, but whose collective energies and aspirations must be handled with care. For Tennyson, the voice of St Simeon, like that of Saint-Simon, did not always set a good example.

The poet's fascination with what the dramatic monologue might be able to make of oratorical dramas found further expression in 'Ulysses'. Some critics have suggested that Ulysses' voice has a political tenor: he 'sounds for all the world like a bored colonial official somewhere in the back of beyond';[84] 'he sounds, in fact, like a colonial administrator turning over the reins to a successor just before stepping on the boat to go home'.[85] These references to what Ulysses 'sounds like' need to be more precisely calibrated, for while the speaker takes part of his tone from colonial rhetoric, the poem also breathes a spirit that takes it beyond such readings (Tennyson's chief source for the poem was Dante's *Inferno*). Writing the poem soon after he learned of Hallam's death, Tennyson is likely to have recalled his friend's views about Dante and Ulysses.

In the 1830s Dante was a live issue in Apostolic circles. Hallam reviewed a book that interpreted the *Commedia* as a political allegory, conceding that 'we by no means contend that there may not be several partial allegories of a political complexion scattered throughout the poem', but adding that 'a character may be allegorical in part, without being so altogether'.[86] On the subject of Ulysses, the canto of the *Inferno* in which he appears is centrally concerned with characters who misuse their powers of eloquence, and draws on a long-standing debate over whether the hero's celebrated powers of

[83] Hallam, *Letters*, 513.

[84] Victor Kiernan, 'Tennyson, King Arthur and Imperialism', in Raphael Samuel and Gareth Stedman Jones (eds.), *Culture, Ideology and Politics: Essays for Eric Hobsbawm* (London: Routledge & Kegan Paul, 1983), 126–48, pp. 131–2.

[85] Matthew Rowlinson, 'The Ideological Moment of Tennyson's "Ulysses" ', *Victorian Poetry*, 30 (1992), 265–76, p. 267.

[86] Hallam, *Writings*, 261, 257.

persuasion are honourable or disreputable.[87] Hallam was conversant with such issues, and also in the habit of comparing Ulysses to contemporary speakers: a letter to Gladstone labelled him a 'divine Ulysses' and started a squabble about whether 'the Homeric statesman' was to be trusted. Gladstone's early Toryism, it would seem, inclined him to see 'dissimulation [and] low cunning' as 'the Whig qualities of Ulysses', while Hallam quoted passages from Homer dwelling on the positive attributes of the speaker to defend his own political principles.[88]

Tennyson's 'Ulysses' remains within ear-shot of political debates, but he also makes it hard for us to decide whether his speaker should be seen as 'divine' or as 'low'. During the 1830s a platform campaign for the abolition of slavery picked up pace.[89] The Abolition Bill was passed in August 1833, two months before Tennyson wrote 'Ulysses'. As in 'St Simeon Stylites', the poet's imagination was fired by a religio-political issue; he supported the Anti-slavery Convention, and at about the same time as he wrote 'Ulysses' he penned 'O mother Britain lift thou up', celebrating the emancipation of those West Indian slaves who worked on the sugar plantations in 'the hills of canes'.[90] The abolition movement revolved around two main considerations. First, there was a debate between those who wanted immediate emancipation of the West Indian slaves and those who supported gradual change over a number of years. Secondly, there were discussions about whether the colonist planters should exercise control over emancipation (Canning had suggested that the matter 'should be left in the hands of the executive government' in the colonies),[91] and about how or whether they should be compensated for the loss of their labour force.[92]

The Abolition Bill established an apprenticeship system: slaves would be seen as technically 'free', but would continue to work for their former masters for some years, while planters were to be given monetary compensation for the loss of their slaves. O'Connell 'objected strongly to the apprenticeships. They were slavery under another name,' and felt that the colonists should gain no compensation for their past 'crimes'.[93] Buxton, the chief supporter of abolition, was less sure. While he too worried about the apprenticeship system and about money and decisions being left to colonial powers, he felt

---

[87] See W. B. Stanford, *The Ulysses Theme: A Study of the Adaptability of a Traditional Hero*, 2nd edn. (Oxford: Blackwell, 1963).

[88] Hallam, *Letters*, 106–13.

[89] See Howard Temperley, *British Antislavery, 1833–1870* (London: Longman, 1972).

[90] See *TP*, ii. 46; H. Tennyson, *Memoir*, i. 41.   [91] *Hansard*, ix. 282 (15 May 1823).

[92] William Green, *British Slave Emancipation: The Sugar Colonies and the Great Experiment, 1830–1865* (Oxford: Clarendon Press, 1976), 99–128.

[93] *Hansard*, xix. 1062 (22 July 1833); xviii. 308 (3 June 1833).

that if concessions were not offered, 'they would lose the colonies'.[94] In one of his most renowned speeches on the issue some years earlier, he had also emphasized the need, not for 'the sudden emancipation of the negro', but for 'slow degrees'.[95] Such measures could be seen as temporizing rather than temperate: apparent liberation edges perilously close to a form of continued possession, for a defence of colonial interests does not sit easily alongside a denunciation of slavery.

'Ulysses' prompts readers to consider the issues involved in such deliberations, and to hear something disconcerting within colonial rhetoric, when the speaker tries to take leave of the need to dole out 'Unequal laws unto a savage race' (l. 4). Ricks rightly senses that 'something goes wrong in terms of the poem's addressees' in the following passage (it was a late addition to the manuscript), and suggests that the lines are 'faultily wooden rather than dramatically revealing'.[96] Considered in relation to contemporary debates, the lines can be heard as both wooden and revealing:

> This is my son, mine own Telemachus,
> To whom I leave the sceptre and the isle—
> Well-loved of me, discerning to fulfil
> This labour, by slow prudence to make mild
> A rugged people, and through soft degrees
> Subdue them to the useful and the good.
> Most blameless is he, centred in the sphere
> Of common duties, decent not to fail
> In offices of tenderness, and pay
> Meet adoration to my household gods,
> When I am gone. He works his work, I mine.

(ll. 33–43)

Ulysses's emphasis on 'slow prudence' and 'soft degrees' is analogous with Buxton's stress on 'slow degrees', but behind this apparent circumspection we also catch the tones of the colonist who refuses to hand over 'this labour'. It seems that, just as the labour force in the Indies was to be kept on even as they were promised freedom, so Ulysses' rugged people are to be kept 'useful'. To 'subdue' a people to 'the useful and the good' is not, after all, the same thing as to raise them to it.

The syntax of this speech is carefully spaced across line-endings in order to allow Ulysses' voice to say two things at once. 'Well-loved of me' could initially refer either to the 'son' or to 'the sceptre and the isle'; the glitch might imply that the king wants to keep political rule and private inclination

[94] Ibid. xix. 1185 (24 July 1833); 20, 136 (29 July 1833).
[95] Ibid. ix. 265 (15 May 1823).   [96] Ricks, *Tennyson*, 117.

intertwined even as he sets off to see the world. Indeed, his handing over of the reins also borders on a fast-and-loose handling of his people: we initially read 'offices of tenderness' as a reference to Telemachus's duty towards his new subjects, but the phrase then seems to point to the son's duty towards his father's established household shrines. A new beginning begins to sound like business as usual, and these verbal feints catch the tone of voices like Canning's: it would seem that the fate of 'a rugged people' is being 'left in the hands of the executive government', even though that government may not itself be mindful of the need for reform.

Tennyson's speaker, then, raises the two main issues of the abolition debate (what is to be done with the slaves? and by whom?). The 1833 parliamentary debates had also often referred to the argument between Buxton and Canning in 1823, when the former first brought his motion before the House, claiming that 'the state of slavery was repugnant to the principles of the Christian religion'. Canning made 'a strong objection to the introduction of the name of Christianity . . . into any parliamentary discussion', before he then hedged his bets: 'God forbid that I should contend that the Christian religion is favourable to slavery'; however, 'it is not true that there is that within the Christian religion which makes it impossible that it should co-exist with slavery in the world'.[97] When Ulysses says 'This is my son . . . Well-loved of me, discerning to fulfil', we can also hear a scriptural allusion behind the political gesture, as if Telemachus's future subduing of the savage race has divine sanction.[98] This resonance may lend an authority to Ulysses' words, an authority about which he cannot know; but, on the other hand, it may prefigure the dangerous self-confidence of those politicians who seek religious backing for imperial policies.

The sense that Tennyson is inviting readers to weigh up the potential dangers that lie behind the eloquence of statesmen is strengthened by the sound and rhythm of the passage. The line-ends carry a series of approaches to rhyme through alliteration and assonance ('isle, mild, mine', 'fulfil, fail, pay', 'good, gods'); it is as though the speaker is employing acoustics as a form of rhetorical seduction—the sound-effects are meant to smooth over differences, to soothe the audience into assent. And yet, a less assured sound also permeates the lines. Perry has observed strings of 'four phrases', establishing 'a rhetorical form which will recur in the poem (ll. 14, 22–3, 70): the three-part phrases normally utilized by the accomplished orator have grown distended, drawn out in a style of fatigued egotism'.[99]

---

[97] *Hansard*, ix. 274–9 (15 May 1823).
[98] See Matt. 3: 17: 'This is my beloved Son, in whom I am well pleased.'
[99] Perry, *Alfred Tennyson*, 76.

The same pattern occurs here, as tripartite structures become long-winded owing to codas beginning with 'and': 'Well-loved, . . . discerning, . . . by slow prudence . . . *and*', 'Most blameless, . . . centred, . . . decent . . . *and*'. Behind the orator's attempt to be accomplished, there is a nagging sense that he's loitering—'and another thing . . . '. A lingering possessiveness is also captured in the slide from three possessives to four, and—just as with St Simeon—'fatigued egotism' is intimated by the long 'I' sound, a hint at the self-centred from within the 'centred': 'my son, mine own . . . my household gods . . . *I mine*'.

As the monologue continues, it becomes harder to trust in the divine right of this 'idle king' (l. 1). Hallam's sense of the 'divine' Ulysses needs to be considered alongside Dante's Ulysses, a man who suffers for his eloquent sins, for it was this hell-bound version of the politician to whom the poet turned when composing the latter half of his monologue. The poised 'political complexion' of the poem can be appreciated by observing how Tennyson interweaves Dante's *Inferno* with a speech that would become the touchstone for colonial endeavour in the late 1820s and 1830s. In Dante's poem, Ulysses delivers an impassioned speech calling his crew to sail westward beyond Spain, and this speech leads captain and sailors to 'the new land' (I quote from the translation Tennyson was using).[100] However, from this new land a storm arises, drowning the sailors (and, by extension, consigning Ulysses to hell). On 12 December 1826, Canning stood up in the Commons to deliver what would become perhaps the most renowned speech in early nineteenth-century political history.[101] His 'New World' address became a key expression of an ethos of confident imperialism. When Canning defended his past refusal to go to war with France over Spain, he too looked past Spain and in the same direction as Dante's Ulysses for his 'new world':

[Now] it was quite another Spain, it was not the Spain, within the limits of whose empire the sun never set . . . Was it necessary . . . that we should blockade Cadiz? No. I looked another way—I sought materials of compensation in another hemisphere. Contemplating Spain, such as our ancestors had known her, I resolved that if France had Spain, it should not be Spain 'with the Indies'. I called the New World into existence, to redress the balance of the Old.[102]

Canning's point is that Spain is not worth defending, and that the colonies in the West Indies contain richer pickings. Though much is taken, much abides.

---

[100] Dante Alighieri, *The Inferno of Dante Alighieri*, trans. H. F. Cary, 2 vols. (London: Carpenter, 1805–6), ii. 165, 167.

[101] For Tennyson on Canning, see H. Tennyson, *Memoir*, i. 41, and 'Will Waterproof's Lyrical Monologue', *TP*, ii. 101.

[102] *Hansard*, xvi. 396–7.

When Tennyson wrote Ulysses' address to his mariners, he heard, I think, the grand sound of voices like Canning's alongside Dante's warnings about the dangerous seductiveness of appeals to the 'new world' as a form of compensation. Tennyson's speaker also looks westward:

> the deep
> Moans round with many voices. Come, my friends,
> 'Tis not too late to seek a newer world.
> Push off, and sitting well in order smite
> The sounding furrows; for my purpose holds
> To sail beyond the sunset, and the baths
> Of all the western stars, until I die.
> It may be that the gulfs will wash us down:
> It may be we shall touch the Happy Isles,
> And see the great Achilles, whom we knew.
> Though much is taken, much abides; and though
> We are not now that strength which in old days
> Moved earth and heaven; that which we are, we are;
>
> (ll. 55–67)

This address, like Canning's, also seeks compensation in another hemisphere. Canning's wavering pronouns ('*we* should blockade, *I* looked, *I* sought, *our* ancestors') signalled both a pride in his policy and a need to get his audience in on the act; Ulysses' pronominal shiftings ('*my* friends, *my* purpose, *I* die, wash *us* down') indicate a similar attempt to create a *rapprochement* between himself and his public. Nevertheless, re-listening to the cadences of an expansionist, adventurous rhetoric, we as readers (not merely auditors) register something more than an appeal to a brave new world. Canning's ardent opposition between 'Old' and 'New' feels less convincing in Ulysses' mouth, as if he only half-believes in the worthiness of his rhetoric: 'old days' attempts to gather strength, but in doing so, mourns the loss of it.[103] Canning's commanding verbosity was captured by his verbs ('I looked, I sought, I resolved, I called'); Ulysses' tone is much harder to gauge. When he calls to his mariners and begins his own 'seeking', announcing that 'my purpose holds', he initially sounds bold; but the poetic form in which this voice is held ensures that his purpose does not quite hold still, for the run-on line sees the verb turn transitive ('my purpose holds | To sail . . . until I die'): the speaker's grand designs are whittled down to an impending sense of his own death. To 'sail beyond the sunset', as Ulysses puts it, is not quite to extend the limits of an empire on which 'the sun never set[s]', as Canning had suggested, because

---

[103] Perry draws attention to 'new*er*' world (not 'new'), which 'beautifully tempers a public call to press on valiantly with a private sense of declining' (*Alfred Tennyson*, 77).

Dante's fearful vision of the future hovers in the back of our minds as we read.

'Ulysses' is a poem that remains, in Hallam's phrase, 'a partial allegory', for it acts as a warning about the probity of grand imperial schemes, and about where they might lead, even as it refuses to pronounce a final judgement on its voluble statesman. On other occasions, Tennyson could be less discerning: in 'The Queen of the Isles', the poet celebrates imperial expansion and offers a toast to the Queen: 'That the voice of a satisfied people may keep | A sound in her ear like the sound of the deep' (ll. 17–18). 'Peop . . . keep . . . deep': this saccharine chiming is out of tune with the more beleaguered, altogether less satisfied tone of 'Ulysses', and Tennyson would later claim that these lines were 'little more than newspaper verse'.[104] Returning to the enduring cadences of his monologue, we hear something less single-minded, as 'voice' becomes 'voices': 'the deep | Moans round with many voices'. The political depth of 'Ulysses' comes from its willingness to allow more than one voice into its form, and from its willingness to weigh expansive ambitions in the balance with the potential cost of such ambitions. Ulysses may order his men to 'smite | The sounding furrows', but the furrows on that well-worn brow of his have led him to a form of expression which involves other kinds of sounding.

Richard Holt Hutton saw in Tennyson's poetry a 'deliberate rejection of single strands of feeling'.[105] The achievements of 'St Simeon Stylites' and 'Ulysses' are built on this commitment to the plural, for Simeon's desire for 'some power with heaven' (l. 141) is not always a laughing matter, and Ulysses' dream of 'some work of noble note' (l. 52) is not always open to suspicion. On occasion, the voices of both speakers strike a noble note; each poem asks us to listen out for how the principles of a public speaker can become entangled in the toils of practice, and to appreciate how religious and political convictions may not sit easily alongside one another. By shaping a voice on the page, the poet asks that his audiences scan the implications of what is being said, for while the publics *in* these poems get only one chance to hear the speakers, the publics *of* them are invited to overhear and to 're-listen' to the speeches again and again. Such acts of renewed attentiveness help to create that audience which Tennyson so wanted to address, one that would allow its immediate political concerns to be tested by a form of eloquence at once passionate and prudent. As such, his poems are a form of political action, even though (or perhaps because) they worry about speakers who counsel immediate action:

---

[104] *TP*, ii. 95.
[105] Richard Holt Hutton, *Aspects of Religious and Scientific Thought: Selected from The Spectator*, ed. Elizabeth M. Roscoe (London: Macmillan, 1901), 375.

the poet impersonates such addresses so that the public might take up the difficult challenge of discriminating between outspoken eloquence and its unspoken limitations.

Walter Bagehot observed that 'The higher faculties of the mind require a certain calm, and the excitement of oratory is unfavourable to that calm'; poems, for instance, require 'a long interval of still and musing meditation'.[106] The terms are similar to those he uses to describe Tennyson's characteristic sound: 'the notion of a slow depositing instinct; day by day, as the hours pass, the delicate sand falls into beautiful forms—in stillness, in peace, in brooding'.[107] Even Tennyson's description of the need for forward movement in 'Ulysses' involves a kind of 'stillness': '[it] was written under the sense of loss and that all had gone by, but that still life must be fought out to the end'.[108] 'Still life': an apt ambiguity for a comment on a poem like 'Ulysses', for it unwittingly voices a need for stillness even as it speaks of a desire for movement (as if one might fight for a 'still life', as well as for a life of imperious action). Recall Alfred Austin's comment on Tennyson: 'Still life—almost uniform still life. There is a motion of a kind—but of what kind?' Austin meant this as a criticism, but it might instead be seen as a compliment, for the 'slow motion' of speech that is the life of these monologues is offered as a necessary prelude to more disinterested political motions in the future.[109]

A CIVIL TONGUE

The 1840s and 1850s witnessed Tennyson's growing popularity and the beginning of his Laureateship, and the poet became increasingly aware of a demand that he speak *for* as well as *to* the public. The Laureate's first collection, *Maud and Other Poems* (1855), is a heartfelt yet also antagonistic response to this demand, and its achievement rests in part on his movement away from the idyllic poetry which he had been writing in the 1840s. Brief consideration of *The Princess* (1847) gives a surer sense of what is so provocative and persuasive about *Maud* (the latter poem was fiercely defended by Tennyson throughout

---

[106] Walter Bagehot, 'Mr Gladstone' (1860), in *Collected Works*, iii. 429, 431.

[107] Bagehot, 'Wordsworth, Tennyson, and Browning; or Pure, Ornate, and Grotesque Art in English Poetry' (1864); cited in John D. Jump (ed.), *Tennyson: Critical Heritage* (London: Routledge, 1982), 230.

[108] Tennyson to James Knowles, cited in *TP*, i. 613.

[109] Hallam's phrase, when drawing attention to 'a majesty of slow motion' in Tennyson's early work (*Writings*, 193).

his life as one of the 'finest things' he ever wrote).[110] It is as though the Laureate first managed to forge a civil tongue that satisfied him by abandoning a tone of chastened civility, as though the finding of an enduring public voice involved a partial loss of voice through a dramatic form that eschewed conciliation for critique.

The pressure on the poet to conciliate was certainly evident in the 1840s. John Sterling (former Apostle and renowned Union speaker) explained:

Look at one of our general elections. The absurdities are plain, no doubt—has not the ocean froth and bubbles? But take the thing altogether, and observe the mixture and spread of interests and faculties brought into action—a nation throws itself into the streets and markets . . . the fools clamour, the poor groan, the rich humble themselves, and all men bring all to judgement, without a moment's fear but that quiet will spring out of the tumult, and a government be born from the mob.[111]

Despite his anxieties about 'the mob', Sterling suggests that the age's cacophony is a vital source of material for poetry. While debaters hope that 'quiet will spring out of the tumult', Tennyson's idyls have—in Sterling's apposite phrase—'a quiet fulness of sound'.[112] *The Princess* seeks to translate the clashes of political 'sound' into the 'quiet fullness' of communion, and its handling of one particular sound amid the contemporary hum of voices is representative of its placatory designs.

Links between Princess Ida's revolutionary college and contemporary feminist and imperialist debates have been explored,[113] but in the year in which Tennyson started to write *The Princess* in earnest (1845), there was a more immediate public debate over the potential dangers of colleges not wholly answerable to state jurisdiction. That summer, Peel's government proposed an increase in the grant to Maynooth College, a training college for Catholic priests in Ireland. The bill was designed to address the growing unrest in Ireland, and it generated considerable debate during the 1845 session.[114] As Donal Kerr observes, 'To Peel belongs the credit of being the first Tory premier to make a serious effort to solve the Irish problem by conciliation.'[115] *The Princess* opens with mention of 'celts and calumets' (I, 17; glossed by Ricks as 'bronze

[110] *TP*, ii. 518.

[111] John Sterling, '*Poems* by Alfred Tennyson' (1842), cited in Jump (ed.), *Tennyson: Critical Heritage*, 105.

[112] Ibid. 122.

[113] See Killham, *Tennyson and The Princess*, and Matthew Reynolds, *The Realms of Verse, 1830–1870: English Poetry in a Time of Nation-Building* (Oxford: Oxford University Press, 2001), 225–45.

[114] See G. I. T. Machin, *Politics and the Churches in Great Britain, 1832 to 1868* (Oxford: Clarendon Press, 1977), 148–80.

[115] Donal Kerr, *Peel, Priests and Politics* (Oxford: Clarendon Press, 1982), 351.

hatchets' and 'pipes of peace') and goes on to consider Ida's right to educate on principles other than those laid down by the ruling state. Such diction and developments ask readers to recall the contemporary Anglo-Irish situation, for the pipes of peace were being played to the Celts by Peel's government.

Tennyson was moving in pro-Peel circles in 1845. He was often talking of 'Peel as a man and a statesman', and Henry Lushington, the man to whom the poet dedicated *The Princess*, was a supporter of Peel.[116] Tennyson and his friend met frequently to discuss the poem, and Lushington got a petition together to back Peel's policy during the summer months.[117] At the height of the public debate, the poet's Irish friend, Aubrey de Vere, recorded in his diary:

[17/18 April 1845] I called on Alfred Tennyson and found him at first much out of spirits . . . complaining much of some writer in 'Fraser's Magazine' who had spoken of the 'foolish facility' of Tennysonian poetry. I went to the House of Commons and heard a good speech from Sir G. Grey—went back to Tennyson . . . Walked with him to his lawyer's: came back and listened to the 'University of Women'.[118]

De Vere's trips from Tennyson's house to the other House and then back again, coupled with his attentiveness to speeches, journals, and poems, outline the environment that informed the writing of *The Princess*. While reading *Fraser's* the discontented poet would have also come across a series on 'Contemporary Orators'. The April issue focused on Peel, reiterating some of the objections to him that had been voiced in Parliament upon the introduction of the Maynooth bill.[119] De Vere, however, supported Peel's move to placate Ireland, and the Grey speech he praises defended the statesman: 'the only principles on which Ireland should be governed were the principles of justice and conciliation'.[120] The debate is pertinent to *The Princess*, for we often find Tennyson's Prince speaking Peel's language.

At the close of the Maynooth debate, Peel took issue with those who wished to exert force on Ireland in an effort to keep her citizens quiet: 'I say, you must break up, in some way or other, that formidable confederacy which exists in that country against the British Government and the British connexion. I do not believe you can break it by force . . . You can do much to break it up by acting in a spirit of kindness, forbearance, and generosity . . . May God avert so great an evil as war!'[121] When faced by his bellicose father's wish to force Ida and her people into submission, the Prince interjects 'Not war, if

---

[116] H. Tennyson, *Memoir*, i. 225.

[117] See John O. Waller, *A Circle of Friends: The Tennysons and the Lushingtons of Park House* (Columbus: Ohio State University Press, 1996), 140–59.

[118] *TL*, i. 237.   [119] [Francis], 'Contemporary Orators'.

[120] *Hansard*, lxxix. 883 (17 Apr. 1845).   [121] Ibid. 1040 (18 Apr. 1845).

possible, | O king' (V, 119–20). I quote his subsequent speech from the first edition of the poem:

> now she lightens scorn
> At him that mars her plan, but then would hate
> (And every voice she talked with ratify it,
> And every face she looked on justify it)
> The general foe. More soluble is this knot,
> Like almost all the rest if men were wise,
> By gentleness than war. I want her love . . .
> I would the old God of war himself were dead.
>
>   (V, 125–39)

The allusion to other 'knots' that are soluble 'if men were wise' suggests that the Prince's speech might prompt in readers a sense of its analogical relation with recent developments. The Prince's '*More* soluble is this knot', like Peel's 'You can do *much* to break it up', does not promise a solution, but instead proposes a step in the right direction. In his speech Peel expressed his hope for 'more kindly relations between Ireland and this country' (he repeated the word 'kindly' three times to emphasize his point).[122] And, as Gama notes of the Prince's speech: 'you talk kindlier' (V, 203).

The Prince's wishful thinking is fulfilled by the plot (just as no lasting offence is taken by combatants in the poem's verbal joustings, so no lives are lost in the jousting tournament in which the Prince is injured). Tennyson is intent on staging a narrative within which a conciliatory rhetoric like Peel's is able to bring about political and social change with very little upheaval. As Matthew Reynolds suggests, 'Tennyson expects his readers to adopt the point of view of the Prince . . . Urging us to take sides in this way, the poem also encourages us to feel that an aesthetically pleasing conclusion to the work will require the fulfilment of the Prince's hopes.'[123] The voices that are 'ratified' by the poem's structure tend to be those that preach 'gentleness'. Yet, it is this peaceable preachiness that feels so unconvincing; Tennyson is rarely at his most persuasive when he is trying to persuade, and one person he seems not to have persuaded was himself. By the time the poem was published, he had already lost heart: 'My book is out and I hate it.'[124] He rightly sensed that his genius was for a different kind of speech in print, one that presents and enquires into mixed feelings, rather than one that merely undergoes them or pretends to have reconciled them. 'I hate it': the way the poet talks about *The Princess* is a portent of the more disturbing voice that confronts readers of *Maud*: 'I hate the dreadful hollow behind the little wood' (i. i. 1).

---

[122] Ibid. 1039.   [123] Reynolds, *Realms of Verse*, 232.   [124] *TL*, i. 281.

Maud is driven by a need to question the communities forged by political voices (indeed, its speaker often senses that such forging may be a forgery), and as a result its structures of address frequently break with rhetorical decorum in order to jolt readers out of potential complacency. The 'monodrama', as Tennyson called it, is a mon-O-drama, for it has particular difficulties with that most oratorical of syllables. The seed of *Maud*—the lyric 'O that 'twere possible' (II. iv. 141)—begins with 'O' and stages within itself a crisis of audience. It opens with the speaker's dream of meeting his loved one, 'her' (l. 145), then jumps to a call to 'thou' (l. 152), then tentatively imagines 'The delight of low replies' (l. 170), then moves back to a sense of 'She' (l. 180), before finally closing on an aching address, as the speaker wishes to weep 'My whole soul out to thee' (l. 238). The drift from 'O' to 'thee' is always accompanied in *Maud* by the bereft sense that there will be no 'low replies'. Throughout the poem the self-lacerating 'O' is used to address people who are absent—'O father' (I. i. 6), 'O child' (I. iv. 118), 'O young lord-lover' (I. xxii. 877)—and, more disturbingly, to speak to another part of the disjointed self, an internalized interlocutor: 'O heart of stone' (I. vi. 268), 'O clamourous heart' (I. xvi. 567), 'O passionate heart' (III. vi. 30). *Maud* never moves with ease from 'O' to 'thee': 'O me' (II. v. 334) is its characteristic calling.

The larger contours of the poem inflect this private drama of address with a sense of public urgency. Classical rhetoric divides oratory into three forms: epideictic (concerned with the present, and with praise or vituperation), judicial or forensic (aimed at past occurrences, and focused on accusation or defence), and deliberative (looking towards the future, with the emphasis on exhortation or dissuasion). The division of *Maud* into parts in the 1859 and 1865 texts echoes and complicates these structures. Take the opening lines of the first two sections: 'I hate the dreadful hollow behind the little wood' displays the epideictic impulse in overdrive, yet it precludes debate—as Griffiths writes, 'Nothing can be answered to these lines. (What could you say—'Oh, really, how fascinating' or 'Yes, yes, so do I, so do I'?)'.[125] The opening of section II—' "The fault was mine, the fault was mine" ' (II. i. 1)—is openly forensic (past tense, accusatory), yet the quotation-marks make it unclear where the speech is coming from. We will learn that Maud's brother said the words, but the speaker's echoing of his speech implies that faultfinding is not an easy business in this arena.

Finally, section III turns towards the future and 'the coming wars' (III. vi. 11); although the speaker mimics a deliberative manner and exhorts himself and others to single-minded action in the Crimean War—'And myself have awaked, as it seems, to the better mind; | It is better to fight for the good than

---

[125] Griffiths, *Printed Voice*, 158.

to rail at the ill' (iii. vi. 56–7)—the voice seems oddly flat. Tennyson said of this utterance: 'Take this with the first where he railed at everything—he is not quite sane—a little shattered.'[126] The movement from railing to rallying-cry (from epideictic to deliberative oratory) lacks the kind of conviction that an audience might be looking for, and while *Maud's* speaker does not know that he is being listened to, the Laureate's publication of such a voice as his nation immersed itself in war constitutes a peculiar form of public speaking. *Maud* is indebted to and haunted by an oratorical impulse, but its speaker's shattered 'O's and his shaken engagements with epideictic, forensic, and deliberative modes turn the poem's addresses from types of performative action into forms of perplexed resistance.

As war fever mounted in 1854, *The Times* proclaimed: 'It is not our business to enquire very exactly into the character of this enthusiasm, or to ask how far everyone of the multitude . . . understands the question at issue . . . It is the whole nation that speaks in this way . . . It never says what it does not mean, and never means what it does not carry out.'[127] The Laureate was not so sure, and *Maud* conducts an enquiry into the character of this enthusiasm by resisting the idea that collective utterance is an undisputable source of authority or self-knowledge at such times. Tennyson listens carefully to those who claim to speak to and for 'the whole nation', before then reviewing their vocal emphases in the searching scepticism of his poetic form. One particular speaker caught his attention from the 1850s onwards: Gladstone.

The long-standing relationship between the two men was to be a point of focus for both when they considered how the public should be addressed through speech and print. Gladstone was a keen reader of Tennyson; while preparing the budget speech in 1859, for example, he was reading 'Tennyson, Tennyson, Tennyson', and a few weeks earlier he 'Read divers pamphlets . . . Hansard's Debates—Tennyson'.[128] The politician wrote reviews of Tennyson's poems, quoted (and misquoted) them in his speeches, and met him frequently. The Laureate, for his part, kept a careful eye on Gladstone's orations in *The Times*, visited the Commons to hear him speak, and wrote letters and poems in which he deigned to offer the statesman political advice. William Allingham talked with Tennyson about 'Gladstone's oratory',[129] and Hallam Tennyson recalled politician and poet discussing

---

[126] *TP*, ii. 584.

[127] Cited in Trevor Royle, *Crimea: The Great Crimean War, 1854–1856* (London: Little, Brown and Co., 1999), 121–2.

[128] William Gladstone, *The Gladstone Diaries*, ed. H. C. G. Matthew and M. R. D. Foot, 14 vols. (Oxford: Clarendon Press, 1968–94), v. 416, 411.

[129] *TL*, iii. 306.

differences between 'poets and literary men . . . and orators'.[130] John Addington Symonds remembered the sound of these voices as they debated political and literary matters: Gladstone would speak in 'an orator's tone' with 'a combative House-of-Commons mannerism', while Tennyson's responses were '*obbligato, sotto voce*, to Gladstone's declamation'.[131]

The *sotto voce* tones of *Maud* are informed by a similar distrust of declamation. Tennyson once said of Gladstone that 'I love the man, but no Prime Minister ought to be an orator',[132] and would later note that the speaker could not 'see all round a thing',[133] as though the sweep of his oratory was associated, in the poet's mind, with something dangerously sweeping. By 1860, Walter Bagehot could remark that 'Mr Gladstone has, beyond any other man in his generation, what we may call the oratorical *impulse*. . . He has the *didactic* impulse. He has the "courage of his ideas". He will convince the audience.'[134] Tennyson is often wary of this singular emphasis on 'the audience', as he observed when outlining the differences between himself and Gladstone:

Before a crowd, which consists of many personalities, of which I know nothing, I am infinitely shy. The great orator cares nothing about all this. I think of the good man, and the bad man, and the mad man, that may be among them, and can say nothing. *He* takes them all as one man. *He* sways them as one man.[135]

It is difficult to gauge where the poet's loyalties lie. That the orator 'cares nothing' is enabling when placed against 'I can say nothing', but this lack of care involves a 'taking' that could be seen as a mistaking. '*He* sways them as one man' primarily suggests that the audience is seen as a unit, but it also suggests that the speaker 'sways' because he conceives himself 'as one man', sees himself as an undivided unity. His being at one with himself as he speaks is an attribute that he transfers to and cultivates in the crowd; it yearns to be a part of such sure-footedness, and so the great orator aims—in the full sense of the phrase—to take the crowd into his confidence.

In *Maud*, the fear of being taken in and the need to take varying points of view into account leads to a public voice that fractures collective addresses and assurance. Tennyson's self-conscious, self-divided speaker (he has something of 'the good man, and the bad man, and the mad man' in him) feels compelled to acknowledge in others the shifting instabilities that he feels within. He is often in search of the 'great orator', but keeps stumbling upon internal hecklers: when voicing a desire for 'one | Who can rule' (I. x. 394–5), he is

---

[130] H. Tennyson, *Memoir*, ii. 278.

[131] J. A. Symonds, 'Recollections of Lord Tennyson: An Evening at Thomas Woolner's' (1893); cited in Bevis (ed.), *Alfred, Lord Tennyson: Lives*, 121–3.

[132] H. Tennyson, *Memoir*, ii. 236.   [133] *TL*, iii. 306.

[134] Bagehot, 'Mr Gladstone', 420.   [135] H. Tennyson, *Memoir*, ii. 280.

drawn to vocabulary that moves away from an emphasis on 'one' to a sense of a self that is always beside itself: 'And ah for a man to arise in me, | That the man I am may cease to be' (I. x. 396–7). 'Ah', not 'O': even the call for a speaker is uttered in muted tones.

Gladstone was worried by where such unmanned utterances led, and his review of Tennyson's work in 1859 considered the differences between *Maud* and the Laureate's other poems by emphasizing the need for the 'manly'. According to the politician, Tennyson's 'manly resolution' and 'manful energies' are displayed in *In Memoriam* as a result of the poet's willingness to speak for the public through a universal lyrical utterance: 'it may be called one long soliloquy, but . . . it never degenerates into egotism—for he speaks typically on behalf of humanity at large'. *Idylls of the King* also displays 'a manly view of human character, life and duty' through an impulse towards the 'universal'.[136] Tennyson's manfulness is enshrined in a language that seeks to express and to forge communion with the public mind, and Gladstone's approval of this language contains within it criteria for judging public speaking that he delineates in his own speaking place.

A few weeks before *Maud* was published, the orator defended a value of a particular type of political rhetoric in the Commons:

It appears to me that when the grave occasion arises—and a very grave one it must be—upon which this House thinks it necessary to pronounce its sentiments in regard to the question of war or peace, it ought, I should say, above all things, it ought to be careful that its sentiments are pronounced in a clear, unequivocal, and unambiguous manner.[137]

The orator's artful repetitions ('when the grave occasion arises—and a very grave one it must be', 'it ought, I should say, above all things, it ought') prime the audience for the confidence of the triadic structure: 'a clear, unequivocal, and unambiguous manner'. Gladstone went on to indulge in another triad (and another repetition) when he stressed that speakers had a responsibility to the public to be 'plain, manly and unequivocal'.[138] His vocabulary puts *Idylls* and *In Memoriam* in the same class, for these works are also felt to honour 'manly' responsibility by following a model of plain-spoken, clear-sighted national rhetoric in a poetic form. When Tennyson writes about peace and war in *Maud*, however, he broaches questions that the politician occludes in the speech above: if a speaker's sentiments are themselves equivocal, should they be pronounced in an unequivocal manner when addressing the public? At what point does a discreet silencing of doubts

[136] William Gladstone, 'Review of *Poems, 1842, The Princess, In Memoriam, Maud, and Other Poems,* and *The Idylls*', *Quarterly Review*, 106 (Oct. 1859), 454–85, pp. 454, 480, 459–60, 468.

[137] *Hansard*, cxxxviii. 1757 (8 June 1855).   [138] Ibid. 1758.

in the name of the national interest become a disreputable avoidance of a necessary debate?

Gladstone's main objection to *Maud* is based on his feeling that it refuses to follow the rules of public speaking as he thinks they should be practised:

We frankly own that our divining rod does not enable us to say whether the poet intends to be in any and what degree sponsor to these sentiments, or whether he has put them forth in the exercise of his undoubted right to make vivid and suggestive representations of even the partial and narrow aspects of some endangered truth. This is at best, indeed, a perilous business, for out of such fervid partial representations nearly all grave human error springs; and it should only be pursued with caution and in season.[139]

The 'great orator' is speaking for all, and taking us all 'as one man', when he leads off with 'We', but Tennyson (in keeping with his general suspicion of collectives in print) was wary of the transference of this oratorical tic into prose, once observing that 'very refreshing likewise is the use of the plain "I" in lieu of the old hackneyed unconscientious editorial "we" '.[140] Moreover, Gladstone is eliding questions of poetic and political representation, for while Tennyson's other poems are seen to support the politician's need for steady but prudent enfranchisement as they cater to 'a popularity at once great, growing and select',[141] *Maud* seems unwilling to address or to represent such a constituency, and instead opts for the 'fervid' and 'partial'. The refusal of the poet to make it clear whether he 'sponsors' the sentiments he has put into print (in contrast to the orator-reviewer's 'We *frankly* own') is also judging the poem by a particular set of oratorical standards. That is, there may be a time and a place for such ambiguously 'suggestive' eloquence, but wartime is not the 'season' for it—poets should be pronouncing 'sentiments' like those speakers in the House, in a 'clear, unequivocal, and unambiguous manner'.

Tennyson's comments on his poem tend to acknowledge these ambiguities without apologizing for them: 'Strictly speaking I do not see how from the poem I could be pronounced with certainty either peace man or war man . . . the man was intended to have an hereditary vein of insanity . . . I do not mean that my madman does not speak truths too.'[142] The relationship between the speaker and the writer of *Maud* is, like the speaker himself, shifting, but not necessarily shifty. The poem represents and enacts the value as well as the danger of being *unable* to 'pronounce with certainty', for a 'season' in which many are nailing their colours to the mast may also be the very time that is most in need of a few awkward questions and equivocal voices.

[139] Gladstone, 'Review of *Poems*', 462.   [140] *TL*, ii. 142.
[141] Gladstone, 'Review of *Poems*', 454.   [142] *TL*, ii. 137–8.

In *Maud*, Tennyson is concerned not so much to 'sponsor' one particular set of sentiments, as to create a dramatic form that can test out the authority of varying allegiances by placing them in close proximity with one another. His poem is investigating positions, not simply taking them; it is calculated to cause debate, rather than to silence it.[143]

Such an investigation frequently takes its cue from the voices in the House. Early in the poem, the speaker snaps: 'Why do they prate of the blessings of Peace? we have made them a curse' (i. i. 21). '[T]hey' refers to the Queen and her ministers; in March 1854 a royal message was read out in Parliament announcing imminent war: 'It is a consolation to her Majesty to reflect that no endeavours have been wanting on her part to preserve for her subjects the blessings of peace.'[144] A few days later, Russell also spoke of 'the blessings of peace'.[145] The speaker of *Maud* often seems to take sides in this way by tussling with the orators' words, but his pronouncements do not stay steady because his imagination is plagued by the very words he wants to resist. His wish to give a piece of his mind is constantly checked by a search for peace of mind, and the word 'peace' echoes through the narrative to highlight this. Although the speaker talks a good fight—'Peace sitting under her olive, and slurring the days gone by' (i. i. 33), 'Is it peace or war? better, war! loud war!' (i. i. 47)—he also expresses a need to escape the fighting talk: 'let a passionless peace be my lot, | Far-off from the clamour of liars belied in the hubbub of lies' (i. iv. 151–2), 'Peace, angry spirit, and let him be' (i. xiii. 487), 'To have no peace . . . is that not sad?' (ii. v. 253).

Gladstone's review of Tennyson's poems objected to repetitions in which, 'though the term is repeated, the sense seems to be changed', and praised instead those repetitions 'which may be called repetitions of emphasis'.[146] That is, he wants the poet to repeat things as an orator might (to hammer home a point, or to create an incantatory conviction—'Education, education, education'). As Adam Piette has noted, '*Maud* bears precocious witness to the cracked obsessiveness that might go along with repeating oneself too much.'[147] Indeed, it is as though this speaker repeats words *because* he lacks confidence in them, senses that they might lead him astray; he needs to hear them again with a slightly different emphasis in order to check up on them, and on himself. His

---

[143] Some reviewers of *Maud* argued that the Laureate was 'for' the Peace Party since he allowed a madman to speak in defence of war, while others insisted that the war passages were evidence of Tennyson's support of England's involvement in the Crimea; see Edgar Shannon, 'The Critical Reception of Tennyson's *Maud*', *PMLA*, 68 (1953), 397–417.

[144] *The Times*, 28 Mar. 1854, 7a.   [145] *The Times*, 31 Mar. 1854, 7a.

[146] Gladstone, 'Review of *Poems*', 476.

[147] Adam Piette, 'Sound-Repetitions and Sense, or How to Hear Tennyson', *SPELL*, 7 (1994), 157–70, p. 163.

repetitions tend towards incredulity or perplexity rather than conviction, and the more we hear a particular word in *Maud*, the less inclined we feel to take it on trust. The poem begins by replaying the words and views of the pro-war orators (and the views of those who saw pacifism as disingenuous masquerade for commercial greed), but even though the speaker drifts towards military service, his language expresses a longing for the blessings of peace.

Tennyson's reading of Gladstone's oratory would also have alerted him to contradictions that were being echoed in the wider public debate about the Crimean war, for while the politician insisted on the importance of reiterative clarity when dealing with 'the question of war or peace', his speeches contained their own equivocations. In 1853 he spoke at Manchester and aligned himself with Bright, Cobden, and the Peace Party when he praised 'commercial freedom' and advised against war with Russia on the grounds that it would be a 'calamity which would disturb the operations of industry'.[148] But Gladstone also came to defend the war; in the same speech he observed that 'there is a necessity for regulating the distribution of power in Europe',[149] and another discrepancy materialized as this economic warning was craftily translated into a moral and religious motive for hostilities when the orator later insisted that 'the original cause of the war [was] the rights of the Greek Christians [in Turkey]'.[150] This is not quite 'manly' according to Gladstone's definition of the term, for although this 'cause' was the pretext for war, the subtext was that Turkey was a key strategic location for Britain's commercial holdings in the East.[151] As *Blackwood's* put it when discussing the apparently 'moral' motives for going to war, 'let us eschew cant in giving our reasons for the war. We go to war because Russia is becoming too powerful.'[152] In addition, Gladstone's sudden switch to a defence of Turkey created further discontinuities, for he had denounced the despotism within the Ottoman Empire in the run-up to the conflict; he uncomfortably acknowledged this point in a later speech: 'I have been reproached for having used at a former time disparaging language in respect to Turkey.'[153]

These changes of opinion and policy did not, according to Gladstone, infringe upon the candid nature of political rhetoric as he conceived it, for each speech might be seen as the cry of its occasion—a firm statement mirroring his views at that particular moment. In *Maud*, Tennyson is interested in something more than the occasional, in part because he senses that being

---

[148] *The Times*, 13 Oct. 1853, 7a.   [149] Ibid. 7c.
[150] *Hansard*, cxxxviii. 1044 (24 May 1855).   [151] See Royle, *Crimea*, 56.
[152] [G. C. Swayne], 'Peace and War, A Dialogue', *Blackwood's Edinburgh Magazine*, 76 (Nov. 1854), 589–98, p. 592.
[153] *Hansard*, cxxxix, 1820 (3 Aug. 1855). Royle acknowledges this shift of opinion in the summer of 1853: 'suddenly it became chic to support the Turks against the Russians' (*Crimea*, 57).

true to the moment is not synonymous with the finding of a moment of truth. Bagehot claimed that 'the orator has a dominion over the critical instant, and the consequences of the decisions taken during that instant may last long after the orator and the audience have both passed away'.[154] *Maud* looks into and beyond the critical instant. Compounding some of the shifts in public rhetoric into a compressed space on the page, the poem asks readers to re-evaluate a language that seeks to take sides in order to find its authoritative 'dominion':

> Below me, there, is the village, and looks how quiet and small!
> And yet bubbles o'er like a city, with gossip, scandal, and spite;
> And Jack on his ale-house bench has as many lies as a Czar;
> And here on the landward side, by a red rock, glimmers the Hall;
> And up in the high Hall-garden I see her pass like a light;
> But sorrow seize me if ever that light be my leading star!

> (I. iv. 108–13)

Alan Sinfield claims that 'the Czar was to recur in Tennyson's work as the figure of a tyrant who could be safely contrasted with the English government'.[155] There is nothing safe about this passage; in July 1855, to align a member of the British public with the Russian leader was to forge an unexpected criticism out of the critical instant. A prevalent feature of political debate during the Crimean conflict was an emphasis on the Tsar as a 'liar' because of his claim that Russia had gone to war to protect the rights of the Greek Christians rather than to seek territorial advantage in the East. But then, this was precisely the same tack that Gladstone and other British orators were taking, hence the comparative rather than contrasting nature of the passage above. The rhetoric of war insists upon differentiation, but *Maud*'s speaker also listens out for discomforting alliances.

Matters are made more intricate by our own uncertainty about where these words are coming from. The speaker feels that he is talking about two different subjects (the first three lines concern public affairs and look down 'there'; the next three lines concern his private love affair 'here'), but the poetic form in which this voice is captured hints at the intermingling of these pronouncements. The rhyme scheme (*abcabc*), the anaphoric line openings ('And', 'And', 'And', 'And'), and the string of semicolons at the line-ends weave the two halves of the stanza together, prompting us to consider the paucity of the 'gossip' alongside the probity of the speaker's own chatter. Would he be speaking about public matters 'below' him in this way, we wonder, if he was able to raise himself 'up' to the level of the 'high Hall-garden' in the

---

[154] Bagehot, 'Mr Gladstone', 421.
[155] Alan Sinfield, *Alfred Tennyson* (Oxford: Blackwell, 1986), 27.

private matter of his own courtship of Maud? Is personal animus informing political animosity? Such questions do not fully undermine the authority of the speaker's political sniping, but they do complicate our response to it. Tennyson's form offers a double challenge to its readers: not only does it prompt us to reconsider some of the unspoken ironies behind a war rhetoric that, for example, saw the Tsar as the only liar; it also asks us to think about *how* political positions are formed. Much to Gladstone's oratorical chagrin, such a poem is not primarily looking for a reader's assent to a line of argument (although it may include that). Rather, it is investigating the ways in which assent is created and maintained.

John Ashbery has suggested that if you go on talking to people they eventually lose interest, but when you start talking to yourself they want to listen in.[156] One reason for this curiosity is, perhaps, that we feel such speakers may tell us something about our own secret lives as well as theirs, blurting out things we have not yet had the opportunity (or the inclination) to say to ourselves. Contemporaries listening to *Maud*'s speaker were being coaxed into asking themselves whether, if Britain was complicit with her enemies, might she not then be at odds with her allies? As we have seen, Gladstone's defence of the Anglo-Turkish alliance jostled alongside his distrust of the Turks—another 'equivocal sentiment' that he and other orators tended to play down during the conflict. Just prior to the Crimean War, Turkish massacres of Christian communities had occurred in the Balkans; in their private correspondence many in the cabinet referred to the Turks as 'the Barbarians' and to their Sultan as 'the despot'.[157] This distrust seethed below the surface of an ostensibly unified public rhetoric that focused principally on the Turkish fight as a 'Christian' cause in need of British support. *Maud* refuses to turn a blind eye to such matters, as the speaker's relations with Maud's brother demonstrate.

The brother is referred to and mocked as 'the Sultan' (I. xx. 790, 825; II. v. 319), labelled as 'barbarous' (I. xiii. 455) and as a 'despot' (I. vi. 231). The 'Sultan' mixes with British politicians at 'A grand political dinner . . . A gathering of the Tory' (I. xx. 817–19), and these references hint at the Anglo-Turkish compact, but the speaker's uncertainty about where he stands in regard to such alliances permeates the narrative. He often spits out his anger towards the Sultan, but at other times he admits, 'I longed so heartily then and there | To give him the grasp of fellowship' (I. xiii. 458–9). To appease Maud, he tries to get along with her sibling, but an uneasy sense emerges that

---

[156] Cited in Adam Phillips, *Promises, Promises: Essays on Literature and Psychoanalysis* (London: Faber & Faber, 2000), 322.

[157] See Royle, *Crimea*, 76.

the speaker is battening down his anger towards the brother in order to get the girl: 'Peace, angry spirit, and let him be! | Has not his sister smiled on me?' (I. xiii. 487–8). The animosity lurking within this attempt at peaceful relations outlines in miniature the tension in the Anglo–Turkish alliance. Moreover, the speaker, like the British government, is particularly aware of territorial issues—'I was crossing his lands' (I. xiii. 449), 'my own dark wood' (I. xvi. 518)—and, given that Maud is often associated with the East in the poem, the implication is that his reasons for seeking the 'grasp of fellowship' are also linked to control of property and territory. He refers to the 'delicate Arab arch' of Maud's feet (I. xvi. 551); in his raptures over her he imagines a 'delicious East' (I. xviii. 614); and, as her British 'lion' (I. vi. 218), he envisages his union with her through a rose-tinted lens that harbours imperial ambitions: 'Blush from West to East . . . Till the West is East' (I. xvi. 591–3).

Such language again brings to the fore aspects of the Crimean conflict that Gladstone would rather have kept in the background—the war was meant to be seen as a moral crusade, not as a way for the West to gain the East. The narrative and the diction of Tennyson's poem replay the rhythms of public oratory back to its audience, but they do so in order to remind it of where its own allegiances may be coming from. The 'great orator' searches out an unperturbed consensus; Tennyson's poem listens out for the potential oversights and costs of such apparent agreement. Indeed, while the orators talked of and to 'Allies', *Maud*'s speaker begins by splicing this word into two of his most repeated monosyllables, voicing them over and over in increasingly vertiginous patterns: '*all* men *lie*' (I. i. 35). Only once does he allow the words to come together, when ruminating over how Maud 'came to be so allied' (I. xiii. 479). Such mutterings do not portend a comforting sense of unity.

In 1856, Gladstone emphasized collective union as he summed up the recent conflict with another cool triad: 'War with Russia was declared. The action at Sinope followed; the public mind was maddened.'[158] At the time, the politician saw this collective maddening as evidence of a stirring national consciousness, and felt that *Maud*'s madman was merely stirring up trouble. Twenty-three years later, however, when republishing his essay on the poem, he graciously added the following footnote: 'I can now see, and I at once confess, that a feeling, which had reference to the growth of the war-spirit in the outer world at the date of this article, dislocated my frame of mind, and disabled me from dealing even tolerably with the work as a work of imagination.'[159] The

---

[158] William Gladstone, 'The War and the Peace', *Gentleman's Magazine* (Aug. 1856), 140–55, p. 145.

[159] Idem., *Gleanings of Past Years, 1843–79*, 7 vols. (London: John Murray, 1879), ii. 146.

shift from confident collective ('the public mind was maddened') to uncertain singular ('dislocated my frame of mind') is apt for an appreciation of *Maud*. The statesman now feels that his mind was dislocated because it was so focused on unity—a little like the speaker at the end of the poem ('not quite sane—a little shattered') when he says: 'We have proved we have hearts in a cause, we are noble still, | And myself have awaked, as it seems, to the better mind' (iii. vi. 55–6). The corollary of this insight is that a speaker who dwells on dislocation may be speaking a strange kind of sense, as *Maud*'s celebrated 'mad-scene' (ii. v) suggests.

During the war Cobden had correctly pointed out that 'the language of ministers was one continual see-saw', while Palmerston glibly countered with the suggestion that the MP should be put in an asylum.[160] The minister's jibe is no laughing matter in *Maud*; while the politician wants awkward observations kept out of ear-shot, Tennyson's speaker, finding himself in an asylum and plagued by the voice of 'a statesman there' (l. 272), longs for an escape from his political insights even as he feels compelled to keep talking. He imagines that he has been buried alive, and the political significance of this imagining is strengthened when we recall that the setting—'a yard beneath the street' (l. 245) in central London—is ominously close to that described in Tennyson's 'Ode on the Death of the Duke of Wellington' (1852, the poet's first separate publication after becoming Laureate). The Laureate had asked:

> Where shall we lay the man whom we deplore?
> Here, in streaming London's central roar.
> Let the sound of those he wrought for,
> And the feet of those he fought for,
> Echo round his bones for evermore.
>
> (ll. 8–12)

This '*sad* and slow' pageant (l. 13; my emphasis), and these '*bones*' under the '*feet*' of '*stream*ing London's central roar', are returned to in *Maud*, but the commemorative publicity that deplores Wellington is now seen and heard as deplorable: 'my *bones* are shaken with pain . . . never an end to the *stream* of passing *feet* . . . To have no peace in the grave, is that not *sad*?' (ll. 243–54; my emphasis). The Ode's triumph of 'for *evermore*' is met by the terror of *Maud*'s '*never* an end': 'to hear a dead man chatter | Is enough to drive one mad' (ll. 257–8). The first readers of *Maud* would have been alerted to these echoes when they bought the poem, for the Ode was republished alongside

---

[160] Richard Cobden and Lord Palmerston, cited in John Vincent, 'The Parliamentary Dimension of the Crimean War', *Transactions of the Royal Historical Society*, 31 (1981), 37–50, pp. 43, 47.

it in the volume. It is as though the Laureate imagines—and asks readers to imagine—the nightmare of having to listen continually to a voice that hymns the praises of statesmen and that sings of national unison.

The dissonance between the assured commentator of the Ode and the anguished speaker of *Maud* hints at the dissonance between the Laureate's sense of his public duties (he said of the Ode, 'I wrote it because it was expected of me to write')[161] and his private reservations about towing the national line. The Ode is more comfortable with the vocative 'O'—'O civic muse' (l. 75)—but the final stanza of the mad-scene in *Maud* presents us with an agonized address and a voice that has had enough of such civility:

> O me, why have they not buried me deep enough?
> Is it kind to have made me a grave so rough,
> Me, that was never a quiet sleeper?
> Maybe still I am but half-dead;
> Then I cannot be wholly dumb;
> I will cry to the steps above my head
> And somebody, surely, some kind heart will come
> To bury me, bury me
> Deeper, ever so little deeper.
>
> (ll. 334–42)

These polished, fraught lines depict both a loneliness and a wish to be alone. Only 'Me' cannot find a corresponding terminal rhyme, instead tiring itself out in a repetition ('O me . . . Me . . . bury me, bury me') that seems to brook no reply. And yet, the sound calls for equivalences, 'bur*ied*', 'd*eep*', 'sl*eep*er', 'Mayb*e*', 'somebod*y*', 'surel*y*', 'bur*y*', 'd*eep*er', equivalences that search out sympathy. Remembering Maud's phrase from long ago, 'rough but kind' (i. xix. 753), the lover's question 'Is it kind to have made me a grave so rough' asks why and how roughness is part of mankind, but the need for 'some kind heart' dreams of another relation, of relation itself. Such suffering pleads for a quiet isolation and a compassionate meeting; in doing so, it stands as eloquent testimony to *Maud*'s need to speak out against those who stress national unity even as it never quite relinquishes the dream of union. Tennyson's decision to publish this voice, a voice that calls for communion while also insisting upon its own inconversability, speaks of a need to be of and apart from what Gladstone refers to as 'the public mind'.

The poem closes with an echo of a war-cry amid 'the clash of jarring claims' (iii. vi. 44), an echo of questionable fidelity that provokes rather than distils thought: 'And myself have awaked, as it seems, to the better mind.' 'Seems'?

---

[161] *TL*, ii. 50.

'The' better mind (not 'a' better mind) sounds oddly unhinged, as though the speaker is not quite sure of his own mind. The stuttering peroration has a sound that Hutton often heard in Tennyson, 'the air of moving through a resisting medium',[162] and also captures the tone that Arnold had complained about in his 1853 Preface: 'the dialogue of the mind with itself', in a situation where 'there is everything to be endured, nothing to be done'.[163] Arnold's phrasing is itself a return: in his review of Tennyson's work, Hallam had noted 'the melancholy which so evidently characterizes the spirit of modern poetry; hence that return of the mind upon itself and the habit of seeking relief in idiosyncrasies rather than community of interest'.[164] *Maud*'s speaker is seeking that community, but we sense that 'the return of the mind upon itself' may return at any moment.

It was precisely this return that Gladstone heard as anti-oratorical. In an early paper on 'Public Speaking', he explained that, in order to sway an audience, 'the great orator must endeavour to get rid of all reflex action of the mind upon itself as he speaks'.[165] Tennyson admired yet resisted the art of 'the great orator'. He never spoke in public, but for the rest of his life he would read *Maud* aloud to select company in his home. *Maud* was a kind of poetic oration that insisted on the importance of listening to the 'reflex action of the mind upon itself', and on the political value of such an action—not necessarily to 'sway' an audience 'as one man', but to ask that audience to consider its self-divisions as well as its unity. As Empson once observed, 'the mind is complex and ill-connected like an audience'.[166] *Maud* speaks of and to that mind, and defends the need to address a national audience in something other than oratorical accents.

THE TONE OF EMPIRE

Tennyson was often an enthusiastic defender of British imperialism, but his poetic voice was not naturally inclined towards enthusiasm. The 'real subject' of *Idylls of the King* (1859–85), as Cecil Lang noted, 'is the British Empire'.[167] Many critics, though, have complained about how the poet handles this subject:

[162] Hutton, 'Tennyson', in *Literary Essays* (1888), cited in Jump (ed.), *Tennyson: Critical Heritage*, 365.

[163] Arnold, 'Preface', in *Poems*, 656.　　[164] Hallam, *Writings*, 190.

[165] William Gladstone, 'Public Speaking' (1838), repr. in *Quarterly Journal of Speech*, 39 (Oct. 1953), 265–72, p. 272.

[166] Empson, *Some Versions of Pastoral*, 68.

[167] Cecil Lang, *Tennyson's Arthurian Psycho-Drama* (Lincoln: Tennyson Research Centre, 1983), 11. See, esp. Reynolds, *Realms of Verse*, 246–73.

'Tennyson saw only heroism, no blundering';[168] the Laureate is 'frequently a more or less crude apologist for an imperialist policy';[169] 'committed to poetry's social responsibility, he set out to be his country's "Public Orator" . . . There is a sombre contradiction at the heart of imperialism; even if Tennyson cannot admit it of his own empire'.[170] Tennyson is frequently an apologist for empire (although 'more or less' is not precise enough about how the apologist may turn into the analyst), but his poem's mixture of hesitation and foreboding when alluding to imperialist policies (not 'policy') gives rise to something less clear-cut than propaganda. He may have set out to be the country's 'Public Orator', but his discomfort with the role was founded on his sense that a commitment to poetry's social responsibility involved the study and expression of contradiction.

When the 'bard' in 'Guinevere' (1859) begins to sing, he starts off as crude apologist: 'the bard | Sang Arthur's glorious wars, and sang the King | As wellnigh more than man, and railed at those | Who called him the false son' (ll. 283–6). So far, so glorious: 'and' is used for cumulative, oratorical effect here, but the 'and' that pervades the *Idylls* often turns from the energetic to the enervated, and within a few lines we learn:

> But even in the middle of his song
> He faltered, and his hand fell from the harp,
> And pale he turned, and reeled, and would have fallen,
> But that they stayed him up; nor would he tell
> His vision.
>
> (ll. 300–4)

The shift from 'railed' to 'reeled' is an informing rhythm of the *Idylls*. Tennyson's poem, like his bard, often desires to sing of the empire on which the sun never sets—its last line is 'And the new sun rose bringing the new year' ('The Passing of Arthur', 469), and the Epilogue 'To the Queen' speaks of the 'sunset and sunrise of all thy realm' (l. 13). Yet, both poem and bard are plagued by the voice of the Queen within, for Guinevere also sees visions:

> she dreamed
> An awful dream; for then she seemed to stand
> On some vast plain before a setting sun
> And from the sun there swiftly made at her
> A ghastly something.
>
> (ll. 73–7)

---

[168] Patrick Brantlinger, *Rule of Darkness: British Literature and Imperialism, 1830–1914* (Ithaca, NY: Cornell University Press, 1988), 205.

[169] Rowlinson, 'Ideological Moment', 268.

[170] Kiernan, 'Tennyson, King Arthur and Imperialism', 130, 147.

A 'ghastly *something*'—it is as though this narrator also refuses, or is unable, to 'tell his vision'. *Idylls of the King* frequently has 'something' in the corner of its eye, and if its narrator aspires to be an orator, his fluency is often checked by what meets his gaze. He wants to say things, but he keeps seeing things, and such nervousness also leads to a perspective that is troubled by whispering voices. The narrator has, as he puts it of King Arthur's knights, 'listening eyes' ('Gareth and Lynette', 320).

In 1862 the Queen presented her Laureate with a volume of the late Prince Consort's speeches, in which the editor draws the reader's attention to the difficulties of speaking in public on political questions. Because Albert is perceived to speak on behalf of the Queen, his 'views had to be compressed and restrained in every direction': 'Of the Prince's speeches, as of much of his life, it may be said that the movement of them was graceful, noble and dignified; but yet it was like the movement of a man in chain armour, which, even with the strongest and most agile person, must ever have been a movement somewhat fettered by restraint.'[171] This could also be a fitting description of the style of the *Idylls*. In his 'Dedication' to the Prince Consort, Tennyson imagines his subject as a knight—'He seems to me | Scarce other than my king's ideal knight' (ll. 5–6)—and praises the 'sublime repression of himself' (l. 18) that Albert effected in his public speech.[172] But the Laureate's alternately burdened and appreciative awareness of a movement somewhat fettered by restraint had implications for his own 'Dedication' (and for the *Idylls* themselves), for he had initially felt the need to allow space for the controversial within the commemorative. Tennyson sent an early version of his poem to another renowned orator, his close friend the Duke of Argyll.[173] It included the following lines:

> he is gone:
> We know him now: those narrow jealousies,
> The sudden fume and petulance of an hour,
> Are silent.
>
> (ll. 14–17)

Argyll was aware that such oratorical paralipsis ('I wouldn't dream of referring to . . .') carried the outspoken within the 'silent', and was quick to reply

---

[171] Prince Consort, *The Principal Speeches and Addresses of His Royal Highness The Prince Consort*, ed. Arthur Helps (London: John Murray, 1862), 10–11.

[172] On Arthurian romance and imperialist politics, see Stephanie Barczewski, *Myth and National Identity in Nineteenth-Century Britain: The Legends of King Arthur and Robin Hood* (Oxford: Oxford University Press, 2000), 201–29.

[173] 'More letters survive from Tennyson to the Duke and Duchess of Argyll than to anyone else except his wife . . . As an *orator* he ranked with Bright, Gladstone, and Disraeli' (*TL*, ii. 562).

with 'a word—not of literary, but of *Political* criticism', advising Tennyson to remove the penultimate line above because 'it is specific and has direct reference to that shameful moment'.[174] The moment to which he refers is late 1853, when the Prince Consort's apparent antipathy to Palmerston's foreign policy was denounced by the press, who labelled Albert as a supporter of Russia in the buildup to the Crimean War and called for his impeachment for treason.[175]

Tennyson acceded to Argyll's requests, and also changed 'those narrow jealousies' to 'all narrow jealousies' to support a move from the 'specific' to the 'general', but he was far from sure as to whether such repressions were 'sublime' when applied to his own public speaking. Argyll's suggestion that the poet's political tact did not affect his literary taste left the Laureate ruminating: 'I am altogether, I assure you, out of love with my Dedication . . . I am much obliged to the Duke for the interest he took in the poem, and I have adopted his omissions, though, I must confess, that in my inner heart I stick to my old readings—at times.'[176] Argyll knew of his friend's concern over how stately silences could threaten '*poetical* value', and the close of his letter to Tennyson regarding the controversy read: 'Let it be forgotten, if possible.'[177] Such a forgetting was not always possible in the *Idylls* themselves.

The first volume of the poem (1859) sold more than any previous collection of Tennyson's work, but it offers something more complex than a eulogy of imperial achievement. As one tale ('Geraint and Enid') attempts to search out the differences between 'the brute Earl' Doorm (l. 711) and Arthur's imperial 'root[ing] out' (l. 937), it expresses a concern about violence committed in the name of empire even as it relishes an imperial forcefulness against the apparently 'lawless tribe' (l. 605). The poem opens with Geraint deciding to pursue imperial military advances in order to avoid the civil unrest created by rumours about the Queen at home:

> He made this pretext, that his princedom lay
> Close on the borders of a territory
> Wherein were bandit earls, and caitiff knights,
> Assassins, and all flyers from the hand
> Of Justice, and whatever loathes a law.
>
> ('The Marriage of Geraint', ll. 33–7)[178]

[174] *TL*, ii. 294.

[175] See Robert Rhodes James, *Albert, Prince Consort* (London: Hamish Hamilton, 1983), 209–27.

[176] *TL*, ii. 294.   [177] Ibid.

[178] The first installment of *Idylls of the King* published 'The Marriage of Geraint' and 'Geraint and Enid' as one poem entitled 'Enid'. For ease of reference, I have kept to the divisions and line numbers of Ricks's edition.

This is characteristic of the *Idylls*: an occasion for speechifying is infused with a sense that not everything is being said. Suspicions are aroused by the word 'pretext', and the indirect report of Geraint's speech is shot through with the speaker's own lack of conviction even as he wishes to take a bold vocal stance. The tidy triad ('earls, knights, Assassins') veers out of control as the 'and's multiply; 'and whatever loathes a law' feels oddly vague, and suggests that the speaker is clutching at straws.

A month before Tennyson began writing his poem, Lord Dalhousie (Governor-General of India) had received much publicity for his annexation of the Muslim state of Oudh. The annexation had been conducted on the grounds of apparent 'misgovernment' within Oudh itself, and Dalhousie's generalship had seen many similar 'reforms', religious, political, and cultural during his tenure (1848–56).[179] The *Times* neatly captured the tones of many politicians, praising the take-over of Oudh: 'Its greatest victory has been the strengthening and consolidation of the empire . . . The undisputed rule of *law* and *justice* has replaced the wild rule of the sword.'[180] Geraint's recourse to the same words when he speaks of consolidating Arthur's empire has implications that do not remain 'undisputed' as Tennyson's poem progresses, for the knight's aggressive tactics turn him into the mirror-image of those from whom he seeks to dissociate himself. When Arthur and his followers finally arrive, one of them addresses him: 'I took you for a bandit knight of Doorm' (l. 785). The speaker of these words, Edyrn, then explains his own past 'lawless hour' (l. 794) in the lands before he was changed by the 'mild heat of holy oratory' (l. 865) with the arrival of Arthur. The king's subsequent speech envisages an imperialist policy that questions the aggressive militarism displayed by Geraint (and by Dalhousie), as he castigates 'a life of violence' (l. 912) and demands peaceful conversions.

Arthur's 'holy oratory' envisages a firm distinction between an imperialism based on the self-discipline of both the colonizer and the people in his charge, and an 'onslaught' (l. 916) that poses a risk to both groups. However, as so often in the *Idylls*, the narrative does not form a perfect fit with the oratory. The end of Tennyson's idyll does not make it entirely clear how peaceful conversions are to take place; we are told that 'Edyrn has done it, weeding all his heart | As I will weed this land before I go' (ll. 905–6), but the analogy confuses rather than clarifies, as it grants Edyrn an agency that Arthur must subdue in other subjects. We are told that the king 'broke the

---

[179] On this administration's contribution to unrest in India, see Bernard Porter, *The Lion's Share: A Short History of British Imperialism, 1850–1970* (London: Longman, 1975), 27–46, and Ronald Hyam, *Britain's Imperial Century, 1815–1914* (London: Batsford, 1976), 206–28.

[180] *The Times*, 4 Mar. 1856, 8f.; my emphasis.

bandit-holds and cleansed the land' (l. 943) through reforms—'He root-ed out the slothful officer . . . and sent a thousand men | To till the wastes' (ll. 937–41)—but this efficient tidying-up seems to down-play the questions the poem has raised regarding the use of force in lands recalcitrant to 'reforms' made in the name of imperial expansion. These questions did not go away; Dalhousie would be the last man to extend the British flag over an Indian state, and four days after Tennyson sent the proofs of his poem to the press, the rebellion of Indian troops against British occupation (10 May 1857) signalled the start of the great Indian Mutiny that, as Hallam records, 'stirred him to the depths'.[181]

'Guinevere' plumbs these depths, and was begun as press coverage of the Mutiny gathered pace in England. Through the queen's revolt against Arthur's empire, Tennyson reviews the implications of the latest political developments in India for his poetic project. As the king points out, Guinevere is an 'imperial-moulded form' (l. 545), and as such, her personal infidelity carries political repercussions. Indeed, her mutiny is so close to home as to be less a war against foreign foes than a civil infighting that blurs the distinctions between accuser and accused. Arthur's agonized sense of revulsion from and devotion to his queen is captured in his possessive pronouns—'I cannot touch thy lips, they are not mine . . . I am thine husband' (ll. 548, 563)—and this mirrors the widespread public reaction to the Indian Mutiny as something at once internal and external; Queen Victoria described it as the work of 'our own people whom we had trusted'.[182] To take ownership of a rebellion against you is to register complicity as well as separation, and the political revolt for which Guinevere is both embodiment and inspiration is, like the Indian Mutiny, a mixed affair.

During the months in which 'Guinevere' was being composed (July 1857–March 1858), the loss of composure on both sides in India forced the British legislature into a difficult position regarding what should be done about the Mutiny. Many took to the platform to engage in the debate: Disraeli worried that 'our soldiers and our sailors will exact a retribution which it may, perhaps, be too terrible to pause upon . . . I protest against meeting atrocities by atrocities'; and a month later Lord Ellenborough (former Governor-General of India) cried for vengeance in a speech to his tenants: 'Do you suppose that, if we could submit to this in India, we should not be threatened with it in England?'[183] The question of whether violence is justified is paused upon

[181] H. Tennyson, *Memoir*, i. 432.

[182] Queen Victoria, cited in Norman McCord, *British History, 1815–1906* (Oxford: Oxford University Press, 1991), 301.

[183] Benjamin Disraeli and Lord Ellenborough, cited in Michael Edwardes, *Red Year: The Indian Rebellion of 1857* (London: Hamish Hamilton, 1973), 161–2, 164.

in Arthur's last speech to Guinevere, a speech in which the king somehow conspires to have it both ways:

> The wrath which forced my thoughts on that fierce law,
> The doom of treason and the flaming death,
> (When first I learnt thee hidden here) is past . . .
> Through the thick night I hear the trumpet blow:
> They summon me their King to lead mine hosts
> Far down to that great battle in the west
> Where I must strike against the man they call
> My sister's son.
>
>   (ll. 534–70)

The division between Arthur's merciful attitude to the queen and his compulsion to strike in battle gives expression to Tennyson's difficulties when considering how to deal with 'imperial-moulded forms' in poetry and politics. The pronouns again mark the crisis, for the proud analogy between 'I' and 'mine' quickly shifts to a situation in which 'I' strikes against 'my'. Arthur had claimed that 'The children born of thee are sword and fire, | Red ruin, and the breaking up of laws' (ll. 422–3), and the personal/political cross-over that Guinevere's mutiny had represented and helped to create has to be fractured, as dealing with the queen seems no longer analogous with dealing with the state. On the one hand, Arthur forgives 'as Eternal God | forgives' (ll. 541–2), and on the other, he will meet the 'Traitor' and 'strike him dead' (l. 572). The speech points to a realm beyond secular politics, but it also acknowledges that imperialist politics demand intervention.

This dispute between a Christian religious imperative and the call for military force had been at the forefront of the public debate over the Indian Mutiny. During November and December 1858 Tennyson was 'full of the Queen's wise proclamation to India',[184] a proclamation widely discussed and translated into seventeen languages. Victoria's own form of 'holy oratory' contains the same tension as Arthur's speech: she begins by appealing to 'the Grace of God' and claims that 'we desire to show our mercy by pardoning the offences of those who have been misled, but who desire to return to the path of duty'; yet she also acknowledges that 'Our power has been shown by the suppression of that rebellion in the field' and notes that, for some offenders, 'the demands of justice forbid the exercise of mercy'.[185] Arthur's speech is a version of this rhetoric, but the narrative in which the speech is placed makes the situation feel more perplexed and perplexing than the Queen's assured cadences had implied.

---

[184] H. Tennyson, *Memoir*, i. 431.   [185] *The Times*, 6 Dec. 1858, 7b.

The 'flaming death' to which Arthur refers above has an analogue in Malory, but where Malory had the king condemn the queen to be burnt to death, Tennyson lessens this severity by allowing Arthur's wrath to pass. The literary revision carries a political charge when we learn that this form of revenge had been widely canvassed by public figures in England soon after the Mutiny occurred. In May 1857, for instance, John Nicholson demanded that parliamentary voices supported his idea for 'a Bill for the flaying alive, impalement, or burning of the murderers of the women and children at Delhi'. Tennyson's revision shows a concern about how such acts of revenge could render the British people a part of what they denounced.

Political events in King Arthur's lands, as in India, are never quite divested of the religious antipathies between the ruling state and its colonies that had helped to foster its wars. The queen's proclamation had also announced Britain's apparent shift away from imperial aggression and religious reform: 'We desire no extension of our present territorial possessions . . . Firmly relying ourselves on the truth of Christianity, and acknowledging with gratitude the solace of religion, we disclaim alike the right and the desire to impose our convictions on any of our subjects.'[186] Tennyson may have been 'full' of this proclamation in late 1858, but when preparing 'Guinevere' and the other idylls for the press in 1859 there are hints that he is moving in another direction: 'I am at present correcting proofs which are a vile nuisance to me, excited as I am about national matters.'[187]

National matters put the proofs to the test, for when Tennyson returns to Arthur's last speech, the religious agenda behind the king's imperial ambitions is made clearer even as we are also asked to hear slight glitches in his oratory:

> I made them lay their hands in mine and swear
> To reverence the King, as if he were
> Their conscience, and their conscience as their King,
> *To break the heathen and uphold the Christ,*
> To ride abroad redressing human wrongs,
> To speak no slander, no, nor listen to it,
> *To honour his own word as if his God's.*

(ll. 464–70; my emphasis)

The opening lines emphasize the Arthur-as-conscience analogy that Tennyson often remarked upon, but 'I made them' and 'as if he were' suggest that the analogy might be open to dispute.[188] The extra syllable in the penultimate line ('no') is a tremulous as well as forceful insistence (perhaps Guinevere was

---

[186] Ibid.   [187] *TL*, ii. 224.
[188] On the instability of the poem's 'parabolic drift', see Reynolds, *Realms of Verse*, 252–3.

about to interrupt Arthur's flow), and the Laureate himself was not always sure where the king's speeches were going. The first italicized line was added when the poet corrected the proofs, and the last appeared in the 1873 Library edition of his works.[189] Both lines are at odds with the tenor of the queen's proclamation, and underline the shifting political alliances of Tennyson's *Idylls* as he composes them. While 'Geraint and Enid' expresses concern over imperialist militarism, 'Guinevere' has less time for such hesitancy as threats to Britain's imperial mission begin to accumulate in the political world from which Tennyson's poem takes its bearings. Both idylls are responsive to contemporary realities, but structural integration between and within them is put under pressure as a result of such responsiveness. That is, the speeches in the poem invite and ward off a sense of it as a sustained political allegory in support of acts conducted in the name of empire.

'To *break* the heathen': Tennyson's poem cannot shake off the sound of this word and its cognates, and as the epic continues it finds itself gravitating towards less purposive voices. The queen's proclamation in 'Guinevere' hints at where Tennyson's imagination is tending:

> Then she stretched out her arms and cried aloud
> 'Oh Arthur!' there her voice brake suddenly,
> Then—as a stream that spouting from a cliff
> Fails in mid air, but gathering at the base
> Re-makes itself, and flashes down the vale—
> Went on in passionate utterance:
> > 'Gone—my lord!
> Gone through my sin to slay and to be slain!
> And he forgave me, and I could not speak.
>
> > (ll. 602–9)

Eric Griffiths notes of the epic simile in this passage ('an old token of rhetorical mastery') that 'Tennyson's skill interposes itself in the gaps of Guinevere's utterance', but adds that his imagination also stops him 'from "spouting" himself in these lines because his skill inhabits her broken voice'.[190] Indeed, the poem is full of speechifiers mouthing 'O's in an effort to rise to the grand style; but this is the only occasion in Tennyson's epic that somebody says 'Oh'. The 'Oh' is an 'O' weighed down with grief—the breaking voice is embodied in the breaking of a typographic rule. In addition, we might expect a stream to 'fall' rather than to 'fail' in mid-air, but Guinevere feels that she has failed Arthur through her fall; it's as though the narrator's own way with words

---

[189] Tennyson, *A Variorum Edition of Tennyson's Idylls of the King*, ed. John Pfordresher (New York: Columbia University Press, 1973), 946.

[190] Griffiths, *Printed Voice*, 105.

has taken on something of the character's internal torment. And when the queen does gather herself up for speech, Tennyson's isolated placement of 'Gone—my lord!' encourages us to think that this is finally the longed-for vocative, that the queen is calling out, and that there may still be another chance for the couple and the political security that their marriage was meant to embody. But, reading the subsequent lines, we realize that 'my lord' is a third-person description, not a second-person address. When the queen sees Arthur ride through the mist 'to slay and to be slain', the vicious circularity of her phrasing reminds us of an uncomfortable truth that Tennyson's epic has been nervously probing: an affection for an 'imperial-moulded form' has set this train of events in motion. Aggression in the name of imperial security might, it seems, be seen as both the model and the catalyst for the violence it deplores in its colonies.

From 'break' the *Idylls* move inexorably towards 'broken': after the Duke of Argyll had read the 1859 collection, he composed his own poetic tribute, praising the Laureate for creating a 'Strong human voice' that could still allow space for 'broken accents'.[191] Guinevere's accents echo through the *Idylls* like a steadily loudening death-knell, turning its own oratorical strains into strainings. The poet manages to hold the sound of the word 'broken' at bay throughout his epic, never allowing its trochaic contours to rupture the beginning of a line, but in 'The Last Tournament' (1871)—a poem that repeats the phrase 'broken music' five times within ten lines (ll. 258–67)—'broken' finally takes control of the line-opening to disrupt the music of the verse. Not once, but three times, and just at those moments when the narrator seeks desperate shelter in euphony:

> The *h*eathen are upon *h*im, *h*is *l*ong *l*ance
> Broken, and his Excalibur a straw . . .
> He *saw* the *laws* that ruled the *tour*nament
> Broken, but spake not . . .
> Flatter *me* rather, *seeing me* so weak,
> Broken with Mark and hate and solitude.
>
> (ll. 87–8, 160–1, 637–8; my emphasis)

The alliterative and assonantal finish of the first lines is met by 'Broken', and the breaking of the epic's stately voice is accompanied by a growing sense that imperial endeavour carries within it the seeds of the savagery that it is attempting to overcome.

---

[191] George Campbell (Duke of Argyll), *Autobiography and Memoirs*, 2 vols. (London: John Murray, 1906), ii. 573.

Remembering the shock that the Indian Mutiny gave to British confidence, the Duke of Argyll lamented: 'The savage slaughter of the officers came at the end of years of sympathy and affection.'[192] The phrasing contains an unwitting ambiguity, for 'the slaughter *of* the officers' could refer to the atrocities committed by them as well as to those that they suffered. The Cawnpore massacre had been covered by *The Times* in leaders that dwelt on atrocities with unprecedented directness: '[The mutineers] killed all ladies, and threw the children alive, as well as the ladies' dead bodies, into a well in the compound . . . Children have been compelled to eat the quivering flesh of their murdered parents, after which they were literally *torn asunder* by the laughing fiends who surrounded them.'[193]

Such reports became the staple of public speeches that demanded retribution; as Ronald Hyam points out: 'The Cawnpore massacre gave sanction to a retributive savagery which is one of the most shameful episodes in British history.'[194] The voices of the orators calling for revenge haunted Tennyson, and when he finally allowed them into his poem, it was to emphasize the violence of the colonizer rather than the colonized. In 'The Last Tournament', Arthur's imperial project meets with an imperious disobedience; the king insists that his knights do not seek revenge for a mutinous uprising, but they disobey his orders. Looking to the East, the horrors of the Indian Mutiny are recalled; only now it is the imperial state's violence that is given prominence. *The Times* had paused to note 'two-inches of blood on the pavement',[195] and Tennyson remembered this detail among others:

> [they] roared
> And shouted and leapt down upon the fallen;
> There trampled out his face from being known,
> And sank his head in mire, and slimed themselves:
> Nor heard the King for their own cries, but sprang
> Through open doors, and swording right and left
> Men, women, on their sodden faces, hurled
> The tables over and the wines, and slew
> Till all the rafters rang with woman-yells,
> And all the pavement streamed with massacre:
> Then, echoing yell with yell, they fired the tower,
> Which half that autumn night, like the live North,
> Red-pulsing up through Alioth and Alcor,
> Made all above it, and a hundred meres
> About it, as the water Moab saw

---

[192] George Campbell (Duke of Argyll), *Autobiography and Memoirs*, 82.
[193] *The Times*, 17 Sept. 1857, 9c.
[194] Hyam, *Britain's Imperial Century*, 224.   [195] *The Times*, 17 Sept. 1857, 9c.

Come round by the East, and out beyond them flushed
The long low dune, and lazy-plunging sea.

So all the ways were safe from shore to shore,
But in the heart of Arthur pain was lord.

(ll. 467–85)

'Saddest of all Victorian epics', Herbert Tucker observes, 'the *Idylls* in their gloomy analytic coherence shadow with equal plangency the losses that empire exacts and the downfall that awaits it.'[196] Such passages refuse to turn away from counting those losses, as the breathless pace of the violence, accentuated by verbs at the end of run-on lines ('sprang', 'hurled', 'slew', 'saw', 'flushed'), is matched by its savagery. Like the other verbs, 'slew' initially seems transitive, but the grammatical shock as we veer into the next line gives gruesome voice to the indiscriminate nature of the killing. What we are asked to dwell on, though, is the monosyllabic drag of the last two lines, isolated on the page, for it is here where imperial supremacy counts the cost of the 'safety' it creates. The callous efficiency of 'So' is almost parodic ('so they all lived happily ever after'), before the 'But' records a heartbeat that has become distempered by the order it has established.

Idylls of the King blends the voice of the 'Public Orator' with that of the broken-hearted observer, and Tennyson worried that his public would listen only to selected aspects of its compound music. Complaining about the forthcoming publication of 'Guinevere', he wrote: 'I know not when . . . it can be made public. Why should it, as I think and fear it may do, in these many tongued days, come out parcel-wise in misquoted quotation.'[197] Volubility is again the marker of a public by which the poet's conception is threatened and to which it frequently has to adapt. Tennyson was right to be nervous, for he would often find words taken out of his mouth during his Laureateship, especially by the orators themselves.

In 1876, a series of massacres by the Turks in the Ottoman province of Bulgaria was publicized in the British press. As Richard Shannon explains, the intensity of the public's indignation was 'derived from a special sense of guilt and complicity created by the pro-Turkish policy of the British government . . . the cause of Turkey had come to be identified predominantly with the maintenance of British Imperial interests'.[198] Gladstone led the charge against the government's inaction, and his combined use of pamphlet and

---

[196] Herbert Tucker, 'Epic', in Richard Cronin, Anthony H. Harrison, and Alison Chapman (eds.), *A Companion to Victorian Poetry* (Oxford: Blackwell, 2002), 25–41, p. 32.

[197] *TL*, ii. 220.

[198] Richard Shannon, *Gladstone and the Bulgarian Agitation 1876* (London: Thomas Nelson, 1963), 15, 17.

platform made his intervention one of the focal points in the history of Victorian public speaking. His pamphlet caused a sensation, selling 40,000 copies within the first four days of publication and 200,000 within the month. In his peroration, the 'great orator' once again reached for his confident 'we', and also took the liberty of inserting a snippet of one of Tennyson's printed speeches into his polemic:

Better, we may justly tell the Sultan, almost any inconvenience, difficulty, or loss associated with Bulgaria,

> 'Than thou reseated in thy place of light,
> The mockery of thy people, and their bane'.[199]

Gladstone is quoting from Arthur's speech to Guinevere (ll. 522–3), one of the two speeches he had praised in his review of Tennyson as 'wonderful . . . They will not bear mutilation: they must be read, and pondered, to be known.'[200] But the politician does mutilate Arthur's speech here by changing the original 'my' to 'thy' in the last line. This 'thy' evades a sense of British imperial possessiveness and complicity. In addition, while a call for honourable intervention may necessitate a distance from the Turkish actions, Gladstone's '*almost* any inconvenience, difficulty, or loss' smacks of shilly-shally in the very act of attack. '[A]lmost' begs the question of how far he is actually prepared to go in order to redress such grievances if it means compromising Britain's imperial authority.[201] Moreover, we have already seen how Arthur's speeches in 'Guinevere' clearly registered an ambivalence over imperial possession and aggression (and how the king's mixture of self-reproach and self-command was registered in his use of possessive pronouns). Gladstone is tub-thumping, but Arthur did not sound so simply righteous; indeed, the king immediately follows the words that Gladstone quotes with a change of heart and direction: 'Yet think not that I come to urge thy crimes, | I did not come to curse thee, Guinevere' (ll. 529–30). This is the first time he has called her by her name, shifting the tone from the 'mockery' of 'thou' to a more intimate verbal caress. Gladstone is trying to evade the discomforting issues that surround these imperious and imperial musings; Tennyson's poem is drawn to staging them.

---

[199] William Gladstone, *Bulgarian Horrors and the Question of the East* (London: Murray, 1876), 62.

[200] Gladstone, 'Review of *Poems*', 477.

[201] Shannon notes the 'strong element of opportunism' in the campaign (*Gladstone*, 110–11); H. C. G. Matthew points out that Gladstone resorted to 'very weak' arguments for non-intervention once he was back in power: 'A reconciliation between the "equal rights of all nations" and the requirements of international order was a highly problematic duty for the Liberal Prime Minister of an imperial power' (*Gladstone, 1809–1878* (Oxford: Clarendon Press, 1997), 376).

In the Epilogue to the *Idylls*, the poet bemoaned the loss of 'the tone of empire' (l. 18) in public rhetoric, but the ominous, burdened cadence of his poem's narrative voice had itself helped to infuse his tone with other concerns. The poet was rarely comfortable with the idea of his being a spokesman, or of his poems as versified speeches that might be slipped easily into ministers' orations. He accepted a literary peerage from Gladstone in 1883—'a historic moment in the recognition by the British state of the claims on it of the world of letters'[202]—but while Gladstone expected Tennyson to vote as a Liberal peer, the poet signalled his intent when he was introduced into the House by taking up a seat on the cross-benches. His later work refused to toe the party line, and when Gladstone reviewed 'Locksley Hall Sixty Years After' in 1887, he was discomforted by its glum refusal to accede to the charm of the 'Orator' (l. 112).

The Prime Minister felt that Lord Tennyson should be hymning the positive aspects of Victorian culture; he accordingly began by complaining about 'a want of tone and fibre' in Tennyson's poem, and ended with the grand assertion that 'Justice does not require, nay rather she forbids, that the Jubilee of the Queen be marred by tragic tones'.[203] But, given that he was speaking to a divided as well as a united public, Tennyson considered it a duty to include more than one tone in his poetry. Despite his registering of the fact that 'some are scared, who mark, | Or wisely or unwisely, signs of storm', the Epilogue to the *Idylls* had closed with a 'poet's blessing' and 'his trust' (ll. 46–9). However, that 'trust' and those 'signs of storm' are returned to in a poem that responds to Gladstone's article, and that stands as an achieved example of Tennyson's reticent eloquence, his ode 'On the Jubilee of Queen Victoria' (1887). As T. S. Eliot once remarked, Tennyson is 'the saddest of all English poets . . . the most instinctive rebel against the society in which he was the most perfect conformist'.[204] This mixture of rebellion and conformity can be heard in the sounds of his ode.

In his reviews of Tennyson's work, Gladstone urged the Laureate to keep an end in sight: the poet should, like the orator, speak clearly in view of a particular goal. Tennyson had a much less assured sense of the ends of poetic speech, of endings, and of the word 'end' itself. It is as though the word inspires in him a divided impulse: nearly half his lines that feature 'end' place it at the end of the line; yet, in most of these instances, the end of the line is not the end of the sentence.[205] For Tennyson, then, the 'end' is frequently something evermore about to be, and the end of his Jubilee ode

---

[202] Richard Shannon, *Gladstone: Heroic Minister* (London: Penguin, 1999), 320.
[203] William Gladstone, ' "Locksley Hall" and the Jubilee', *Nineteenth Century*, 21 (Jan. 1887), 1–18, pp. 1, 18.
[204] Eliot, 'In Memoriam', 337.
[205] See Arthur Baker (ed.), *A Concordance to the Poetical and Dramatic Works of Alfred, Lord Tennyson* (London: Kegan Paul, 1914), 176.

draws out the political implications of this unfinished yet purposive craft. The poem begins by following Gladstone's lead, honouring the fifty years 'Since our Queen assumed the globe, the sceptre' (l. 3), and rejoicing 'At this glad Ceremonial | And this year of her Jubilee' (ll. 37–8). Sceptres and ceremonials have their place, but Tennyson decided to end the poem with something more than a sound bite:

> Are there thunders moaning in the distance?
> Are there spectres moving in the darkness?
> Trust the Hand of Light will lead her people,
> Till the thunders pass, the spectres vanish,
> And the Light is Victor, and the darkness
> Dawns into the Jubilee of the Ages.
>
> (ll. 66–71)

John Bayley has suggested that Tennyson's poetry 'is instinct with incongruities all the more compelling for not being overt',[206] and these lines hold implicit provocations. Tennyson's ear, as so often, bespeaks his capacious mind; for being jubilant about achievement involves an awareness of how the power of the 'sceptre' can glide into the presence of 'spectres', and how behind the 'ceremonial'—if one listens carefully enough—one can hear 'moaning'. The last two lines also break the end-stopped pattern of the stanza's previous lines in order that the reader might register the oddity of 'darkness | Dawns': 'day', 'morning', or 'light' normally 'dawns', not 'darkness'. It's as though the darkness is no longer quite so firmly in the distance, as though it replaces 'the Light' rather than being dissipated by it. The syntax seems to drag its heels against the force of the imagined victory.

In Tennyson's poems, judgements—like sounds—are often transitive. Edgar Allan Poe observed of Tennyson that 'he has neglected to make precise investigation of the principles of metre; but, on the other hand, so perfect is his rhythmical instinct in general, that . . . he seems *to see with his ear*'.[207] In the last line of his Jubilee ode, in contrast to the confident last sentence of Gladstone's article, Tennyson creates a minute rhythmical lapse, adding an extra syllable ('the') to disrupt the steadily falling rhythms of the trochaics he had been so careful to establish in the earlier lines.[208] The last line is exemplary in more than just its syllable count; the previous lines never go beyond a

---

[206] John Bayley, 'Tennyson and the Idea of Decadence', in Hallam Tennyson (ed.), *Studies in Tennyson*, (London: Macmillan, 1981), 186–205, p. 202.

[207] Edgar Allan Poe, 'The Poetic Principle', cited in Jump (ed.), *Tennyson: Critical Heritage*, 418.

[208] One might read 'th'Ages' in order to elide the syllable, but the rhythmic tremor would still be audible.

disyllabic word, nor do any of these disyllables begin with an unstressed syllable ('Jubilee' and 'into' break with this prosodic ceremony). These tiny fractures of poetic decorum insist upon the integrity of a public speech that refuses to become too eloquent, too polished, through an appeal to 'Trust'.

William Allingham once noticed 'a peculiar *incomplete* cadence at the end' when the poet read his work aloud.[209] The cadence suits a poet who mulls over the ends of speech, and his last words here speak of the difficulty of smooth perorations, as his 'seeing with his ear' involves a mediation between the aspiring and the apprehensive. For the Laureate, sound political judgement was also a matter of judging sounds. Keeping a civil tongue in his head required a negotiation between a self that has a right to its own peculiar accents and a self that speaks for the people in a voice not entirely its own.

[209] William Allingham, *William Allingham's Diary*, introd. Geoffrey Grigson (Fontwell: Centaur Press, 1967), 158.

4

Joyce's Breathing Space

GOVERNING THE TONGUE

In 1890, news broke of Charles Parnell's affair with Mrs Katharine O'Shea. Parnell was the leader of the Irish Parliamentary Party, and a meeting was called in Dublin to give a demonstration of support for the Chief. Tim Healy, soon to prove himself one of the most gifted and influential orators in the party, stood up and asked:

Is it now in this moment within sight of the promised land that we are to be asked to throw our entire organisation back once more into the melting pot? . . . Were Mr Parnell tomorrow to resign his seat for Cork would he not be instantly re-elected? . . . If we joined in with this howling pack would that be a noble spectacle before the nations (cheers)?[1]

The second question raises an option by pretending to consider it unnecessary: although Healy claims to be against those calling for Parnell's head, he is insinuating the possibility that the leader might stand down. Most of the audience missed the orator's ruse, but one member of the crowd spotted it: Joyce's father stood up and shouted, 'You're an imposter! You're only waiting for the moment to betray him!,' before being forcibly removed from the hall as he continued to protest.[2]

This interruption was prescient, as Healy would turn on the Chief and lead the anti-Parnellite faction of the Irish party. Joyce Senior's ability to read between the lines of Healy's artful appeal to 'we' (apparently against the 'pack', yet archly working to foster a pack mentality) was a result of the listener's suspicion of rhetorical posturing, but this suspicion was itself built on his attraction to political oratory. Once an aspiring politician, John Joyce had been elected Secretary of the Liberal Club in 1878, and his volubility during

---

[1] *Freeman's Journal*, 21 Nov. 1890.
[2] Richard Ellmann, *James Joyce*, rev. edn. (Oxford: Oxford University Press, 1983), 33; *Evening Telegraph*, 21 Nov. 1890.

the 1880 election helped to see both Liberal candidates returned for the first time in Dublin's history. In 1885 it was even suggested that John might stand as an electoral candidate alongside his hero, Parnell.[3]

These voices haunted James Joyce's acoustic imagination; his first composition, 'Et Tu, Healy', seized on his father's appetite for direct address (Stanislaus Joyce referred to the poem as an 'echo' of the 'political rancours' that surrounded the artist as a young man).[4] John would later say that he was proud of his son because 'he could hold his own on a platform'.[5] 'I often told Jim to go for the Bar', he reminisced, 'for he had a great flow of language and he speaks better than he writes.'[6] From *Dubliners* to *Finnegans Wake*, Joyce's flow of language is marked by a particular attention to oratorical display; this display is a source of his writing's energy, and a threat to its endeavour. When Healy speaks of a '*howling* pack' as a '*spectacle* before the nations', his curious translation of sound into sight is a microcosm of recurring Joycean preoccupations: the relationships between ear and eye, hearing and reading. Joyce was frequently drawn to the idea that his print might turn 'howling' into 'spectacle', and that such a transformation could be a political contribution to the life of his nation.

Oratory was a national obsession as well as a family hand-me-down. Since the Act of Union that saw Irish politicians enter Westminster in 1801, more governments were defeated on Irish issues than on any other topic debated in the Commons.[7] Growing Irish demands for 'Home Rule' (the creation of a subsidiary Irish parliament within the United Kingdom) led to calculated disruptions of business at Westminster until these demands were met: the obstructive tactics honed to a fine art by Parnell's Irish party were reliant on oratorical fluency. By 1893, Henry Lucy could observe that 'all Parliamentary roads lead to Ireland',[8] while the *Fortnightly Review* grumbled about the 'disastrous Irish speciality . . . oratory', and noted that members now talked more 'than even Irishmen had talked since the beginning of human speech'.[9] Prolixity became a weapon in the fight for political

[3] John Wyse Jackson and Peter Costello, *John Stanislaus Joyce: The Voluminous Life and Genius of James Joyce's Father* (London: Fourth Estate, 1997), 84, 87, 134.

[4] Stanislaus Joyce, *My Brother's Keeper: James Joyce's Early Years*, ed. Richard Ellmann (New York: Viking, 1958), 45.

[5] Cited in Mary and Patrick Colum, *Our Friend James Joyce* (New York: Doubleday, 1958), 78.

[6] John Joyce, cited in Robert Scholes and Richard M. Kain (eds.), *The Workshop of Daedalus: James Joyce and the Raw Materials for A Portrait of the Artist as a Young Man* (Evanston, Ill. Northwestern University Press, 1965), 123.

[7] Brian Farrell (ed.), *The Irish Parliamentary Tradition* (Dublin: Gill & Macmillan, 1973), 23.

[8] Henry Lucy, *Diary of the Home Rule Parliament, 1892–1895* (London: Cassell, 1896), 38.

[9] Anon., 'The Rhetoricians of Ireland', *Fortnightly Review*, 54 (1 Dec. 1893), 713–27, pp. 713, 718.

freedom, and the example of the Irish MPs was followed by those outside Parliament.[10]

For some, the fall of Parnell and the subsequent split of the party demonstrated the inefficacy of a parliamentary solution to the Irish question; for others, Irish garrulity indicated an eloquence that was self-defeating on account of its self-promotions. Standish O'Grady felt that the Irish were 'stupefied by too much oratory',[11] while D. P. Moran lamented ' "Speeches from the Dock" and all that . . . We are happy on the strength of one another's bombast.'[12] Moran observed that Irish public speaking had been corrupted 'into one string of uncomplimentary adjectives applied to the English, and another string of an opposite description applied to Ireland'.[13] If oratory conjured community into being and enhanced the possibility of nationalist progress in Ireland, it also served as a distraction from, and as a simplification of, the problems that the country faced. Dublin was at the centre of these debates about debate; Irish papers contained ample reports of nationalist oratory, and the city was the second largest distribution centre for *The Times* after London. A contemporary recalled one of the capital's favourite pastimes—reading, reciting, and discussing fragments of public speeches—and declared that 'the city was oral as no other in Western Europe was'.[14]

Joyce could be scathing about Dublin's orality—a 'race of charlatans . . . That is why the English Parliament is full of the greatest windbags in the world'[15]—but in his public speeches he spoke approvingly of what the Irish penchant for 'endless speeches' could achieve in the socio-political realm, whilst also acknowledging that, 'though the Irish are eloquent, a revolution is not made of human breath'.[16] His journalism also displays a qualified regard for Ireland's way with words; the country, 'poor in everything else . . . rich solely in political ideas, perfected the tactics of obstructionism', and yet, 'listening again to the speeches [of Parnell] . . . it is useless to deny that all the eloquence and all those triumphs of strategy begin to smell stale'.[17] This reflects the disillusionment of the post-Parnellian generation with parliamentarianism, yet the grudging concession and the fact that Joyce feels that he is 'listening again' (not 'reading again') suggests that his mind's ear continues to be drawn by the potential of such voices. In addition, other nationalisms were beginning to make themselves heard—Douglas Hyde's

---

[10] See Philip H. Bagenal, *The Irish Agitator in Parliament and on the Platform* (Dublin: Hodges, Foster & Figgis, 1880), 107.

[11] Standish O'Grady, *The Story of Ireland* (London: Methuen, 1893), 181.

[12] D. P. Moran, *The Philosophy of Irish Ireland* (Dublin: James Duffy, 1905), 24, 15.

[13] Moran, 'The Battle of Two Civilizations' (1901), cited in David Pierce (ed.), *Irish Writing in the Twentieth Century: A Reader* (Cork: Cork University Press, 2000), 34.

[14] Colum and Colum, *Our Friend*, 57.   [15] Cited in Ellmann, *James Joyce*, 217.

[16] *JCW*, 168, 174.   [17] Ibid. 195, 226.

Gaelic League, Moran's espousal of an 'Irish Ireland' in *The Leader*, Arthur Griffith's Sinn Féin movement—although, as Paul Bew has observed, aspects of the new nationalism were open to the charge of being 'increasingly exclusive, introspective and intolerant: the emotional mirror-image, albeit understandably, in certain important respects, of the "imperialism" it sought to replace'.[18]

Joyce's appreciation of how these nationalisms could act as 'counterparts' to imperialism, as well as resistances to it, has been well documented.[19] Joseph Valente envisages Joyce's characteristic impetus as trans-national, and defines his 'aesthetic project' in these terms: 'to transcend the ideological limits of so-called national culture or art, unfolding the hybrid and contradictory elements of Irish life in ever more capacious designs, but to contrive against losing the local and, yes, national particularity of those elements in elevating them to the dignity of the universal'.[20] This balancing act requires a nuanced sense of how appeals to a national community might be both coercive and constructive. One way of appreciating the significance of Joyce's designs is to focus on the lines of convergence and divergence between his work and Irish oratory, for it was through oratory—a medium that draws on and is drawn to collectives—that Irish nationalism made its most potent as well as its most specious appeals.[21] The trajectory of Joyce's writing career would be governed by the search for an eloquence that could unite without producing a false or pernicious homogeneity, and that could acknowledge and explore difference without being merely divisive. As he put it in one of his own speeches, 'Our civilization is a vast fabric, in which the most diverse elements are mingled . . . Nationality . . . must find its reason for being rooted in something that surpasses and transcends and informs changing things like blood and the human word.'[22]

Joyce's quest for this 'something' is thrown into sharper relief by pausing on the difficulties that Yeats had when attempting to adumbrate the relation of literary craft to rhetorical conflict: 'out of the quarrel with others we

---

[18] Paul Bew, *Conflict and Conciliation in Ireland, 1890–1910: Parnellites and Radical Agrarians* (Oxford: Clarendon Press, 1987), 6.

[19] See Vincent J. Cheng, *Joyce, Race, and Empire* (Cambridge: Cambridge University Press, 1995); Leo Platt, *Joyce and the Anglo-Irish: A Study of Joyce and the Literary Revival* (Atlanta: Rodopi, 1998); and Derek Attridge and Majorie Howes (eds.), *Semicolonial Joyce* (Cambridge: Cambridge University Press, 2000).

[20] Joseph Valente, 'Joyce's Politics: Race, Nation, and Transnationalism', in Jean-Michael Rabaté (ed.), *Palgrave Advances in James Joyce Studies* (Basingstoke: Palgrave Macmillan, 2004), 73–96, pp. 87, 95.

[21] There is, of course, another form of oratory that Joyce is drawn to in his work: the sermon. See Cheryl Herr, *Joyce's Anatomy of Culture* (Urbana and Chicago: University of Illinois Press, 1986), 222–55.

[22] *JCW*, 165–6.

make rhetoric; out of the quarrel with ourselves we make poetry. Unlike the rhetoricians, who get a confident voice from remembering the crowd they have won or may win, we sing amid our uncertainty.'[23] The distinction is a valuable one, but Yeats's voice is itself confident, and the rhetorical appeal to 'we' and 'our' is intent on addressing and winning us over as a crowd (the pronouns also make it unclear where 'ourselves' end and where 'others' begin). Yeats's love affair with the rhetorical was more enduring (and more quarrelsome) than his renowned formulation might suggest; he hoped 'to find in Ireland an uncorrupted & imaginative audience trained to listen by its passion for oratory', but he was also anxious lest such passion corrupt the imaginative impulse: 'the Irishman of our times' so deeply loves 'ready talking, effective speaking to crowds, that he has no thought for the arts which consume the personality in solitude'.[24] In Yeats's letter to the *United Ireland*, the oscillations are heard again:

Though fondness for oratory is inevitable and necessary in a country like Ireland, it is none the less a danger and a cause of many evils . . . Too often there are none but certainties in the world of the orator . . . We are a nation of orators, and must suffer the defects of our quality with a good grace, but . . . Is not our social life ruined by the oratorical person . . . his scorn of delicate half lights and quiet beauty[?][25]

But Yeats, so often drawn to the role of combative spokesman and leader, was to become senator as well as sage. 'Rhetoric' may be the enemy, but the poet was frequently given to the rhetorical question—as seen in the quotation above, and in a speech delivered in 1914: 'I have been driven into public life—how can I avoid rhetoric?'[26]

The young Joyce was a cautiously admiring reader of Yeats and of the *United Ireland*, so when he asked his own questions of the poet on their first meeting, he was quarrelling with himself as well as with others. Yeats recalled: 'He asked me "Why did I make speeches? Why did I concern myself with politics?" '[27] The queries voice a distance, but they also intimate a closeness, for Joyce too was aiming to forge a public speech that could concern itself with politics without reducing the artist to a mere mouthpiece of one nationalist

[23] W. B. Yeats, 'Anima Hominis' (1917), repr. in *Mythologies* (London: Macmillan, 1959), 331.

[24] Yeats, cited in R. F. Foster, *W. B. Yeats: A Life*, i: *The Apprentice Mage, 1865–1914* (Oxford: Oxford University Press, 1997), 184, 146.

[25] In *The Collected Letters of W. B. Yeats*, i: *1865–1895*, ed. John Kelly and Eric Domville (Oxford: Clarendon Press, 1986), 372–3.

[26] Yeats, speech at *Poetry* banquet, Chicago, 1 Mar. 1914; reported in *Inter-Ocean*, 2 Mar. 1914.

[27] Yeats, cited in Foster, *Apprentice Mage*, 276.

grouping. Hugh Kenner has observed that 'there were few things that could hold James Joyce's attention like the spectacle of a man speaking in public'.[28] Again, note the image of 'speaking' as 'spectacle': Joyce's writing, like Yeats's, took its bearings from 'the world of the orator', and the figures of speech in his work were indebted to one figure in particular.

Yeats acknowledged that Parnell was 'that lonely and haughty person below whose tragic shadow we of modern Ireland began to write'.[29] Joyce's imaginative investment in the Chief is well known.[30] Yet Parnell's principal bequest to the writer was a stylistic repertoire replete with political connotations, and despite the recent crop of readings of Joyce that mention his 'literary Parnellism',[31] or his being 'at heart a Fenian Parnellite',[32] or the fact that 'the shade of Parnell . . . haunts all of Joyce's texts',[33] there has been little consideration of how the shade finds its way into the shadings of his style. Joyce felt that Parnell was 'perhaps the most formidable man that ever led the Irish',[34] and his close reading of speeches and biographies alerted him to how this strength was expressed most eloquently through a studied avoidance of eloquence. He noted that Parnell's 'short and fragmentary speeches lacked eloquence, poetry, and humour', and that 'The applause and the anger of the crowd . . . never perturbed the melancholy serenity of his character'.[35] Parnell's oratory was built on a resistance to one version of the 'rhetorical': the stereotype of the fluent, fiery Irishman. 'There was nothing of rhetorical eloquence in his utterance . . . The epigrammatic brilliance, the emotional appeal with which one associates Irish oratory were almost wholly lacking.'[36] Parnell always spoke slowly, with little emphasis in his voice, and had a 'horror of speaking loudly'.[37] His first biographer noted that 'He took no pleasure in oratory'.[38] This resistance to crowd pleasing was precisely what pleased the

---

[28] Hugh Kenner, *Joyce's Voices* (London: Faber & Faber, 1978), 39.

[29] Yeats, cited in Foster, *Apprentice Mage*, 462.

[30] See Dominic Manganiello, *Joyce's Politics* (London: Routledge & Kegan Paul, 1980), 3–8, 14–23, 39.

[31] James Fairhall, *James Joyce and the Question of History* (Cambridge: Cambridge University Press, 1993), 43.

[32] Peter Costello, *James Joyce: The Years of Growth, 1882–1915* (London: Kyle Cathie, 1992), 99.

[33] Emer Nolan, *James Joyce and Nationalism* (London: Routledge, 1995), 131.

[34] *JCW*, 162.   [35] Ibid. 225.

[36] Claude G. Bowers, *The Irish Orators: A History of Ireland's Fight for Freedom* (Indianapolis: Bobbs-Merrill, 1916), 502.

[37] John Howard Parnell, *Charles Stewart Parnell: A Memoir* (London: Constable, 1916), 175–7.

[38] R. Barry O'Brien, *The Life of Charles Stewart Parnell, 1846–1891*, 2 vols. (London: Smith & Elder, 1898), i. 86.

crowds; Parnell's frequent asides—'it is not my fault if I cannot charm the multitude with gifts of oratory', 'I have never pretended in my public life to any eloquence or what is called oratorical power'[39]—inspired conviction through the speaker's very refusal to employ the usual Irish methods of convincing. He embodied an example rather than merely arguing a case; discussing Parnell's 'reticence and calm', one reporter suggested that 'the Irish believed in him because he possessed those negative qualities which they are without'.[40]

When Joyce's brother wrote that 'all his work is permeated by a kind of litotes which . . . signifies much more than it says',[41] and when John Macy observed that Joyce's stories imply a vast deal that is not said',[42] they seized on central aspects of his writing. Stephen Dedalus, for example, seems not only to think in litotes, but also to think about why he thinks in this way ('The corridor was dark and silent but not unwatchful. Why did he feel that it was not unwatchful?').[43] The implicatory understatement and litotes, in particular, were also vital parts of Parnell's orchestrated ambiguities, for such forms helped him to create room for manœuvre between the constitutional demands of his party and the more radical, potentially violent agitation of the Fenians and advanced nationalist groups. Parnell once noted that 'a true revolutionary movement in Ireland should . . . partake of both a constitutional and an illegal character',[44] and his speeches brought these dual allegiances into fruitful dialogue.[45] Litotes became a means of withstanding while drawing on the stridency of certain types of Fenian rhetoric.[46] A speech delivered in Dublin highlights this poise:

If our constitutional movement today is broken down, sundered, separated, discredited, and forgotten, England will be face to face with that imperishable force which tonight gives me my vitality and power (*loud and prolonged cheers*) . . . And if Ireland leaves this path upon which she has trodden until she is almost within sight of victory, I will not for my part say that I will not accompany her further (*cheers*); but I shall claim for myself the right which each one of you has to consider the future, to be warned by the mistakes of the past, and to shape his course as the side lights and

---

[39] *Freeman's Journal*, 28 Apr. and 6 June 1891.   [40] *Spectator*, 27 Dec. 1890.

[41] S. Joyce, *My Brother's Keeper*, 34.

[42] John Macy, 'James Joyce', *Dial*, June 1917, cited in Robert H. Deming (ed.), *James Joyce: The Critical Heritage*, 2 vols. (London: Routledge & Kegan Paul, 1970), i. 109.

[43] James Joyce, *A Portrait of the Artist as a Young Man*, ed. Jeri Johnson (Oxford: Oxford University Press, 2000), 155. Subsequent page references are given parenthetically in the text.

[44] Charles Parnell, cited in F. S. L. Lyons, *Charles Stewart Parnell* (London: HarperCollins, 1978), 106.

[45] See Conor Cruise O'Brien, *Parnell and his Party, 1880–90* (Oxford: Clarendon Press, 1957), 9–10.

[46] On litotes as a figure peculiarly adapted to judicious mediation between opposed impulses, see Freya Johnston, *Samuel Johnson and the Art of Sinking, 1709–1791* (Oxford: Oxford University Press, 2005), 165–81.

guide lights and head lights may best direct for the future success and prosperity of Ireland.[47]

'It is not a difficult thing to get an Irish crowd to cheer,' Moran once tittered.[48] However, one contemporary noted that Parnell had a way of 'constantly moderating a sweeping sentence that had been uproariously cheered . . . As one heard him . . . one felt that the standard for Irish public assertion was rising.'[49] In this speech, the standard is set when the cheers are followed by a 'but', as Parnell modulates his tone from the threatening to the thoughtful. Even his threat—couched in a contorted double negative ('I will not for my part say that I will not accompany her further')—intimates without committing to an abandonment of the constitutional solution to the Irish question.

Joyce admired how Parnell employed the hint of Fenian 'force' in his speeches as a way of 'treading on the verge of insurrection',[50] and the suppleness of this speech is palpable in the orator's very use of the word 'force': 'England will be face to face with that imperishable force which tonight gives me my vitality and power.' '[F]orce' refers to the orderly crowd, but Parnell also invests it with a glint of Fenian intent—a physical force movement to stand within and behind the mass of people who stand before him. '[F]ace to face' might sound figurative, yet—spoken before so many faces—it conjures up a literal scene, a threat of war-like numbers to resist English encroachment. The speaker also allows urgent collective callings and sober individual counsel to take the measure of one another. The opening appeal to 'our' movement is met by Parnell's sense of what he might 'claim for myself' and how another man might choose 'to shape his course' differently. That is, an initial resistance to 'sundering' and 'separation' finds room to accommodate other standpoints. The collective address refuses to elide or ignore differences, and—as so often in Parnell's oratory—the speech elaborates a cherished solitude amid a dream of community.

'If the young men of Ireland have trusted me it is because they know that I am not a mere parliamentarian,' Parnell observed in another speech.[51] Understatement again embodies poise: the Chief defends the parliamentary process even as he hints at its limitations. This stylistic balancing act was the vehicle for many other Parnellian emphases: his resistance to a supremacist Catholic Ireland via a defence of the pluralistic treatment of the Protestant minority (Parnell was himself a Protestant), his refusal to define Home Rule merely in terms of the working through of land purchase, his fight against

---

[47] *Freeman's Journal*, 17 Dec. 1890.
[48] Moran, *Philosophy of Irish Ireland*, 82.
[49] *Manchester Guardian*, 8 Oct. 1891.
[50] *JCW*, 227.
[51] *Freeman's Journal*, 22 Dec. 1890.

Irish clerical and English Liberal 'dictation' alike—all these stances offered a compound of principle and plurality for which Joyce was searching.[52] Parnell's speaking style itself encompassed this fusion, for his refusal merely to pander to the crowd as a homogeneous entity, his simultaneous mastery of and discomfort with the collective appeal, could be conceived as a template for how Ireland might speak to and of itself with more amplitude.

The orator's 'moderation of sweeping sentences' was also translated into the moderated action of his speaking body:

> I was much struck by his appearance when he spoke. He had one hand behind his back, which he kept closing and opening all the time. It was curious to watch the signs of nervous excitement and tension which one saw looking from the back, while in front he stood like a soldier on duty, frigid, impassive, resolute—not a trace of nervousness or emotion. He did not seem to care about putting himself in touch with his audience.[53]

Other reporters also highlighted the peculiar effectiveness of Parnell's suppressed emotion.[54] Touching the audience by not quite being 'in touch' with them, the orator asks his listeners to govern their enthusiasms through the way he attempts to govern his own. In doing so, he is not only an advocate; he becomes a catalyst by embodying a model of civic conduct. It was this model of self-government that Joyce set himself to emulate and explore in his own speaking and writing.

The Literary and Historical Society at University College Dublin, of which Joyce was a member, was one of Ireland's most important training grounds for orators. There was a ' "British House of Commons" atmosphere during debates'; the Society acted as a miniature parliament—a prelude to a career in Westminster, and a model of the parliament that nationalists hoped to see instituted in Ireland.[55] Recalling *St Stephen's* (the university magazine), one contemporary termed it 'our *Hansard*'.[56] This Hansard tended to report and discuss speeches from members of the growing Catholic movement. Moran's brand of Catholic cultural nationalism had a strong impact on the society during Joyce's university days; he appeared at several meetings and obtained a following among the most prominent orators there.[57] When Joyce voiced his

---

[52] See Frank Callanan, *The Parnell Split, 1890–91* (Cork: Cork University Press, 1992).

[53] Cited in R. B. O'Brien, *Life of Parnell*, ii. 178.

[54] See Alan O'Day, 'Parnell: Orator and Speaker', in George D. Boyce and Alan O'Day (eds.) *Parnell in Perspective* (London and New York: Routledge, 1991), 201–20.

[55] See Senia Paseta, *Before the Revolution: Nationalism, Social Change and Ireland's Catholic Elite, 1879–1922* (Cork: Cork University Press, 1999), 64.

[56] Cited in James Meenan (ed.), *Centenary History of the Literary and Historical Society of University College Dublin, 1855–1955* (Tralee: Kerryman, 1955), 46.

[57] See Willard Potts, *Joyce and the Two Irelands* (Austin: University of Texas Press, 2000), 30.

opinions in this parliament, it was clear that he 'did not seem to care about putting himself in touch with his audience'.

The writer's eloquence was deliberately shorn of magniloquence. Stanislaus recalled that he spoke slowly and—like Parnell—'without emphasis'.[58] Joyce referred to his speaking style as 'a tone of metallic clearness',[59] and he also adopted the Chief's signature tunes in other ways. In his journalism, when discussing Parnell's behaviour in the Commons, the writer remarked on his 'cold and formal bearing' and his composure when faced with 'the denunciations . . . of the British ministers'.[60] One contemporary remembered Joyce speaking in 'passionless tones' and remaining 'cold and undisturbed by interruptions (and he had many)'.[61] Joyce's first oration also saw him break 'parliamentary' rules, as he continued to speak for half an hour after the bell sounded—thus acting out his own kind of Parnellian obstructionism.[62]

The lack of declamatory emphasis in Joyce's public speaking is related to the suspicion of declamation that informs the subject of those speeches. In one, he questioned the idea of 'the votaries of the antique school' that art should merely 'to use their stock phrase . . . instruct, elevate, and amuse . . . . I do not say that drama may not fulfil any or all of these functions, but I deny that it is essential that it should fulfil them.'[63] The calculated resistance to the classical emphasis on the three duties of the orator—*docere, movere, delectare*—aims to keep art distinct from certain kinds of persuasive utterance. Joyce also suggested that an enabling approach to art is 'not to look for a message but to approach the temper which has made the work . . . to see what there is well done and how much it signifies'.[64] The distinction between what is 'signified' and a 'message' is a distinction between a literary politics that sounds things out and one that merely sounds off.

Such oratory may seem far removed from nationalist debates, but in both speeches Joyce was channelling Parnellian techniques and preoccupations into the cultural realm. The first counselled against eliding art with the 'sphere of religion', where it 'generally loses its true soul in stagnant quietism'; the second noted that his subject, 'James Clarence Mangan', was 'little of a patriot' and warned against a 'narrow and hysterical nationality'.[65] The resistance to 'dictation' from church and state was not missed by the predominantly Catholic nationalist crowd assembled before him. When Joyce looked out

---

[58] S. Joyce, *My Brother's Keeper*, 128.
[59] James Joyce, *Stephen Hero*, ed. Theodore Spencer, John J. Slocum, and Herbert Cahoon (New York: New Directions, 1963), 101. Subsequent page references are given parenthetically in the text.
[60] *JCW*, 225.   [61] Meenan (ed.), *Centenary History*, 69–70.
[62] See Scholes and Kain (eds.), *Workshop*, 151–2.   [63] *JCW*, 43.   [64] Ibid. 75.
[65] Ibid. 43, 76, 82.

into the house with his own form of 'melancholy serenity' and said that 'art cannot be governed by the insincerity of the compact majority',[66] he was both courting and criticizing the heckles he received from the compact majority seated before him. This oratorical stance was shaped by Parnell's example, and would in turn shape the dispassionate provocations of Joyce's prose—a governance of art indebted to a speaker who had learned to govern his tongue. In 1927, Italo Svevo noted that, if you looked closely enough, 'you see Joyce walking through the world with one sole comrade in faith, Parnell'.[67] Joyce's writing is the test and the fulfilment of that faith.

CROWD TROUBLE

One reviewer of *Dubliners* pleased Joyce by referring to the oddly compelling effect of a narrational voice that displayed 'the cold detachment of an unamiable god',[68] while Pound praised 'the curiously seductive interest of clear-cut and definite sentences' in his work.[69] Commentators on Parnell's oratory noted how his 'old-blooded, businesslike speeches . . . fired the people more than the wild rhetoric of some of his more inflammable colleagues'.[70] What Joyce termed Parnell's 'short and fragmentary speeches' and his 'cold and formal bearing' might be considered as an analogue for the poised coolness of his own short, fragmentary stories. His letters hint at potential conversings between speech and print; writing to a potential publisher of *Dubliners*, he insisted that 'the book be published by you not later than 6th October 1912'.[71] Joyce was fussy about dates, and this one meant that the book would be published not later than the twenty-first anniversary of Parnell's death, Ivy Day 1912. *Dubliners*, it was hoped, would come of age by making an elegant bow to its political forbear.[72]

The title of *Dubliners* suggests that the book offers itself as a form of political speech and as a written series. Joyce had spotted that a novel, *The Londoners*, had recently been published,[73] but by omitting a definite article from the title of his collection, he forged a rich ambiguity: *Dubliners* is an appellative, but it

---

[66] *JCW*, 44.

[67] Italo Svevo, cited in Livia Veneziani Svevo, *Memoir of Italo Svevo*, trans. Isabel Quigly (London: Libris, 1989), 154.

[68] Gerald Gould, cited in Deming (ed.), *James Joyce: The Critical Heritage*, i. 63.

[69] Ezra Pound, *Pound/Joyce: The Letters of Ezra Pound to James Joyce, with Pound's Essay on Joyce*, ed. Forrest Read (New York: New Directions, 1967), 135.

[70] R. B. O'Brien, *Life of Parnell*, i. 193.   [71] *JL*, ii. 310.

[72] For Joyce's interest in the structuring principle of twenty-one years, see *JCW*, 193–6.

[73] See *JL*, ii. 122; Robert Hichens, *The Londoners* (London: Heinemann, 1898).

could also be a vocative, a kind of call ('Friends, Dubliners, countrymen . . . '). The title, then, is a name and an address. Joyce envisaged the collection as a form of invocation: 'I am writing a series of epicleti—ten—for a paper. I call the series *Dubliners*.'[74] To 'call' them is not merely to name them, but to call upon them, for an epiclesis (part of the prayer of the Consecration) comes from the Greek meaning 'to call upon, to invoke'.

The oratorical inflections of the volume are also suggested by Joyce's renowned description of its style—a 'scrupulous meanness'.[75] From his scrupulous reading of Skeat's *Etymological Dictionary* (1882) and of Cicero's works, he would have known that the history of the word 'scruple' contained within it an oratorical flourish: Skeat cites the root as '*scrupule*, "a little sharp stone . . . in a mans shooe," . . . hence an uneasiness, difficulty, small trouble, doubt',[76] and the *OED* gives 'dim. of *scrupus* rough or hard pebble, used. fig. by Cicero for a cause of uneasiness of anxiety'. The word recalls an eloquent speaker, but it also reminds us that a truly scrupulous style should not be enamoured of its own eloquence, and should be drawn to entertain perplexities and doubts.[77] The *OED* sees in the word 'scrupulous' a combination of care ('minutely exact'), moral probity ('characterized by a strict and minute regard for what is right'), and tentativeness ('prone to hesitate or doubt')—three qualities that Joyce felt were lacking in much contemporary nationalist oratory. 'Meanness' hints at a mediatory as well as a severe style, for one *OED* definition is 'the condition of being between two extremes'. As well as 'coming between, intermediate . . . see Mediate', Skeat also suggests an etymology for 'mean' that takes us closer to *Dubliners'* sustained enquiry into the collective and the communal; 'common, general'[78] (the *OED* gives 'communion, fellowship' and 'land held in common'). The collection's title contains another aural pun that embodies 'the condition of being within two extremes'; *Dubliners* is a call to and description of a community, but it is also a chastisement and a judgement of the parochial nature of that community: Dublin errs.

Oratory creates and divides communities through the ministration and manipulation of crowds, and Joyce often registered a Parnellian dislike of collectives alongside an urgent need to find a way of influencing them.[79] He praised a depiction of one scene because 'To paint such a crowd one must

---

[74] *JL*, i. 55.   [75] Ibid. ii. 134.

[76] Walter W. Skeat, *An Etymological Dictionary of the English Language* (Oxford: Clarendon Press, 1882), 535.

[77] On Joyce's knowledge of Cicero, see R. J. Schork, *Latin and Roman Culture in Joyce* (Gainesville: University Press of Florida, 1997), 108–20.

[78] Skeat, *Etymological Dictionary*, 361.

[79] On modernism's relations with 'the crowd mind', see Michael Tratner, *Modernism and Mass Politics: Joyce, Woolf, Eliot, Yeats* (Stanford, Calif.: Stanford University Press, 1995).

probe humanity with no scrupulous knife',[80] and this combination of litotes and scrupulosity is characteristic of Joyce. He observed that 'the artist, though he may employ the crowd, is very careful to isolate himself'.[81] The mixture of employment and isolation was a crucial aspect of Parnell's speeches, and the mobile figure of the narrator in *Dubliners* might be conceived as a kind of literary orator—a speaker who, though not always directly making an appeal to us, is seeking to embody an indirect circumspection that may prompt a critical self-reflection in the audience. Indeed, the 'employment' of the crowd in *Dubliners* is particularly marked; although the shortest of Joyce's major works, in it the word 'crowd' appears more frequently than in any of the others.[82]

In 'A Little Cloud', Chandler passes through a little crowd: 'for the first time in his life he felt himself superior to the people he passed'.[83] And yet, this feeling soon shifts into another kind of impulse:

[He] pitied the poor stunted houses. They seemed to him a band of tramps, huddled together along the river-banks...He wondered whether he could write a poem to express his idea...If he could give expression to it in a book of poems perhaps men would listen. He would never be popular: he saw that. He could not sway the crowd but he might appeal to a little circle of kindred minds. (p. 55)

Chandler's imagination gravitates towards collective engagement. The 'book of poems' is conceived in terms that verge on the oratorical: 'perhaps men would *listen*' (not just 'read'); he 'might *appeal* to a little circle' ('appeal' also hints at vocal address). He is crossing Grattan Bridge as he indulges in his dream of eloquence (named after one of Ireland's most famous orators, whose name was associated with the pre-Union Irish House of Commons, 'Grattan's Parliament'). The location, then, may prompt Chandler's ambitions. Further, the idea that inspires Chandler's wonderings is an oratorical figure that turns a plural medley ('poor stunted houses') into a collective singular, a vignette of a crowd ('band of tramps'). Chandler is enacting the cherished ideals of the artist-orator embedded in the narratorial voice of *Dubliners*; at once a literary loner and an aspiring speaker, he shuns the crowd and reshapes his surroundings into crowd scenes.

This fragile epiphany is swamped by the other pressures in Chandler's life, and his story echoes the rhythm of the volume as a whole. The narrator often

---

[80] *JCW*, 35.   [81] Ibid. 69.

[82] 'Crowd' and its cognates appear twenty-three times in *Dubliners*, eight times in *A Portrait of the Artist as A Young Man*, twelve times in *Ulysses* (not including eighteen occasions in the 'Circe' episode where it is used merely as part of the machinery to designate who is speaking), and ten times in *Finnegans Wake*.

[83] James Joyce, *Dubliners*, ed. Jeri Johnson (Oxford: Oxford University Press, 2000), 55. Subsequent page references are given parenthetically in the text.

gives us glimpses of people who are trying to rise above the crowd, only to imply that they also need to be seen as involved in it. Such a negotiation frequently carries with it a political resonance; in 'Araby', we find ourselves in the middle of another crowd:

We walked through the flaring streets, jostled by drunken men and bargaining women, amid the curses of labourers, the shrill litanies of shop-boys who stood on guard by the barrels of pigs' cheeks, the nasal chanting of street-singers, who sang a *come-all-you* about O'Donovan Rossa, or a ballad about the troubles in our native land. These noises converged in a single sensation of life for me: I imagined that I bore my chalice safely though a throng of foes. (p. 20)

The speaker individuates himself by homogenizing the crowd (plural 'noises' converge into a 'single' sensation; different figures become a collective singular, a 'throng of foes'). The song he hears, in contrast, aims to draw him back into the crowd; a *come-all-you* (with its conventional opening line 'Come all you gallant Irishmen and listen to my song') is a musical oratory of sorts that seeks to draw the 'you' into community with 'all'. This one, sung in the character of the infamous Fenian speaker and agitator (nicknamed 'Dynamite Rossa') celebrates the violent separatist strand of Ireland's nationalist history, a history from which the boy sees himself removed by his passion for Mangan's sister. However, his casualness about the songs he hears belies a deeper commitment to their memory, for a phrase from the most well-known *come-all-you* about Rossa seeps into the prose here: 'My friends and me we did agree | Our native land to save.'[84] When the narrator refers to the troubles of 'our native land', his collective pronoun raises, without fully registering, the question of his own involvement in these troubles.

The boy imagines himself above nationalist address, but the narrator of the tale is plagued by oratorical demons that remind him how even his quest on behalf of Mangan's sister is influenced by the pressures of history. Critics have emphasized 'the patriotic hints in his devotions',[85] mainly by teasing out links between Mangan's sister and James Mangan's 'Dark Rosaleen' (1846), the girl who stood for the nation's woes in a lyric that mourned Ireland's subjection to England.[86] The poem was dear to Joyce (he wrote a musical accompaniment for it), so when Parnell's nemesis and the star speaker of the Irish Party, Tim Healy, stood up in the Commons a couple of years before 'Araby' was written and employed the poem for his own ends, the writer's ears would have pricked up.

[84] See Colm o Lochlainn, *Irish Street Ballads* (Dublin and London: Constable, 1939), 68.
[85] Donald T. Torchiana, *Backgrounds for Joyce's Dubliners* (Boston: Allen & Unwin, 1986), 62.
[86] See Heyward Ehrlich, ' "Araby" in Context: The "Splendid Bazaar," Irish Orientalism, and James Clarence Mangan', repr. in Joyce, *Dubliners*, ed. Margot Norris (New York: Norton, 2006), 261–82.

Healy's defence of the Land Purchase Act would become one of his most widely acclaimed speeches, largely on account of his peroration:

You cannot deal with this question merely as. . . £ s. d. It strikes hard a chord in the Irish character other than the sordid note of finance, it marks a reversal of a long period of dismal oppression and awful sorrow. . . This Bill will change more than Ireland, it will change England too, and with that change I hope to see a brighter light in the eyes of dark Rosaleen.[87]

Playing on 'note' to revise it from its economic context into part of a musical chord, Healy's vision of a brave new world played up the achievements of parliamentary nationalism, but talk of a 'reversal' obscured how 'the sordid note' would continue to be a crucial aspect of Anglo-Irish relations (in 1907 Joyce pointed out that 'the Irish Parliamentary party has gone bankrupt . . . the fruit of its agitation is that Irish taxes have gone up 88 million francs and the Irish population has decreased a million').[88]

In 'Araby', the quest for booty to lay at the feet of the boy's Dark Rosaleen ends at a bazaar where an Irish girl is beguiled by 'English accents' (p. 23) and where 'porcelain vases and flowered tea-sets' (p. 23) seem to be the only things on sale ('porcelain and tea, as commodities of the Far East trade . . . were obvious emblems of British economic colonialism').[89] The ending of Joyce's story recalls Healy's peroration on finance and 'the brighter light in the eyes of dark Rosaleen', but it transposes talk of money, eyes, darkness, and brightness into another register. The narrator insists on counting the specific cost of his situation in '£ s. d.':

I allowed the two pennies to fall against the sixpence in my pocket . . . the light was out. The upper part of the hall was now completely dark.
    Gazing up into the darkness I saw myself as a creature driven and derided by vanity; and my eyes burned with anguish and anger. (p. 24)

As so often in *Dubliners*, the ending of the tale refuses us the satisfactions of a smooth peroration. The boy will return with nothing to his Dark Rosaleen, and the brighter light in his eyes bespeaks something other than gratitude.

A few years before this tale was set, O'Donovan Rossa had spoken against English domination, uttering his usual refrain: 'I take no stock in Parliamentary agitation.'[90] By taking stock of Healy's emphasis on the parliamentary route to progress, it would seem that Rossa's ghost has come back to haunt this tale with an intimation of what may not be settled through these means. As we read the story in solitude, rather than being addressed as part of any

[87] *Hansard*, cxxii. 66 (7 May 1903).   [88] *JCW*, 195–6.
[89] Ehrlich, ' "Araby" in Context', 273.
[90] O'Donovan Rossa, cited in 'O'Donovan Rossa and Mr Parnell', *Irish Times*, 3 Jan. 1891.

single crowd, the narratorial voice allows us to reflect on the efficacy and limitations of different kinds of nationalist appeal, be they constitutional or Fenian. When Joyce spoke in public around this time about political advances that had been made in his homeland in the past, he observed that it was 'thanks partly to the endless speeches and partly to Fenian violence'.[91] 'Araby' does not take the 'part' of any one grouping (it is not *advocating* anything), but instead attempts to raise an enabling awareness of the complexity of the Irish troubles—economic as well as political. Hovering between the solitary absorption of a frustrated quest narrative and the collective stridency of a *come-all-you*, the tale picks the boy out of the crowd only to hint that he will return to it with a more nuanced appreciation of where those curses, litanies, chantings, and songs are coming from.

The embattled, laconic eloquence of *Dubliners* invites readers to sense community where they may at first glance have seen only division. Yet, Joyce's ruminating over crowds also explores how group mentalities can ignore fissures and frictions within their own structures, and how the unacknowledged fragility of such groupings can act as the impetus for intolerance. In many of the stories, the crowd acts to repress division and as a catalyst for divisiveness; Freud would later suggest that 'the social sense is based on reversing an initially hostile emotion to become a positively stressed attachment that has the character of an identification'.[92] That 'hostile emotion' does not evaporate; it reorients itself towards external targets the better to disguise to itself the unstable sources of its own identification. The crowd augurs uncertainty as well as safety in numbers.

Dubliners was written as mass psychology and crowd theory prompted debates about the value and danger of appeals to 'public opinion', the strengths and limitations of parliamentary systems, and the uses and abuses of oratory. Books by Hippolyte Taine and Scipio Sighele, and the English publication of Gustave Le Bon's *The Crowd* in 1896 (its final chapters were on 'Electoral Crowds' and 'Parliamentary Assemblies'), emphasized the rise of mass socialist movements and envisaged 'the age of the crowd' both as a threat to parliamentary democracy and as its consummate expression.[93] By 1905, Martin Conway could assert that 'Democracy is nothing else than the enthronement of the crowd': 'All the assemblies in the world are themselves

[91] *JCW*, 168. See also Joyce's comment: '[Fenians] maintain (and in this assertion history fully supports them) that any concessions that have been granted to Ireland, England has granted unwillingly, and, as it is usually put, at the point of a bayonet' (ibid. 188).

[92] Sigmund Freud, *Mass Psychology and Other Writings*, trans. J. A. Underwood, introd. Jacqueline Rose (London: Penguin, 2004), 75.

[93] See Jaap Van Ginneken, *Crowds, Psychology, and Politics, 1871–1899* (Cambridge: Cambridge University Press, 1992).

crowds, subject to the vices of crowds, the passions of crowds.'[94] Much crowd theory sought to find ways to control the apparently capricious throng and to combat the threats of socialism and mob rule. Le Bon claimed that 'man descends several rungs in the ladder of civilization. Isolated, he may be a cultivated individual; in a crowd he is a barbarian.'[95]

However, the socialist, irredentist, and syndicalist crowds in which Joyce was moving in Trieste and Rome took up Le Bon's lines of enquiry while declining to take up his tone. They conceived crowd trouble as something more than merely troubling, and focused also on the positive value of mass movements and collective behaviour.[96] Le Bon's definition of a crowd included not just parliamentary assemblies, but also extended to the microcosmic (a small group of people) and the macrocosmic ('a nation').[97] Variations aside, the minimum number required for a group to constitute a 'crowd' was generally agreed by the theorists to be ten.[98] Joyce wrote 'Ivy Day in the Committee Room' with a sense of how the dynamics of committee, parliament, and nation could intersect and overlap in the ambivalent figure of the crowd. Nine people have been in Joyce's Committee Room that day, but there is also one absent-present figure who never seems to have left the space and who makes up the ten: the shade of Parnell.

'Ivy Day' explores the oversights of group mentalities even as it laments the loss of an enabling sense of civic community. As this group of Dublin canvassers may stand as a synecdoche of parliament or nation (an intima-tion of the loss of bearings of the Irish Parliamentary Party (IPP) and of the Irish nationalist movement), so their gossip and chit-chat may act as an index to the state of the nation's public speech. Joyce's story hints at these intersections; not only does the 'Committee Room' recall the room in Westminster where Parnell was ousted as leader, but we are told that 'It was the sixth of October, dismal and cold out of doors' (p. 92). 'Out of doors' can carry a parliamentary resonance—'Outside or beyond the confines of the Houses of Parliament' (*OED*)—and was often used in reference to oratory (the *OED* gives an example from the *Daily News* in 1897: 'out-of-doors or extra Parliamentary speaking'). This room in Wicklow Street becomes a miniature parliament, and the men sometimes adopt parliamentary termi-nology as they talk with one another; the Orangeman Crofton, for instance,

---

[94] Martin Conway, 'Is Parliament a Mere Crowd?', *Nineteenth Century and After*, 57 (June 1905), 898–911, pp. 910, 905.

[95] Gustave Le Bon, *The Crowd: A Study of the Popular Mind* (London: Unwin, 1896), 36.

[96] See Van Ginneken, *Crowds*, 76, 87–95, 185. On Joyce's absorption of these cultures and his 'socialistic tendencies', see *JL*, ii. 68, 89, 148, 173–4, and John McCourt, *The Years of Bloom: James Joyce in Trieste, 1904–1920* (Madison: University of Wisconsin Press, 2000), 65–70.

[97] Le Bon, *The Crowd*, 27.   [98] Conway, 'Is Parliament a Mere Crowd?', 898.

says of Parnell that 'Our side of the house respects him because he was a gentleman' (p. 102).

The speech-tics of these peripatetic orators are revealing in other ways, for Joyce's exploration of this crowd's talk as at once inconsequential and portentous is pursued through a figure that resonates across the tale and throughout Irish politics: the 'address'. We are told that 'The walls of the room were bare except for a copy of an election address' (p. 93), and so reminded that the printed text of this tale is immersed in an insistently oral culture. Joyce was in Dublin during 1902 for the municipal elections on which the story was based; he probably heard election addresses by the socialist James Connolly, and these speeches informed his brief discussion of the working-class candidate Colgan and his tale's preoccupation with how the drink trade was corrupting Irish politics and the IPP.[99] The only man in the story who sees through this state of affairs is Hynes, and he is also the only man whose speaking is accorded the dignity of the verb 'address': 'Hasn't the working-man as good a right to be in the Corporation as anyone else . . . Isn't that so, Mat? said Mr Hynes, *addressing* Mr O'Connor' (p. 93; my emphasis).

As well as being part of the tale's stylistic shorthand, 'the address' is also its subject. The crowd discusses whether there should be 'an address of welcome to Edward Rex' (p. 94) when the new king visits Ireland (this was the central issue of the 1902 election campaign). One meaning of 'address' is 'a formal speech . . . *esp.* the formal reply of the House of Lords or Commons to the Royal Speech at the opening of Parliament' (*OED*). An address of welcome, therefore, implied loyalty to the Crown and acceptance of British rule (political and parliamentary). The king would visit Ireland in 1903, so the tale's composition and publication after the event asks readers to consider the consequences of the reception that the Irish crowd gave to the monarch, and to reflect on what kind of public speech the nation might adopt in order to conduct relations with the British. Henchy is in favour of the address because it will bring 'capital' (p. 102), while Hynes—following the Parnellian precedent of refusing to acknowledge such visits—is against it (p. 94).[100]

Press coverage of the visit throws light on these disagreements. Under pressure from 'The People's Protection Committee'—founded to protest against the king's visit—the Dublin Corporation had voted to refuse an address of welcome. *The Times* portrayed pressure on the Corporation as unrepresentative crowd trouble and emphasized that it should be seen in opposition to the behaviour of the crowds out-of-doors.[101] 'Unfortunately . . . the influences of

---

99 See Fairhall, *James Joyce*, 92–104.
100 On Joyce's admiration of Parnell's stance, see *JCW*, 227.
101 Joyce was a regular reader of *The Times*; see *JL*, i. 87, 106.

the demagogue and of mob oratory still linger in Ireland, and triumphs of unreason may still be snatched from popular assemblies hardly as yet awake to the responsibilities of self-government.'[102] Another report contrasted this behaviour with that of the Dublin crowds: 'The people were determined to give THEIR MAJESTIES a cordial greeting . . . . They were united in Dublin yesterday as with one voice the immense crowd which had gathered at the entrance to the city at Leeson bridge supplied the welcome which the Corporation ought to have dutifully given.'[103] This language carries its own traces of demagoguery and 'mob oratory', for the emphasis on Dublin's 'one voice' is built on a refusal to acknowledge that the city's tentative approaches to parliamentary proceedings—its 'popular assemblies'—should be credited with the name of 'self-government' unless such proceedings involve submission to being governed by England. Reports also portrayed those against the address as part of the 'Physical Force Party' or as mere 'roughs who overawed the city fathers'.[104]

Joyce's story picks up on these emphases by having Henchy refer to Hynes behind his back as one of 'these hillsiders and fenians' (p. 96), yet while the tale links Hynes to the ebbing Phoenix flame (and so to Fenianism) via his closeness to the fire in the Committee Room,[105] it does so only to emphasize the principled dignity of his shivering figure. O'Connor points out that 'poor Joe' should be seen as a representative rather than a 'rough': 'he's hard up like the rest of us' (p. 96). In a story of addresses, it is noteworthy that the two men who gang up against Hynes (Henchy and Jack) often refuse to address him. On arriving, Henchy only 'nodded curtly to Mr Hynes' (p. 94), and the narrator makes a point of telling us that he does not say goodbye to him (p. 95), while old Jack—in anticipation of Hynes's return to the room—says that 'He doesn't get a warm welcome from me when he comes' (p. 96). The men will support an address to the representative of a state intent on subduing their own nationalist aspirations, but they cannot summon up the courtesy of an address to a local who shares their problems (as Freud once observed of crowds, 'it is a curious fact that mass intolerance often finds stronger expression against small differences than against fundamental ones').[106] The English press reports may have emphasized the 'one voice' of Dublin—indeed, they claimed that the crowd's welcome was 'nowhere . . . more demonstrative than from the throng formed of the poorer orders of the people'[107]—but the forensic eye of Joyce's narrator shows that these 'poorer orders' are not unified on the issue, and that those who support the welcome are suffering from a politically impoverished sense of what their own modes of address are ignoring.

---

[102] *The Times*, 21 July 1903, 8e.   [103] *The Times*, 22 July 1903, 9d.
[104] *The Times*, 21 July 1903, 8d; 22 July 1903, 9d.
[105] See Torchiana, *Backgrounds*, 176–87.   [106] Freud, *Mass Psychology*, 253.
[107] *The Times*, 22 July 1903, 9c.

King Edward's address to Dubliners paid tribute 'to the death of the POPE' as a way of calling for an Ireland 'united' in grief and future hope.[108] The use of the church in a state address to emphasize unity would have rankled Joyce ('I do not see what good it does to fulminate against the English tyranny while the Roman tyranny occupies the palace of the soul').[109] The speech that closes his tale—Hynes's versified oration to 'Erin' (p. 103)—mourns instead 'the Death of Parnell' and offers a revised address to a king: 'Our Uncrowned King is dead' (p. 103). This appellation was first used to refer to Parnell in a speech by Tim Healy, the orator who subsequently did most to ensure that the king was never crowned, and Joyce was often drawn to the phrase.[110] Hynes's literary effort—at once spoken and written—takes its bearings from oratorical precedent even as it acts as a riposte to Healy's legacy, a legacy embodied in the paucity of the miniature parliament gathered before him. Angered by political and religious crowd cultures ('the fell gang | Of modern hypocrites' and the 'rabble-rout | Of fawning priests' (p. 104)), yet haunted by the need to forge a collective address that might be worthy of Parnell's leadership ('*Our* uncrowned king . . . O, *Erin*, mourn . . . *Erin*, list . . . (pp. 104–5; my emphasis)), Hynes's speech distils the rhythm of simultaneous repulsion from and attraction to the crowd's oratorical enthusiasms that is present throughout *Dubliners*.

Critics have tended to feel that the poem is simply an embarrassment,[111] but Stanislaus's approach to Hynes's awkward, shaken eloquence is more discriminating: 'the poem . . . strikes a faint note of pathos and prevents the story from being cynical . . . despite the hackneyed phrases and tawdry literary graces, one feels in it a loyalty to the departed chief and a real sorrow'.[112] This sorrowful loyalty is heard most acutely in the narrator's voice during the aftermath of the address, a voice that speaks as if it were one of the crowd while also intimating a perspective beyond it:

Mr Hynes sat down again on the table. When he had finished his recitation there was a silence and then a burst of clapping: even Mr Lyons clapped. The applause continued for a little time. When it had ceased all the auditors drank from their bottles in silence.

Pok! The cork flew out of Mr Hynes' bottle, but Mr Hynes remained sitting, flushed and bareheaded on the table. He did not seem to have heard the invitation. . .

—What do you think of that, Crofton? Cried Mr Henchy. Isn't that fine? What?

Mr Crofton said that it was a very fine piece of writing. (p. 105)

---

[108] Ibid. 9d.   [109] *JCW*, 173.   [110] See ibid. 228.
[111] See Seamus Deane, 'Dead Ends: Joyce's Finest Moments', in Attridge and Howes (eds.), *Semicolonial Joyce*, 21–36, p. 32.
[112] S. Joyce, *My Brother's Keeper*, 206.

When we are told that Hynes 'did not seem' to have heard the invitation, the lack of omniscience from the narratorial voice implies that the observer sees things as one of the men in the room might see them. And yet, this scrupulous meanness carries within it other tones and perspectives. Hynes's poem closes with a call to 'Pledge in the cup . . . the memory of Parnell' (p. 105), but his refusal of a drink points to his resistance to the principles that inform this parliament, for the core of Parnell's policy was the independence of the IPP. Here, the drink is provided from Tierney's pub, and Hynes's imperviousness to the address—'*Pok!*'—from the bottle is a refusal to be bribed. As is often the case in Joyce's work, the action of abstaining (from drink as well as from speech) does not mark political apathy, but politic commitment.

The apparently neutral descriptions of the men's applause are also charged with Joyce's sure feel for the power of understatement. There was 'a burst of clapping' (not 'the men clapped'), 'When it had ceased' (not 'when they had ceased'); these passive structures intimate the narrator's passive resistance, for such plaudits are the epitome of the mechanical, unprincipled herd instinct that Hynes has been criticizing in his address. To be clapped by 'auditors' (an apposite pun to capture the decline of a civically responsible audience—these men are paid to support a particular political line) is scant consolation, and Hynes's isolated response to this adulation has a Parnellian ring to it. To recall Joyce on Parnell: 'The applause and the crowd . . . never perturbed the melancholy serenity of his character.' Hynes's melancholy serenity is emphasized here by the narrator's own form of address: 'Mr Hynes's bottle, but Mr Hynes remained sitting'. A simple 'he' would have sufficed in the second clause, but the formal repetition of Hynes's name accentuates his distance from the crowd and the narrator's respect for that distance. Partially at odds with the applause he inspires, unbeguiled by his own eloquence even though moved by it, Hynes is aware that more than words are needed at this moment in Irish history. When his poem ends with a hope that Parnell's spirit may 'Rise, like the Phoenix from the flames' (p. 105), he—like the Chief—is employing Fenian iconography to hint at the need for something more than hot air.

The story closes with an ambiguous address. The final sentence is the only time that the narrator opts for an indirect representation of speech (as if he cannot bring himself to speak in Crofton's voice—a printed retort to a disingenuous public speech). The Orangeman may be bowing to crowd pressure despite his pro-British sympathies, but his tone—perhaps begrudging, with an arch swoop on 'writing'—may imply that writing is all this moment is, emptying out the crowd's sense of Hynes's piece as a moving oral performance and hinting at a reservation about its politics ('the writing is very fine in its own way, I suppose, but . . .'). Crofton's attempt to play down the urgency of Hynes's oration (just as he had played down Parnell's oratorical challenges and Fenian links by referring to him as a 'gentleman' in the 'house') has an analogue in the way the press reports attempted to minimize the Irish troubles when discussing the royal address during the king's visit. The trip coincided with the passing of the 1903 Land Bill, and *The Times* linked the cheers of the Dublin crowd out-of-doors with the 'chorus of approval and congratulations' from the gentlemen inside the Commons.[113] This elision of the 'one voice' of the Irish populace with the 'chorus' of the British Parliament—the homogenization of both groups and subsequent absorption of an Irish crowd into London's in-crowd—is precisely what Joyce's less stridently oratorical narrator resists.

Hynes's poem speaks of 'the dawning of the day' (p. 105) as dusk settles on the city, and his glance out-of-doors is a call to this parliament to look beyond its four walls and to respond to other voices, for the crowd in the room is 'in the dark' (p. 92) in more than one sense. As one commentator observed, Parnell 'introduced Fenianism into parliament, and injected parliamentarianism into the Fenians'.[114] As a defender and questioner of the parliamentary process, Hynes's voice echoes the dual inflections of his hero and the compounded tones of *Dubliners* as a whole. Such a voice creates echoes of its own; by the time 'Ivy Day' was being written, the People's Protection Committee had evolved into the basis for Arthur Griffith's Sinn Féin, a movement that would respond to the demands of speakers like Hynes with something more than dismissive nonchalance or faint praise.

Dubliners is replete with understatements meant to set the crowd thinking; a fine piece of writing, when heard, may also be a fine piece of righting. The claustrophobic weight of the stories is meant to inspire in readers—as it does in Hynes—a need for fresh air. Air is dwelt upon in the final story, 'The Dead', to accentuate the link between breathing space and an improvement in public speech that the whole volume has been deftly exploring. 'A cold fragrant air from *out-of-doors*' (p. 139; my emphasis) slips into the hall, and the phrase's political inflection should be kept in mind as Gabriel makes a speech on Irish matters in this 'House'. Just before he begins to speak, he wonders, 'People, perhaps, were standing in the snow... The air was pure there' (p. 159). It is as if he is already fighting for another kind of breath, dimly aware of the limitations of his own eloquence, and the air that 'the people' breathe continues to haunt him. Bartell D'Arcy's rendition of 'The Lass of Aughrim' ('the old Irish tonality... the cadence of the air with words expressing grief' (pp. 165–6)) and Michael Furey's fading breath (he caught his death of cold in the night air) form elegantly understated heckles to Gabriel's airs and

---

[113] *The Times*, 22 July 1903, 9d.   [114] Bowers, *Irish Orators*, 425.

graces, and his journey from orotund crowd-pleaser to his enlightened sense of himself as 'orating to vulgarians and idealizing his own clownish lusts' (p. 173) relies on a move from in-house speechifying to a registering of lives and deaths out-of-doors.

Dubliners ends with a glance towards the window, as Gabriel finally takes his cue from Gretta. Recalling her example ('she was looking out of the window' (p. 169), 'She went on to the window and stood there, looking out' (p. 171)), he feels that 'The air of the room chilled his shoulders' (p. 176), and a few taps of snow upon the pane 'made him turn to the window' (p. 176). This is not merely window-shopping; *Dubliners* closes with a sense that if Gabriel is to improve his orations (and his relations with his wife and country), he will do so by listening and responding to the preoccupations of more than one crowd—those outdoors as well as inside, who may breathe a more bracing and less refined air.

Elliot Paul once recalled Joyce in company; he sat apart, 'near the only window', but 'his attitude showed that he was listening intently and was trying to isolate himself from the slight commotion of the crowd'.[115] To be listening intently *and* to be isolating oneself from the crowd is a characteristically Joycean stance, and this poise offers us an apposite figure for the civil yet self-protective impulse of *Dubliners*. When describing Joyce's writing, Virginia Woolf wrote: 'in order to breathe he must break the windows . . . the determined and public-spirited act of a man who needs fresh air'.[116] This is astute, but not quite true to Joyce's art—which operates in the space between inside and outside—and we might revise Woolf's vocabulary in a Joycean spirit: not 'breaking' windows, but 'opening' them. The first speech he delivered to the Literary and Historical Society ended a vision of what art might do for Ireland:

> The sooner we understand our true position, the better; and the sooner then will we be up and doing on our way. In the meantime, art . . . may help us to make our resting places with a greater insight and a greater foresight, that the stones of them may be bravely builded, and the windows goodly and fair. ' . . . what will you do in our Society, Miss Hessel?' asked Rörlund—'I will let in fresh air, Pastor.'—answered Lona.[117]

Dubliners breathes this air and invites its reader-listeners to do the same. It is characteristic of Joyce's insight and foresight to envisage such construction in terms that are at once collective (*'we* understand *our* true position . . . will *we*

---

[115] Elliot Paul, 'Farthest North: A Study of James Joyce', *Bookman*, May 1932, cited in E. H. Mikhail (ed.), *James Joyce: Interviews and Recollections* (Basingstoke: Macmillan, 1990), 125.

[116] Virginia Woolf, 'Mr Bennett and Mrs Brown' (1923), in *The Captain's Death Bed and Other Essays* (New York: Harcourt Brace Jovanovich, 1950), 116.

[117] *JCW*, 46. The reference is to Ibsen's play *Pillars of Society*. See also Joyce's comment: 'One cannot but observe in Ibsen's later work a tendency to get out of closed rooms' (ibid. 66).

be up . . . *our* resting places . . . help *us*') and individual ('*I* will let in fresh air'). Such a resting place is the foundation for a speaking place (a *parle-ment*), yet the emphasis is not exactly on mobilizing opinion, but rather on encouraging mobility of opinion. The narrative voice of *Dubliners* is at once a collective representative of what Dublin's citizens are and might be, and a diffident but imperturbable figure on the outskirts of the crowd. From within the marooned yet implicated tones of the volume's eloquence, we hear Joyce's whispered admission that if crowds and communities are to be enriched, they will need to be resisted as well as joined, led as well as followed.

STEPHEN'S HEROES

While writing *Stephen Hero*, Joyce asked: 'Do you not think the search for heroics damn vulgar—and yet how are we to describe Ibsen?'[118] This may describe Ibsen as heroic *because* he is searching for heroics; Joyce's wary defence of an impulse as itself a form of achievement finds expression in his portrayal of Stephen Dedalus—a character whose self-auditing imagination embodies his author's search for an example that might act as a model of leadership for crowds. His early essay, 'A Portrait of the Artist', noted that Stephen's 'reluctance to debate . . . was not without a satisfactory flavour of the heroic'.[119] This 'reluctance' requires a distance from what Stephen refers to as 'the phrases of the platform' (p. 56) in *Stephen Hero*. However, litotes ('not without') bespeaks hesitancy amid determination, and Stephen's egoism might be conceived as a catalyst for political change: 'Though his taste for elegance and detail unfitted him for the part of demagogue . . . from his general attitude he might have been supposed not unjustly an ally of the collectivist politicians' (p. 147). Litotes again embodies a balancing act—a search for an individualism that takes care to avoid haranguing others whilst also taking pains to engage with them.[120]

Stephen is frequently drawn to a connoisseurship and criticism of eloquence. In *Stephen Hero*, he is described as an '*orator*' (p. 106), his talk as an '*oration*' (p. 126), and his companion as an '*auditor*' (p. 144). In *A Portrait of the Artist as a Young Man*, he adopts the role of the Speaker in the House even as he

---

[118] *JL*, ii. 80–1.

[119] James Joyce, 'A Portrait of the Artist', cited in Scholes and Kain (eds.), *Workshop*, 61.

[120] Such emphases are influenced by anarchist and socialist thought; see Jean-Michel Rabaté, *James Joyce and the Politics of Egoism* (Cambridge: Cambridge University Press, 2001), and David Weir, *Anarchy and Culture: The Aesthetic Politics of Modernism* (Amherst: University of Massachusetts Press, 1997), 210–27.

announces his 'reluctance to debate': 'That question is out of order . . . Next business' (p. 164). Stephen's 'business'—like Joyce's—is the creation of an order at once aesthetic and political. Pound suggested: 'If more people had read *The Portrait* . . . there might have been less recent trouble in Ireland . . . the rhetoric of later Rome [was] the seed and the symptom of the Roman Empire's decadence and extinction. A nation that cannot write clearly cannot be trusted to govern, nor yet to think.'[121] Stephen's educational environment is founded on a similar sense of the value of literary and oratorical dialogue. When Joyce observed that Roman life was civilized because 'the men of action and the men of imagination are the complement of each other',[122] he was echoing the lessons of his schooling. The Clongowes prospectus noted that 'the best prize in the college is still the Large Medal for Oratory',[123] and the school magazine was called *The Rhetorician*.[124] At Belvedere, Jesuit teaching was based on the *Ratio Studiorum*, in which rhetorical teaching 'spans two major fields, oratory and poetry, with oratory taking the place of honour'; students wrote speeches and poems to be read out in class; prelection—the core principle of teaching—involved texts being read aloud as a prelude to analysis, for 'Nothing, in fact, so develops resourcefulness of talent as frequent individual practice in speaking from the platform'.[125] For the artist as a young man, the practice of writing was intimately associated with 'the phrases of the platform'.

Stephen Heath suggests that 'Joyce's writing is a questioning (in the sense of an active interrogation, a dispersion, a hesitation) of rhetoric'.[126] *A Portrait* is one such dispersion and hesitation, for the structure of the novel is built on rhetorical teaching that relates to the construction of a classical speech. Hugh Kenner has shown how 'the first two pages, terminating in a row of asterisks, enact the entire action in microcosm'.[127] But what these pages also enact is a *progymnasmata*, a set of fourteen exercises to prepare students of rhetoric for the creation of speeches. Aphthonius wrote the canonical version (used by the Jesuits), and a brief comparison of his text with the opening of *A Portrait* is revealing.

[121] Pound, *Pound/Joyce*, 90.

[122] Arthur Power, *Conversations with James Joyce* (Dublin: Lilliput Press, 1999), 84.

[123] Cited in Kevin Sullivan, *Joyce among the Jesuits* (New York: Columbia University Press, 1958), 232.

[124] Bruce Bradley, *James Joyce's Schooldays* (Dublin: Gill & Macmillan, 1982), 4.

[125] Allan P. Farrell (trans.), *The Jesuit Ratio Studiorum of 1599* (Washington: Conference of Major Superiors of Jesuits, 1970), 72–5, 79.

[126] Stephen Heath, 'Ambiviolences: Notes for Reading Joyce', in Derek Attridge and Daniel Ferrer (eds.), *Post-Structuralist Joyce: Essays from the French* (Cambridge: Cambridge University Press, 1988), 31–68, p. 41.

[127] Hugh Kenner, *Dublin's Joyce* (Boston: Beacon Press, 1962), 14.

A Portrait opens with a series of parallels that recall and domesticate the contours of the *progymnasmata*. The first exercise is 'Fable', and—according to Aphthonius—often 'Aesopic' in nature, it links animal and human life;[128] *A Portrait* begins with 'Once upon a time...there was a moocow' who 'met a nicens little boy named baby tuckoo'. Second is 'Narration'; the next paragraph of the novel begins 'His father told him that story'. Aphthonius gives an example of 'a dramatic narrative concerning the rose'; Stephen's song '*O, the wild rose blossoms*' sees him beginning to tell his own stories (Stephen's first spoken word in the novel is '*O*'—an epic vocative, address, and shorthand for his role as budding Orator). Next is the 'Chreia', or anecdote, 'a brief recollection, referring to some person in a pointed way'; Stephen's recollective point runs: 'He sang that song. That was his song.' Then, the 'Maxim', 'a summary statement in declarative sentences, urging or dissuading something', followed by the 'Refutation', which is 'the overturning of some matter at hand'; Stephen's suitably gnomic utterance combines these: 'When you wet the bed first it is warm then it gets cold.' Then comes the 'Confirmation', 'the corroboration of some matter at hand', which should reverse the procedure of the previous refutation; Stephen notes: 'His mother put on the oilsheet.' Next follows the 'Common-Place', which focuses on negative attributes; Stephen seizes on the oilsheet: 'That had the queer smell.' Then the 'Encomium', expounding 'inherent excellences', and 'so called from singing in villages (*kômai*) in ancient times'; Stephen blends praise with a recollection of music: 'His mother had a nicer smell than his father. She played on the piano the sailor's hornpipe for him to dance.'

'Invective' follows (some versions of the *progymnasmata* omit this section, and it is absent from the opening of *A Portrait*). Next is 'Syncrisis', or comparison, 'made by setting things side-by-side'; Stephen thinks to himself: 'Uncle Charles and Dante clapped. They were older than his father and mother but uncle Charles was older than Dante.' Then comes 'Ethopoeia', the 'imitation of the character of a proposed speaker', echoed by Stephen's singing the sailor's hornpipe. Then comes 'Ecphrasis', descriptive language, 'bringing what is shown clearly before the eyes'; Stephen's eye wanders to Dante's 'maroon velvet' and 'green velvet' brushes, along with the 'cachou' she gave him whenever he brought her 'a piece of tissue paper'. Next is the 'Thesis'; Aphthonius gives what he calls a 'political' example, 'Whether one should marry.' This is followed by the final exercise, the 'Introduction of a Law', which

---

[128] Aphthonius, in George A. Kennedy (ed. and trans.), *Progymnasmata: Greek Textbooks of Prose Composition and Rhetoric* (Atlanta: Society of Biblical Literature, 2003), 96–124. All references are to this edition, and all references to the opening paragraphs of *Portrait* are from p. 5.

should include both advocacy of and opposition to a piece of legislation. The prose style again parallels Aphthonius's text, for Stephen's thesis is itself an opposition to the Catholic 'legislation' of his elders and centres on marriage: 'When they were grown up he was going to marry Eileen.' The section ends as Stephen is ordered to say sorry, while he sits under the table chanting rhyming variations on the word 'Apologise' (p. 6). His first 'poem', then, is also a defiant speech of sorts; as Fritz Senn notes, the young boy's 'Apologise' has its roots in the *apologia*—a speech made in one's defence.[129] This opening is a 'microcosm', but an even more minutely crafted one than Joyce scholars have realized: a domesticated *progymnasmata* that hints at how the artist as a young man is being conceived, shaped, and recalled through oratorical models.

Stephen's classical heritage permeates the novel. Rhetorical treatises linked the training of the orator to the story of the education and civilization of the individual; the texts were a kind of pedagogical-biographical hybrid, and Joyce blends his *Bildungsroman* with a vision of The Orator's Progress to suggest that Stephen's coming into his own is also a coming to terms with the artist's civic calling. Teaching enumerated five canons of speech making: *inventio* (the finding of something to say), *dispositio* (the arrangement/order of the subject-matter in the speech), *elocutio* (the style in which the speech will be couched), *memoria* (the committing of the speech to memory and the storing up of commonplaces and quotations), and *actio* (the delivery of the speech, including tone of voice and body language). The seed of Joyce's novel, his essay 'A Portrait of the Artist', evokes this pattern with subtle insistence. We are informed that Stephen's 'rhetoric proclaimed transition', and the transitions of the piece are rhetorical: it begins with the search 'through some art, by some process of the mind as yet untabulated' (*inventio*); next comes the attempt to locate the 'formal relation of . . . parts' (*dispositio*); then 'the enigma of a manner' and 'the rhythms of phrase and period' are formed (*elocutio*). Stephen subsequently undergoes 'meditative hours', during which he calls on another rhetorician for aid as 'he *remembered* a sentence in Augustine' (my emphasis). After this exercise in *memoria*, the essay ends on *actio*: 'amid the general paralysis of an insane society, the confederate will issues in *action*' (my emphasis).[130]

This trajectory from invention to action is allowed more space in *A Portrait*, where the five parts of the novel (the roman numerals at the heading of each section hint at the classical structure) expand the rhythms of the earlier piece. Section I outlines the search for something to say—'When would he be

---

[129] Fritz Senn, *Joyce's Dislocutions: Essays on Reading as Translation*, ed. John Paul Riquelme (Baltimore and London: Johns Hopkins University Press, 1984), 43.

[130] Joyce, 'A Portrait', cited in Scholes and Kain (eds.), *Workshop*, 67, 60, 61, 64, 65, 68.

like the fellows in poetry and rhetoric?,' Stephen wonders (p. 13). Section II centres on composition (pp. 58, 66) as the boy begins to order his materials. Section III is a *tour de force* of *elocutio*, as the style of Father Arnall's sermon penetrates Stephen's consciousness and produces his prayer—his longest piece of direct, albeit internal, speech in the novel so far (p. 117). Section IV sees Stephen remembering snatches of rhetoricians (p. 138) and turning *memoria* to advantage, as recollection of past experiences on the beach begins his conversion to his artistic vocation (pp. 141–2). Section V brings *actio* to the fore, as Stephen delivers more speeches in this section than in any other, expounding theories while keeping a self-critical eye on his own rhetorical postures: 'Talked rapidly of myself and my plans. In the midst of it unluckily I made a sudden gesture of a revolutionary nature. I must have looked like a fellow throwing a handful of peas into the air' (p. 213).

The air that Stephen breathes is oratorical, but—as the last quotation suggests—the protagonist is also wary of a style that seeks to make an impression through an overt need to impress. This may account for why 'Invective' was the section of the *progymnasmata* missing from the opening, as though from the beginning Stephen avoids the particular skill for which his countrymen had become renowned. One danger of rhetorical power is a recapitulation that signifies only capitulation; Joyce observed that 'the poet who hurls his anger against tyrants would establish upon the future an intimate and far more cruel tyranny'.[131] Accordingly, all sections of *A Portrait* end with a balance between outspoken utterance and internal musing. The first closes with an oratorical victory of sorts; after Stephen's pandying, the boys demand justice: 'The Senate and the Roman people declared that Dedalus had been wrongly punished' (p. 44). Stephen's speech to the Rector sees him acting as tribune, yet while the boys offer him loud congratulations, 'The cheers died away . . . He was alone . . . He would be very quiet' (p. 49). Section II ends with a sexual liberation as a 'cry' 'broke from him like a wail of despair . . . a cry for an iniquitous abandonment' (p. 84), yet this utterance again modulates into silence in Stephen's encounter with the prostitute: 'his lips parted though they would not speak' (p. 85). Section III draws to a close with another speech, Stephen's confession; however, the final scene observes the eloquent hero open-mouthed yet silenced as he is about to take communion (p. 123). Section IV ends with Stephen's dedication to his artistic calling, and words are enunciated before we realize that they are internalized: '—Heavenly God! Cried Stephen's soul, in an outburst of profane joy . . . no word had broken the silence of his ecstasy' (pp. 144–5). The novel ends with an address even as we approach it in the most inwardly private of forms, the diary: 'Old father,

---

[131] *JCW*, 82.

old artificer, stand me now and ever in good stead' (p. 213). This feels at once like a note from Stephen to himself, and the peroration of a speech in the presence of his father.

The stylistic architecture of *A Portrait* houses a protagonist who seeks to employ and revise oratorical standards. Stephen's search for a hero (in himself and in others) is in many ways the search for a speaker, and his Parnellian leanings draw him towards a hero who excels in a similar kind of revision. One contemporary summed up Parnell as 'everything the typical Irishman is not—taciturn, calculating and retiring'.[132] Stephen's own triad—his renowned defence of 'silence', 'cunning', and 'exile' (p. 208) in *A Portrait*—is a fitting analogue to such testimonials. His earliest reading is of the Parnell scandal (p. 13), and when he gazes up at the Land League orator, Mr Casey, at the Christmas dinner-table, finds himself imagining the man 'making speeches from a wagonette' (p. 31) and feels 'the glow rise to his own cheek as the spoken words thrilled him' (p. 32), he is responding to the man reputed to be the last in Ireland to have shaken hands with the Chief.[133]

The dovetailing of classical rhetorical ambitions and contemporary setting is seen throughout the novel. Take, for example, Stephen's big day:

Stephen's mother and his brother and one of his cousins waited at the corner of quiet Foster Place while he and his father went up the steps . . . When they had passed into the great hall and stood at the counter Stephen drew forth his orders on the governor of the bank of Ireland for thirty and three pounds; and these sums, the moneys of his exhibition and essay prize, were paid over to him rapidly by the teller in notes and in coin respectively. He bestowed them in his pockets with feigned composure and suffered the friendly teller, to whom his father chatted, to take his hand across the broad counter and wish him a brilliant career in after life. He was impatient of their voices and could not keep his feet at rest . . . Mr Dedalus lingered in the hall gazing about him and up at the roof and telling Stephen, who urged him to come out, that they were standing in the house of commons of the old Irish parliament.

—God help us! he said piously, to think of the men of those times, Stephen, Hely Hutchinson and Flood and Henry Grattan and Charles Kendal Bushe, and the noblemen we have now, leaders of the Irish people at home and abroad. Why, by God, they wouldn't be seen dead in a tenacre field with them. (p. 81)

Stephen's unease is more than mere boredom or shyness. 'Foster Place' raises an oratorical ghost through topographic detail even before we enter the former parliament. The dead-end street was named after John Foster, the last Speaker of the Irish House of Commons and the Chancellor of the Exchequer for

---

[132] Bowers, *Irish Orators*, 424.

[133] Mr Casey is based on John Kelly, a close friend of Joyce's father and a renowned orator; see Jackson and Costello, *John Stanislaus Joyce*, 166.

Ireland. Foster gave anti-Union speeches in his homeland before switching sides to support the measure after 1801; he was handsomely compensated for his losses resulting from the abolition of the Irish parliament, and accused by contemporaries and historians of time-serving and venality. '[Q]uiet' Foster Place, then, marks the purchased silence of a Speaker who had once defended Ireland's right to a parliament of its own.

Stephen perhaps senses the broader relevance of his outing even before his father recounts the glories of Ireland's rhetorical tradition. To accept money for his own exercises in eloquence in a building that has shifted from pre-Union legislative chamber to post-Union bank is to register a potential complicity. Members of the parliament had voted for the abolition of their own speaking place as a result of financial bribery—as Joyce put it, 'a parliament corrupted and undermined with the greatest ingenuity by the agents of the English prime minister'.[134] One condition of the sale of the building to the bank was that it be redecorated so as to suppress visual allusion to its parliamentary past.[135] However, given that Stephen's father mentions the celebrated pre-Union voice of the patriot orator Henry Flood, and that we are told that it is 'October' (p. 81), we might detect an aural allusion in the prose.

In October 1763 Flood rose in the room that Stephen is standing in to speak against the 'court sycophant' and those who 'concur in the distribution of pecuniary gratifications to individuals at the expense of the nation'. Like Stephen's father, he talked of forefathers: 'In this age of vanity and dissipation, men are corrupted by even less than a promise; a trivial compliment, a familiar and a gracious smile, or a squeeze by the hand, are deemed valuable considerations for those inestimable blessings which our forefathers procured for us, at the expense of treasure, of ease, of health, and even life itself.'[136] When Stephen takes a compliment as well as a 'hand' from the familiar and 'friendly teller' who wishes him well in 'after life', it is as though the memory of Flood's voice judges and finds him wanting, as though the artist is not living up to his oratorical heritage, betraying the rhetorical expectation that the form of the novel has been nurturing. The narration records no direct speech while the men are in this erstwhile speaking-place, and Stephen's only reported utterance is a call to leave it. Perhaps he is 'impatient of their voices' because they unwittingly remind him of political losses as well as of pecuniary gains.

---

[134] *JCW*, 162.

[135] Don Gifford, *Joyce Annotated: Notes for Dubliners and A Portrait of the Artist as a* Young Man 2nd edn. (Berkeley: University of California Press, 1982), 174.

[136] Henry Flood, cited in Frederick Bussy and G. Ralph Hall Kane (eds.), *Gems of Oratory: And Notable Passages from the Lips of British and Irish Statesmen and Orators* (London: Collier, 1909), 6, 5, 7.

As so often in the labyrinthine layerings of *A Portrait*, the style of the narration also hints at a principled stance within the boy's nervousness. Stephen's 'feigned composure' is carried into the oddly finessed composition of the writing: the opening catalogue of 'and's sets the tone; then he draws 'thirty and three pounds' (not 'thirty-three'); rapid payment is handled in a peculiarly unrapid narrative manner ('in notes and in coin respectively'); and Stephen does not simply 'put' his hands in his pockets, he 'bestowed' them there. Such prolonged periods may highlight the excruciating nature of the boy's experience, but 'suffered' also has its tinge of pride, and—given that this event takes place around Ivy Day—there is perhaps another oratorical example hovering in the margins of the prose. One of Joyce's favourite anecdotes involved the occasion on which Parnell received money from the Irish people in return for his eloquent endeavours on their behalf: 'When the Irish people presented him with a national gratuity of 40,000 pounds sterling in 1887, he put the cheque into his billfold, and in the speech which he delivered to the immense gathering made not the slightest reference to the gift which he had received.'[137]

Joyce admired these superb silences, for they encapsulated the orator's refusal to tailor his eloquence to the crowd's expectations even as they maintained a tacit and dignified acceptance of their support. At this moment in the bank, Stephen's silence may, then, also take its cue from a Parnellian example with which he is honoured to be associated. The prose is woven together with monitory voices and exemplary precedents; the heroic ghosts of Flood and Parnell jostle for attention and remind us of the complexity of the young artist's task, for he too is searching for a way to be of benefit to his country without being beholden to it. Stephen's subsequent use of the prize-money expresses his civic ambition: he 'drew up a form of commonwealth for the household by which every member of it held some office, [and] opened a loan bank for his family' (p. 82). This fledging vision of Irish independence—where 'members' of the 'house' *do* hold office in their own country—is an attempt to revise the contours of Stephen's private drama at the bank. Here, as elsewhere in *A Portrait*, the sequestered artist shelters the unacknowledged legislator. Just as Stephen's internal musings and maturation are nurtured in a *Bildungsroman* whose structure evokes the shape of a classically formed speech, so individual scenes ask readers to see (and hear) how Stephen's very isolation is a protean form of political engagement.

A Portrait frequently hints at Stephen's hidden oratorical depths; *Ulysses* (1922) plumbs them. The figures of the artist and the orator are coordinated and competing vocations, and the later novel opens with oratory on the tip

---

[137] *JCW*, 225. See also Ellmann, *James Joyce*, 32.

of its tongue. Buck Mulligan was based on a platform-speaker (Oliver St John Gogarty), which is perhaps why John Eglinton referred to Mulligan's 'oratory' when discussing *Ulysses*.[138] Gogarty was Arthur Griffith's closest friend and political ally at the time the novel was set (Griffith was the leader of Sinn Féin as well as a frequent visitor to Martello Tower), and the former would become senator in 1922. He spoke alongside Griffith at the first annual convention of Sinn Féin in 1905, and the memory of his senatorial swagger makes its way into *Ulysses*. Arguing that 'the language of Ireland was suppressed, the history of Ireland was ignored or mis-stated, the attention of Ireland was turned to a foreign country', Gogarty emphasized the importance of turning to 'ourselves alone' and championed Sinn Féin's focus on Irish independence: 'The first thing to understand was that the difficulty of nationality was the most important: one had to identify himself mentally several times a day, and recall to mind to whom he belonged, if he would avoid being changed into one of those nationless nonentities such as the Universities in Ireland were tending to produce.'[139] Amongst other things, this is a demand for a particular kind of interior monologue, one in which the self comes into being only through a sense of national belonging. *Ulysses* resists this assumption about identity, and the identity politics on which it is based, by conceiving the mind as a realm in which the politic 'I' can question as well as confirm itself.

Joyce's technical innovation has often been discussed as if it were a mode that enshrines privacy—as 'unpublic speech' and as something that 'seems not to assume the presence of an audience . . . as if the character were simply being overheard'.[140] Yet this privacy is often conceived in public terms, as if to highlight how the mind itself might be considered a debating chamber. Stephen has a habit of mulling over how his thoughts might be received by an audience. His inward critique of 'Words Mulligan had spoken a moment since' ends with his listening out for a potential reception for his own sagacity: 'Hear, hear! Prolonged applause.'[141] Much of the internal action in the first episode—and in the novel as a whole—evokes the image of a public assembly from within the mind's private imaginings. When Mulligan tries to chivvy Stephen by taking his arm and telling him, 'if you and I could only work together we might do something for the island. Hellenise it' (1. 157–8),

---

[138] John Eglinton, *Irish Literary Portraits* (London: Macmillan, 1935), 137.

[139] Cited in Ulick O'Connor, *Oliver St John Gogarty: A Poet and his Times* (London: Jonathan Cape, 1964), 91.

[140] Vincent Sherry, *James Joyce: Ulysses* (Cambridge: Cambridge University Press, 1994), 26; Marilyn French, *The Book as World: James Joyce's Ulysses* (Cambridge, Mass.: Harvard University Press, 1976), 58.

[141] James Joyce, *Ulysses*, ed. Hans Walter Gabler (London: Bodley Head, 2002), 1. 660–1, 665. All subsequent references are cited via episode and line number.

the Hellenic reference, Stephen's immediate thought, 'His arm' (1. 159),
and subsequent action, 'Stephen freed his arm' (1. 182), echo *The Odyssey*.
Telemachus (who has already announced that 'public speech shall be . . . my
concern most of all') stands in the assembly and delivers this riposte to
Mulligan's precursor: 'Antinous, among all you roisterers I can never eat
undistressed . . . So speaking, he snatched his hand from Antinous' hand.'[142]
The cut and thrust of the debating chamber is translated into the movements
of Stephen's mind. His keeping of his own counsel is an echo of debates in
council, as internalized soliloquy is modelled on political colloquy.

The first appearance of interior monologue in *Ulysses* carries an oratorical
charge. Just after Mulligan ends his speech with the command 'Silence, all'
(1. 23), Stephen catches sight of his teeth glistening 'with gold points'; his
mind then opens its mouth, as it were, to say: 'Chrysostomos' (1. 26). The
word, meaning 'golden-mouthed', was a classical epithet of praise for orators.
Stephen's phrasing mocks the mocker, whittling down Mulligan's delusions of
oratorical grandeur to a reflection on the corrupt state of his mouth. Moreover,
although the interior monologue may be a way of muttering things under your
breath, it is also a chance to say two things in the same breath, for Stephen's
golden-mouthed word also recalls Dio Chrysostom, a speaker who placed an
emphasis on the value of literary learning as the basis for cultured political
speech.[143] That is, Stephen's thought may be a reminder of the oratorical ideal
he is striving for, as well as a resistance to that ideal's debasement by the glib
rhetorician before him.

Interior monologue springs into life in *Ulysses*, then, at the moment oratory
is both resisted and defended. Derek Attridge has observed how Joyce's writing
sometimes aims to 'take advantage of the tonelessness of print',[144] and the tonal
ambiguity of interior monologue is also a way of ensuring that unequivocal,
univocal speech does not take advantage of the enquiring consciousness. Print
allows Joyce to reach beyond the limitations of the spoken word even as
he asks us to imagine what such thoughts *sound* like. Either a back-biting
scepticism or a nostalgic longing can be heard in Stephen's 'Chrysostomos';
or rather, we might hear a coalescence of both tones, for the form allows us
to register complexities that speech may sometimes miss. (Mulligan is never
allowed an interior monologue in *Ulysses*, and therefore becomes something
of a 'nonentity' himself; it is as though his public speech is impoverished

---

[142] Homer, *The Odyssey*, trans. Walter Shewring (Oxford: Oxford University Press, 1998)
9, 19.

[143] See George Kennedy, *The Art of Rhetoric in the Roman World, 300 BC–AD 300* (Princeton:
Princeton University Press, 1972), 566–82.

[144] Derek Attridge, *Joyce Effects: On Language, Theory, and History* (Cambridge: Cambridge
University Press, 2000), 47.

precisely because it has no private convictions and questionings against which to test itself.) As a silent resistance to Mulligan's call for 'silence', Stephen's 'unpublic speech' acts as a criticism of and a template for political eloquence: the interior monologue becomes a trial run or blueprint for a renovated and replenishing oratorical endeavour.

As in *A Portrait*, classical structure underpins contemporary political engagement, for Stephen's tussle with Mulligan's voice is a resistance to Orator Gogarty's commitment to the intolerant emphases of Griffith's Sinn Féin platform. At the movement's inception, Joyce had cautiously approved its cultivation of Irish independence, but questioned the way in which this rhetoric could slide into national, racial, and religious prejudice. He pointed out that Gogarty's public rants against English 'venereal excess' in *Sinn Féin* were hypocritical,[145] that his references to the 'Jew mastery of England' were ill-founded,[146] and that his publicly servile attitude to the Church would help to condemn 'generations to servitude'.[147] Indeed, in the opening episode Stephen is more concerned than Mulligan about threats to independence, as the latter pays rent to the British Secretary of State for War for the peaceable yet distinctly impure life of his ivory tower, toadies to the anti-Semitic Englishman Haines, and glides easily over the artist's inward wrestling with the Church's influence on Ireland. These quotidian details act as awkward footnotes to the sweeping gestures of the Sinn Féin platform, and by inviting the reader to overhear Stephen's views on Mulligan's eloquence, Joyce asks that we resist the beguiling orator and pause upon the silences that echo around his voluble figure.

Stephen's reticent heroism in response to the disingenuous volubility of those like Mulligan reaches its zenith in the 'Aeolus' episode, set in the *Freeman's* newspaper office (Joyce designated the art of the episode as 'Rhetoric').[148] Stephen's resistance to being press-ganged into service for the *Freeman's* crowd involves him—and us—casting an appreciative yet sceptical eye over what is received by the ear. When J. J. O'Molloy tells him, 'One of the most polished periods I think I ever listened to in my life fell from the lips of Seymour Bushe. It was in that case of fracticide, the Childs murder case' (7. 747–9), the shift to Stephen's consciousness is a glimpse into the mind's eye: '*And in the porches of mine ear did pour*' (7. 750). The allusion to *Hamlet* (the ghost is telling the prince how Claudius murdered him (1. v. 63) shows Stephen's literary cast of mind warding off the seductions of the spoken word, as oratory is equated with poisonous phial. However, the inclusion of Bushe's speech in *Ulysses* is a result of Joyce's appreciation of its artistry; the author

[145] *JL*, ii. 191.   [146] See Manganiello, *Joyce's Politics*, 129–35.   [147] *JL*, ii. 148.
[148] See Stuart Gilbert, *James Joyce's 'Ulysses': A Study* (New York: Vintage, 1955), 194–8.

was present at the trial and took copious notes of the oration.[149] The effect on Stephen is similarly compelling as he hears it: 'Stephen, his blood wooed by grace of language and gesture, blushed' (7. 776).

This alloy of wary admiration is mirrored in his response to the men's discussion and rendition of John F. Taylor's speech (originally delivered in 1901) in which he defended the study of the Irish language—and, by extension, the value of Irish nationalism. Joyce attended this speech and another by Taylor, and it was reported that, although the orator's style was like that 'of our own Joyce at his best', during the speech 'Dreamy Jimmy and J. F. Byrne, standing on a window-sill, looked as if they could say things unutterable'.[150] For Joyce, the printed voice of the interior monologue was a place for unutterable things to be 'said'. Stephen listens carefully:

Noble words coming. Look out. Could you try your hand at it yourself? . . . Gone with the wind. Hosts at Mullaghmast and Tara of the kings. Miles of ears of porches. The tribune's words howled and scattered to the four winds. A people sheltered within his voice. (7. 836–7, 880–3)

Yeats saw Joyce's use of the interior monologue as 'an entirely new thing— neither what the eye sees nor the ear hears',[151] and such a technique—reliant on both ear and eye yet beholden to neither—is a form well suited to an enquiry into how a writer might seek to respond to oratorical achievement. Here, Stephen's staccato snatches of thought embody a mental pause for breath even as the speech takes his breath away. The tonal ambiguity of the prose registers divided allegiances: 'Look out' initially seems to be Stephen's warning to himself to beware of nationalist rhetoric, but—reading the following sentence—it also may be a call to look outwards, a quick reminder to listen carefully so that he might emulate Taylor in future. Similarly, 'Gone with the wind' would first seem to point to the effervescence of such words (lost on the air), but then also hints at the enduring political enthusiasms they can inspire. Listening to 'Miles of ears of porches' as well as reading it, we can catch how it revisits and revises '*And in the porches of mine ear did pour*'. Stephen is now balancing his sense of oratory as a poisoning of minds with a feeling for such addresses as part of the architecture of a nation's progress and protection. As so often in *Ulysses*, an act of hindsight is a form of re-hearing; just as Stephen looks back over his oratorical heritage with a renewed appreciation of its benefactions, so the reader's backward glance over previous sentences allows for the complication of our first impressions. By inviting us to overhear the

---

[149] See Ellmann, *James Joyce*, 91.
[150] *St Stephen*', Feb. 1902; cited in Ellmann, *James, Joyce*, 90–1.
[151] Yeats, cited in Deming (ed.), *James Joyce: The Critical Heritage*, i. 172.

thoughts of others, the interior monologue also becomes a space where we are able to hear ourselves think—and to hear *how* we think.

'Mullaghmast and Tara': Stephen is remembering Daniel O'Connell's orations calling for the repeal of the Union, and behind this recollection lies Joyce's reading of an anthology of oratory edited by his friend Thomas Kettle MP: 'The dainty egotism of certain young men among us—"literary" men, if only by the baptism of desire—leads them to cry down O'Connell and his successors as a tribe of demagogues. The thunders of the Titan were often vulgar . . . But he took his people by the twenty and the two hundred thousand, and shouted slaves into the status of manhood.'[152] For Joyce, as for Stephen, Taylor's voice (itself a reverberation of O'Connell's nationalist demands) was a vital model for his own 'literary' aspirations and eloquence.[153] When the author agreed to a sole recording of himself reading *Ulysses*, he chose the rendition of Taylor's speech (7. 827–69), foregrounding the oratorical indebtedness of his writing alongside that writing's ability to give enhanced and renewed life to oratory. Indeed, other surviving reports of the speech pale in comparison with Joyce's polished-up version,[154] which is perhaps why, when John Joyce requested a copy of his son's recording, he referred to the 'gramophone record of Jim's oratory'.[155]

Joyce's stately, graceful reading of 'his' oratory accentuates the dignity of Taylor's speech—a speech built on an analogy between the Irish under English rule and the Jews in Egypt—and the peroration movingly aligns members of the Irish audience with the brave figure of the 'youthful Moses' (7. 862) who will lead his 'chosen people out of the house of bondage' (7. 865). Yet the author also includes in his reading other printed interruptions to the reader's reception of the speech: Stephen's interior monologues, the newspaper headlines, a narratorial report of the speaker's 'belch of hunger' (7. 860). Such interruptions are not heckles, exactly, but sounds to keep us on our guard against the compelling cadences of the oratory. Gilbert observed how rhetorical sleights of hand in the speech employ false analogies between the Irish and the Jewish situations even as he admitted that one could not hear the speech 'without being in some measure convinced by the speaker's argument'.[156]

---

[152] Thomas Kettle (ed.), *Irish Orators and Oratory* (London: Gresham, [1915]), pp. 291, xii.

[153] Stephen's 'blood' is perhaps 'wooed' because oratory is in his blood (the Joyces had married into the O'Connell family). 'I have O'Connell blood in me' (Stanislaus Joyce, *The Complete Diary of Stanislaus Joyce*, ed. George H. Healey (Ithaca, NY, and London: Cornell University Press, 1971), 72).

[154] See Ellmann, *James Joyce*, 91, and Scholes and Kain (eds.), *Workshop*, 156–7.

[155] Jackson and Costello, *John Stanislaus Joyce*, 399.

[156] Gilbert, *James Joyce's 'Ulysses'*, 288.

This 'measure' is mercurial, for the text is favourable report and thoughtful commentary, designed to encourage our admiration and our scepticism. Heard in the mind's ear, Taylor's words serve as a needful spur to nationalist sympathies; seen by the reader's eye, the same words may be reread and critically evaluated by taking time that the initial listeners did not have available to them. This key moment in *Ulysses* is at once a testament to and a judgement of Ireland's oratorical heritage, as Taylor's poetic licence is conceived as the kernel of an enabling political action and an excuse for the newspaper cronies to wallow in and perpetuate their parochial reminiscences. When the recitation ends, we read: 'J. J. O'Molloy said not without regret:—And yet he died without having entered the land of promise' (7. 872–3). Mark the litotes: Parnell is once again the presiding judge and victim standing behind this scene.

Stephen's first words after hearing the speech are telling: 'Gentlemen . . . As the next motion on the agenda paper may I suggest that the house do now adjourn?' (7. 885–6). His parliamentary witticism calls for a trip to the pub, yet the words also echo Taylor's call for someone to lead 'the chosen people out of the house of bondage'. That is, Stephen's oratorical *bon mot* quietly takes up the mantle of Taylor's challenge even as it would seem that he is changing the subject. If he is to influence these men and others like them, he will need to work within the vocabularies they know. At the same time, he'll need to coax them into engaging with a form of expression that offers them something more than mere entertainment or copy for the next *Freeman's*. His 'Parable of the Plums' is one such attempt (parable as 'parabola', meaning 'speech, talk' (*OED*)). Stephen's thought just before he begins his rendition is 'Dubliners' (7. 922; like *Dubliners*, an address and an appellation—the internal monologue again announces oratorical ambitions). Although he calls his story a 'vision' (7. 917), the fact that he recites it aloud points to his sense of it as a contribution to the preceding debate about oratory. The tale ends when two Irish women, having climbed Nelson's pillar and looked down on Dublin only to argue 'about where the different churches are' (7. 1011), and having then become dizzy by peering up at 'the statue of the onehandled adulterer' (7. 1018), finally become 'too tired to look up or down or to speak' (7. 1024). They settle down to eat their plums and spit 'the plumstones slowly out between the railings' (7. 1027). 'Dubliners': unable to look up to the oppressive state that governs them, unwilling to survey their own territory without breaking into religious wrangling, reduced to silence as they spit on unfruitful ground.

One title of Stephen's piece is '*A Pisgah Sight of Palestine*' (7. 1058), and the professor immediately says, 'I see . . . Moses and the promised land. We gave him that idea' (7. 1061). He does not 'see' because he has not been listening carefully enough: Stephen is implementing the rhetorical emphasis of Taylor's speech, but with the awareness that both he and Taylor are building on Parnell's example, for the orator had popularized the image that Healy had employed in the speech with which this chapter opened.[157] In the Committee Room where he was betrayed, Parnell closed his defence in reply to Healy's attack with a faltering yet firm litotes: 'I should like—and it is not an unfair thing for me to ask—that I should come within sight of this "promised land". '[158] In Dublin he again employed litotes, 'I know that having come this far with me you, our warm-hearted race, will not forbid me to lead you to this promised land,'[159] and the 'promised land' was his refrain during his last campaign in 1891.[160]

These speeches were reported in the very paper that these newsmen worked for, the paper that finally turned against the Chief in September 1891 and supported the anti-Parnell faction. This is one reason why Stephen aims to remove himself and his audience from the 'house of bondage' that is the newspaper office. Despite their emphasis on cherishing the good old days, the pressmen's selective amnesia about their most promising oratorical forbear and about the factors that have brought them to this pass mean that they miss the point of Stephen's Parnellian parable. When Stephen's story threatens to offend the editor's distinctly public sense of sexual decency, the latter chips in: 'Easy . . . no poetic licence. We're in the archdiocese here' (7. 1015–16). This aside is a microcosm of the paper's decision to bow to the force of the Church in 1891 (it had condemned Parnell for his affair with O'Shea)—a decision that helped to bring down its own Moses. Stephen's reference to the 'onehandled adulterer' also points out the hypocrisy of a British state that demanded Parnell step down when the divorce scandal broke. As so often, the artist-orator's poetic licence is also political.

Although drawn to Taylor's patriotic devotion, Joyce was aware of the sectarian intolerance that such a compound of political and religious rhetoric had the potential to inspire, if unaccompanied by a Parnellian circumspection. Talk of the promised land envisages the Irish as 'a chosen people', and since the Parnell scandal, the originator of the trope—Healy—had cultivated precisely this kind of exclusivity in Irish nationalism on an unprecedented scale.[161] Stephen's eloquence is, therefore, reservedly diagnostic rather than resolutely prophetic. While the editor asks him to take up an entrenched position, his parable—like the novel in which it appears—is more concerned

---

[157] Joyce was fond of the image; see *JCW*, 225. [158] *Freeman's Journal*, 2 Dec. 1890.

[159] *Freeman's Journal*, 11 Dec. 1890. [160] *Freeman's Journal*, 6 July 1891.

[161] '[Healy's] rhetoric constitutes arguably the single most remarkable corpus of rhetoric in the history of nationalism . . . Healy minted the coin of modern chauvinistic nationalism . . . The pervasiveness of his rhetoric can hardly be overstated' (Frank Callanan, *T. M. Healy* (Cork: Cork University Press, 1996), 258).

to foster the grounds for a disinterested disposition. Valéry Larbaud noted that Telemachus, as the etymology of his name signified, was 'far from the war': 'all his resources absorbed by the task of knowing, of understanding and of expressing'.[162] 'Public speaking' may be, as Telemachus says in the *Odyssey*, 'my concern most of all', but Stephen's grappling with this concern is only just beginning, a tacit expression of Joyce's view that 'the problem of my race is so complicated that one needs to make use of all the means of an elastic art to delineate it—without solving it'.[163]

The elasticity of this art requires that we keep our ears as well as our eyes open. In the 'Eumaeus' episode, Stephen quips: 'We can't change the country. Let us change the subject' (16. 1171). This apparent lack of concern enshrines a principle to which Stephen is heroically committed and which he saw embodied in Parnell, for Joyce's print again asks us to *hear* double: 'let us not start by changing the country, but by changing the individual *subject*'. A truly nationalist endeavour will, like charity, begin at home, with a change of conscience as a vital prelude to the shaping of the national conscience. Stephen's isolated stance is couched in collective terms ('let *us*'), for his search for heroics has often been an internal cultivation and an external beckoning—an artistic calling and an oratorical call. William Empson pointed out that '[Stephen] knows he is only an avatar of the needed culture-hero'.[164] Such a hero will be, like Stephen, informed by a rhetorical culture. To change the subject, though, Joyce's novel implies that he—and we—will need to remain cognizant of another kind of eloquence. The man to whom Stephen speaks these words is, unbeknown to him, an analogue for the most celebrated orator in classical literature and his 'favourite hero'.[165] As Joyce once observed: 'Ulysses was always my hero. Yes, even in my tormented youth, but it has taken me half a lifetime to reach the necessary equilibrium to express it.'[166]

HOUSE RULES

'I see that John Dillon at the Galway election alluded to Capt. Shawe Taylor as a bastard *and* a blackguard. Note the discrimination. I thought of beginning

---

[162] Valéry Larbaud, cited in Deming (ed.), *James Joyce: The Critical Heritage*, i. 256.

[163] *JL*, i. 118.

[164] William Empson, *Using Biography* (Cambridge, Mass.: Harvard University Press, 1984), 208.

[165] Joyce chose Ulysses as the subject of his school essay 'My favourite Hero'; see Herbert Gorman, *James Joyce: The Definitive Biography* (New York: Farrar and Rinehart, 1939), 45.

[166] Cited in Power, *Conversations*, 46.

my story *Ulysses*: but I have too many cares at present.'[167] It is fitting that Joyce's first recorded reference to his 'story' by name should come after a discriminating reflection on the phrases of the platform. Karen Lawrence hears a spoken accent in the novel's many styles, writing of 'the oratory of the narrative', of 'the oratorical quality' of the 'Oxen of the Sun' episode, of characters who 'orate to one another', and of the 'oratory of English prose styles' in 'Circe'.[168] Indeed, two-thirds of *The Odyssey* is devoted to speeches. When Stuart Gilbert noted that the Achaeans were 'orators, lovers of noise, of debates and fine words' and quoted Bérard's sense of them as 'garrulous orators . . . lusty debaters, natural politicians',[169] he was drawing the reader's attention to an aspect of the classical source that fascinated Joyce. The most revered of these politicians was Ulysses. Telemachus is not indulging in flattery when he says to his father: 'you have the name of the deepest counsellor in the world'.[170] Aristotle and Quintilian also accorded Ulysses the laurel when seeking to inculcate the finest examples of public speech.[171]

Bringing Ulysses closer to home, the nineteenth century witnessed an appropriation of the orator into political vocabularies. In the 'Royal Readers'—textbooks read all over the Empire—tales included the conquest of Ireland as well as Odysseus outwitting the Cyclops, and the hero was frequently envisaged as an avatar for British imperialist endeavour.[172] Gladstone projected a vision of Victorian liberalism on to Homer, seeing in ancient Greece 'a spirit, that still lives and breathes in our own institutions', where 'visible traces of the patriarchal mould' coexisted with 'political liberties of more recent fashion'. Ulysses was a 'gentleman' whose words most clearly embodied this ideal of liberal gradualism in a 'parliamentary' context.[173] He would later write: 'The character of Odysseus, as a whole, is admirably balanced between daring and prudence.'[174] When contemporaries thought of Ulysses, they often thought of Gladstone. An article in *The Times*, 'The Modern Ulysses', proclaimed that Gladstone was 'the first orator in the world',[175] and in the Commons Whiteside referred to the 'first orator' as having 'the

---

[167] *JL*, ii. 190.

[168] Karen Lawrence, *The Odyssey of Style in Ulysses* (Princeton: Princeton University Press, 1981), 130, 124, 146.

[169] Gilbert, *James Joyce's 'Ulysses'*, 95, 121.   [170] Homer, *Odyssey*, 279.

[171] See Aristotle, *On Rhetoric*, I. vi. 22, II. iii. 16; Quintilian, *Institutio*, II. xvii. 8, XII. x. 64–5.

[172] See Edith Hall, 'No Man's Lands: Modern Myths of the Cyclops', *Times Literary Supplement*, 26 May 2006, 14–15.

[173] William Gladstone, *Studies on Homer and the Homeric Age*, 3 vols. (Oxford: Oxford University Press, 1858), iii. 3, 31, 48. See also David Bebbington, *The Mind of Gladstone: Religion, Homer, and Politics* (Oxford: Oxford University Press, 2004), 142–77.

[174] William Gladstone, *Juventus Mundi: The Gods and Men of the Heroic Age* (London: Macmillan, 1869), 498.

[175] *The Times*, 18 Jan. 1859, 4d.

cunning of an Ulysses'.[176] Such references continued throughout the period
and into the twentieth century.[177] Debates on the 1912 Home Rule Bill (which
Joyce followed closely) saw Asquith again compare Gladstone to Ulysses.[178]
The links were underlined by grand old man himself; defending Home Rule,
Gladstone famously said in the House that he was 'fast bound to Ireland as
Ulysses to his mast'.[179]

The orator's metaphor portrays him as steadfast Irish saviour and implies
that the sirens are those opposed to Home Rule, but—leaning on the idea
of Ulysses as colonial champion—it also apprehends Ireland's rightful place
as being *within* British imperial rule. The *OED*'s definition of 'Ulyssean' is
'characteristic of, or resembling, Ulysses in craft or deceit', and the 'or' points
to a long-standing question: was his eloquence a marker of exalted wisdom
or low cunning? The first word describing him in *The Odyssey* is 'polytropos',
meaning 'much turned, of many turns'; multi-troped, then, like the word
itself, which can also mean 'versatile, manifold', or 'shifty, fickle'.[180] The word
is an emblem of the larger debate; Ulysses as sophisticated or sophistical, wily
or wise, or a combination of both. When discussing Gladstone, Joyce's sense of
the untrustworthy side of the many-turned Ulyssean voice gains prominence:
'he temporized . . . contradicting and justifying himself in turn, he always
maintained (as much as he was capable of it) a sincere admiration for liberty
in the house of others. It is necessary to keep in mind this elastic quality of
Gladstone's liberalism in order to understand the nature and the magnitude
of Parnell's task.'[181] As Joyce began to shape his Ulysses, he did so with the
intention of making him the complement of Parnell, wresting the figure away
from the privileged oversights of Gladstone's Liberal polity and from a recent
history that had conceived the hero as a colonial English gentleman abroad.
Leopold Bloom's advocacy of 'liberty in the house' is a much less safe affair,
elastic in an altogether more provocative sense.

The entrance of Bloom's voice into the novel announces his oratorical
heritage in one lovely and loving breath: 'O, there you are' (4. 17). His first
word is the same as Stephen's in *A Portrait*: 'O', not 'Oh'. Bloom's call to
his pussens is a homely version of the epic *O*, an address, a shorthand for
his Odyssean roots and for his figure as Orator. Joyce often insisted that

---

[176] *The Times*, 8 May 1861, 6b.

[177] See *The Times*, 6 Feb. 1864, 6b; 18 Jan. 1875, 10b; 18 Aug. 1892, 9e.

[178] *The Times*, 12 Apr. 1912, 12a. Joyce often refers to Gladstone's speeches; see *JCW*, 193, 195, 223, 226–7.

[179] Cited in G. R. Searle, *A New England? Peace and War, 1886–1918* (Oxford: Clarendon Press, 2004), 162.

[180] See Fritz Senn, 'Book of Many Turns', in Derek Attridge (ed.), *James Joyce's Ulysses: A Casebook* (Oxford: Oxford University Press, 2004), 33–54, p. 43.

[181] *JCW*, 226.

Bloom was 'all-round . . . a complete man . . . a good man'.[182] His roundness is captured in the 'O', the seed of an eloquent exemplar—curious, kindly, benign. Charles Peake suggests that 'When Joyce said that Bloom was "a good man" . . . he seems to have used "good" in a vague and unparticularized sense'.[183] But the *vir bonus*, template for the classical orator, was the model as well as the advocate for ethical conduct. Quintilian conceived the orator as the civilizing hero: 'The first essential for such an one is that he should be a good man . . . before all else a good man.'[184] In *Ulysses*, Bloom strives to live up to this estate; we learn that he has been 'a *quasi* aspirant to parliamentary honours' (16. 1582), and Molly remembers that 'the Doyles said he was going to stand for a member of Parliament' (18. 1186–7). His ambitions are evident from one of the anagrams he composes on his name, 'Old Ollebo, M. P.' (17. 409); yet the '*quasi*' element of these aspirations is intimated by the fact that this nomenclature is not a complete fit with the letters from 'Leopold Bloom'. The civic pseudonym is missing an 'O'—a fitting omission for a fledgling orator whose utterances are sometimes a little short of breath.

Kenner suggests that 'Bloom is the Ciceronian *doctus orator* in final decay. He goes through the day uttering an immensely intricate monologue that no one hears'.[185] When he thinks about his situation, Bloom's interior voice, 'Useless: can't move' (4. 448), carries with it an unwitting acoustic memory of his forbear. 'Useless' feels like another of Bloom's botched anagrams ('Ulysses'),[186] and one of the classical orator's powers ('to move', *movere*) is often beyond our hero: 'Bloom sang dumb' (11. 776). Yet, the dumb show of interior monologue is heard by us, and is on occasion the basis for an enlightened attempt to 'move': Bloom muses with 'a kind of inward voice' that considers 'moving a motion' (16. 1463–4). Budgen observed that 'The unspoken thoughts of Bloom are often political' and saw him 'reforming the world by the force of the spoken word . . . turning private woe into a source of public weal'.[187] Bloom's predicament is not only evidence of the decay of the *doctus orator*, for the intricacy of his monologue is also an opportunity for him and us to reconsider things by re-hearing the orators. 'Flat Dublin voices bawled in his head' (5. 279); Bloom's mind is a kind of parliament—engaged in public session as

[182] Joyce, cited in Frank Budgen, *James Joyce and the Making of 'Ulysses' and Other Writings*, introd. Clive Hart (Oxford: Oxford University Press, 1972), 18.

[183] Charles H. Peake, *James Joyce: The Citizen and the Artist* (London: Edward Arnold, 1977), 324.

[184] Quintilian, *Institutio*, I. Pr. 9, XII. i. 27.   [185] Kenner, *Dublin's Joyce*, 214–15.

[186] Joyce referred to Ulysses as the 'usylessly unreadable Blue Book of Eccles' in *Finnegans Wake* (1939; repr. London: Penguin Classics, 2000), 179; a 'Blue' book is 'sad' and 'indecent', but also—fittingly—'one of the official reports of Parliament' (*OED*). Subsequent page references are given parenthetically in the text.

[187] Budgen, *James Joyce and the Making of 'Ulysses'*, 152, 168.

well as in private secession. In a letter to Budgen, discussion of Bloom led to a
warm Joycean flourish: '(prolonged cheers from all parts of the house)'.[188] The
parliamentary enthusiasm marks the civic potential of Bloom's inward voice.

The cheers in 'the house' bring into earshot a figure that resonates throughout *Ulysses*. Images of 'the House' (the Houses of Parliament, Dublin's public
houses and whorehouses, Bloom's house) permeate the novel, as do figures
of 'the Home', for 'Home Rule' is at once a private and a public matter.
When Stephen quips 'Let us change the subject', Bloom is stumped, and mulls
over the boy's domestic circumstances: 'Probably the homelife to which Mr
B attached the utmost importance had not been all that was needful' (16.
1177–8). In *A Portrait*, the young artist thinks: 'arguing at home . . . That
was called politics' (p. 13), and—following up clues from both novels—the
10-year-old Stephen first invites Bloom to his house in January 1892, just a
month after the row over Parnell at the Christmas dinner-table (17. 471).
That is, part of what has always been 'needful' in Stephen's 'homelife' is
Bloom—a father-figure who might be able to negotiate a path through the
arguing. Similarly, Bloom's request to Stephen to 'Come home' (15. 4511) is
expressive of his own search for a homely enrichment. His invented name for
his clandestine correspondence with Martha Clifford ('Henry' means 'ruler
of the home') hints at the need for a 'home rule' that may only be achieved
through partnership, for Bloom's dream of a son involves the thought 'Hear
his voice in the house' (6. 75–6). In *Ulysses*, a son in the house is often a
sun over the house: 'homerule sun rising up' (4. 102). The interpenetration
of these voices in these houses carries a political charge. The combined force
of Odysseus and Telemachus is a domestic and civic enterprise; when each
thinks of the state of his home, he is also thinking of how he might properly
define and manage the home of his state.

Joyce composed *Ulysses* as Irish nationalism become increasingly drawn
to figures of house and home. The Irish leader in the Commons, Isaac Butt,
had spoken enthusiastically of the 'magic words, "Home Rule"', and named
the Irish parliament as 'that "Old House and Home" . . . which is associated
with the memories of great Irishmen'.[189] By 16 June 1904, Arthur Griffith was
busy writing the book that would become the Sinn Féin bible, in which he
stated that 'the policy of parliamentarianism has been materially and morally
disastrous to the country' and outlined a policy that would 'end the usurped
authority of a foreign Senate to legislate for Ireland'.[190] By the 1910s, calls
for abstention from the foreign Senate had developed into the central rallying

---

[188] *JL*, i. 126.   [189] Isaac Butt, cited in Bowers, *Irish Orators*, 423.
[190] Arthur Griffith, *The Resurrection of Hungary: A Parallel for Ireland* (Dublin: Duffy, 1904),
91, 96.

cry of the Sinn Féin orators: 'we'll be masters in our own house'.[191] That house signified a national parliament as well as an Irish state divested of British influence. Debates on the third Home Rule Bill (1911–14) seemed to offer a parliamentary solution to the Irish question within an imperial framework—Yeats had high hopes for this route, and decided that 'Ireland is no longer a sweetheart but a house to be set in order'.[192]

However, the failure of the Home Rule negotiations in 1916 and the aftermath of the Easter Rebellion ushered in the demise of the Irish Parliamentary Party as the republican agenda of Sinn Féin began to dominate nationalist consciousness. Roger Casement's speech from the dock after the failed rebellion took up the figure of the home to mark the shift: 'if charity begins at home, "Empire" begins in other men's homes'.[193] *Ulysses* was written, then, with parliamentarianism on the wane, and with a separatist rhetoric beginning to outweigh Home Rule emphases. Critics have tended to emphasize Joyce's antipathy to the process at Westminster;[194] but while Joyce found 'all talk, no action' routes intolerable, he was also aware of how ungoverned talk out-of-doors could lead to intolerant action. The problem with 'we'll be masters in our own house' lay in the narrowness of Sinn Féin's definition of 'we' and 'our' as it began to set its house in order. The movement's commitment to an abstract Ireland took unity for granted (the 'we' tended to be an exclusively southern, Gaelic, and Catholic construct), while the emphasis on separatism led to a militarization of politics, to a rhetoric that blended religion and violence, and to a call for 'partition' that Joyce distrusted.[195]

After 1916, as Enda Duffy points out, Joyce was writing a novel in which his hero was wandering down Dublin streets that had already been half-destroyed in the Easter Rising.[196] Backdating *Ulysses* to the year in which Sinn Féin began its inexorable progress constitutes an exploration of what has been gained and lost since the movement's inception. As he listens to the talk in Dublin's public houses, Bloom cogitates on what it might mean to be 'master in the house' (how should one relate to 'strangers in the house' like Boylan, say? or how far should one avoid possessiveness when dealing with one's own 'sweetheart', like Molly?). These questions are also ways into considering the oversights as well as the insights of public rhetoric. Andrew Gibson has traced Joyce's antagonism

[191] Cited in Michael Laffan, *The Resurrection of Ireland: The Sinn Féin Party, 1916–1923* (Cambridge: Cambridge University Press, 1999), 214.

[192] Yeats, cited in Foster, *Apprentice Mage*, 513.

[193] Roger Casement, cited in Michael McLoughlin (ed.), *Great Irish Speeches of the Twentieth Century* (Dublin: Poolbeg, 1996), 57.

[194] Manganiello, *Joyce's Politics*, 125.

[195] See Laffan, *Resurrection*, 214–65, and Charles Townshend, *Easter 1916: The Irish Rebellion* (London: Penguin, 2006), 28–59, 324–59.

[196] Enda Duffy, *The Subaltern Ulysses* (Minneapolis: University of Minnesota Press, 1994), 2.

towards British imperialism alongside his refusal to give unwavering allegiance to Catholic nationalist culture, seeing 'the delicate course between Scylla and Charybdis' as 'the most apposite figure for Joyce's negotiations in the sphere of cultural politics', yet also noting that this figure is 'frequently traced with such subtlety as to seem full of contradictions'.[197] Prudent mediations have their costs (lives were lost when Ulysses sailed between Scylla and Charybdis), and, as Bloom admits when congratulating himself on his 'presence of mind', 'Can't always save you, though' (15. 644–5). Still, *Ulysses* is a commitment to the peril and the potential of such courses, and to the value of facing 'contradictions'. Bloom's peregrinations are therefore not straightforwardly pro- or anti- 'House and Home', but a kind of compound attraction towards and backing off from the figure.

In 'Calypso' we see that 'In the act of going he stayed to straighten the bedspread' (4. 308–9). 'In the act of going he stayed', and in the act of returning he delays: Bloom's voyage, like that of Odysseus, is at once purposive and digressive. The heroes may be lovers of home rule, but they are also explorative wanderers; in a notebook Joyce wrote, 'Ulysses not a Homer',[198] and also pointed out that 'He romances about Ithaca . . . and when he gets back it gives him the pip'.[199] The unhoused condition is at once a cause of suffering and a chance to enlarge one's horizons. Bloom can sadly acknowledge that 'The Irishman's house is his coffin' (6. 821–2), yet also dream up 'the house of keys . . . Innuendo of home rule' (7. 149–50). Joyce's novel is built on a negotiation between centripetal and centrifugal yearnings that allows his hero to weigh up the desire to institute forms of Home Rule alongside the need for more expansive gestures.

Bloom's eloquence is the deliberative counterpart to Stephen's forensic interventions.[200] While Stephen tends to look back (he thinks about the causes of things in order to think more clearly about *how* political causes might be supported), Bloom is forward-thinking in the sense that the novel's backdating asks readers to appreciate him as a man who is a little before his time, and whose prescience acts as a warning about where Ireland might be heading. As he puts it himself, 'Coming events cast their shadows before' (8. 526). Bloom is, above all, 'a prudent member' (12. 437); on every occasion that the adjective appears in *Ulysses* to describe a person's attitude, it refers to Bloom

---

[197] Andrew Gibson, *Joyce's Revenge: History, Politics and Aesthetics in Ulysses* (Oxford: Oxford University Press, 2002), 145.

[198] Joyce, cited in R. J. Schork, *Greek and Hellenic Culture in Joyce* (Gainsville: University Press of Florida, 1998), 131.

[199] Joyce, cited in Ellmann, *James Joyce*, 471.

[200] Classical 'forensic' oratory was oriented towards the past, deliberative speech towards the future.

(one etymology for 'prudent', according to the *OED*, is the Latin adjective for 'foreseeing'). As a cardinal virtue, it is chiefly associated with the exercise of sound judgement in practical affairs. When, for example, Bloom looks back over his recent treatment at the hands of the Sinn Féin 'orators' in Barney Kiernan's pub, he is also seeing forward to the violence of language and gesture that such rhetoric will encourage in the buildup to and aftermath of 1916:

Got my own back there. Drunken ranters what I said about his God made him wince. Mistake to hit back? Or? No. Ought to go home and laugh at themselves. Always want to be swilling in company. Afraid to be alone like a child of two. Suppose he hit me. Look at it the other way round. Not so bad then. Perhaps not to hurt he meant. (13. 1216–19)

This is characteristic of Bloom's stuttering eloquence—valuable precisely because it is what the citizen would denounce as 'tonguetied' (12. 1200), an answering accent to the loose tongues of the nationalists in drunken session.[201] Moving from thoughts of vengeance ('Got my own back') to a principled yet hesitant resistance ('Mistake to hit back? Or? No') to a sympathetic hope ('Perhaps not to hurt he meant'), his mind becomes a parliament that allows differing voices room for manœuvre and debate. The very syntax of 'Perhaps not to hurt he meant' embodies the act of looking at it the other way round, for the phrase is a form of anastrophe, a departure from the normal word order. The phrasing is more generous than merely 'Perhaps he didn't mean to hurt', for it could also mean that he actively 'meant *not* to hurt'. 'Look at it the other way round' is a commitment to seeing things in the round; the 'all-round' Bloom is often in two minds because of his ability to imagine what it might be like to be inside another mind. Like Joyce's writing, he is curious about the side he is not taking, frequently trying to entertain opinions that he does not necessarily share.

Bloom's day is punctuated by attenuated aphorisms that resist what a commitment to the words 'Sinn Féin' might portend (literally 'we ourselves', sometimes translated as 'ourselves alone'). *Finnegans Wake* glosses: 'Ourselves, oursouls alone' (623). 'Oursouls': that is, 'arseholes', speaking out of their arse, in contrast to Bloom's more hesitant sense of self: 'Pause. If we were all suddenly somebody else' (6. 835–6); 'Am I like that? See ourselves as others see us' (8. 662); 'Never know whose thoughts you're chewing' (8. 717–18); 'Daresay she felt I. When you feel like that you often meet what you feel' (13. 828–9); 'Think you're escaping and run into yourself. Longest way round is the shortest way home' (13. 1110–11). Bloom's 'home' truths hit home

---

[201] Joyce observed that Parnell was 'tongue-tied'; see *Poems and Exiles*, ed. J. C. C. Mays (London: Penguin, 1992), 354.

because they imagine and defend a permeable, multi-layered sense of himself, not fully beholden to identity politics or to group psychologies: 'Ought to go home and laugh at themselves. Always want to be swilling in company. Afraid to be alone'. If they are to be fully 'themselves', the Sinn Féiners will need to find a way of being themselves 'alone' that allows for a little more amplitude. As so often in *Ulysses*, the act of 'going home' (as in Bloom's case) should involve an accommodation to complex relations. Bloom's mind practises what his tongue preaches; he frequently gives the benefit of the doubt, because he is often counselling for the benefits *of* doubt.

Reference to the dangers of 'swilling in company' brings together two forms of Irish facility with the mouth that saturated nationalist politics: talking and drinking. Joyce once observed: 'The Dubliner spends his time ceaselessly babbling in bars, pubs and whorehouses, never tiring of the concoction which he is served and which is always made up of the same ingredients: whiskey and Home Rule.'[202] *Ulysses* is structured around this triad of babbling establishments: the bar ('Sirens'), the pub ('Cyclops'), the whorehouse ('Circe'), are all 'houses' where varieties of Home Rule are broached, and where Bloom's consideration of house rules becomes a way of exploring how pub opining might be transformed into responsible public opinion. Drink and licensing laws were themselves crucial aspects of the Irish question: while the English press emphasized the Irish propensity to drink as one reason for their need to be governed,[203] others pointed out that this problem was the effect of, rather than a cause for, English rule. The 'nationalist' view of intemperance stressed that the Irish were driven to excessive drinking by political and economic oppression, and encouraged in their habit in order to raise taxes and to keep the people servile.[204]

In addition, the Irish drink trade encompassed varying political commitments: the pub was an integral part of Fenian culture (serving as meeting-place and recruiting station).[205] Yet much of the funding for the increasingly supine Irish Parliamentary Party came from the drink trade, and publicans exerted a huge pressure on its political dealings.[206] Events at the public house, then, could be seen as a prelude to political mobilization, or as an abject continuance

---

[202] Joyce, cited in Willard Potts (ed.), *Portraits of the Artist in Exile: Recollections of James Joyce by Europeans* (Seattle and London: University of Washington Press, 1979), 28.

[203] See R. F. Foster, *Paddy and Mr Punch: Connections in Irish and English History* (London: Penguin, 1993), 173.

[204] See Elizabeth Malcolm, *'Ireland Sober, Ireland Free': Drink and Temperance in Nineteenth-Century Ireland* (Dublin: Gill & Macmillan, 1986).

[205] R. V. Comerford, *The Fenians in Context: Irish Politics and Society, 1848–82* (Dublin: Wolfhound, 1998), 111.

[206] F. S. L. Lyons, *Culture and Anarchy in Ireland, 1890–1939* (Oxford: Clarendon Press, 1979), 59.

of a socio-economic predicament—as a starting-point for progress or as a site of paralysis. As David Lloyd has remarked, 'drinking is, as Joyce clearly grasped it, the shadowy figure of nationalism's own articulation of resistance and dependence'.[207]

This rhythm is observable in an issue that impinges on the many plots of *Ulysses*, and on the eloquence and politics that Bloom is trying to nurture: temperance. The oratory of Fr James Cullen, the exclusion of drink from Gaelic League meetings, the fierce teetotalism of Patrick Pearse—all emphasized how temperance had become intertwined 'with the most extreme elements in the nationalist movement of the time . . . preached by catholic nationalists, often with markedly revolutionary overtones'.[208] Parnell had been as averse to extreme 'preaching' as he had been wary of revolutionary overtones when unaccompanied by temperate undertones. Unwilling to alienate either the Irish drink industry or the temperance movement, but also unwilling to conflate the voice of the politician with that of the moral and religious guardian or to assent to the caricatures of 'Irishness' that informed these discussions, his speeches in the Commons were characteristic of his measured mediations: 'I am a temperance man,' he conceded, but immediately added: 'I cannot admit for a single moment that the Irish are a less temperate people than the English or the Scotch.'[209] 'Scotch', not 'Scottish': a spry oratorical tipple.

Bloom's wanderings and wonderings are informed by these voices, and by a Parnellian circumspection. The 'I' of 'Cyclops' reports Bloom 'talking about the Gaelic league and the antitreating league and drink, the curse of Ireland . . . Ireland sober is Ireland free' (12. 683–4, 692). Our Ulysses is again leaning on the orators; in a speech in the Commons in 1881, J. A. Blake instituted a catch-phrase: 'Drink was the greatest curse of Ireland.'[210] Yet Bloom is no teetotaller (as his partiality for a good burgundy attests), and we also overhear him thinking how 'Selfish those t.t's are' (8. 366). Earlier he thinks: 'drink his health. Pass round the consolation. Elixir of life' (6. 430–1). Drink is consolation as well as curse, elixir as well as atrophy. The spirit giveth life, or—as Joyce puts it in *Finnegans Wake*—'Ireland sober is Ireland stiff' (214).

Bloom is frequently aware of the complex relations between drink and political speech. As his sharp eye glances over a newspaper, it is no accident

---

[207] David Lloyd, 'Counterparts: *Dubliners*, Masculinity and Temperance Nationalism', in Attridge and Howes (eds.), *Semicolonial Joyce*, 128–49, p. 144.

[208] Elizabeth Malcolm, 'Temperance and Irish Nationalism', in F. S. L. Lyons and R. A. J. Hawkins (eds.), *Ireland under the Union: Varieties of Tension: Essays in Honour of T. W. Moody* (Oxford: Clarendon Press, 1980), 69–114, p. 114.

[209] *Hansard*, cccxxv. 1788, 1785 (9 May 1888).

[210] J. A. Blake, cited in Malcolm, 'Temperance', 92.

that he considers 'pubs' ads, speeches' (7. 198–9) alongside one another, and his suggested advertisement for the House of Keyes combines the public house with the parliamentary one: 'Alexander Keyes, tea, wine and spirit merchant . . . You know, councillor, the Manx parliament. Innuendo of home rule . . . Highclass licensed premises. Longfelt want. So on' (7. 143, 149–50, 157–8). The '[L]ongfelt want' is also a thirst for licensed parliamentary premises in Ireland, yet the growth of the separatist platform in opposition to Home Rule rhetoric was to be built on the refusal to seek permission for a licence from the English 'landlord'; the republicans were to have no truck with the publicans. Bloom is not always above the duplicities and compromised principles he observes in his countrymen (his advert could be seen as an expedient way of manipulating political activism into the realm of private consumption—a cynical blend of 'whiskey and Home Rule'). However, his struggle to see things from more than one perspective is often an attempt to separate himself from the blurred double vision of the Dublin drinker-orators. Hearing them, we often hear the drink talking; overhearing him, we listen to a speaker who is trying to resist coming under the influence.

The first 'House' Bloom visits is in 'Sirens', as we find him bound to his mast in a civilizing mission on behalf of Irish house and home, but—*contra* Gladstone—the siren voices are those of the nationalists themselves. The whole chapter is as wary of sonority as it is drawn to it; the overture warns, 'Decoy. Soft word. But look' (11. 14). The technique sees through speech by forging a breathing space around and between the sounds of words, so that a conversation between the reader's ear and eye might resist those 'enthusiasts' who are, as Bloom puts it, merely 'all ears' (11. 1192–3). Sounds are 'Alluring', yes, 'But look'—observe the notes that make up the word: 'Ah, lure!' (11. 26). Both Gilbert and Budgen pointed out a link between the Irish love of singing and of oratory.[211] As Joyce's father acknowledged, '[Jim] had a great flow of language and he speaks better than he writes,' but, as Bloom observes, 'Means something, language of flow' (11. 298). When he thinks to himself, 'It's in the silence after you feel you hear' (11. 793), his mind—like Joyce's silently sonorous page—dwells on 'flow' in order to still it. Bloom 'seehears' (11. 1002), and as we 'seehear' the phrase, slowing it down through reading, we can hear the colloquial riposte 'but *see here*'—a gentle resistance to the seductions of uninterrupted flow.

'The Croppy Boy' tells of an English captain disguised as a priest who tricks a young Irish rebel out of his life. The barflies' rendition of the song is, Bloom reflects, a 'kind of drunkenness' (11. 1191), and he breaks house rules by

---

[211] See Gilbert, *James Joyce's 'Ulysses'*, 240; Budgen, *James Joyce and the Making of 'Ulysses'*, 137.

refusing to stay until the end of the song: 'General chorus off for a swill to wash it down. Glad I avoided' (11. 1144–5). Joyce was fond of the song, but advised: 'When you sing it, be sure to hold the balance equal between the captain and the young man . . . This is not a patriotic song . . . You could sing it just as well at Sheffield as at Cork.'[212] This balance is not held by those in the Ormond Hotel bar, who drown out such poised accents as they drown their sorrows. The focus on the croppy boy's martyrdom is an excuse for self-pity and self-congratulation—an oblique yet insistent overture to sounds in political rhetoric which lay much closer to home, and which Joyce asks readers to reconsider when he has Bloom make what is perhaps the most pronounced engagement with oratory in the writer's work: namely, with Robert Emmet's speech from the dock.

As the leading orator of the new generation, and one of the leading forces behind the Easter Rebellion, Patrick Pearse's eloquence was as intemperate as it was divisive. When Joyce's first readers overheard Bloom's response to Emmet's speech, they would also have recalled Pearse, for he had placed Emmet first in his pantheon of failed Irish revolutionaries. His speech at the Emmet commemoration in 1914 praised 'the noble trade of arms', and in other orations he emphasized that 'bloodshed is a cleansing and sanctifying thing', constantly equating religious and political fervour and defending a sacral view of patriotic death.[213] Emmet's failed rebellion and execution had 'redeemed Ireland from acquiescence in the Union', and, according to Pearse, his last words were 'the most memorable words ever uttered by an Irishman'.[214]

The end of 'Sirens' 'seehears' a memorable engagement with those memorable words. Bloom is recalling the speech and preparing to fart (Joyce's italics highlight Emmet's peroration):

When my country takes her place among.
Prrprr.
Must be the bur.
Fff! Oo. Rrpr.
Nations of the earth. No-one behind. She's passed. *Then and not till then.* Tram kran kran kran. Good oppor. Coming. Krandlkrankran. I'm sure it's the burgund. Yes. One, two. *Let my epitaph be.* Kraaaaaa. *Written. I have.*
Pprrpffrrppffff.

Done.   (11. 1284–94)

When discussing his brother's 'calm, supreme contempt for violence', Stanis-laus noted: 'Men can begin to cultivate that attitude in peacetime by quietly

[212] *JL*, iii. 335–6.   [213] See Townshend, *Easter 1916*, 50, 40, 114–15.
[214] Padraic Pearse, *Collected Works of Padraic H. Pearse: Political Writings and Speeches* (Dublin: Maunsel & Roberts, 1922), 69–70.

breaking wind from behind, as Mr. Bloom does, when they listen to patriotic speeches.'[215] Joyce's prose cheekily enacts Bloom's action, for it too breaks wind by breaking up the hot air of Emmet's rhetoric into isolated gusts, giving the reader the opportunity to see round and through the rhetoric. Emmet's words seek to absorb selfhood into nationhood; Bloom's mind moves in the opposite direction, translating nationalist aspirations into the preoccupations of the subject. His 'rendition' of the speech—unlike that of the men in the bar—slows down its pace and choreographs its figures according to the rhythms of his concerns. Emmet looks forward to Ireland among '*nations of the earth*' as Bloom glances behind him; Emmet says '*Then and not till then*', but we hear Bloom inside that phrase as he waits for the moment when 'She's passed'; Emmet said 'Let my epitaph be written', but the disruption to his polished period in Bloom's mind creates space for another meaning. '*Let my epitaph be*' means 'Let it be'; that is, 'let it be, let it have its place', but also 'Let it be, leave it alone', let the past be past rather than allowing voices like Pearse's to write Emmet's epitaph in blood.

The oppressive logic of Emmet's oratory is that the self can be inscribed with meaning only through the inception of the nation—the individual comes to be as the nation comes into being. Yet, his words also mean that the birth of the nation is the commemoration of the self's death, its epitaph, making his utterance feel like the contorted christening of a death-wish. This is not quite a readiness to die, but an aspect of what Yeats sensed in Pearse, 'a man made dangerous by the Vertigo of Self-Sacrifice. He has moulded himself on Emmett.'[216] The men in the bar embody such vertigo in a minor key. The rendition of 'The Croppy Boy' ended with their raised glasses and their chants from a drinking song, whereas Bloom's sense that his flatulence comes from the burgundy is a comical acknowledgement of the corporeal consequences of high spirits. Drinking in patriotic speeches and letting off steam have their place; perhaps there is reason, though, to engage in such activities 'quietly'—as Stanislaus suggests—if you are concerned about how you might live in a community as well as die for it.

'*Written. I have*': he has. This arch Joycean counter-signing is testimony to the quiet confidence of his written page, a page that acts as a more disinterested epitaph for Emmet than does Pearse's rhetoric because it allows space for questioning amid commemoration. The chapter is '*Done*' at the same moment that Emmet ends his speech; the writing is not above and beyond that speech, then, but times itself alongside as well as against it. Odysseus,

---

[215] S. Joyce, *My Brother's Keeper*, 218–19.
[216] Yeats, cited in R. F. Foster, *W. B Yeats: A Life*, ii: *The Arch-Poet, 1915–1939* (Oxford: Oxford University Press, 2003), 46.

after all, could have followed his advice to his sailors and remained deaf to the siren voices, but he chose to remain attentive and within ear-shot. The final monosyllable is flushed with movement, for it acts as a confluence of voices—Emmet's, Pearse's, Bloom's, Joyce's—and therefore as a dextrous example of how the last word need not go to just one person, or to one political standpoint. 'It's in the silence after you feel you hear.'

Bloom's departure from 'the House' in *Ulysses* is always the prelude to a return, just as his search for a breathing space for politic evacuation is the precursor to his voyage towards political engagement. He is soon in Barney Kiernan's pub in 'Cyclops' arguing with the citizen about 'Robert Emmet and die for your country' (12. 499–500). Listening intently, one can hear premonitions of Pearse in the voice of the citizen, as if the novel is again warning readers of how it all starts. Pearse's funeral oration over the grave of O'Donovan Rossa in 1915 (the largest nationalist manifestation since the funeral of Parnell) became the most renowned speech of Irish modern times, and summed up the spirit of those times: 'we pledge to Ireland our love, we pledge to English rule in Ireland our hate'.[217] During the argument about Emmet, the citizen proclaims: '*Sinn Fein!* ... *Sinn fein amhain!* The friends we love are by our side and the foes we hate before us' (12. 523–4). Bloom's thoughts and words throughout the day are a resistance to such rhythms: in 'Sirens' he thinks, 'Hate. Love. Those are names' (11. 1069), and in 'Cyclops' he insists on 'Love ... I mean the opposite of hatred' (12. 1485). Such a resistance is not without it own weaknesses (Bloom's call for 'Love' is parodied by the narration as saccharine). But then, parody is itself a mode of fellow-feeling that allows for difference—unlike the voice of the citizen, which insists on taking 'sides'.

In *The Odyssey*, Polyphemos was fooled after being plied with alcohol, and his Cyclopic eye was also blind to the arts of civic government. The citizen extends Joyce's interest in the relations between drink and oratory as he 'ups with his pint to wet his whistle' (12. 1505). Even the way in which the men order their drinks is soaked in the phrases of the platform. After the citizen requests a Guinness, Joe asks 'I' what he wants: 'Ditto MacAnaspey, says I' (12. 146). At the time of the Parnell split, MacAnaspey made a lengthy speech at a public meeting, and the speaker who followed him simply said: 'Ditto MacAnaspey.'[218] This drinking culture—ostensibly Fenian and against the shilly-shally of constitutional nationalism, seeing it as beholden to the English—is, on closer inspection, feeding off the very tradition it would claim

---

[217] Pearse, cited in McLoughlin (ed.), *Great Irish Speeches*, 40.
[218] See Don Gifford, *Ulysses Annotated: Notes for James Joyce's Ulysses*, 2nd edn. (Berkeley: University of California Press, 1988), 320.

to despise. The citizen is against 'The pledgebound party on the floor of the house' (12. 219); yet this public house is another miniature parliament of sorts (a 'licensed premises' (12. 395)), and the drinkers follow house rules. When the Dublin MP Nannetti is discussed, Alf follows parliamentary procedure, 'I won't mention any names' (12. 826); Bloom is 'a prudent member' (12. 437); agreement among the men is expressed with 'Hear, hear to that' (12. 1317); and even breaks in decorum have a parliamentary ring to them—'I' tells the citizen to 'sit down on the parliamentary side of your arse' (12. 1792).

Most tellingly, when the citizen gets into full Fenian swing, he says, 'we want no more strangers in our house' (12. 1150–1). He is summing up a tradition of Irish resistance ('strangers' was Irish slang for the English, and Yeats's *Cathleen ni Houlihan* sees the heroine bemoan 'too many strangers in the house').[219] However, 'strangers in the house' also has a parliamentary sense: 'One who is not a member or official of the House, and is present at its debates only on sufferance' (*OED*). When MPs called out 'strangers in the house', they were usually calling for a cessation of debates (often to stop the press reporters taking down speeches). That is, the citizen's inveighing against the English is itself an imitation and perpetuation of the enemy's own house rules. Joyce's satire is prescient: the first Irish Dáil instituted in 1919 showed the same pattern: 'Politically, Sinn Féin attempted to duplicate the institutional framework it was dedicated to destroy . . . the Dáil was from the outset a Westminster import.'[220]

The resistance to British culture belies an indebtedness to it; the Sinn Féin sense of self is shown to be a refusal to acknowledge roots, paradoxically rendering it less able to articulate a productive sense of difference. Bloom is at once more open-minded about the advantages of British 'civilisation' (12. 1196) and more resistant to house rules, pledge-bound to a less intoxicated view of Anglo-Irish relations (he won't accept the offer of a drink, and nor does he stand one). His talk on the floor of this house becomes a form of obstructionism, as 'I' observes: 'if you took up a straw from the bloody floor and if you said to Bloom: *Look at, Bloom. Do you see that straw? That's a straw.* Declare to my aunt he'd talk about it for an hour so he would and talk steady' (12. 893–6). Splitting straws in this parliament becomes a Parnellian gesture, a way of standing between competing interests, and Parnell hovers in the wings of the episode's denouement: 'Your God was a jew. Christ was a jew like me . . . —By Jesus, says he, I'll brain that bloody jewman for using the holy name. By Jesus, I'll crucify him so I will. Give us that biscuitbox here' (12. 1808–12). Kenner feels that 'Joyce had little use for the oratory that

²¹⁹ See Don Gifford, *Ulysses Annotated: Notes for James Joyce's Ulysses*, 195.
²²⁰ Brian Farrell, 'The First Dáil and After', in *Irish Parliamentary Tradition*, 208–20 (p. 210).

fuelled hotheadedness', while Emer Nolan insists that 'surely we must at least concede that Joyce had indeed a great deal of *use* for this kind of language'.[221] But talk of 'little' use or a 'great deal' of use needs refining through a consideration of where these words come from.

Early in the chapter, the citizen has lamented the loss of Parnell (12. 221), but here we catch him echoing one of the most infamous moments in the Parnell row in Committee Room 15, the first time that decorum was fractured as the party began to move towards abandoning its saviour: 'Mr. John O'Connor: Crucify him (*cries of 'Oh, Oh'*). Mr. Condon: I think that is an expression that should not be made use of (*hear hear*).'[222] Adam Piette has considered the acoustic potential of Joyce's prose styles and written of how 'the sounds of words can harbour evaded memories' in his work.[223] Frequently in *Ulysses*, these sounds are also housed in the characters' unwitting allusions to Ireland's oratorical past. Here, the citizen is being condemned to repeat history because of his refusal to understand the significance of his own history—previously mimicking English parliamentary traditions that he claimed to despise, and now echoing Irish political betrayals that he has been denouncing.

The Parnellian Bloom is the offer of a second chance and a second coming. One of the reasons for the strength of the citizen's anger is that he has a submerged sense that Bloom's refusal to play by house rules constitutes a more persuasive (and therefore more provocative) form of Fenianism than his own. Likewise with 'I', who frequently wants to translate Bloom's timely equipoise into time-serving equivocations, moaning about 'Bloom with his *but don't you see?* and *but on the other hand*' (12. 515). Bloom is drawn to 'but's—'But, says Bloom' (12. 1360), 'Perfectly true, says Bloom, but' (12. 1376), 'But it's no use, says he' (12. 1481)—but this House stands in need of these ifs and buts. As Joyce acutely remarked: 'You see, "I" is really a great admirer of Bloom who, besides being a better man, is also more cunning, a better talker, and more fertile in expedients.'[224] This is the governing rhythm of the 'Cyclops' episode: animosity masks covert admiration or implication. An oratory built on self-deceived and deceiving appeals to 'love' and 'hate' stands in danger of becoming self-hating through the very vehemence with which it attacks the strangers in its own house.

The fertile expedients of Bloom become ever more Parnellian as the day wears on. The parallels between the two men have been quietly developed

---

[221] Nolan, *James Joyce and Nationalism*, 94.   [222] *Freeman's Journal*, 5 Dec. 1890.

[223] Adam Piette, *Remembering and the Sounds of Words: Mallarmé, Proust, Beckett, Joyce* (Oxford: Clarendon Press, 1996), 172.

[224] Joyce, cited in Budgen, *James Joyce and the Making of 'Ulysses'*, 169.

throughout the novel, as Joyce's reading of biographies of the Chief is allowed to permeate Bloom's story. Not only does Bloom think *about* Parnell, he also thinks *like* him. The latter detested funerals,[225] and in 'Hades' Bloom's dislike of such ceremonies reaches new levels of discomfort when Hynes suggests that they walk past Parnell's grave (6. 932). The Chief was superstitious about the number 13 (he would not draft bills with thirteen clauses, and refused to dine with thirteen at the table);[226] Bloom displays a similar concern: 'Twelve. I'm thirteen. No. The chap in the macintosh is thirteen' (6. 827). Such aversions are common enough, but Katharine O'Shea's book on Parnell's life also bears on Bloomian enthusiasms; the Chief was fond of rescuing stray dogs, wrote love poems, and was fascinated by astronomy (he was an avid reader of Robert Ball and Herschel).[227] Bloom feeds stray retrievers (15. 660), pens amorous verses (17. 412), and is a keen star-gazer—he reads Ball's *The Story of the Heavens* (17. 1373) and mulls over Herschel's discoveries (17. 1110). Parnell's involvement in adultery, his adoption of an assumed name ('Mr Fox') when conducting his clandestine relationship, and the fact that he and Katharine lost a child a few months after it was born, are all mirrored in Bloom's private life (from his own love triangles, to his pseudonym 'Henry Flower', to his lost son Rudy).[228]

From 'Circe' on, these curious fragments begin to coalesce. The last sentence of O'Brien's biography of Parnell ran: 'He brought Ireland within sight of the Promised Land. The triumph of the national cause awaits other times, and another Man.'[229] Bloom dreams of being that man; after his 'stump speech' (15. 1353), he imagines John Parnell crying 'Illustrious Bloom! Successor to my famous brother!' before he borrows a Parnellian turn of phrase to speak of 'Erin' as 'the promised land' (15. 1513–16). The mob, however, seems less certain, and homes in on Bloom's guilty secrets: 'He's as bad as Parnell was. Mr Fox!' (15. 1761). Bloom structures his own apotheosis and imagined downfall through Parnell's life story (the trial featuring Bloom's sexual misdemeanours in 'Circe' echoes the press reports of the divorce proceedings). At the time of the scandal, Parnell refused to respond in detail to the allegations and said 'my defence will be known some day'.[230] 'Circe' is that defence; the fact that Bloom's psychodrama is represented as a series of defence speeches and political addresses again highlights how his mind is envisaged as a kind of uncensored debating chamber where his house rules allow for unruly inhabitants.

[225] See Parnell, *Charles Stewart Parnell*, 265.   [226] R. B. O'Brien, *Life of Parnell*, ii. 344.
[227] Katharine O'Shea, *Charles Stewart Parnell: His Love Story and Political Life*, 2 vols. (London: Cassell, 1914), ii. 243, i. 192, ii. 113.
[228] Ibid. i. 244.   [229] R. B. O'Brien, *Life of Parnell*, ii. 367.
[230] *Freeman's Journal*, 11 Dec. 1890.

Bella Cohen's whorehouse is, then, another house in which the motions of the parliament of the mind involve consideration of Ireland's own requirements for a parliament—an apparition of Alexander Keyes asks Bloom, 'When will we have our own house of keys?' (15. 1683). Bloom's orated response—a hotchpotch manifesto including 'no more patriotism of barspongers . . . free love and a free church in a free lay state' (15. 1692–3)—also countenances and stages a series of heckles to itself, so that the buoyant comedy of the scene is built on the speaker's winning mixture of self-promotion and self-doubt. His mind is a half-way house; overhearing it, we are asked to dwell less on *when* the house of keys will be instituted, more on *how* the handling of domestic dramas might provide the keys to unlock the country's potential. Bloom's mulling over his marital situation and his sex life becomes an analogue of larger political crises, as Parnell's engagement with house and home informs his own attempts to create a new set of house rules. Listening in on Bloom's state of mind provides an opportunity for a critical engagement with the mind of the state.

One contemporary orator archly recalled that Parnell was deposed 'for the sin he committed against the home, such as that home was, in smart English circles'.[231] That is, the 'home' was a sham: Captain O'Shea and his wife had been estranged for years, and the husband had turned a blind eye to the affair because it suited his own political ambitions. Bloom acknowledges that Parnell forgot 'home ties' (16. 1383), but offers a similar gloss on the inadequate state of those ties: 'it was simply a case of the husband not being up to the scratch' (16. 1380). The triangle in *Ulysses* sees Bloom in O'Shea's position, Boylan as Parnell, and Molly as Katharine. However, Bloom's Parnellian leanings mean that the emotional contours of this situation are revised; for rather than acting as a disingenuous representative of outraged Victorian Liberal opinion (O'Shea's tactic), Bloom's mixture of 'envy, jealousy, abnegation, equanimity' (17. 2155) in the face of the affair becomes a more even-handed way of dealing with house and home.

The huge body of oratory surrounding the Parnell scandal—instigated and inspired by Healy—stressed the links between private and public morality: '[Healy's] bleak comedy of sexual allusion was a dominant feature of his rhetoric . . . the Parnell myth became a pornographic conceit.'[232] The Chief's sin against the home became a synecdoche of his inability to lead in the House and his indifference towards Home Rule. To adopt Healy's phrase, the toppling of the Parnell myth was to be seen as a series of 'home truths'.[233] The whole structure of *Ulysses* adopts Healy's analogical technique, but resists

---

[231] Jasper Tully, reported in *Roscommon Herald*, 24 Oct. 1903.
[232] Callanan, *T. M. Healy*, 300, 307.   [233] *National Press* 7 Mar. 1891.

its conclusions. Bloom's internalized oratory has its own bleak comedy, but it moves us in a different political direction, for the end of the novel will build on Parnellian precedent in order to focus a more measured attention on two key aspects of the political debate: house-breaking and home-making.

Bloom's meeting with Parnell is more than a meeting of minds. He recalls picking up the Chief's hat for him—and the latter's 'perfect *aplomb*' in reply, '*Thank you, sir*' (16. 1522–3)—during the fracas outside the offices of the *United Ireland* in 1890. Parnell had returned to Dublin to retake control of the paper (it had swapped sides and had begun to support Healy's faction), and his attempt to storm the building meant that he too became an Odyssean figure, returning to Ithaca to challenge the suitors and to set his house in order. This parallel was made explicit in Katharine O'Shea's biography, which likened the scene to 'a Homeric struggle'.[234] *The Times* told the story as a break-in to 'the house' from 'the rear',[235] while O'Brien explained, 'Parnell suddenly realised that the fort might be carried from the area door. In a moment he was on the point of vaulting the railings'; once inside, he then reappeared to address the crowd, but 'his hat was off'.[236] Bloom's arrival at his Ithaca is modelled on the scene. Finding himself locked out of his house, 'he climbed over the area railings', gaining 'retarded access' via 'the area door' before reappearing 'without his hat' to let Stephen in (17. 84–117). Moreover, Bloom and Parnell depart from Odyssean precedent in one important way. There is to be no slaying of the suitors in this house; once inside the *United Ireland*, Parnell 'had specially directed that no violence should be used to any hostile person found on the premises',[237] and Bloom's mental accommodation with Molly's suitors is in keeping with his own consistent avoidance of violence: 'Assassination, never' (17. 2201). These house rules are moving in a different orbit from those that animated 1916 and its aftermath.

O'Shea's biography told of how Parnell and she got a house together: 'He then turned his attention to making a smooth lawn in our little garden, spending hours pulling a roller up and down, while I sat on the steps writing from his dictation "A Proposed Constitution for the Irish and English Peoples".'[238] Bloom's day draws to a close as he imagines in minute detail the layout of his ideal house and garden, seeing himself 'trundling a weed-laden wheelbarrow . . . ameliorating the soil, multiplying wisdom, achieving longevity' (17. 1584–7). As a follower of 'the constitutional agitation of Charles Stewart Parnell' (17. 164), we see 'Bloom of Flowerville' (17. 1581) as both 'gardener' and as 'Bloom, Leopold P., M. P.' (17. 1609–12) in his united

---

[234] O'Shea, *Charles Stewart Parnell*, ii. 180.

[235] *The Times*, 12 Dec. 1890, 3e.

[236] R. B. O'Brien, *Life of Parnell*, ii. 295–6.

[237] *The Times* 12 Dec. 1890, 3e.

[238] O'Shea, *Charles Stewart Parnell*, ii. 112.

kingdom—imagining schemes to resist 'all orotund instigators of international persecution' (17. 1631). Such flights of fancy are to be taken with a
pinch of salt, and Bloom indulges in them as a needful prelude to a good
night's sleep: '[they] alleviated fatigue and produced as a result sound repose
and renovated vitality' (17. 1757–8). Yet the rhythms of his imaginings, his
Parnellian inheritance throughout *Ulysses*, are meant to be conceived as the
seeds for a polity that might resist recent developments in Joyce's homeland.
Indeed, what Empson termed 'the Bloom Offer' (Bloom's offer of Molly to
Stephen, to save Stephen from himself and to spur husband and wife into
conceiving a child) has a political resonance, for it offers an undoing of the
painful denouement of the Parnell affair alongside hope for a future generation: '[Bloom] is confident that to offer Stephen his wife is a good action,
a rescue for Stephen as well as being needed for his own problems.'[239] The
'homerule sun rising up' (4. 102) may be a son as well as a sun.

Despite Bloom's voyeurism and his occasional appetite for punishment, his
condoning of Molly's adultery and his permissiveness should be seen for what
they really are: an act of 'free love' (15. 1693)—a figure for the regeneration
of a nation and a template for a kind of Parnellian tolerance and open-
mindedness that Ireland chose *not* pursue with the establishment of the Irish
Free State in the year that *Ulysses* was published. The Free State constitution
repeatedly sounded the note of 'freedom', but in a different key from Bloom's
emphasis on a 'free lay state': 'The free profession and practice of religion
are, *subject to public order and morality*, guaranteed to every citizen . . . The
right of free expression of opinion . . . is guaranteed *for purposes not opposed
to public morality*' (my emphasis).[240] In practice, 'public order and morality'
did not leave much room for manœuvre. On the opening of the Free State
parliament, William Cosgrave emphasized the importance of the House as
a space to resuscitate 'the Gaelic spirit and the Gaelic civilisation'.[241] That
spirit would involve a blend of conservatism, censorship, and Catholicism that
the house of Bloom's mind—and Joyce's house of fiction—had been intent
on resisting.[242] In the Irish Free State, the unholy trinity of Stephen, Bloom,
and Molly (Artist, Jew, and Woman) were not to be granted the freedom,
sympathy, and consideration that Joyce's novel had both recommended and
embodied from the outset.

---

[239] Empson, *Using Biography*, 246.

[240] Cited in Alan O'Day and John Stevenson (eds.), *Irish Historical Documents since 1800*
(Dublin: Gill & Macmillan, 1992), 181.

[241] William Cosgrave, cited in Arthur Mitchell and Pádraig Ó Snodaigh (eds.), *Irish Political
Documents, 1916–1949* (Dublin: Irish Academic Press, 1985), 145.

[242] On the Free State, see R. F. Foster, *Modern Ireland, 1600–1972* (London: Penguin, 1989),
516–35.

Neither *Ulysses* nor Bloom is under any illusions about the power of the spoken word. In the 'Aeolus' episode, Bloom listens to the newsmen mocking Dan Dawson's oratory and thinks to himself: 'All very fine to jeer at it now in cold print but it goes down like hot cake that stuff' (7. 338–9). Joyce's print is not cold to those charms, although his writing from *Dubliners* onwards is characterized by a suspicion of heated speakers. W. S. Graham wrote appreciatively of language that 'goes on speaking again and again beyond behind its speaking words, a space of continual messages behind the words like behind Joyce's words'.[243] This 'space' is a breathing space in two senses: an acoustic space that often breathes the air of the political orators, demanding to be heard as well as read, and a printed space in which voices can be seen for what they are, an arena in which both author and reader might pause for breath from oratorical seductions. In an interview in 1922, Joyce spoke of *Ulysses* in terms that announced his sense of his masterpiece as a confirmation of, and a counterpoint to, his oratorical heritage. His well-chosen words are a fitting tribute to the literary art of eloquence between the early nineteenth and twentieth centuries: 'They are all there, the great talkers, they and the things they forgot.'[244]

---

[243] W. S. Graham, 'Notes on a Poetry of Release', in *The Nightfisherman: Selected Letters of W. S. Graham*, ed. Michael and Margaret Snow (Manchester: Carcanet, 1999), 382.

[244] Joyce to Djuna Barnes, *Vanity Fair*, 18 (Apr. 1922), 65.

Coda: An Eyed Ear

'I'd like to have seven tongues . . . and put them all in my cheek at once,' Joyce mused.[1] 'Only seven?,' replies the reader of *Finnegans Wake* (1939). Voices combine, sounds ricochet, languages swap tall tales and ideas; there are so many tongues and so many cheeks that it often feels as though this book is merely content to talk to itself. But one of the most esoteric, dizzying texts in modern literature is also one of the most insistently vocal and oratorical, for it is often on the lookout for how it might make an appeal (and be appealing)—full of 'ahems and ahahs, imeffible tries at speech unasyllabled' (p. 183). When Stanislaus finally lost patience with his brother's work in progress, he put his tongue in his cheek to ask 'whether it was likely to go on until somebody asked a question in Parliament about it'.[2] This quip also highlights the civic ambitions of Joyce's final work, for although *Finnegans Wake* may initially seem a world away from the literary art of eloquence that this book has been exploring, in many ways it is the exaggerated summation of that art—at once its most challenging example and its *reductio ad absurdum*. A brief excursion through the pages of the *Wake* can serve to highlight the characteristic rhythms and concerns of this art of eloquence—and to underscore the dangers and opportunities that may attend it.

Shem the penman is 'all ears' (p. 169). He collects the chatter of his society's talkers with his 'ear-waker's pensile' (p. 173), locks himself up in 'his inkbattle house' (p. 176), and—although wary of 'the tong warfare' (p. 177) out-of-doors—keeps it in mind as he begins to compose. The artist is at once engaged and distanced—all ears, but also eyeful of those who give you an earful. This is one reason why we need our ears and our tongues when reading *Finnegans Wake*, so that we might follow the artist's lead and test out the voices for ourselves. Contemporary reviewers immediately picked up on the life that is breathed into Joyce's book when it is read aloud.[3] Others drew attention to the author's photographic ear and his obsession with sounds; Max

---

[1] Joyce, cited in Mikhail (ed.), *James Joyce: Interviews*, 132.
[2] Stanislaus Joyce, cited in Manganiello, *Joyce's Politics*, 184.
[3] See Deming (ed.), *James Joyce: The Critical Heritage*, ii. 412, 495, 652, 662, 676, 683, 689, 711, 720.

Eastman observed that 'You feel that he lives in a world of spoken sounds, through which he goes hearing as acutely as a dog goes smelling', while Harry Levin noted that 'His resources of observation are largely auditory... The detachment which can look upon the conflicts of civilization as so many competing vocables is wonderful and terrifying.'[4] The book itself is a kind of 'optophone' (p. 13; a machine that allows the blind to read by sound); it makes us an 'earwitness' (p. 5), and its hero has learned to 'talk earish with his eyes shut' (p. 130). Joyce claimed: '[this] transposition—from sight to sound—I insist, is the very essence of art'.[5]

On the other hand, the writer also insisted on transpositions that move in the opposite direction—from sound to sight—referring to the 'hallucinations of the ear' caused by his work.[6] We are prompted to develop an 'earsighted view' (p. 143) and a 'listener's eye' (p. 174), but things are both seen and heard here—'seenheard' (p. 61)—and Joyce often seems to suggest that we might have new ideas if we cultivated eyed ears. The title *Finnegans Wake* highlights the dual provocations of this acoustic imagining. Christopher Ricks writes: 'the human voice cannot unequivocally say "*Finnegans Wake*" (it might be saying "Finnegan's Wake," the source ballad) . . . it is only if those words are thrown on the page that they can exactly be put'.[7] Seeing is believing; the transposition from sound to sight—voice to page—allows for an exactness we should appreciate. However, once we have arrived here, we still need an ear to pick up on the ambiguity of 'Wake' (is it an indicative or an imperative?). As Adorno puts it, 'In every punctuation mark thoughtfully avoided, writing pays homage to the sound it suppresses.'[8] Yes—imagine, for instance, if the title read *Finnegans! Wake!* The journey back from sight to sound—re-listening to what we see—allows us to hear the title as an address (as in *Dubliners*): 'Friends, Finnegans, Countrymen—You must Wake!' Paying homage to the sound it suppresses, Joyce's page sends us back to voice—to a sense of writing as urgent public call.

Jacques Derrida has observed how the printed pages of *Finnegans Wake* preserve various forms of indecision that would have to be settled either one way or another if we were to read the book aloud: 'the written form retains polyglossia by placing the tongue at risk'.[9] Derrida's emphasis on grammatology often involves a privileging of writing over speech, but John Bishop has suggested that 'Vision . . . becomes, in the *Wake*, a sense whose

---

[4] See Deming (ed.), *James Joyce: The Critical Heritage*, ii. 490, 702.

[5] Joyce, cited in Potts (ed.), *Portraits*, 226.   [6] *JL*, i. 331.

[7] Christopher Ricks, *Reviewery* (London: Penguin, 2003), 23.

[8] Theodor Adorno, 'Punctuation Marks', in *Notes to Literature*, ii. 97.

[9] Jacques Derrida, 'Two Words for Joyce', in Attridge and Ferrer (eds.), *Post-Structuralist Joyce*, 145–59, p. 156.

developed forms are preceded and made possible by hearing'.[10] Garrett Stewart responds to these tussles between eye and ear with a discriminating sense of the dangers of privileging either: the novel stages 'a dialectic between graphic and phonic . . . a continuous modality of auditing not entirely marshalled by the contrary modality of script'; it retains 'an aural modality even in the mode of silence'.[11] Stewart is taking aim at deconstruction's deaf spot, arguing for 'gramophonology' rather than grammatology, and allowing for the claims of each 'modality' (eye and ear) when reading.[12] This balance needs to be kept in mind if we are to appreciate the way in which the book conducts its political enquiries.

If writing wards off the decisiveness of the tongue, it also asks us to try out its words on our tongues so that we might develop our sense of what is at stake in the process of our decision-making. This is perhaps why Joyce opts for 'soandso many counterpoint words. What can't be coded can be decorded if an ear aye seize what no eye ere grieved for' (p. 482). Such writing asks us to keep our ears open in order that we may see ('aye' is also 'eye'). An ear-eye *sees* things by '*sei*zing' on sounds, then, and such an act of seizing may lead to a more capacious sense of the griefs and grievances to which we should be attending while reading. And yet, we can probably only pick up on this airing of grievance and mull over its significance because we are able to see it on the page, because our eyes are given the opportunity to slow down the pace of our listening. Joyce's 'Book of Breathings' (p. 415) solicits and shies away from voicing; the writing asks us to hesitate, and makes its 'points' by getting us to go through the compound motions of counterpointed words, words that in many ways resist the 'code' of speech.

Such hesitancy is a form of political as well as aesthetic conduct. Samuel Beckett astutely observed that *Finnegans Wake* 'is not to be read—or rather it is not only to be read. It is to be looked at and listened to. His writing is not *about* something; *it is that something itself.*'[13] As an example, Beckett focused on those moments when Joyce aims for a 'sensuous suggestion of hesitancy' in language, noting that the phrase 'in twosome twiminds' captures a sense of doubt better than the word 'doubt' itself.[14] It is fitting that Beckett

[10] John Bishop, *Joyce's Book of the Dark: Finnegans Wake* (Madison: University of Wisconsin Press, 1986), 289.

[11] Garrett Stewart, *Reading Voices: Literature and the Phonotext* (Berkeley: University of California Press, 1990), 251–2, 257.

[12] For a defence of the importance of the phonic, and a cogent engagement with deconstruction's critique of the spoken, see Donald Wesling and Tadeusz Slawek, *Literary Voice: The Calling of Jonah* (Albany, NY: State University of New York Press, 1995).

[13] Samuel Beckett, 'Dante . . . Bruno. Vico. Joyce', in *Disjecta: Miscellaneous Writings and a Dramatic Fragment* (London: John Calder, 1983), 19–34, p. 27.

[14] Ibid. 28.

should gravitate towards a consideration of 'hesitancy' when thinking about the novel, because the word and the idea are diffused throughout *Finnegans Wake*. It was the misspelling of the word 'hesitancy' that led to the downfall of Richard Pigott in 1889; Pigott had composed forged letters which purported to show that Parnell had condoned the Phoenix Park murders. One letter had included 'Parnell's' instruction: 'Let there be an end of this hesitency. Prompt action is called for.' Pigott's misspelling helped to give the game away; as Joyce put it, the word became a 'catchword' for the attempted betrayal of the Irish leader.[15]

Pigott's slip might be said to come from a penmanship that is not careful enough about how the sounds of words might trip one up, whereas Parnell's statesmanship was informed by a hesitancy that sought to shape progress by offering principled resistance to certain calls for 'prompt action'. In *Finnegans Wake*, the gyrations of the letters HCE keep Piggot's misspelling in the back of our minds. The continual squabble between the brothers Shem and Shaun is often staged as a pitched battle between writer and orator, and—as the crowd reminds Shaun when he's in full flow—Shem's 'penmarks' are full of 'hesitancy' (p. 421). Shaun is infuriated by this, and his fury leads him into Pigott's slip of the pen and tongue: 'HeCitEncy! Your words grates on my ares' (p. 421). The *OED* reminds us that 'hesitancy' comes from '*hæsitare*: to stick fast, stammer in speech, be undecided'. *Finnegans Wake* asks us to stutter over and through its pages in order that we might see the benefits of indecision, and that we might become alert to the dangers of certain kinds of decisiveness. We are encouraged to listen and look out for 'two thinks at a time' (p. 583); such a phrase—like much of the book—requests that we hear what isn't quite being said in order to work out what is. 'Two thinks' at a time is a twist of 'two things' at a time, and to spot this we have to *do* what the phrase is talking about (take in two things/thinks at a time). Indeed, we are also being prompted to consider the relations between a 'think' and a 'thing'—as if thought itself might be conceived as a tangible force.

By talking to us in this strangely uncivil tongue, *Finnegans Wake* is offering itself as a civic resource. As one contemporary reviewer suggested, 'Read Joyce, and you will come back to . . . your newspaper with a greed for reading, a delight in words you never had before'; or, as Harold Nicolson put it, 'once you have absorbed the Joyce climate, you begin to notice things in your own mind which had never occurred to you before'.[16] Noticing new things in your own mind may lead to an enlarged sense of the methods that others employ when they seek to change it. In the *Wake*, 'two thinks' at a time is often a chance to

---

[15] See *JL*, i. 241.
[16] Cited in Deming (ed.), *James Joyce: The Critical Heritage*, ii. 514, 562–3.

spot what the orators are up to when they urge you to think in one way. When, for example, Shaun says to the crowd, 'I have of coerce nothing in view to look forward at' (p. 410), Joyce is asking readers to consider how even a seemingly throwaway phrase like 'of course' may be a cover-up for a certain kind of coercion ('of course' is a phrase that takes things for granted—audiences included). Similarly, when we hear Shaun begin a speech with 'I apologuise' (p. 414) we are alerted to how an 'apology' may sometimes seek to disarm an audience even as it seems to pander to them (hubris is being disguised as humility).

These little things portend bigger ones. As commentators have noted, *Finnegans Wake* is shot through with references to the wranglings over the Irish Free State, and Shaun is often linked to the leading spokesman of the age, Éamon de Valera.[17] De Valera's Ireland was built on an alliance with the Church and a defence of a rural utopianism (divorce was made illegal, working mothers were discouraged). His vision of Ireland tended to emphasize the kinds of intolerance that Joyce had been battling throughout his life, and the sound of the politician's voice is grappled with throughout the *Wake*; with de Valera, we face 'the devil era' (p. 473). Ireland is full of 'ire', yet Joyce's forms of expressiveness in the novel are meant to encourage two other thinks: an 'eye-r-land' might be of benefit to an 'ear-land'. The country should heed the hesitancies of the writer as well as the stridency of the speaker.

Our hero, Humphrey Chimpden Earwicker, failed to get elected to public office in the past. *Finnegans Wake* draws to a close, though, with his wife Anna Livia Plurabelle predicting that 'Next peaters poll you will be elicted . . . And I'll be your aural eyeness' (pp. 622–3). This 'aural eyeness' (royal highness) is a crucial part of the book, and—to reverse Beckett's point—it is not only *that something itself*, but also what it is *about*. The Treaty debates saw orators fiercely debating whether the new Free State should swear an oath of allegiance to his royal highness the King (the oath became a key issue in the resulting Irish civil war that divided the pro- and anti-Treaty sides). De Valera led the anti-Treaty party with the rallying cry: 'You may sneer at words, but I say words mean . . . if you take this, you are presuming to set the bounds on the onward march of a nation.'[18] He was quoting Parnell, and Michael Collins objected: 'There is no man here that has more regard for dead men than I have. I don't think it is fair to be quoting them against us.'[19] Erskine Childers

---

[17] See John Garvin, *James Joyce's Disunited Kingdom and the Irish Dimension* (Dublin: Gill & Macmillan, 1976), 121–219; Manganiello, *Joyce's Politics*, 174–89.

[18] Eamon de Valera, *Speeches and Statements by Eamon de Valera, 1917–73*, ed. Maurice Moynihan (Dublin: Gill & Macmillan, 1980), 91.

[19] Michael Collins, cited in McCloughlin (ed.), *Great Irish Speeches*, 102.

then reiterated de Valera's point: 'Parnell once said that no man has the right to set a boundary to the onward march of a nation. Parnell was right.'[20]

Childers and de Valera were not doing justice to the poise of Parnell's initial utterance. The Chief's words—some of which were engraved on his tombstone—were delivered in his most famous speech in Cork in 1885:

No man has the right to fix the boundary to the march of a nation (great cheering); no man has the right to say to his country "Thus far shalt thou go and no further", and we have never attempted to fix the *ne plus ultra* to the progress of Ireland's nationhood, and we never shall (cheers).[21]

As F. S. L. Lyons has noted, these words could be a call for complete independence, but they are also designed to sound 'agreeably constitutional' to some parts of the audience.[22] (Note that de Valera and Childers misquote Parnell—adding 'onward' to 'march' so as to make him sound just that little bit more strident.) Parnell was attempting to mediate between different interests, trying to create a 'march' and a 'progress' that was enriched rather than enervated by competing claims. This is why—as is so often the case with Parnell—the 'cheers' were followed by a 'But', as he then counselled the audience to 'avoid difficulties and contentions amongst each other'.[23] As Joyce fully appreciated, the tone of the Treaty debates and subsequent developments in Ireland were not part of the Chief's balanced bequest. Accordingly, the writer's 'aural eyeness' in the *Wake* neither swears full allegiance nor abandons the idea of partial allegiance (to say the words 'aural eyeness' is to gesture towards the oath without 'fixing' it to the 'march' of your tongue). When Joyce comes to defend his own literary eloquence against those who would seek to limit him to what they define as 'common sense' (p. 292), it is characteristic of him that he should do so via an allusion to Parnell: 'no mouth has the might to set a mearbound to the march of a landsmaul' (p. 292).[24] Such a defence of literary craft through recourse to oratorical statecraft is a reminder to readers that these pages are conceived as a certain kind of political intervention.

In its fascination with orators, in its desire to be heard as well as seen, and in its attempt to create a disinterested form of political expression in print, *Finnegans Wake* condenses many aspects of the literary eloquence that I have been exploring in these pages. Joyce's hope that his audience would be willing to attend to such 'aural eyeness' may have been optimistic, but such optimism is part of the novel's point, and it echoes the proud cry with which this book

[20] Michael Collins, cited in McCloughlin (ed.), *Great Irish Speeches*, 108.
[21] *The Times* 22 Jan. 1885, 10a.   [22] Lyons, *Charles Stewart Parnell*, 261.
[23] *The Times*, 22 Jan. 1855, 10a.
[24] HCE later delivers his own apologia to the crowd and notes that 'No mum has the rod to pud a stub to the lurch of amotion' (p. 365).

began. Recall Disraeli, raising his voice above the mockery and laughter of a hostile House: 'the time will come when you will hear me.' After giving his paper on Mangan at the Literary and Historical Society, one contemporary remembered Joyce answering back to the hecklers: 'the time would come when his audience would hear him'.[25] Mary and Patrick Colum later recalled Joyce discussing the hostile reception of his literary works: '[he] made the defiant prophecy associated with Disraeli of a time coming when he would be heard'.[26] Again, Joyce's adoption of an orator's words even as he conceives his work as standing back from the expectations and requirements of the audience is a strikingly apt figure for the literary art of eloquence. This art is informed by an oratorical culture, but it also seeks to reform that culture by resisting some of its established rules of debate. Disinterested yet not disengaged, such eloquence is both a response and a stimulus.

Empson felt that 'Joyce did mosaic a lot of grumbling about local politics' into *Finnegans Wake*, but objected: 'surely it was very absurd for Joyce . . . to make political recommendations in a style which could not affect votes'.[27] The politics were more than 'local', and such a style may aim to affect more than 'votes'; but one can understand this impatience with the vertiginous pyrotechnics of Joyce's book. Yet, a page later, when thinking about the covert provocations of *Ulysses*, Empson seizes on a vital aspect of such literary politics when he senses the reason why the author's work does not always yield up its secrets immediately: 'only if the public worked out the meaning for themselves, by a gradual process of debate and turmoil, would it enter deeply into their minds'.[28]

This 'working out' is, I think, more readily available to readers of *Ulysses* than to those of *Finnegans Wake*, but the principle still stands. Indeed, it is a principle to which all four writers in this book remained committed. This 'gradual process of debate and turmoil' would often involve the entertaining, testing, and staging of contradiction in forms that resisted the immediate demands of their audiences. But then, as Empson also wrote, 'all noble art, all art that suggests a better life, is based on some sort of contradiction'.[29] Joyce shared this sentiment; in the first work he ever published, he was drawn to describe what he most valued in literary art: 'a deep sympathy with the cross-purposes and contradictions of life, as they may be reconcilable with a hopeful awakening'.[30]

---

[25] Cited in Ellmann, *James Joyce*, 96.   [26] Colum and Colum, *Our Friend*, 26.
[27] Empson, *Argufying*, 476–7.   [28] Ibid. 478.   [29] Ibid. 545.   [30] *JCW*, 66.

Bibliography

This bibliography does not include individual volumes of *Hansard* or newspapers (*The Times, Freeman's Journal, Morning Chronicle*, etc.) that have been cited in the footnotes. Nineteenth- and early twentieth-century articles in journals are given in Primary Sources. For more recent articles in edited volumes, I have given only the volumes themselves and their general editors in Secondary Sources. Primary sources cited in other volumes are not listed separately.

Primary Sources

ALIGHIERI, DANTE, *The Inferno of Dante Alighieri*, trans. H. F. Cary, 2 vols. (London: Carpenter, 1805–6).

ALLINGHAM, WILLIAM, *William Allingham's Diary*, introd. Geoffrey Grigson (Fontwell: Centaur Press, 1967).

ANON., 'Charles Dickens and his Works', *Fraser's Magazine*, 21 (April 1840), 381–400.

ANON., 'Charles Dickens as a Reader', *Critic*, 4 September 1858.

ANON., *Live and Learn: A Guide for All Who Wish to Speak and Write Correctly*, 28th edn. (London: Shaw, 1872).

ANON., 'Loose Thoughts', *Fraser's Magazine*, 18 (October 1838), 495–504.

ANON., 'Review of *The Bride of Abydos* and *The Corsair*', *Antijacobin Review*, 46 (March 1814), 209–37.

ANON., 'Review of *Childe Harold's Pilgrimage*', *Christian Observer*, 11 (June 1812), 376–86.

ANON., 'Review of *The Corsair*', *Critical Review*, 5 (February 1814), 144–55.

ANON., 'Review of *Don Juan*, XII–XIV', *Monthly Review*, 103 (February 1824), 212–15.

ANON., 'The Rhetoricians of Ireland', *Fortnightly Review*, 54 (1 December 1893), 713–27.

ANON., 'The School of Saint Simon', *Englishman's Magazine*, 1 (May 1831), 192–9.

ANON., *Speech*, 1.1 (October 1989), 1.

ANON., *Talking and Debating* (London: Groombridge, 1856).

ARISTOTLE, *On Rhetoric: A Theory of Civic Discourse*, ed. and trans. George Kennedy (Oxford: Oxford University Press, 1991).

ARNOLD, MATTHEW, *The Poems of Matthew Arnold*, ed. Miriam Allott, 2nd edn. (London: Longman, 1979).

——*Culture and Anarchy and Other Writings*, ed. Stefan Collini (Cambridge: Cambridge University Press, 1993).

AUDEN, W. H., *Tennyson: An Introduction and a Selection* (London: Phoenix House, 1946).

AUSTIN, GILBERT, *Chironomia; or, a Treatise on Rhetorical Delivery* (London: Davies, 1806).

BAGEHOT, WALTER, *The Collected Works of Walter Bagehot*, ed. Norman St John-Stevas, 15 vols. (London: The Economist, 1965–86).

_____ *The English Constitution*, ed. Miles Taylor (Oxford: Oxford World's Classics, 2001).

BAGENAL, PHILIP H., *The Irish Agitator in Parliament and on the Platform* (Dublin: Hodges, Foster & Figgis, 1880).

BARRETT BROWNING, ELIZABETH, *Casa Guidi Windows*, ed. Julia Markus (New York: Browning Institute, 1977).

_____ *Aurora Leigh*, ed. Margaret Reynolds (New York: Norton, 1996).

BECKETT, SAMUEL, *Disjecta: Miscellaneous Writings and a Dramatic Fragment* (London: John Calder, 1983).

BENTHAM, JEREMY, *The Works of Jeremy Bentham*, ed. John Bowring, 11 vols. (Edinburgh: Tait, 1843).

BEVIS, MATTHEW (ed.), *Alfred, Lord Tennyson: Lives of Victorian Literary Figures* (London: Pickering & Chatto, 2003).

BLAIR, HUGH, *Lectures on Rhetoric and Belles Lettres*, 3rd edn., 3 vols. (London: Strahan & Cadell, 1783).

BOSWELL, JAMES, *Boswell's Life of Johnson*, ed. George Birkbeck Hill and L. F. Powell, 6 vols. (Oxford: Oxford University Press, 1934–50).

BRIGHT, JOHN, *Speeches on Questions of Public Policy by John Bright, M.P.*, ed. J. E. T. Rogers, 2 vols. (London: Macmillan, 1868).

BROWNING, ROBERT, *Robert Browning: Poems*, i, ed. John Pettigrew (London: Penguin, 1981).

BULWER–LYTTON, EDWARD, 'On Art in Fiction', *The Monthly Chronicle*, 1 (April 1838), 138–49.

_____ *England and the English* (1833), ed. Standish Meacham (Chicago: University of Chicago Press, 1970).

BURKE, EDMUND, *The Correspondence of Edmund Burke*, ed. Thomas W. Copeland *et al.*, 10 vols. (Cambridge: Cambridge University Press, 1960–78).

_____ *Reflections on the Revolution in France*, ed. Leslie G. Mitchell (Oxford: Oxford University Press, 1999).

BUSSY, FREDERICK, and KANE, G. RALPH HALL (eds.), *Gems of Oratory: And Notable Passages from the Lips of British and Irish Statesmen and Orators* (London: Collier, 1909).

BYRON, GEORGE GORDON, LORD, *Byron's Letters and Journals*, ed. Leslie A. Marchand, 11 vols. (London: John Murray, 1973–81).

_____ *Lord Byron: The Complete Miscellaneous Prose*, ed. Andrew Nicholson (Oxford: Clarendon Press, 1991).

_____ *Lord Byron: The Complete Poetical Works*, ed. Jerome McGann, 7 vols. (Oxford: Clarendon Press, 1980–93).

CAMPBELL, GEORGE, *The Philosophy of Rhetoric* (Newbury Port: Wait and Whipple, 1809).

CAMPBELL, GEORGE (Duke of Argyll), *Autobiography and Memoirs*, 2 vols. (London: John Murray, 1906).

CARLYLE, THOMAS, 'Lockhart's *Life of Scott*', *The London and Westminster Review*, 28 (January 1838), 293–345.

—— *The Works of Thomas Carlyle*, ed. H. D. Traill, 30 vols. (London: Chapman & Hall, 1896–9).

—— *Carlyle: Selected Writings*, ed. Alan Shelston (London: Penguin, 1971).

—— *Latter-Day Pamphlets*, ed. M. K. Goldberg and J. P. Seigel (Ottawa: Canadian Federation for the Humanities, 1983).

CHESTERTON, G. K., *Charles Dickens* (1906; repr. London: Methuen, 1956).

—— *Criticisms and Appreciations of the Works of Charles Dickens* (1911) (London: Stratus, 2001).

—— *The Victorian Age in Literature* (1913) (Denton: Edgeways, 2001).

CICERO, *De Oratore*, trans. E. W. Sutton and H. Rackham, 2 vols. (London: Heinemann, 1976).

COBBETT, WILLIAM, *The Political Proteus: A View of the Public Character and Conduct of R. B. Sheridan, Esq.* (London: Cox and Baylis, 1804).

—— *Biographia Literaria: Or Biographical Sketches of My Literary Life and Opinions*, ed. George Watson (London: Dent, 1980).

COLERIDGE, SAMUEL TAYLOR, *The Collected Works of Samuel Taylor Coleridge*, iii: *Essays on his Times in the Morning Post and the Courier*, ed. David V. Erdman, 3 vols. (Princeton: Princeton University Press, 1979).

—— *The Collected Works of Samuel Taylor Coleridge*, xvi: *Poetical Works*, Part 1, ed. J. C. C. Mays (Princeton: Princeton University Press, 2001).

COLLINS, PHILIP (ed.), *Dickens: Interviews and Recollections*, 2 vols. (London: Macmillan, 1981).

COMERFORD, R. V., *The Fenians in Context: Irish Politics and Society, 1848–82* (Dublin: Wolfhound, 1998).

CONWAY, MARTIN, 'Is Parliament a Mere Crowd?', *Nineteenth Century and After*, 57 (June 1905), 898–911.

COX, EDWARD, *The Arts of Writing, Reading and Speaking* (London: Crockford, 1863).

DALLAS, ROBERT, *Recollections of the Life of Lord Byron* (London: Knight, 1824).

DE VALERA, EAMON, *Speeches and Statements by Eamon de Valera, 1917–73*, ed. Maurice Moynihan (Dublin: Gill & Macmillan, 1980).

DICKENS, CHARLES, 'The Uncommercial Traveller', *All the Year Round*, 30 June 1860, 274–8.

—— *Charles Dickens: The Public Readings*, ed. Philip Collins (Oxford: Clarendon Press, 1975).

—— *The Posthumous Papers of the Pickwick Club*, ed. Robert Patten (London: Penguin, 1986).

—— *Hard Times*, ed. Grahame Smith (London: Everyman, 1988).

—— *The Speeches of Charles Dickens: A Complete Edition*, ed. K. J. Fielding (Brighton: Harvester, Press, 1988).

—— *Nicholas Nickleby*, ed. David Parker (London: Dent, 1994).

—— *Oliver Twist*, ed. Steven Connor (London: Dent, 1994).

—— *Barnaby Rudge*, ed. Donald Hawes (London: Dent, 1996).

—— *Bleak House*, ed. Nicola Bradbury (London: Penguin, 1996).

—— *Christmas Stories*, ed. Ruth Glancy (London: Dent, 1996).

—— *Great Expectations*, ed. Charlotte Mitchell (London: Penguin, 1996).

—— *The Pickwick Papers*, ed. Malcolm Andrews (London: Dent, 1998).

—— *The Christmas Books*, ed. Sally Ledger (London: Dent, 1999).

—— *Little Dorrit*, ed. Angus Easson (London: Dent, 1999).

—— *The Dent Uniform Edition of Dickens' Journalism*, ed. Michael Slater, 4 vols. (London: Dent, 1994–2001).

—— *The Pilgrim Edition of the Letters of Charles Dickens*, ed. Graham Storey, Kathleen Tillotson, and Madeline House, 12 vols. (Oxford: Clarendon Press, 1982–2002).

DICKENS, MAMIE, *My Father as I Recall Him* (London: Roxburghe, 1897).

DISRAELI, BENJAMIN, *Disraeli's Reminiscences*, ed. Helen M. Swartz and Marvin Swartz (New York: Stein and Day, 1976).

DOLBY, GEORGE, *Charles Dickens as I Knew Him* (London: Unwin, 1885).

EGLINTON, JOHN, *Irish Literary Portraits* (London: Macmillan, 1935).

ELIOT, GEORGE, *The George Eliot Letters*, ed. Gordon Haight, 9 vols. (New Haven and London: Yale University Press, 1954–78).

—— *Felix Holt: The Radical*, ed. Lynda Mugglestone (London: Penguin, 1995).

—— *Middlemarch*, ed. David Carroll (Oxford: Oxford World's Classics, 1998).

ELIOT, T. S., *Selected Essays*, 3rd edn. (London: Faber & Faber, 1951).

ELWIN, WARWICK (ed.), *Some XVIII. Century Men of Letters*, 2 vols. (London: John Murray, 1902).

ENFIELD, WILLIAM, *The Speaker* (London: Johnson, 1774).

ESCOTT, T. H., *Platform, Press, Politics and Play* (Bristol: Arrowsmith, 1895).

FARRELL, ALLAN P. (trans.), *The Jesuit Ratio Studiorum of 1599* (Washington: Conference of Major Superiors of Jesuits, 1970).

FAUVELET DE BOURRIENNE, LOUIS ANTOINE, *Memoirs of Napoleon Bonaparte*, ed. R. W. Phipps, 3 vols. (London: Bentley, 1885).

FIELD, KATE, *Pen Photographs of Charles Dickens's Readings: Taken from Life* (1868; repr. New York: Whitston, 1998).

FORSTER, JOHN, *The Life of Charles Dickens*, 3 vols. (London: Chapman & Hall, 1872–4).

[FRANCIS, G. H.], 'Contemporary Orators: Sir Robert Peel', *Fraser's Magazine*, 31 (April 1845), 379–91.

—— *Orators of the Age* (London: Nickisson, 1847).

FREUD, SIGMUND, *Mass Psychology and Other Writings*, trans. J. A. Underwood, introd. Jacqueline Rose (London: Penguin, 2004).

FRITH, W. P., *My Autobiography and Reminiscences*, 3 vols. (London: Bentley, 1887–8).

FROUDE, JAMES, *Thomas Carlyle: A History of his Life in London*, 2 vols. (London: Longman, 1884).

GAMMAGE, R. G., *History of the Chartist Movement, 1837–1854* (London: Truslove & Hanson, 1894).

GARDEN, FRANCIS, *Christian Rememberancer*, 4 (July 1842), 42–58.

GISSING, GEORGE, *Charles Dickens: A Critical Study* (London: Blackie, 1898).

GLADSTONE, WILLIAM, 'The War and the Peace', *Gentleman's Magazine*, August 1856, 140–55.

_____ 'The Declining Efficiency of Parliament', *Quarterly Review*, 99 (September 1856), 521–60.

_____ *Studies on Homer and the Homeric Age*, 3 vols. (Oxford: Oxford University Press, 1858).

_____ 'Review of *Poems, 1842, The Princess, In Memoriam, Maud, and Other Poems*, and *The Idylls*', *Quarterly Review*, 106 (October 1859), 454–85.

_____ *Juventus Mundi: The Gods and Men of the Heroic Age* (London: Macmillan, 1869).

_____ *Bulgarian Horrors and the Question of the East* (London: John Murray, 1876).

_____ *Gleanings of Past Years, 1843–79*, 7 vols. (London: John Murray, 1879).

_____ '"Locksley Hall" and the Jubilee', *Nineteenth Century*, 21 (January 1887), 1–18.

_____ 'Public Speaking' (1838), repr. in *Quarterly Journal of Speech*, 39 (October 1953), 265–72.

_____ *The Gladstone Diaries*, ed. H. C. G. Matthew and M. R. D. Foot, 14 vols. (Oxford: Clarendon Press, 1968–94).

GOODRICH, CHAUNCEY, *Select British Eloquence* (London: Sampson Low, 1852).

GRAHAM, W. S., *The Nightfisherman: Selected Letters of W. S. Graham*, ed. Michael and Margaret Snow (Manchester: Carcanet, 1999).

GRIFFITH, ARTHUR, *The Resurrection of Hungary: A Parallel for Ireland* (Dublin: Duffy, 1904).

GROVE, WILLIAM, 'Robert Browning at Home: A Chat with a Former Servant of the Poet', *Pall Mall Budget*, 19 December 1889, 1625.

HALLAM, ARTHUR, *The Writings of Arthur Hallam*, ed. T. H. Vail Motter (London: Oxford University Press, 1943).

_____ *The Letters of Arthur Henry Hallam*, ed. Jack Kolb (Columbus: Ohio State University Press, 1981).

HAZLITT, WILLIAM, 'On the Present State of Parliamentary Eloquence', *London Magazine*, 2 (October 1820), 373–84.

_____ *The Complete Works of William Hazlitt*, ed. P. P. Howe, 21 vols. (London: Dent, 1930–4).

HELPS, ARTHUR, 'In Memoriam', *Macmillan's Magazine*, 22 (1870), 236–40.

HICHENS, ROBERT, *The Londoners* (London: Heinemann, 1898).

HILL, GEOFFREY, *Selected Poems* (London: Penguin, 2006).

HOBHOUSE, JOHN CAM, *A Trifling Mistake* (London: Stoddart, 1819), 49.

_____ *Recollections of a Long Life*, ed. Lady Dorchester, 6 vols. (London: John Murray, 1909–11).

_____ *Byron's Bulldog: The Letters of John Cam Hobhouse to Lord Byron*, ed. Peter Graham (Columbus: Ohio State University Press, 1984).

HODGSON, JOHN, 'Review of *The Corsair*', *Monthly Review*, 73 (February 1814), 189–200.

HOMER, *The Odyssey*, trans. Walter Shewring (Oxford: Oxford University Press, 1998).

HOPKINS, GERARD MANLEY, *The Letters of Gerard Manley Hopkins to Robert Bridges*, ed. Claude Coller Abbott (London: Oxford University Press, 1935).

HOWE, M. A. DE WOLFE, *Memories of a Hostess* (London: Unwin, 1923).

HUTTON, RICHARD HOLT, *Aspects of Religious and Scientific Thought: Selected from the Spectator*, ed. Elizabeth M. Roscoe (London: Macmillan, 1901).

JENNINGS, GEORGE HENRY, *An Anecdotal History of the British Parliament* (London: Cox, 1899).

JEPHSON, HENRY, *The Platform: Its Rise and Progress*, 2 vols. (1892; repr. London: Cass, 1968).

JERROLD, BLANCHARD, 'On the Manufacture of Public Opinion', *Nineteenth Century*, 13 (June 1883), 1080–92.

JOYCE, JAMES, *The Critical Writings of James Joyce*, ed. Ellsworth Mason and Richard Ellmann (New York: Viking, 1959).

——— *Stephen Hero*, ed. Theodore Spencer, John J. Slocum, and Herbert Cahoon (New York: New Directions, 1963).

——— *Letters of James Joyce*, ed. Stuart Gilbert and Richard Ellmann, 3 vols. (London: Faber & Faber, 1957–66).

——— *Poems and Exiles*, ed. J. C. C. Mays (London: Penguin, 1992).

——— *Dubliners*, ed. Jeri Johnson (Oxford: Oxford University Press, 2000).

——— *Finnegans Wake* (1939; repr. London: Penguin Classics, 2000).

——— *A Portrait of the Artist as a Young Man*, ed. Jeri Johnson (Oxford: Oxford University Press, 2000).

——— *Ulysses*, ed. Hans Walter Gabler (London: Bodley Head, 2002).

——— *Dubliners*, ed. Margot Norris (New York: Norton, 2006).

JOYCE, STANISLAUS, *My Brother's Keeper: James Joyce's Early Years*, ed. Richard Ellmann (New York: Viking, 1958).

——— *The Complete Diary of Stanislaus Joyce*, ed. George H. Healey (Ithaca, NY, and London: Cornell University Press, 1971).

JUMP, JOHN D. (ed.), *Tennyson: Critical Heritage* (London: Routledge, 1982).

KANT, IMMANUEL, *Critique of the Power of Judgment*, ed. Paul Guyer, trans. Paul Guyer and Eric Matthews (Cambridge: Cambridge University Press, 2000).

KENNEDY, GEORGE A. (ed. and trans.), *Progymnasmata: Greek Textbooks of Prose Composition and Rhetoric* (Atlanta: Society of Biblical Literature, 2003).

KENT, CHARLES, *Charles Dickens as a Reader* (London: Chapman & Hall, 1872).

KETTLE, THOMAS (ed.), *Irish Orators and Oratory* (London: Gresham, [1915]).

KINNEAR, ALFRED, 'Parliamentary Reporting', *Contemporary Review*, 87 (March 1905), 369–75.

LE BON, GUSTAVE, *The Crowd: A Study of the Popular Mind* (London: Unwin, 1896).

LEWES, GEORGE H., *Versatile Victorian: Selected Writings of George Henry Lewes*, ed. Rosemary Ashton (London: Bristol Classical Press, 1992).

LOCHLAINN, COLM, *Irish Street Ballads* (Dublin and London: Constable, 1939).

LOVELL, ERNEST J. (ed.), *His Very Self and Voice: Collected Conversations of Lord Byron* (New York: Macmillan, 1954).

LUCY, HENRY, *Diary of the Home Rule Parliament, 1892–1895* (London: Cassell, 1896).

MACAULAY, THOMAS BABINGTON, 'The Life and Writings of Addison', *Edinburgh Review*, 78 (July 1843), 193–260.

MACY, JOHN, 'James Joyce', *Dial*, 62 (14 June 1917), 525–7.

[MAGINN, WILLIAM], 'Place-Men, Parliament-Men, Penny-a-Liners, and Parliamentary Reporters', *Fraser's Magazine*, 2 (October 1830), 282–94.

——— 'Poets of the Day', *Fraser's Magazine*, 8 (December 1833), 658–70.

MAINE, HENRY, *Popular Government: 4 Essays* (London: Murray, 1885).

MARX, KARL, *Marx: Later Political Writings*, ed. and trans. Terrell Carver (Cambridge: Cambridge University Press, 1996).

MASSON, DAVID, '*Pendennis* and *Copperfield*: Thackeray and Dickens', *North British Review*, 15 (1851), 57–89.

MAY, THOMAS ERSKINE, *A Treatise on the Law, Privilege, Proceedings and Usage of Parliament* ([1844]; repr. London: Clowes, 1893).

MCCARTHY, JUSTIN, *Portraits of the Sixties* (London: Unwin, 1903).

MCLOUGLIN, MICHAEL (ed.), *Great Irish Speeches of the Twentieth Century* (Dublin: Poolbeg, 1996).

MEDWIN, THOMAS, *Medwin's Conversations of Lord Byron* (1824), ed. Ernest J. Lovell (Princeton: Princeton University Press, 1966).

MEREDITH, GEORGE, *Beauchamp's Career*, 2 vols. (London: Constable, 1910).

MIKHAIL, E. H. (ed.), *James Joyce: Interviews and Recollections* (Basingstoke: Macmillan, 1990).

MILL, JOHN STUART, *On Liberty and Other Essays*, ed. John Gray (Oxford: Oxford World's Classics, 1991).

——— *Collected Works of John Stuart Mill*, ed. J. M. Robson *et al.*, 33 vols. (1963–91; repr. London: Routledge & Kegan Paul, 1996).

MITCHELL, ARTHUR, and Ó SNODAIGH, PÁDRAIG (eds.), *Irish Political Documents 1916–1949* (Dublin: Irish Academic Press, 1985).

MOORE, THOMAS, *Memoirs of the Life of the Right Honourable Richard Brinsley Sheridan* (London: Longman, 1825).

MORAN, D. P., *The Philosophy of Irish Ireland* (Dublin: James Duffy, 1905).

O'BRIEN, R. BARRY, *The Life of Charles Stewart Parnell, 1846–1891*, 2 vols. (London: Smith & Elder, 1898).

O'DAY, ALAN, and STEVENSON, JOHN (eds.), *Irish Historical Documents since 1800* (Dublin: Gill & Macmillan, 1992).

O'GRADY, STANDISH, *The Story of Ireland* (London: Methuen, 1893).

O'SHEA, KATHARINE, *Charles Stewart Parnell: His Love Story and Political Life*, 2 vols. (London: Cassell, 1914).

PARNELL, JOHN HOWARD, *Charles Stewart Parnell: A Memoir* (London: Constable, 1916).

PEARSE, PADRAIC, *Collected Works of Padraic H. Pearse: Political Writings and Speeches* (Dublin: Maunsel & Roberts, 1922).

[PHILLIPS, WILLIAM], 'Parliamentary Eloquence (No. II): House of Commons', *Fraser's Magazine*, 3 (July 1831), 744–57.

PIERCE, DAVID (ed.), *Irish Writing in the Twentieth Century: A Reader* (Cork: Cork University Press, 2000).

POTTS, WILLARD (ed.), *Portraits of the Artist in Exile: Recollections of James Joyce by Europeans* (Seattle and London: University of Washington Press, 1979).

POUND, EZRA, *Pound/Joyce: The Letters of Ezra Pound to James Joyce, with Pound's Essay on Joyce*, ed. Forrest Read (New York: New Directions, 1967).

POWER, ARTHUR, *Conversations with James Joyce* (Dublin: Lilliput Press, 1999).

PRATI and FONTANA, *St Simonism in London* (London: Effingham Wilson, 1833).

PRIESTLEY, JOSEPH, *A Course of Lectures on Oratory and Criticism* (London: Johnson, 1777).

PRINCE CONSORT, *The Principal Speeches and Addresses of His Royal Highness The Prince Consort*, ed. Arthur Helps (London: John Murray, 1862).

QUINTILIAN, *Institutio Oratoria*, trans. H. E. Butler, 4 vols. (London: Heinemann, 1968).

REDE, LEMAN THOMAS, *Memoir of the Right Honorable George Canning* (London: Virtue, 1827).

REEVE, HENRY, 'Earl Grey on Parliamentary Government', *Edinburgh Review*, 108 (July 1858), 271–97.

REIMAN, DONALD H. (ed.), *The Romantics Reviewed: Contemporary Reviews of British Romantic Writers*, 5 vols. (New York and London: Garland, 1972), Part B: Byron and Regency Society Poets.

RUSKIN, JOHN, *The Library Edition of the Works of John Ruskin*, ed. E. T. Cook and Alexander Wedderburn, 39 vols. (London: George Allen, 1903–12).

SCHOLES, ROBERT, and KAIN, RICHARD M. (eds.), *The Workshop of Daedalus: James Joyce and the Raw Materials for A Portrait of the Artist as a Young Man* (Evanston, Ill.: Northwestern University Press, 1965).

SHAW, GEORGE BERNARD, *Shaw on Dickens*, ed. Dan H. Laurence and Martin Quinn (New York: Ungar, 1985).

SHELLEY, PERCY BYSSHE, *The Letters of Percy Bysshe Shelley*, ed. Frederick L. Jones, 2 vols. (Oxford: Clarendon Press, 1964).

——— *Shelley's Poetry and Prose*, ed. Donald H. Reiman and Sharon B. Powers (New York: Norton, 1977).

SHERIDAN, RICHARD, *Speeches of the Late Right Honourable Richard Brinsley Sheridan*, ed. 'A Constitutional Friend', 3 vols. (London: Bohn, 1842).

SHERIDAN, THOMAS, *A Course of Lectures on Elocution* (London: Strahan, 1762).

SIDGWICK, HENRY, 'The Prophet of Culture', *MacMillan's Magazine*, 16 (August 1867), 271–80.

SKEAT, WALTER W., *An Etymological Dictionary of the English Language* (Oxford: Clarendon Press, 1882).

SMILES, SAMUEL, *A Publisher and his Friends: Memoir and Correspondence of the Late John Murray*, 2 vols. (London: John Murray, 1891).

——— *Self-Help: With Illustrations of Character, Conduct, and Perseverance*, ed. Peter W. Sinnema (Oxford: Oxford World's Classics, 2002).

[SOUTHEY, ROBERT], 'Doctrine de Saint Simon: New Distribution of Property', *Quarterly Review*, 45 (July 1831), 407–50.

St Simon, Henri De, *New Christianity by Henri de St Simon*, trans. Elimatet Smith (London: Effingham Wilson, 1834).

Strachan, John, and Stones, Graham (eds.), *Parodies of the Romantic Age*, 5 vols. (London: Pickering & Chatto, 1999).

——and Jones, Steven (eds.), *British Satire, 1785–1840*, 5 vols. (London: Pickering & Chatto, 2003).

[Swayne, G. C.], 'Peace and War, A Dialogue', *Blackwood's Edinburgh Magazine*, 76 (November 1854), 589–98.

Swinburne, Algernon Charles, *Essays and Studies* (London: Chatto & Windus, 1875).

——*The Swinburne Letters*, ed. Cecil Lang, 6 vols. (New Haven: Yale University Press, 1956–62).

Tennyson, Alfred, Lord, *A Variorum Edition of Tennyson's Idylls of the King*, ed. John Pfordresher (New York: Columbia University Press, 1973).

——*The Poems of Tennyson*, ed. Christopher Ricks, 2nd edn., 3 vols. (London: Longman, 1987).

——*The Letters of Alfred Lord Tennyson*, ed. Cecil Y. Lang and Edgar F. Shannon Jun., 3 vols. (Oxford: Clarendon Press, 1982–90).

Tennyson, Hallam, *Alfred, Lord Tennyson: A Memoir by his Son*, 2 vols. (London: Macmillan, 1897).

Traill, Henry, 'The Plague of Tongues', *National Review*, 6 (January 1886), 616–30.

Trench, Melesina (ed.), *Richard Chenevix Trench, Archbishop: Letters and Memorials*, 2 vols. (London: Kegan Paul, 1888).

Trollope, Anthony, *An Autobiography* (1883; repr. London: Williams & Norgate, 1946).

——*Can You Forgive Her?* (1876), ed. Andrew Swarbrick (Oxford: Oxford World's Classics, 1982).

——*Phineas Redux*, ed. John C. Whale, 2 vols. (Oxford: Oxford World's Classics, 1983).

——*Phineas Finn*, ed. David Skilton and Hugh Osborne (London: Dent, 1997).

Twiss, Horace, *The Public and Private Life of Lord Eldon*, 3 vols. (London: John Murray, 1844).

Vassall, Henry Richard, *Further Memoirs of the Whig Party 1807–1821, With Some Miscellaneous Reminiscences*, ed. Lord Stavordale (London: John Murray, 1905).

Watson, Robert, *The Life of Lord George Gordon* (London: Symonds, 1795).

White, William Hale, *The Inner Life of the House of Commons*, ed. Justin McCarthy, 2 vols. (London: Unwin, 1897).

Whitty, E. M., *History of the Session, 1852–3: A Parliamentary Retrospect* (London: Chapman, 1854).

Woolf, Virginia, *The Captain's Death Bed and Other Essays* (New York: Harcourt Brace Jovanovich, 1950).

Wordsworth, William, *The Prelude: A Parallel Text*, ed. J. C. Maxwell (Harmondsworth: Penguin, 1984).

_____ *William Wordsworth: The Major Works*, ed. Stephen Gill (Oxford: Oxford University Press, 2000).

YEATS, W. B., *Mythologies* (London: Macmillan, 1959).

_____ *The Collected Letters of W. B. Yeats, i: 1865–1895*, ed. John Kelly and Eric Domville (Oxford: Clarendon Press, 1986).

YOUNG, G. M., and HANDCOCK, W. D. (eds.), *English Historical Documents, 1833–1874* (1956; repr. London: Routledge, 1996).

Secondary Sources

ADORNO, THEODOR, *Notes to Literature*, ed. Rolf Tiedemann, trans. Shierry Weber Nicholsen, 2 vols. (New York: Columbia University Press, 1991–2).

_____ *Aesthetic Theory*, ed. Gretel Adorno and Rolf Tiedemann, trans. Robert Hullot-Kentor (London: Athlone, 1997).

ALLEN, PETER, *The Cambridge Apostles: The Early Years* (Cambridge: Cambridge University Press, 1978).

ALTICK, RICHARD, *Writers, Readers and Occasions: Selected Essays on Victorian Literature and Life* (Columbus: Ohio State University Press, 1989).

_____ *The Presence of the Present: Topics of the Day in the Victorian Novel* (Columbus: Ohio State University Press, 1991).

ANDERSON, AMANDA, *The Powers of Distance: Cosmopolitanism and the Cultivation of Detachment* (Princeton: Princeton University Press, 2001).

ANDERSON, BENEDICT, *Imagined Communities: Reflections on the Origins and Spread of Nationalism* (London: Verso, 1991).

ANDREWS, MALCOLM, *Charles Dickens and his Performing Selves: Dickens and the Public Readings* (Oxford: Oxford University Press, 2006).

ARMSTRONG, ISOBEL, *Victorian Poetry: Poetry, Poetics and Politics* (London: Routledge, 1993).

ARMSTRONG, NANCY, *Desire and Domestic Fiction: A Political History of the Novel* (Oxford: Oxford University Press, 1987).

ASHTON, ROSEMARY, *George Eliot: A Life* (London: Penguin, 1996).

ATTRIDGE, DEREK, *Joyce Effects: On Language, Theory, and History* (Cambridge: Cambridge University Press, 2000).

_____ (ed.), *James Joyce's Ulysses: A Casebook* (Oxford: Oxford University Press, 2004).

_____ and FERRER, DANIEL (eds.), *Post-Structuralist Joyce: Essays from the French* (Cambridge: Cambridge University Press, 1988).

_____ and HOWES, MARJORIE (eds.), *Semicolonial Joyce* (Cambridge: Cambridge University Press, 2000).

BAINBRIDGE, SIMON, *Napoleon and English Romanticism* (Cambridge: Cambridge University Press, 1995).

BAKER, ARTHUR (ed.), *A Concordance to the Poetical and Dramatic Works of Alfred, Lord Tennyson* (London: Kegan Paul, 1914).

BAKHTIN, MIKHAIL, *The Dialogic Imagination: Four Essays*, ed. Michael Holquist, trans. Caryl Emerson and Michael Holquist (Austin: University of Texas Press, 1981).

BARCZEWSKI, STEPHANIE, *Myth and National Identity in Nineteenth-Century Britain: The Legends of King Arthur and Robin Hood* (Oxford: Oxford University Press, 2000).

BARTON, ANNE, *Byron: Don Juan* (Cambridge: Cambridge University Press, 1992).

BAYLY, C. A., *Imperial Meridian: The British Empire and the World, 1780–1830* (London: Longman, 1989).

BEBBINGTON, DAVID, *The Mind of Gladstone: Religion, Homer, and Politics* (Oxford: Oxford University Press, 2004).

BELCHEM, JOHN, 'Radical Language and Ideology in Early Nineteenth-Century England: The Challenge of the Platform', *Albion*, 20 (1988), 246–60.

___ and EPSTEIN, JAMES, 'The Nineteenth-Century Gentleman Leader Revisited', *Social History*, 22 (May 1997), 174–93.

BEW, PAUL, *Conflict and Conciliation in Ireland 1890–1910: Parnellites and Radical Agrarians* (Oxford: Clarendon Press, 1987).

BIAGINI, EUGENIO, *Liberty, Retrenchment and Reform: Popular Liberalism in the Age of Gladstone, 1860–1880* (Cambridge: Cambridge University Press, 1992).

BIALOSTOSKY, DON H., and NEEDHAM, LAWRENCE D. (eds.), *Rhetorical Traditions and British Romantic Literature* (Indianapolis: Indiana University Press, 1995).

BISHOP, JOHN, *Joyce's Book of the Dark: Finnegans Wake* (Madison: University of Wisconsin Press, 1986).

BLAKE, ROBERT, *Disraeli* (London: Eyre & Spottiswoode, 1966).

BOURDIEU, PIERRE, *Distinction: A Social Critique of the Judgement of Taste*, trans. Richard Nice (London: Routledge & Kegan Paul, 1984).

BOWERS, CLAUDE G., *The Irish Orators: A History of Ireland's Fight for Freedom* (Indianapolis: Bobbs-Merrill, 1916).

BOYCE, GEORGE D., and O'DAY, ALAN (eds.), *Parnell in Perspective* (London and New York: Routledge, 1991).

BRADLEY, BRUCE, *James Joyce's Schooldays* (Dublin: Gill & Macmillan, 1982).

BRANTLINGER, PATRICK, *Rule of Darkness: British Literature and Imperialism, 1830–1914* (Ithaca, NY: Cornell University Press, 1988).

BRETT, JAMES, 'Political Dinners in Early Nineteenth-Century Britain: Platform, Meeting Place and Battleground', *History*, 81 (October 1996), 527–52.

BRIGGS, ASA, *Victorian People: A Reassessment of Persons and Themes, 1851–67* (New York: Harper & Row, 1955).

BRISTOW, JOSEPH (ed.), *The Victorian Poet: Poetics and Persona* (London: Croom Helm, 1987).

BROERS, MICHAEL, *Europe under Napoleon, 1799–1815* (London: Arnold, 1996).

BROMWICH, DAVID, *A Choice of Inheritance: Self and Community from Edmund Burke to Robert Frost* (Cambridge, Mass.: Harvard University Press, 1989).

___ *Hazlitt: The Mind of a Critic*, 2nd edn. (New Haven and London: Yale University Press, 1999).

BROOKS, PETER, *Reading for the Plot: Design and Intention in Narrative* (Oxford: Clarendon Press, 1984).

BROWN, MARSHALL (ed.), *The Cambridge History of Literary Criticism*, v: *Romanticism* (Cambridge: Cambridge University Press, 2000).

BRUNDAGE, ANTHONY, *The Making of the New Poor Law: The Politics of Inquiry, Enactment, and Implementation, 1832–39* (London: Hutchinson, 1978).

BUDGEN, FRANK, *James Joyce and the Making of "Ulysses" and Other Writings*, introd. Clive Hart (Oxford: Oxford University Press, 1972).

CALLANAN, FRANK, *The Parnell Split, 1890–91* (Cork: Cork University Press, 1992).

—— *T. M. Healy* (Cork: Cork University Press, 1996).

CAMERON, KENNETH NEILL (ed.), *Romantic Rebels: Essays on Shelley and his Circle* (Cambridge, Mass.: Harvard University Press, 1973).

CANNON, JOHN, *Parliamentary Reform, 1640–1832* (Aldershot: Gregg Revivals, 1994).

CAREY, JOHN, *The Violent Effigy: A Study of Dickens' Imagination*, 2nd edn. (London: Faber & Faber, 1991).

CHANCELLOR, VALERIE, *The Political Life of Joseph Hume, 1777–1855* (Stratford-on-Avon: Bloomfield, 1986).

CHENG, VINCENT J., *Joyce, Race, and Empire* (Cambridge: Cambridge University Press, 1995).

CHILDERS, JOSEPH W., *Novel Possibilities: Fiction and the Formation of Early Victorian Culture* (Philadelphia: University of Pennsylvania Press, 1995).

CHITTICK, KATHRYN, *Dickens and the 1830s* (Cambridge: Cambridge University Press, 1991).

CHRISTENSEN, JEROME, *Lord Byron's Strength: Romantic Writing and Commercial Society* (Baltimore: Johns Hopkins University Press, 1993).

CLARK, ANNA, 'Queen Caroline and the Sexual Politics of Popular Culture in London, 1820', *Representations*, 31 (Summer 1990), 47–68.

—— *Scandal: The Sexual Politics of the British Constitution* (Princeton: Princeton University Press, 2004).

CLARK, TIMOTHY, *The Theory of Inspiration: Composition as a Crisis of Subjectivity in Romantic and Post-Romantic Writing* (Manchester: Manchester University Press, 1997).

COHEN, EMMELINE W., *The Growth of the British Civil Service, 1780–1939* (London: Cass, 1965).

COHN, DORRIT, *Transparent Minds: Narrative Modes for Presenting Consciousness in Fiction* (Princeton: Princeton University Press, 1984).

COHN, NORMAN, 'The Saint-Simonian Portent', *Twentieth Century*, 152 (October 1952), 330–40.

COLLINI, STEFAN, *Public Moralists: Political Thought and Intellectual Life in Britain, 1850–1930* (Oxford: Oxford University Press, 1991).

COLLINS, IRENE, *Napoleon and his Parliaments, 1800–1815* (London: Edward Arnold, 1979).

COLLINS, PHILIP, (ed.), *Dickens: The Critical Heritage* (London: Routledge & Kegan Paul, 1971).

—— *Reading Aloud: A Victorian Métier* (Lincoln: Tennyson Society, 1972).

—— 'Dickens the Citizen', in *Politics in Literature in the Nineteenth Century* (Lille: Editions Universitaires, 1974), 61–82.

COLUM, MARY, and COLUM, PATRICK, *Our Friend James Joyce* (New York: Doubleday, 1958).

COSTELLO, PETER, *James Joyce: The Years of Growth, 1882–1915* (London: Kyle Cathie, 1992).

CRONIN, RICHARD, *The Politics of Romantic Poetry: In Search of the Pure Commonwealth* (London: Macmillan, 2000).

—— *Romantic Victorians: English Literature, 1824–1840* (Basingstoke: Palgrave, 2002).

—— HARRISON, ANTHONY H., and CHAPMAN, ALISON (eds.), *A Companion to Victorian Poetry* (Oxford: Blackwell, 2002).

CURRAN, STUART, *Poetic Form and British Romanticism* (Oxford: Oxford University Press, 1986).

DAVIS, PHILIP, *The Victorians* (Oxford: Oxford University Press, 2002).

DE BOLLA, PETER, *The Discourse of the Sublime: Readings in History, Aesthetics and the Subject* (Oxford: Blackwell, 1989).

DE MAN, PAUL, *Aesthetic Ideology*, ed. Andrzej Warminski (Minneapolis: University of Minnesota Press, 1996).

DEACON, RICHARD, *The Cambridge Apostles* (London: Royce, 1985).

DEMING, ROBERT H. (ed.), *James Joyce: The Critical Heritage*, 2 vols. (London: Routledge & Kegan Paul, 1970).

DERRIDA, JACQUES, 'Economimesis', *Diacritics*, 11 (June 1981), 3–25.

DUFFY, ENDA, *The Subaltern Ulysses* (Minneapolis: University of Minnesota Press, 1994).

DUFFY, MICHAEL, 'World-Wide War and British Expansion, 1793–1815' in P. J. Marshall (ed.), *The Oxford History of the British Empire: The Eighteenth Century* (Oxford: Oxford University Press, 1998), 184–207.

EAGLETON, TERRY, *The Ideology of the Aesthetic* (Oxford: Blackwell, 1990).

—— *After Theory* (London: Allen Lane, 2003).

EDWARDES, MICHAEL, *Red Year: The Indian Rebellion of 1857* (London: Hamish Hamilton, 1973).

EHRLICH, HEYWARD, ' "Araby" in Context: The "Splendid Bazaar," Irish Orientalism, and James Clarence Mangan', repr. in *Dubliners*, ed. Margot Norris (New York: Norton, 2006), 261–82.

ELLEDGE, PAUL, *Lord Byron at Harrow School: Speaking Out, Talking Back, Acting Up, Bowing Out* (Baltimore and London: Johns Hopkins University Press, 2000).

ELLISON, ROBERT H., *The Victorian Pulpit: Spoken and Written Sermons in Nineteenth-Century Britain* (Selinsgrove: Susquehanna University Press, 1998).

ELLMANN, RICHARD, *James Joyce*, rev. edn. (Oxford: Oxford University Press, 1983).

EMPSON, WILLIAM, *Some Versions of Pastoral* (1935; repr. New York: New Directions, 1974).

—— *Using Biography* (Cambridge, Mass.: Harvard University Press, 1984).

—— *Argufying: Essays on Literature and Culture*, ed. John Haffenden (London: Chatto & Windus, 1987).

—— *Seven Types of Ambiguity* (1930; repr. London: Hogarth, 1991).

EPSTEIN, JAMES, *The Lion of Freedom: Feargus O'Connor and the Chartist Movement 1832–1842* (London: Croom Helm, 1982).

—— 'The Constitutional Idiom: Radical Reasoning, Rhetoric and Action in Early Nineteenth-Century England', *Journal of Social History*, 23/3 (1990), 553–74.

—— *Radical Expression: Political Language, Ritual and Symbol in England, 1790–1850* (Oxford: Oxford University Press, 1994).

ERDMAN, DAVID V., 'Lord Byron and the Genteel Reformers', *PMLA*, 56 (1941), 1065–94.

FAIRHALL, JAMES, *James Joyce and the Question of History* (Cambridge: Cambridge University Press, 1993).

FARRELL, BRIAN (ed.), *The Irish Parliamentary Tradition* (Dublin: Gill & Macmillan, 1973).

FOOT, MICHAEL, *The Politics of Paradise: A Vindication of Byron* (London: Collins, 1988).

FOSTER, R. F., *Modern Ireland, 1600–1972* (London: Penguin, 1989).

—— *Paddy and Mr Punch: Connections in Irish and English History* (London: Penguin, 1993).

—— *W. B. Yeats: A Life*, i: *The Apprentice Mage, 1865–1914* (Oxford: Oxford University Press, 1997).

—— *W. B. Yeats: A Life*, ii: *The Arch-Poet, 1915–1939* (Oxford: Oxford University Press, 2003).

FRANKLIN, CAROLINE, *Byron's Heroines* (Oxford: Clarendon Press, 1992).

FRENCH, MARILYN, *The Book as World: James Joyce's Ulysses* (Cambridge, Mass.: Harvard University Press, 1976).

FULFORD, ROGER, *The Trial of Queen Caroline* (London: Batsford, 1967).

GARIS, ROBERT, *The Dickens Theatre: A Reassessment of the Novels* (Oxford: Clarendon Press, 1965).

GARVER, EUGENE, *Aristotle's Rhetoric: An Art of Character* (Chicago: University of Chicago Press, 1994).

GARVIN, JOHN, *James Joyce's Disunited Kingdom and the Irish Dimension* (Dublin: Gill & Macmillan, 1976).

GIBSON, ANDREW, *Joyce's Revenge: History, Politics and Aesthetics in Ulysses* (Oxford: Oxford University Press, 2002).

GIBSON, MARY ELLIS (ed.), *Critical Essays on Robert Browning* (New York: Hall, 1992).

GIFFORD, DON, *Joyce Annotated: Notes for Dubliners and A Portrait of the Artist as a Young Man*, 2nd edn. (Berkeley: University of California Press, 1982).

—— *Ulysses Annotated: Notes for James Joyce's Ulysses*, 2nd edn. (Berkeley: University of California Press, 1988).

GILBERT, STUART, *James Joyce's 'Ulysses': A Study* (New York: Vintage, 1955).

GOLDING, ROBERT, *Idiolects in Dickens: The Major Techniques and Chronological Development* (London: Macmillan, 1985).

GOODHEART, EUGENE, *The Reign of Ideology* (New York: Columbia University Press, 1997).

GOODMAN, PAUL, *Speaking and Language: Defence of Poetry* (New York: Random House, 1971).

GORMAN, HERBERT, *James Joyce: The Definitive Biography* (New York: Farrar and Rinehart, 1939).

GRAB, ALEXANDER, *Napoleon and the Transformation of Europe* (Basingstoke: Palgrave Macmillan, 2003).

GRAY, ERIK, *The Poetry of Indifference from the Romantics to the Rubáiyát* (Amherst and Boston: University of Massachusetts Press, 2005).

GREEN, WILLIAM, *British Slave Emancipation: The Sugar Colonies and the Great Experiment 1830–1865* (Oxford: Clarendon Press, 1976).

GREENE, GRAHAM, *The Lost Childhood and Other Essays* (London: Eyre & Spottiswoode, 1954).

GRIFFITHS, ERIC, *The Printed Voice of Victorian Poetry* (Oxford: Clarendon Press, 1989).

GUYER, PAUL, *Kant and the Experience of Freedom: Essays on Aesthetics and Morality* (Cambridge: Cambridge University Press, 1993).

HABERMAS, JÜRGEN, *The Structural Transformation of the Public Sphere: An Inquiry into a Category of Bourgeois Society*, trans. Thomas Burger (Cambridge: Polity, 1989).

HALL, EDITH, 'No Man's Lands: Modern Myths of the Cyclops', *Times Literary Supplement*, 26 May 2006, 14–15.

HANHAM, H. J., *The Nineteenth Century Constitution, 1815–1914* (Cambridge: Cambridge University Press, 1969).

HEANEY, SEAMUS, 'A Hundred Years After', *Times Literary Supplement*, 2 October 1992, 8.

HERR, CHERYL, *Joyce's Anatomy of Culture* (Urbana and Chicago: University of Illinois Press, 1986).

HILL, GEOFFREY, *The Lords of Limit* (London: André Deutsch, 1984).

HILTON, BOYD, *A Mad, Bad, and Dangerous People? England, 1783–1846* (Oxford: Clarendon Press, 2006).

HINDE, WENDY, *George Canning* (London: Collins, 1973).

HOLLANDER, JOHN, *Melodious Guile: Fictive Patterning in Poetic Language* (New Haven: Yale University Press, 1988).

HOLLIS, PATRICIA (ed.), *Pressure from Without in Early Victorian England* (London: Arnold, 1974).

HOOVER, BENJAMIN BEARD, *Samuel Johnson's Parliamentary Reporting: Debates in the Senate of Lilliput* (Berkeley and Los Angeles: University of California Press, 1953).

HOPPEN, THEODORE, *The Mid-Victorian Generation, 1846–1886* (Oxford: Clarendon Press, 1998).

HORNER, WINIFRED (ed.), *The Present State of Scholarship in Historical and Contemporary Rhetoric* (Columbia: University of Missouri Press, 1990).

HOUSE, HUMPHRY, *The Dickens World*, 2nd edn. (Oxford: Oxford University Press, 1942).

HOWARTH, PATRICK, *Questions in the House: The History of a Unique British Institution* (London: Bodley Head, 1956).

Howe, Anthony, *Free Trade and Liberal England, 1846–1946* (Oxford: Clarendon Press, 1997).

Howell, Wilbur Samuel, *Eighteenth-Century British Logic and Rhetoric* (Princeton: Princeton University Press, 1971).

Hyam, Ronald, *Britain's Imperial Century, 1815–1914* (London: Batsford, 1976).

Inkster, Ian (ed.), *The Steam Intellect Societies: Essays on Culture, Education and Industry, c.1820–1914* (Nottingham: Nottingham University Press, 1985).

Jackson, John Wyse, and Costello, Peter, *John Stanislaus Joyce: The Voluminous Life and Genius of James Joyce's Father* (London: Fourth Estate, 1997).

Jagger, Peter (ed.), *Gladstone* (London: Hambledon, 1998).

James, Robert Rhodes, *Albert, Prince Consort* (London: Hamish Hamilton, 1983).

Jarvis, Simon, *Adorno: A Critical Introduction* (Cambridge: Polity, 1998).

Jenkins, T. A., *Parliament, Party and Politics in Victorian Britain* (Manchester: Manchester University Press, 1996).

Johnson, Edgar, *Charles Dickens: His Tragedy and Triumph*, 2 vols. (New York: Simon & Schuster, 1952).

Johnston, Freya, *Samuel Johnson and the Art of Sinking, 1709–1791* (Oxford: Oxford University Press, 2005).

Jordon, John O. (ed.), *The Cambridge Companion to Dickens* (Cambridge: Cambridge University Press, 2001).

Joseph, M. K., *Byron the Poet* (London: Gollancz, 1964).

Karlin, Daniel, and Woolford, John, *Robert Browning* (Harlow: Longman, 1996).

Keach, William, 'Political Inflections in Byron's *Ottava Rima*', *Studies in Romanticism*, 27 (Winter 1988), 551–62.

Kellsall, Malcolm, *Byron's Politics* (Brighton: Harvester Press, 1987).

——— 'Lord Byron', in David Pirie (ed.), *The Romantic Period* (Harmondsworth: Penguin, 1994), 289–310.

Kelly, Linda, *Richard Brinsley Sheridan: A Life* (London: Sinclair-Stevenson, 1997).

Kennedy, George, *The Art of Rhetoric in the Roman World, 300 BC–AD 300* (Princeton: Princeton University Press, 1972).

Kenner, Hugh, *Dublin's Joyce* (Boston: Beacon Press, 1962).

——— *Joyce's Voices* (London: Faber & Faber, 1978).

Kerr, Donal, *Peel, Priests and Politics* (Oxford: Clarendon Press, 1982).

Killham, John, *Tennyson and The Princess: Reflections of an Age* (London: Athlone, 1958).

Kivy, Peter (ed.), *Essays on the History of Aesthetics* (New York: University of Rochester Press, 1992).

Knight, George Wilson, *The Burning Oracle: Studies in the Poetry of Action* (Oxford: Oxford University Press, 1939).

Kreilkamp, Ivan, *Voice and the Victorian Storyteller* (Cambridge: Cambridge University Press, 2005).

Laffan, Michael, *The Resurrection of Ireland: The Sinn Féin Party, 1916–1923* (Cambridge: Cambridge University Press, 1999).

LAMBERT, MARK, *Dickens and the Suspended Quotation* (New Haven: Yale University Press, 1981).

LANG, CECIL, *Tennyson's Arthurian Pyscho-Drama* (Lincoln: Tennyson Research Centre, 1983).

LAWRENCE, KAREN, *The Odyssey of Style in Ulysses* (Princeton: Princeton University Press, 1981).

LEASK, NIGEL, *British Romantic Writers and the East: Anxieties of Empire* (Cambridge: Cambridge University Press, 1992).

LEE, STEPHEN J., *Aspects of British Political History, 1815–1914* (London: Routledge, 1994).

LEVINE, GEORGE (ed.), *Aesthetics and Ideology* (New Brunswick, NJ: Rutgers University Press, 1994).

LLOYD, T., 'Uncontested Seats in British General Elections, 1852–1918', *Historical Journal*, 8/2 (1965), 260–5.

LOPATIN, NANCY, *Political Unions, Popular Politics and the Great Reform Act of 1832* (Basingstoke: Macmillan, 1998).

LOWE, BRIGID, *Victorian Fiction and the Insights of Sympathy: An Alternative to the Hermeneutics of Suspicion* (London: Anthem Press, 2006).

LUBENOW, WILLIAM C., *The Cambridge Apostles, 1820–1914: Liberalism, Imagination and Friendship in British Intellectual and Professional Life* (Cambridge: Cambridge University Press, 1998).

LYONS, F. S. L., *Charles Stewart Parnell* (London: HarperCollins, 1978).

―― *Culture and Anarchy in Ireland, 1890–1939* (Oxford: Clarendon Press, 1979).

―― and HAWKINS, R. A. J. (eds.), *Ireland under the Union: Varieties of Tension: Essays in Honour of T. W. Moody* (Oxford: Clarendon Press, 1980).

MCCALMAN, IAIN, 'Controlling the Riots: Dickens, *Barnaby Rudge* and the Romantic Revolution', *History*, 84 (July 1999), 458–76.

MCCORD, NORMAN, *British History, 1815–1906* (Oxford: Oxford University Press, 1991).

MCCOURT, JOHN, *The Years of Bloom: James Joyce in Trieste, 1904–1920* (Madison: University of Wisconsin Press, 2000).

MCGANN, JEROME, *Don Juan in Context* (London: John Murray, 1976).

―― *Byron and Romanticism*, ed. James Soderholm (Cambridge: Cambridge University Press, 2002).

MACHIN, G. I. T., *The Catholic Question in English Politics, 1820 to 1830* (Oxford: Clarendon Press, 1964).

―― *Politics and the Churches in Great Britain, 1832 to 1868* (Oxford: Clarendon Press, 1977).

MALCOLM, ELIZABETH, *'Ireland Sober, Ireland Free': Drink and Temperance in Nineteenth-Century Ireland* (Dublin: Gill & Macmillan, 1986).

MANDLER, PETER, *Aristocratic Government in the Age of Reform: Whigs and Liberals, 1830–52* (Oxford: Clarendon Press, 1990).

MANGANIELLO, DOMINIC, *Joyce's Politics* (London: Routledge & Kegan Paul, 1980).

MANNING, PETER, *Reading Romantics* (Oxford: Oxford University Press, 1990).

MARCHAND, LESLIE A., *Byron: A Biography*, 3 vols. (London: John Murray, 1957).

MARSHALL, P. J. (ed.), *The Oxford History of the British Empire: The Eighteenth Century* (Oxford: Oxford University Press, 1998).

MATTHEW, H. C. G., *Gladstone 1809–1878* (Oxford: Clarendon Press, 1997).

MEE, JOHN, *Romanticism, Enthusiasm, and Regulation: Poetics and the Policing of Culture in the Romantic Period* (Oxford: Oxford University Press, 2003).

MEENAN, JAMES (ed.), *Centenary History of the Literary and Historical Society of University College Dublin, 1855–1955* (Tralee: Kerryman, 1955).

MEISEL, JOSEPH S., *Public Speech and the Culture of Public Life in the Age of Gladstone* (New York: Columbia University Press, 2001).

MERMIN, DOROTHY, *The Audience in the Poem: Five Victorian Poets* (New Brunswick, NJ: Rutgers University Press, 1983).

MILLER, D. A., *The Novel and the Police* (Berkeley: University of California Press, 1988).

MITCHELL, LESLIE G., *Holland House* (London: Duckworth, 1980).

—— *Charles James Fox* (Oxford: Oxford University Press, 1992).

MONYPENNY, W. F., and BUCKLE, G. E., *The Life of Benjamin Disraeli, Earl of Beaconsfield*, 6 vols. (London: John Murray, 1910–20).

MORTIMER, ANTHONY (ed.), *The Authentic Cadence: Centennial Essays on Gerard Manley Hopkins* (Fribourg: Fribourg University Press, 1992).

MUGGLESTONE, LYNDA, *'Talking Proper': The Rise of Accent as Social Symbol* (Oxford: Clarendon Press, 1995).

MULVIHILL, JAMES, *Upstart Talents: Rhetoric and the Career of Reason in English Romantic Discourse, 1790–1820* (Newark: University of Delaware Press, 2004).

MURPHY, WILLIAM S., *The Genesis of British War Poetry* (London: Simpkin, Marshall & Co., 1918).

NEW, C. N., *The Life of Henry Brougham to 1830* (Oxford: Clarendon Press, 1961).

NICHOLSON, ANDREW, 'The Princess of Wales and Byron in 1813', *Byron Journal*, 30 (2002), 54–66.

NOLAN, EMER, *James Joyce and Nationalism* (London: Routledge, 1995).

NUSSBAUM, MARTHA, *Poetic Justice: The Literary Imagination and Public Life* (Boston: Beacon Press, 1995).

O'BRIEN, CONOR CRUISE, *Parnell and his Party, 1880–90* (Oxford: Clarendon Press, 1957).

—— *The Great Melody: A Thematic Biography and Commentated Anthology of Edmund Burke* (London: Sinclair-Stevenson, 1992).

O'CONNOR, ULICK, *Oliver St John Gogarty: A Poet and his Times* (London: Jonathan Cape, 1964).

O'GORMAN, FRANK, *Voters, Patrons and Parties: The Unreformed Electoral System of Hanoverian England, 1734–1832* (Oxford: Clarendon Press, 1989).

—— 'Campaign Rituals and Ceremonies: The Social Meaning of Elections in England 1780–1860', *Past and Present*, 135 (May 1992), 79–115.

ONG, WALTER, *Orality and Literacy: The Technologizing of the Word* (London: Methuen, 1982).

PAGE, NORMAN, *Speech in the English Novel*, 2nd edn. (London: Macmillan, 1988).

PANKHURST, RICHARD, 'Saint-Simonism in England', *Twentieth Century*, 152 (December 1952), 499–512.

—— 'Saint-Simonism in England: II', *Twentieth Century*, 153 (January 1953), 47–58.

PARES, RICHARD, and TAYLOR, A. J. P. (eds.), *Essays Presented to Sir Lewis Namier* (London: Macmillan, 1956).

PAROISSIEN, DAVID, *The Companion to Oliver Twist* (Edinburgh: Edinburgh University Press, 1992).

PASETA, SENIA, *Before the Revolution: Nationalism, Social Change and Ireland's Catholic Elite, 1879–1922* (Cork: Cork University Press, 1999).

PEAKE, CHARLES H., *James Joyce: The Citizen and the Artist* (London: Edward Arnold, 1977).

PERRY, SEAMUS, *Alfred Tennyson* (Tavistock: Northcote House, 2005).

PHILLIPS, ADAM, *Promises, Promises: Essays on Literature and Psychoanalysis* (London: Faber & Faber, 2000).

PICKER, JOHN M., *Victorian Soundscapes* (Oxford: Oxford University Press, 2003).

PIETTE, ADAM, 'Sound-Repetitions and Sense, or How to Hear Tennyson', *SPELL*, 7 (1994), 157–70.

—— *Remembering and the Sounds of Words: Mallarmé, Proust, Beckett, Joyce* (Oxford: Clarendon Press, 1996).

PIRIE, DAVID (ed.), *The Romantic Period* (Harmondsworth: Penguin, 1994).

PLATT, LEO, *Joyce and the Anglo-Irish: A Study of Joyce and the Literary Revival* (Atlanta: Rodopi, 1998).

PLOTZ, JOHN, *The Crowd: British Literature and Public Politics* (Berkeley: University of California Press, 2000).

PORTER, BERNARD, *The Lion's Share: A Short History of British Imperialism, 1850–1970* (London: Longman, 1975).

POTTS, WILLARD, *Joyce and the Two Irelands* (Austin: University of Texas Press, 2000).

POWELL, J. (ed.), *Liberal by Principle: The Politics of John Wodehouse, 1st Earl of Kimberley, 1843–1902* (London: Historians' Press, 1996).

RABATÉ, JEAN–MICHEL, *James Joyce and the Politics of Egoism* (Cambridge: Cambridge University Press, 2001).

—— (ed.), *Palgrave Advances in James Joyce Studies* (Basingstoke: Palgrave Macmillan, 2004).

RAVEN, JAMES, SMALL, HELEN, and TADMOR, NAOMI (eds.), *The Practice and Representation of Reading in England* (Cambridge: Cambridge University Press, 1996).

READ, DONALD, *Cobden & Bright: A Victorian Political Partnership* (London: Camelot, 1967).

READ, JAN, *War in the Peninsula* (London: Faber & Faber, 1977).

REID, CHRISTOPHER, *Edmund Burke and the Practice of Political Writing* (Dublin: Gill & Macmillan, 1985).

—— 'Whose Parliament? Political Oratory and Print Culture in the Later Eighteenth Century', *Language and Literature*, 9 (May 2000), 122–34.

REYNOLDS, MATTHEW, *The Realms of Verse, 1830–1870: English Poetry in a Time of Nation-Building* (Oxford: Oxford University Press, 2001).

RICKS, CHRISTOPHER, *Tennyson*, 2nd edn. (Basingstoke: Macmillan, 1989).

——— *Allusion to the Poets* (Oxford: Oxford University Press, 2002).

——— *Reviewery* (London: Penguin, 2003).

RIDENOUR, GEORGE, *The Style of Don Juan* (New Haven: Yale University Press, 1960).

ROBINSON, PETER, *Poetry, Poets, Readers: Making Things Happen* (Oxford: Clarendon Press, 2002).

ROBSON, J. M., *What Did He Say? Editing Nineteenth-Century Speeches from Hansard and the Newspapers* (Lethbridge: University of Lethbridge Press, 1988).

ROGERS, NICHOLAS, *Crowds, Culture, and Politics in Georgian Britain* (Oxford: Clarendon Press, 1998).

ROWLINSON, MATTHEW, 'The Ideological Moment of Tennyson's "Ulysses" ', *Victorian Poetry*, 30 (1992), 265–76.

ROYLE, TREVOR, *Crimea: The Great Crimean War, 1854–1856* (London: Little, Brown and Co., 1999).

RUSH, MICHAEL, *The Role of the Member of Parliament since 1868: From Gentlemen to Players* (Oxford: Oxford University Press, 2001).

RUTHERFORD, ANDREW (ed.), *Byron: The Critical Heritage* (London: Routledge & Kegan Paul, 1970).

——— (ed.), *Byron: Augustan and Romantic* (Basingstoke: Macmillan, 1990).

SAMUEL, RAPHAEL, and STEDMAN-JONES, GARETH (eds.), *Culture, Ideology and Politics: Essays for Eric Hobsbawm* (London: Routledge & Kegan Paul, 1983).

SANDERS, ANDREW, *Dickens and the Spirit of the Age* (Oxford: Clarendon Press, 1999).

SCHLICKE, PAUL (ed.), *Oxford Reader's Companion to Dickens* (Oxford: Oxford University Press, 1999).

SCHORK, R. J., *Latin and Roman Culture in Joyce* (Gainesville: University Press of Florida, 1997).

——— *Greek and Hellenic Culture in Joyce* (Gainsville: University Press of Florida, 1998).

SCHRAMM, JAN–MELISSA, *Testimony and Advocacy in Victorian Law, Literature, and Theology?* (Cambridge: Cambridge University Press, 2000).

SEARLE, G. R., *A New England? Peace and War, 1886–1918* (Oxford: Clarendon Press, 2004).

SENN, FRITZ, *Joyce's Dislocutions: Essays on Reading as Translation*, ed. John Paul Riquelme (Baltimore and London: Johns Hopkins University Press, 1984).

SHANNON, EDGAR F., *Tennyson and the Reviewers* (Cambridge, Mass.: Harvard University Press, 1952).

——— 'The Critical Reception of Tennyson's *Maud*', *PMLA*, 68 (1953), 397–417.

SHANNON, RICHARD, *Gladstone and the Bulgarian Agitation 1876* (London: Thomas Nelson, 1963).

——— *Gladstone: Heroic Minister* (London: Penguin, 1999).

SHAW, W. DAVID, *Origins of the Monologue: The Hidden God* (Toronto: University of Toronto Press, 1999).

SHERRY, VINCENT, *James Joyce: Ulysses* (Cambridge: Cambridge University Press, 1994).

SILVESTER, CHRISTOPHER (ed.), *The Literary Companion to Parliament* (London: Sinclair-Stevenson, 1996).

SINFIELD, ALAN, *Alfred Tennyson* (Oxford: Blackwell, 1986).

SKINNER, QUENTIN, *Reason and Rhetoric in the Philosophy of Hobbes* (Cambridge: Cambridge University Press, 1996).

SLATER, MICHAEL (ed.), *Dickens 1970: Centenary Essays* (London: Chapman and Hall, 1970).

SMITH, H. P., *Literature and Adult Education a Century Ago: Pantopragmatics and Penny Readings* (Oxford: Smith, 1960).

ST CLAIR, WILLIAM, *The Reading Nation in the Romantic Period* (Cambridge: Cambridge University Press, 2004).

STABLER, JANE, *Byron, Poetics and History* (Cambridge: Cambridge University Press, 2002).

STANFORD, W. B., *The Ulysses Theme: A Study of the Adaptability of a Traditional Hero*, 2nd edn. (Oxford: Blackwell, 1963).

STEDMAN JONES, GARETH, *Languages of Class: Studies in English Working Class History 1832–1982* (Cambridge: Cambridge University Press, 1983).

STEFFAN, TRUMAN GUY, *Byron's Don Juan: The Making of a Masterpiece*, 2nd edn., 4 vols. (Austin: University of Texas Press, 1971).

STEWART, GARRETT, *Reading Voices: Literature and the Phonotext* (Berkeley: University of California Press, 1990).

STEWART, ROBERT, *Henry Brougham, 1778–1868: His Public Career* (London: Bodley Head, 1986).

STONEHOUSE, J. H. (ed.), *The Catalogue of the Library of Charles Dickens* (London: Picadilly, 1935).

STÜRZL, ERWIN A., and HOGG, JAMES (eds.), *Byron: Poetry and Politics* (Salzburg: Salzburg University Press, 1981).

SULLIVAN, KEVIN, *Joyce among the Jesuits* (New York: Columbia University Press, 1958).

SUTHERLAND, JOHN, *The Longman Companion to Victorian Fiction* (Harlow: Longman, 1988).

SVEVO, LIVIA VENEZIANI, *Memoir of Italo Svevo*, trans. Isabel Quigly (London: Libris, 1989).

SWINDELLS, JULIA, *Glorious Causes: The Grand Theatre of Political Change, 1789 to 1833* (Oxford: Oxford University Press, 2001).

TAYLOR, MILES, *The Decline of British Radicalism, 1847–1860* (Oxford: Clarendon Press, 1995).

TEMPERLEY, HOWARD, *British Antislavery, 1833–1870* (London: Longman, 1972).

TENNYSON, HALLAM (ed.), *Studies in Tennyson* (London: Macmillan, 1981).

THOMAS, P. D. G., *The House of Commons in the Eighteenth Century* (Oxford: Clarendon Press, 1971).

THOMAS, WILLIAM, *The Philosophic Radicals: Nine Studies in Theory and Practice, 1817–1841* (Oxford: Clarendon Press, 1979).

THOMPSON, DAVID (ed.), *Performance of Literature in Historical Perspectives* (Lanham, Md.: University Press of America, 1983).

THOMPSON, DOROTHY, *The Chartists: Popular Politics in the Industrial Revolution* (Aldershot: Wildwood, 1986).

THORNE, R. G. (ed.), *The House of Commons, 1790–1820*, 5 vols. (London: Secker & Warburg, 1986).

TILLY, CHARLES, *Popular Contention in Great Britain, 1758–1834* (Cambridge, Mass.: Harvard University Press, 1995).

TORCHIANA, DONALD T., *Backgrounds for Joyce's Dubliners* (Boston: Allen & Unwin, 1986).

TOWNSHEND, CHARLES, *Easter 1916: The Irish Rebellion* (London: Penguin, 2006).

TRATNER, MICHAEL, *Modernism and Mass Politics: Joyce, Woolf, Eliot, Yeats* (Stanford, Calif.: Stanford University Press, 1995).

TUCKER, HERBERT, *Tennyson and the Doom of Romanticism* (Cambridge, Mass.: Harvard University Press, 1988).

VAN GINNEKEN, JAAP, *Crowds, Psychology, and Politics, 1871–1899* (Cambridge: Cambridge University Press, 1992).

VICKERS, BRIAN, *In Defence of Rhetoric* (Oxford: Oxford University Press, 1988).

VINCENT, DAVID, *Literacy and Popular Culture: England, 1750–1914* (Cambridge: Cambridge University Press, 1989).

VINCENT, JOHN, 'The Parliamentary Dimension of the Crimean War', *Transactions of the Royal Historical Society*, 31 (1981), 37–50.

VLOCK, DEBORAH, *Dickens, Novel Reading and the Victorian Popular Theatre* (Cambridge: Cambridge University Press, 1998).

WALKER, JEFFREY, *Rhetoric and Poetics in Antiquity* (Oxford: Oxford University Press, 2000).

WALLER, JOHN O., *A Circle of Friends: The Tennysons and the Lushingtons of Park House* (Columbus: Ohio State University Press, 1996).

WALLER, PHILIP (ed.), *Politics and Social Change in Modern Britain: Essays Presented to A. F. Thompson* (Brighton: Harvester Press, 1987).

—— *Writers, Readers, and Reputations: Literary Life in Britain, 1870–1918* (Oxford: Oxford University Press, 2006).

WARD, A. W., and WALLER, A. R. (eds.), *The Cambridge History of English Literature*, xiv: *The Nineteenth Century* (Cambridge: Cambridge University Press, 1916).

WEIR, DAVID, *Anarchy and Culture: The Aesthetic Politics of Modernism* (Amherst: University of Massachusetts Press, 1997).

WESLING, DONALD, and SLAWEK, TADEUSZ, *Literary Voice: The Calling of Jonah* (Albany, NY: State University of New York Press, 1995).

WOLFSON, SUSAN, *Formal Charges: The Shaping of Poetry in British Romanticism* (Stanford, Calif.: Stanford University Press, 1997).

ZEGGER, ROBERT E., *John Cam Hobhouse: A Political Life, 1819–1852* (Columbia: University of Missouri Press, 1973).

Index